European Policies on Competition, Trade and Industry

European Policies on Competition, Trade and Industry

Conflict and Complementarities

Edited by
Pierre Buigues, Alexis Jacquemin and André Sapir

Edward Elgar
Aldershot, UK - Brookfield, US

Published by
Edward Elgar Publishing Limited
Gower House
Croft Road
Aldershot
Hants GU11 3HR
UK

Edward Elgar Publishing Company
Old Post Road
Brookfield
Vermont 05036
US

British Library Cataloguing in Publication Data
European Policies on Competition, Trade
and Industry: Conflict and
Complementarities
I. Buigues, P.
338.6048094

Library of Congress Cataloguing in Publication Data
European policies on competition, trade and industry: conflict and complementarities / edited by Pierre Buigues, Alexis Jacquemin, André Sapir.
400p. 23cm.
"Proceedings of the conference on 'EC Policies on Competition, Industry, and Trade: Complementarities and Conflicts,' held in Louvain-la-Neuve on 27–28 October 1994'—P.
Includes index
1. European Union countries—Commercial policy—Congresses. 2. Industrial policy—European Union countries—Congresses. 3. Dumping (International trade)—European Union countries—Congresses. 4. Antitrust law—European Union countries—Congresses. 5. Competition, International—Congresses. I. Buigues, P. II. Jacquemin, Alex. III. Sapir, André.
HF 1531.E84 1995 95–19501
330.94'0559—dc20 CIP

ISBN 1 85898 315 0

Printed and bound in Great Britain by
Hartnolls Limited, Bodmin, Cornwall

Contents

Preface

This book documents the proceedings of the conference on 'EC Policies on Competition, Industry and Trade: Complementarities and Conflicts', held in Louvain-la-Neuve on 27-28 October 1994.

The studies presented at the Conference were funded by the European Commission's Directorate General for Economic and Financial Affairs, and the Forward Studies Unit.

We are grateful to the Catholic University of Louvain for providing excellent conference facilities. The support of Pierre Dehez, Chairman of Economics Department, and Cia Rosenqvist was very useful. We also express our gratitude to Montse Berges, Gianni Contestabile, Chantal Mathieu and Margaret O'Donovan, whose patience and skilled secretarial work have played a crucial role in the production of the book. The contributions of participants other than the authors of papers and comments were essential to the success of this volume. In particular, we acknowledge Raymond De Bondt, Robert Lawrence, Jean-François Marchipont and Agne Pantelouri. Last but not least, we are especially grateful to Karel Van Miert, European Commissioner in charge of competition policy, who delivered the Opening Address. It is important to recall here his central message:

> Coherence between the major microeconomic policies, competition, trade and industry, is a necessary condition for their efficiency and their credibility. This importance is even greater once we adopt a dynamic outlook. Indeed, the growing globalization of our economies implies that the distinction between 'internal' and 'external' competition is becoming more and more blurred. It is illustrated by the transcontinental nature of direct investments and the importance of intrafirm trade, the increasing mixing up of the local and international content of final products, the continuous process of relocation of activities all over the world.
>
> As a corollary, the distinction between external and internal policies is also becoming less clear. It is therefore crucial to adapt and transform our policies, so that they are able to respond to the new challenges.
>
> One particular issue in which the Communities' experience may have an important lesson to offer is with regard to the relationship between competition

> law and industrial policy. I believe that Community experience has proven that modern industrial policy and competition policy are complementary, mutually dependent policies. This is no less true in the context of the global economy than within the confines of the Community. The primary aim of both policies, as is acknowledged in the Maastricht Treaty, is the maintenance and furthering of an open, competitive market and the creation of the consumer benefits which ultimately derive from such a system. On a global basis both policies are also necessary in the creation of an open world trading environment.
>
> Concerning trade policy, one area that has often been spoken of as being potentially inconsistent with an international competition regime is anti-dumping law. My view is that a global antitrust regime may over time reduce the number of anti-dumping actions and therefore has the potential to lessen the trade friction often generated by unilateral anti-dumping actions. I am not however advocating the replacement of anti-dumping with competition rules, but rather over time I see competition policy playing a larger role in this area, with anti-dumping becoming ever more a remedy of last resort, covering only instances of unfair trade which would not necessarily be addressed by the application of an international competition law.
>
> It is clear in my mind that no inherent inconsistency exists between modern industrial or trade policies and competition policies, but that the effective integration of these policies will require further discussion and study.

The contributions to this volume are a first step in the direction outlined by the Commissioner.

List of Contributors

BOURGEOIS, Jacques, *Lawyer, Brussels*
BRAUN, Fernand, *Special Adviser, European Commission*
BUIGUES, Pierre, *Head of Unit, European Commission*
DE GHELLINCK, Elisabeth, *Professor, UCL, Louvain-la-Neuve*
DEACON, David, *Head of Unit, European Commission*
DEMARET, Paul, *Professor, Université de Liège*
FORAY, Dominique, *CNRS, IRIS-TS, Université Paris Dauphine and OECD*
GLAIS, Michel, *Professor, Institut des Sciences Economiques de Brest*
GUAL, Jordi, *Professor, IESE, Barcelona and Advisor, European Commission*
HOLMES, Peter, *Professor, University of Sussex, UK*
HUVENEERS, Christian, *Professor, UCL, Louvain-la-Neuve*
JACQUEMIN, Alexis, *Chief Adviser, European Commission and Professor, UCL, Louvain-la-Neuve*
KLEPPER, Gernot, *Doctor, Institute of World Economics, Kiel*
LAUSSEL, Didier, *Professor, Université d'Aix-Marseille II, France*
MAVROIDIS, Pietros, *Advisor, GATT Legal Service, Geneva*
MESSERLIN, Patrick A., *Professor, Institut d'Etudes Politiques, Paris*
MONTET, Christian, *Professor, Université de Montpellier-I*
PURVIS, Colin M., *Director General of the C.I.R.F.S. (International Rayon and Synthetic Fibres Committee), Brussels*
RUTSAERT, Pauline, *Postdoctoral Research Fellow, Tinbergen Institute, Rotterdam*
SAPIR, André, *Professor, ULB, President of the Institut d'Etudes Européennes, Brussels*
SMITH, Alasdair, *Professor, University of Sussex, UK*
SOETE, Luc, *Director of MERIT (Maastricht Economic Research Institute on Innovation and Technology), University of Limburg, Maastricht*
WAELBROECK-ROCHA, Elisabeth, *Director, DRI-Europe, Brussels*

Introduction: Complementarities and Conflicts in EC Microeconomic Policies

Pierre Buigues, Alexis Jacquemin and André Sapir

All public authorities must be concerned by the problem of coherence among their policies, be they micro or macroeconomic. Contradictions between them lead to inefficiencies of each instrument, put into question their credibility and create a climate of insecurity for private as well as public actors.

Conversely, exploiting the possible complementarity between the various public policies can correct each others' specific deficiencies, facilitate their enforcement and increase institutional credibility.

This book is the first one that seeks to investigate systematically the relationships between the microeconomic policies of competition, trade and industry at the EC level. These policies play a central role in the efficiency of any market economy and from that point of view the rich European experience provides useful lessons.

In this introduction, we first contrast in general terms the optimal mix of targets and instruments with the effective use and interactions of policies that can be observed in the real world. The second section is devoted to the European Union experience, its institutional framework and the evolving use of instruments. In the third section, it is shown, in the light of four case studies that, in spite of important progress, gaps remain between economic prescriptions and application in the EC. This leads to some normative conclusions.

WHICH INTERACTIONS?

In an ideal scheme, market failures and structural adjustment issues should be the preserve of industrial policy, whilst competition policy fights monopolization, collusion and other restrictive practices, and trade policy's broad objective is to progress steadily towards free trade. However, this best policy-mix is not very realistic. Often the persons in charge of the policies will ignore the optimal actions or simply prefer to implement other policies for political reasons. Competition policy is the result of forces different from the simple objective of promoting efficiency: for example several competition laws aim more towards the defence of small firms against big business; conversely, by using an 'efficiency defence' or a lax application of the rules in domains such as mergers or cooperative agreements, restriction of competition can be accepted to support national champions. Industrial policy is greatly influenced by interest groups and regulatory capture is especially likely to result when, in contrast with a horizontal policy, the benefits of industrial policy are concentrated upon a relatively small number of sectors and firms. Creeping protectionism in new forms, such as voluntary export restraints and orderly marketing agreements, counters the liberalization trend. One important general implication is that, even if each country has found some form of (unstable) equilibrium between industrial, trade and competition policies, a confusion within as well as amongst them is frequent.

These problems have been intensified by the globalization of the economy. In the transnational context there is no specific industrial policy so that the temptation is to use competition policy and trade policy, especially anti-dumping actions, as substitutes. The tendency is to favour domestic firms and domestic location at the expense of foreign ones, and maximize only national welfare. Even though the overall costs of market power may outweigh its overall benefits at the global level, to the national economy the costs may be lower than its benefits. National authorities are then tempted to distort their policies in an effort to improve their 'competitive' advantage on international markets. A kind of 'strategic trade policy' becomes part of both competition and industrial policies, i.e. both policies might be used in a protectionist or promotional manner. Figure 1 presents in a more systematic way a typology of these observed interactions.

Figure 1: Competition, industrial and trade policies

COMPETITION POLICY
⇓

Degree of severity			
	HIGH	A Open trade policy based on low external and internal barriers; efforts to establish world-wide control of restrictive practices	B Strong domestic competition policy coupled with a relatively protective external trade policy
	LOW	C Passive adaptation to international division of labour and submission to multinationals' strategies	D Internal interventionism including discrimination against foreign firms; protectionism affecting external trade and mitigating internal competition
		LOW	HIGH ⇒Industrial Policy

Degree of interventionism

Case A is a situation where the guiding principles are liberalism (minimal restrictions on international transactions) and symmetry (all nations and corporations should be treated the same). It is also characterized by efforts to reinforce the complementarity between regional and multilateral integration, and to provide common rules of the game for all market participants. In case D, external and domestic competition is constrained by public strategies intended to favour domestic firms over foreign rivals. Through various forms of tariff and non-tariff barriers, the internal and external dimensions of these strategies interact to reduce trade and foreign direct investment. Case C relies on the ideal world of perfect competition. Nations and industries must passively adapt to given static comparative advantages produced by exogenous factor endowments. Foreign direct investments are viewed as dictated exclusively by efficiency considerations complementing the mobility of factors, and not related to market power. Strategic considerations are excluded. In case B, conflicts between public policies can lead to various scenarios, the most probable being maintenance of competition at home and use of various tools (safeguard provisions, anti-dumping duties, countervailing duties, VERs and so on) to limit domestic market access.

The criterion of economic efficiency is insufficient to explain this variety of cases. A much wider configuration of incentive structure underlies the content of the three policies. For example, a movement towards more economic openness, however potentially welfare improving, can be perceived as inimical to national interest, because of its income distribution effects. The welfare-improving character of the change may imply the theoretical possibility of compensating any loss, but this may not be a politically feasible option. Or a priority other than wealth creation may be paramount, such as national security considerations or the preservation of national identity.

To understand the real basis of the policies effectively adopted, necessitates a positive approach. The positions of the major players must be identified to highlight sources of resistance with respect to potentially-improving changes. In other words, it can be important to elucidate the underlying payoff structure as perceived by the players which have significant impact on the outcome, and to know the determinants of those structures.

Finally, differences in the content and use of the three policies may be explained by a country's specific economic and socio-cultural characteristics. For example, contrary to large countries, small developed open economies having small effects, if any, on the prices of traded goods maximize their real income level by a policy of free trade; and, in this situation, antitrust policy is not usually operating as international trade provides a very effective source of discipline on market performance. In developing countries, on the other hand, the infant industry argument is often used to justify protection against imports as well as the adoption of various forms of industrial policy restricting competition at home.

More profoundly, there are differences in attitudes towards economic power (private or public), freedom of contract and trade, efficiency and equity, which are grounded in dissimilarities in political, cultural and moral history. The predominant American view has relied upon the interplay of selfish motives in competitive markets converted by Adam Smith's invisible hand into public virtues. In Japan, it is well known that there is a poor record of punishing antitrust violators and a very low number of launched procedures: one explanation for this lies in the crucial role of consensus in Japanese society. In recent years, European attitudes about the market have changed and there exists today a broad agreement that competition exercises a positive influence on social welfare. Nevertheless, it is also argued that the existence of market imperfections and market failures plays a crucial role in many activities: this includes the problems created by monopolistic behaviour, the existence of important externalities and public goods, the strong asymmetries between economic agents, and the role of equity and redistribution. Awareness of the limits of the market has created a large consensus in favour of a communitarian model for Europe, namely the social market economy.

It is in this context that we may examine the explicit goals and instruments of EU policy in the domains of competition, industry and trade.

WHICH COMMUNITY INSTITUTIONAL FRAMEWORK?

By comparing the respective status of the common policies in competition, industry and trade, we shall see the extent to which these three policies do or do not benefit from clear objectives and instruments. The danger of perverse applications and interactions will depend on that situation.

Concerning *competition policy*, the Treaty of Rome gives a clear mandate to the Commission to ensure that competition in the Common Market is not distorted. As stated in the first report on competition policy (1972), 'Competition is the best stimulant of economic activity, it enables enterprises continuously to improve their efficiency, which is the sine qua non for a steady improvement in living standards'.

When we look at the instruments, the mission is also clear. By using Article 85 of the Treaty of Rome, which prohibits cartels and other restrictive agreements between firms, Article 86 condemning abuses of dominant positions, the Merger Regulation prohibiting larger mergers creating a dominant position, and Article 92 which forbids state aids that distort trade between Member States, the Commission is theoretically able to implement a strict and coherent policy.

However, there are a certain number of exemptions giving rise to different interpretations. In the case of Article 85, for example, exemptions are accepted if a number of conditions are fulfilled (Table 1).

Concerning state aids, the situation is even more delicate. The concept of state aid in the Treaty is very broad and covers not only direct grants but also low-interest loans, tax relief and any gratuitous advantage in general. Furthermore, derogations are accorded on the basis of a large body of derived legislation, in particular Commission guidelines. These guidelines clearly show that, contrary to the other articles, the Community's state aid policy is profoundly influenced by other policy objectives in such diverse fields as industrial and research policy, regional development or protection of the environment.

The use of instruments has also evolved. For example, there has been an increasing use of Article 85: 27 decisions in the sixties, 109 in the seventies, 148 in the eighties. However, the large majority of these decisions cover the manufacturing sector (88 per cent), services only represent 12 per cent. Moreover, Article 86 decisions and use of the Merger regulation are relatively recent. As for state aids, the number of notifications has also increased, from 605 in the seventies to 1987 in the eighties.

Concerning *industrial policy*, it was only in 1990 that the Commission presented Community guidelines. The Maastricht Treaty, agreed in December 1991, provided for the first time an institutional framework for such a policy. The objective of industrial policy is not defined in relation to existing market failures needing removal by public intervention. Instead, it refers to a broad and multidimensional concept: 'ensuring that the conditions necessary for the competitiveness of Community's industry exist' (Article 130, EU Treaty). Furthermore, Article 130 concludes that EC industrial policy 'does not provide a basis for the introduction by the Community of any measure which may distort competition'.

Table 1: Competition, Industrial and Trade Policy: objectives and instruments

Policy	Main objectives and instruments	Other policy considerations
Competition	• Art. 85 (cartels and prohibition of other restrictive agreements).	• Art. 85 inapplicable in the case of cartels and other restrictive agreements 'which contributes to improving the production or distribution of goods or to promoting technical or economic progress, while allowing consumers a fair share of the resulting benefit'.
	• Merger control and Art. 86 (abuse of dominant position).	• The Commission shall take into account 'the development of technical and economic progress provided that it is to consumers' advantage and does not form an obstacle to competition'.
	• Art. 92 to 94 (state aid control).	• Guidelines explicitly profoundly influenced by industrial policy, regional development, protection of the environment.
Industrial	• R&D programme	• Only at pre-competitive level because of possible conflict with state aid control.
	• Internal market directives: public procurement liberalisation, banking, insurance, air transport, road transport...	• Based both on industrial and competition considerations.
Trade	• Progressive trade liberalization	• Anti-dumping, VER, quotas based on industrial policy considerations.

When we look at the instruments of industrial policy, it appears that Article 130 has not yet been used. Of course, other instruments such as the European Framework Programme on R&D, not traditionally considered an industrial instrument, clearly does have industrial policy implications. However, EC research support is limited by other policy considerations.

For example, it is granted only at the pre-competitive stage (basic and fundamental research) leading eventually to product innovations. There is no possibility of financing product development, because this would conflict with competition policy (state aid control). Moreover, the total amount of financial support available under the third Framework Programme on R&D was 8.8 billion ECU, which corresponds to around 1.75 billion ECU per year. Despite its growth in recent years (from 3.1per cent of the EC budget to 3.8 per cent), research support at the EC level remains relatively modest by comparison with national research spending. It corresponds to less than 5 per cent of public, or 2 per cent of public and private R&D expenditure in Member States.

Policies for completion of the internal market also play a major role in the competitiveness of the European economy (standardization and public procurement) but are rarely viewed as instruments of industrial policy.

Concerning *trade policy*, the Treaty of Rome leaves unclear the objectives of EC trade policy, providing only that there should be a common policy. Only Article 110 states the desirability of 'progressive abolition of restrictions on international trade and the lowering of customs barriers'.

Moreover, some instruments of trade policy are not related to the objective abolishing restrictions on international trade. For example, anti-dumping measures are permitted under the GATT. The test of dumping is whether prices in the export market are below prices in the exporter's home market. Identifying dumping allows importing countries to charge anti-dumping duties in the case of material injury. However, such calculations are highly dependent on data and definition of costs. Moreover, prices under production costs could reflect factors other than just predatory pricing (business cycles, price equal to marginal cost). So anti-dumping actions are often justified instead by the maintenance of domestic firms' market share against increased foreign competition and other policy considerations. The number of anti-dumping measures implemented has been relatively stable (around 20) since 1985.

To sum up, there are different degrees of clarity in the objectives and instruments between the three policies: clear and consistent for competition policy, relatively unclear and fragmented for industrial policy, unclear and partly inconsistent for trade policy. These could have been mitigated if there had been a single body able to reconcile the objectives of the three policies. However, the roles of the Commission, the Council and the Member States differ from one policy to another.

In *competition policy*, two institutions play the dominant role: the Commission and the EC Court of Justice. The Council of Ministers only plays a basic legislative role when regulations are expanded or amended. Moreover, the Commission can act on its own initiative and upon all kinds of formal and informal complaints. Firms and Member States must give full collaboration for any investigation decided by the Commission. Refusal to cooperate is in itself an infringement of Community law. Finally, the EC Court rules as an appeal court for Member States and firms. Over time, the EC Court has played a major role in widening the scope of EU competition policy.

In *industrial policy*, the Council of Ministers plays the dominant role. For example, Article 130 needs unanimity in the Council. The Framework Programme is adopted by the Council of Ministers and the European Parliament, on the basis of a Commission proposal, but the Council decision on the Framework Programme and its various components must be unanimous. Under the Maastricht Treaty, however, specific programmes will be adopted by the Council, acting by qualified majority, after consultation with the European Parliament. The process of decision-making is therefore complex. As stated in the communication 'From the Single Act to Maastricht and Beyond: the means to match our ambitions' (COM(92)2000), 'The procedures, which normally involve both the Council and Parliament are too cumbersome. The effectiveness of a research programme is substantially reduced when over two years are required for its adoption'.

For *trade policy*, the Commission and the Council are the relevant institutions, the latter being more important than the former. The Commission proposes initiatives for trade agreements, multilateral agreements and GATT negotiations' but in close collaboration with the 113 Committee, consisting of the Directors General for trade policy in the Member States. It is the Council that gives the mandate for negotiation to the Commission and concludes any agreements. On these matters, the Council decides by qualified majority.

WHAT LESSONS FOR THE FUTURE?

The previous discussion suggests that the current design of EC industrial, competition and trade policies may not prevent perverse interactions between them. As explained in the chapters by Jordi Gual, and by Jacques Bourgeois and Paul Demaret, there are several causes for possible conflicts between these different EC policies. Some relate to the industrial characteristics of modern markets, but others relate to the Community's institutional framework.

The case studies analysed in this volume focus on some 'problem sectors', where there are clear gaps between the prescription proposed by economic theory and the reality observed inside the Community.

Public policy towards the EC car industry seems to have been motivated by two main factors: its importance in the economy (15 per cent of EC industrial employment) and decline in competitiveness relative to Japanese producers. In their chapter, Peter Holmes and Alasdair Smith admit that there may well be market failures in the EC car industry requiring appropriate industrial policies. They find, however, that such policies have been on a modest scale at the EC level in the past, with only small financial support for retraining workers and collaborative R&D activity. On the other hand, the Community's trade policy has been rather protectionist and competition policy somewhat lax. Trade measures have included, in addition to the 10 per cent common external tariff, quantitative restrictions (QRs) and voluntary export restraints (VERs) on Japanese cars in several Member States. These have been replaced, since 1993, by an EC-wide VER due to be phased out on 31 December 1999. Protectionist measures have been buttressed by a competition policy granting a 'block exemption' to selective and exclusive car dealership arrangements prevailing in the Community. The exemption, which expires in 1995, has been extended for another ten-year term.

In chemical fibres, EC public policy has long been dominated by problems of over-capacity. In their chapter, Elisabeth de Ghellinck and Christian Huveneers report that a crisis cartel has been in place inside the EC since the early 1970s with the blessing of the Commission, although EC competition authorities only sanctioned it in 1984. At the same time, the latter have strictly regulated national state aids to the industry. To help enforce the cartel, the Commission has also implemented protectionist trade measures against imports of synthetic fibres (through several anti-dumping (AD) actions) and synthetic garments (through VERs agreed under the Multi-Fibre Arrangement).

Similar policies have been adopted in the steel industry, which also has suffered from over-capacity for many years. In his chapter, Michel Glais documents how, in 1980, the Commission proceeded to a 'public cartelization' of the sector, while at the same time conducting strict control over national state aids. As in the case of chemical fibres, enforcement of the cartel required the imposition of restrictions on foreign suppliers. This was mainly achieved through AD actions, which were generally terminated by price and/or quantity undertakings given to the Commission by foreign firms. Today's EC competition policy is different: public cartelization no longer exists and private cartel behaviour is repressed by the Commission. On the other hand, trade policy has remained fairly unchanged: foreign suppliers continue to face AD actions and other protectionist measures which encourage collusive behaviours.

Two conclusions emerge from examination of sectoral policies towards cars, chemical fibres and steel. First, the actual design of EC industrial policy, competition policy and trade policy towards these sectors is far removed from the prescription of economic theory. There has been little intervention which qualifies as 'industrial policy' in the sense of taxes or subsidies targeted at externalities or other market imperfections. Moreover, there have been plenty of competition policy and trade policy measures, but few that aim at improving efficiency. In all three sectors, competition policy has been fairly lax and trade policy rather protectionist.

Second, in spite of this suboptimal design, there is little evidence of conflicts in the actual implementation of the three policies. However, their aim seems to have been to allow a 'breathing space' for EC producers rather than encourage efficiency. In particular, the lax competition policy and protectionist trade policy were designed to boost profit margins, thereby producing financial resources for the necessary restructuring. The danger in terms of efficiency is that, by sheltering EC producers from the rigour of (internal or external) competition, this approach may instead have delayed the inescapable restructuring. In other words, a coherent approach to industrial policy, competition policy and trade policy is a necessary but not sufficient condition for efficiency.

The situation in telecommunications services contrasts sharply with that in cars, chemical fibres and steel. As shown in the chapter by Dominique Foray, Pauline Rutsaert and Luc Soete, there is strong coherence in the design of EC industrial, competition and trade policies in this sector. A key aspect of this situation is consensus on the need to increase competition in the EC telecommunication services market. The authors highlight, however, various problems regarding the actual implementation by Member States of policies correctly designed at the Community level.

As already indicated, there are two major institutional factors which account for any discrepancy between the actual design of EC policies and the precepts of economic theory in the 'problem sectors' analysed previously. One relates to the EC Treaty, the other to the functioning of EC institutions. Concerning the latter, the Commission is clearly the only body at the centre of the industrial-competition-trade policy triangle, and, as such, the only one potentially able to solve the problem of coordination among these three policies and between the different layers of decision.

Although necessary, coordination is certainly not sufficient to ensure that the three policies are conceived and implemented so that markets efficiently allocate resources and maximize welfare. There is no denial that coordination among the relevant Commission services is a problem, yet without additional measures there is no guarantee that the efficiency objective would be met.

Within the Commission, three services are each responsible for one of the three policies: DG I for trade policy, DG III for industrial policy, and DG IV for competition policy.[1] There are different degrees of consultation between these three services and with DG II (in charge of economic analysis) and of analysis of individual measures. At one extreme, decisions on state aids and mergers involve close cooperations between DG II, DG III and DG IV. At the other, decisions on AD and VERs or QRs involve DG I and DG III, but no consultation with DG II and DG IV, let alone any cost/benefit analysis.

In addition, there is insufficient transparency of the links between the three policies, not only in the Commission but also in the Council. As a result, dubious industrial policy interventions sometimes take the shape of trade policy actions. It is obviously much easier for firms to lobby for generally non-transparent trade measures than to seek the help of more transparent industrial policy measures, especially when they involve highly visible budgetary outlays.

Over the years, EC policy has moved closer to economic prescriptions, especially since the liberalization undertaken to complete the internal market. Nonetheless, a certain number of problems remain which are illustrated by the case studies.

We make two recommendations to improve the role of the Commission in designing and implementing more rational industrial, competition and trade policies. First, we follow Jacques Bourgeois and Paul Demaret in calling for greater cooperation among Commission services responsible for the three policies. In particular, DG I, DG III and DG IV should each, together with DG II, play a formal role in all three policies. This does not mean that the three DGs should be merged into a single MITI-like super-body. Diversity of viewpoints among the three services is a healthy state of affairs which should be fully utilized in examining actions pertaining to either of the three policy areas. The new Santer Commission has taken a step in this direction by establishing committees grouping relevant commissioners whose aim is to improve coherence. Second, we recommend that a separate service be given the responsibility of evaluating the costs and benefits associated with the positions of the three respective DGs and drawing recommendations for the Commission. This service would be akin to the Council of Economic Advisors in the United States.

Finally, we recognize that the objective of the EC is not, nor should it be, restricted to economic efficiency. Employment, solidarity and protection of the environment are (some of the) other objectives pursued by the EC, and rightly so. However, these objectives require their own set of instruments.

---

1 DG stands for Directorate General.

The proper assignment of instruments requires that industrial policy, competition policy and trade policy be used for improving efficiency, while other instruments be assigned for employment, solidarity and the environment.

PART I

A LAW AND ECONOMICS OVERVIEW

1. The three common policies: an economic analysis

Jordi Gual

INTRODUCTION

Industrial policy, competition policy and trade policy are becoming increasingly interrelated in the European economic policy scene. This is the result of economic and political trends such as internationalization and trade liberalization, but also a consequence of the statutory and institutional framework within which these policies are currently designed and implemented.

This chapter assesses the coherence and conflicts between these policies in the European Union. This assessment is undertaken from the perspective of the optimal deployment of economic policies as prescribed by economic analysis and takes into consideration the legal mandate and the institutional constraints imposed by EU treaties and regulations.

The first section of the chapter is devoted to an analysis of the optimal use of the three policies and a discussion of the contradictions which may arise even in a theoretical world where policies can be deployed without statutory or political restrictions.

The second section analyses the regulatory framework which determines the policy assignments in the European Union. Both the legal mandate as well as the allocation of competences across institutions are discussed. The analysis focuses on the implications for economic policy design and it may be viewed as complementary to the legal approach adopted by Bourgeois and Demaret (1994).

The third section of the chapter draws upon the previous analyses and presents the main contradictions inherent in the statutory and institutional design of EC policy. The discussion focuses on the potential conflict between policies. Nonetheless, some attention is also paid to inconsistencies in practice since in many cases these conflicts reveal shortcomings in policy design which are often the consequence of statutory constraints.

The chapter concludes with a few remarks pointing out the changes in policy assignment and implementation which could increase efficiency by alleviating the most harmful policy conflicts.

I. TRADE, COMPETITION AND INDUSTRIAL POLICIES: A NORMATIVE VIEW

This section of the chapter discusses the general objectives of trade, competition and industrial policies from a broad perspective and draws attention to the areas where conflict between policies may arise. The allocation of policies to the different objectives and how conflicts can best be resolved are discussed from a normative viewpoint.

This section also provides general definitions of trade, competition and industrial policies which will be used as guidelines for the analysis of EC policies discussed in the rest of the chapter. Although the policy definitions are quite general, an effort is made to analyse specific policy instruments to allow for a detailed discussion of policy conflicts.

Optimal Trade Policies.

Trade policy can be defined as including all taxes (or subsidies) levied on goods traded by a country with the rest of the world, other trade-related regulations (such as quotas or non-tariff barriers - antidumping, countervailing duties -) and trade-related foreign investment measures, also known as TRIMS (such as local factor content requirements). This definition could be expanded to include also preferential financing arrangements such as export credit subsidies as well as national procurement policies.[1]

Trade policy modifies the allocation of resources which would result from free trade. Goods and factors of production will be allocated differently between the country and its trading partners and, as a result, also within the domestic economy. Of course, this may be also the consequence of other domestic policies. What defines narrowly trade policy is the fact that it achieves these results by way of imposing taxes and/or regulations on foreign goods, services or investments which do not

---

1 See Krugman and Obstfeld, 1992, p. 202.

apply to their domestic counterparts.[2] Note, also, that this definition of trade policy includes not only (protectionist) policies that impose trade barriers, but also (liberal) policies that remove trade restrictions.

From a normative viewpoint, it is well known that a protectionist trade policy only makes sense under a limited set of circumstances. The traditional reference is the work of Bhagwati (1971).[3]

Consider first, the case of perfectly competitive markets. The generalized theory of distortions shows that free trade is the best policy except if the country is comparatively large and, as a consequence, enjoys monopoly power in trade. In that situation, there is a difference between the marginal foreign rate of transformation and the marginal rates of transformation in domestic production.[4] The optimal policy dictates the exploitation of the large-country advantage when setting tariffs, which is tantamount to a policy intervention that eliminates the market-induced distortion.

Even when the country is large, the possibility of retaliation has to be considered and may question the attractiveness of optimal tariff policies. Optimal tariffs are lower if the trading partners can retaliate.[5] We can think of this from a game-theoretic perspective. Within a static approach the situation is akin to a prisoner's dilemma where tariffs are set at the optimal level by both countries, which end up worse off relative to a tariff-free equilibrium. In a dynamic setting one may expect, on average, lower tariffs because there will be equilibria where tacit cooperation between trading partners is sustained by the threat of reverting to a protectionist policy.[6]

The generalized theory of distortions shows that other types of distortions that may arise are best dealt with what we define as part of industrial policy. That is, taxes/subsidies on production/consumption which target the source of the distortion and do not alter domestic prices relative to international prices. For example, if the production of a good is insufficient from the social point of view (the marginal rates of substitution in consumption and of transformation in domestic production

2 Procurement policies will be relevant in this chapter and certainly should fall under the heading of trade policy to the extent that they involve discrimination between national and foreign providers of goods. Nonetheless, procurement policies within the EC are considered as part of industrial policy. See section below.

3 See also Caves (1987) for a summary including more modern developments.

4 Which itself equals the marginal rate of substitution in consumption if no other distortions are present.

5 See, for example, Anderson (1994) or Laussel and Montet (1994).

6 See also Dixit (1987). Note that both the static prisoner's dilemma and the repeated games usually assume that the two trading partners are symmetric.

are different), the optimal policy is a production subsidy rather than a tariff, since the subsidy avoids the negative consumption effects induced by the tariff.

Within the framework of perfectly competitive markets, two traditional distortions have been considered in the literature:[7] the presence of industry-wide external economies (or diseconomies),[8] and the existence of distortions in input markets.[9] In both cases, however, theoretical analysis shows that the use of trade policy to correct these distortions is second best.

Distortions in input markets will be explicitly considered under industrial policy. Consider, for the moment, an industry where externalities are generated at the industry level, and are thus not being captured by the firms. The divergence between the marginal social cost and the supply curve of the industry implies that a strictly positive tariff would be welfare improving. However, the introduction of such a tariff would introduce a consumption distortion since it would raise the domestic price of the good above its international level. Thus, trade policy is second best to an alternative industrial policy which, in this case, would be a subsidy. More generally, the appropriate intervention is a subsidy or a tax depending on the sign of the externality.

If we allow for imperfectly competitive industries, two more reasons for active trade policy arise. These are sometimes called rent-extracting and rent-shifting.[10]

The extraction of (foreign) rent takes place when a country faces a foreign monopolist[11] who is the sole supplier of a good in the domestic market (for details see Helpman and Krugman (1989), Chapter 4).[12] In these conditions, the optimal policy calls for a ceiling on the price of

---

7 Note also that some measures of contingent protection have received justification in terms of insurance. Eaton and Grossman (1985) show that commercial policy can partially substitute for missing insurance markets. Contingent protection will be optimal for a small country when it faces uncertain terms of trade and some factors are immobile. However, as the authors themselves have pointed out, it must be reminded that trade policy is also second best in this case since the first-best policy is to redistribute income directly without distorting consumer and producer prices.

8 For details see Helpman and Krugman (1985), Chapter 3 or Smith (1994).

9 See Brecher (1974) and Neary (1982).

10 See, for example, Laussel and Montet (op. cit.) or Krugman (1990, Chapter 14).

11 If the country faces a foreign oligopoly, the results are similar, but of course the number of firms in the foreign industry will matter. In fact the optimal tariff falls to zero as the number of firms of the foreign oligopoly grows to infinity.

12 These authors also explore the case of a foreign monopoly facing a competitive domestic fringe. In that case the choice of optimal trade policy is substantially more complex since the demand facing the monopolist is kinked.

imports such that the monopolist prices at marginal cost. Additionally, a lump-sum tax on the monopolist is needed to capture the producer surplus. Of course, this type of import policy is not usually implemented, but with a tariff/subsidy[13] the domestic country obtains also some of the rent-extraction effect. Although a tariff raises further the price to domestic consumers, under certain conditions on the demand function the increase in tariff revenue compensates for the loss in consumer surplus. When that is not the case, the optimal policy is a subsidy. In that instance the cost of the subsidy is compensated by the increase in consumer surplus.[14]

The idea of rent-shifting is a very simple one.[15] Consider the simplest case where two firms from different countries compete in a third market as a duopoly. That kind of market structure causes what Eaton and Grossman (1986) have denoted as a strategic distortion. Both firms perceive a marginal revenue curve different from the one they would really face if they were to commit to a certain output (or price, depending on the nature of the game) before competition takes place. The optimal policy for this strategic distortion is an export (or production) subsidy when firms compete in quantities and a tax when they compete in prices.[16] The optimal policy is again contingent on the (residual) demand function (or on the perceived marginal revenue function), and that is why it will be different in quantity or price competition.

A full discussion of the optimality of policies, however, has to drop the assumption that the two firms sell only in a third market. That is, we have to incorporate the consumption effects.[17]

When firms sell in a third market but also domestically, the design of the optimal policy involves both a consumption tax/subsidy, and production and export tax/subsidies which in this case need not be equivalent. Since

---

13 We refer here to specific tariffs. The results are slightly different for 'ad valorem' tariffs. See Helpman and Krugman (op. cit.) section 4. 8.

14 Note, also, that quotas usually do worse than tariffs, since the rents cannot be collected by the government (although in this instance the results are not easily extended to a foreign oligopoly).

15 For a complete treatment see, for example, Helpman and Krugman (op. cit., chapter 5).

16 The fact that the optimal policy changes so drastically with the type of competition has worried many discussants of strategic trade policy. Maggi (1993) has explored a model where the price-quantity decision is endogenized and depends on the importance of the capacity constraints. The government has incomplete information about this critical parameter but can design incentive-compatible policies which induce the firms to reveal their information and which result in subsidies to increase productive capacity and increase the welfare of the home country.

17 Additionally, we would have to consider the possibility of retaliation (see Helpman and Krugman, op. cit., section 5.6).

we have at least two markets (the third market and the domestic market) a key issue is the extent to which the two markets remain segmented or are integrated via arbitrage.

With segmented markets[18] the optimal policies for the duopoly case are simple and intuitive. The consumption tax/subsidy is set to confront the monopoly distortion,[19] while the export tax/subsidy is used to offset the strategic distortion.

When markets are linked through arbitrage, the consumption tax/subsidy targets the monopoly distortion, but production and export taxes/subsidies have to deal not only with the strategic distortion, but also with the linkage effects on foreign markets resulting from domestic tax/subsidies.

Overall, it is not at all clear to what extent one can advocate an optimal trade (or industrial) policy on the basis of what is known about international competition in imperfectly competitive markets. From the theoretical viewpoint, the results are quite sensitive to detailed information on market structure and conduct, which is unlikely to be available to the policy-maker.[20] Apart from the degree of segmentation of markets and the type of competition between firms, theoretical research has shown that the extent of potential entry is also important (see Horstman and Markusen, 1986). Similarly, the eventual positive welfare effects of the policies may be substantially reduced in the presence of a scarce factor (such as scientists) intensively used in the production of the subsidized good and in other potentially targeted industries.[21]

From the perspective of the policy-maker, it is also relevant to consider the practical importance of strategic trade policy in terms of its quantitative effect on welfare when applied in the real world. Most of the

---

18 This is a situation which does not appear to be very realistic, see Helpman and Krugman (op. cit., p. 153).

19 If there are several domestic competitors, there is an additional terms of trade effect, since firms do not internalize the effect of their output decisions on the price faced by domestic firms. This terms of trade effect calls for a tax/subsidy on exports which has the opposite sign of the tax/subsidy used for the strategic distortion. For example, with Cournot competition the strategic effect requires a subsidy, but the terms of trade effect a tax, in order to avoid excessive competition among domestic firms. See Krishna and Thursby (1991).

20 Another set of theoretical work deals with industries where R&D competition is important and there are positive R&D externalities. Export subsidies may then be optimal (Brander and Spencer, 1983) although the design of the policy requires in this instance detailed acknowledgement of the impact of R&D effort on the competitive outcome and of the extent and scope of R&D spillovers. The discussion of this kind of policy intervention is related to the infant-industry argument which we take up below.

21 See Dixit and Grossman (1986). Ulph and Winters (1994) have looked at the case where scientific manpower is internationally mobile. These authors show that the potential benefits of an R&D policy may then be quite large, although the result depends crucially on the degree of mobility of scientists.

research in this area has been undertaken through the use of calibration techniques given the limited data sets available for econometric research. The results, recently synthesized in a research volume (see Krugman and Smith, 1994) show that a) the effects of unilateral trade policy are indeed positive for the economy undertaking the intervention; b) that these effects, nonetheless, are of non-significant quantitative importance; but, most importantly, c) that if retaliation takes place the welfare-reducing impact on all trading partners may be quite significant (see Krugman and Smith, op. cit.).

Summarizing, theoretical analysis and empirical evidence provide few arguments for an active trade policy. The new international economics implies that the optimality of free trade is not taken for granted any more. But even within the realm of theoretical models and formal empirical analysis, the optimality of trade intervention is far from clear (even when combined with taxes and subsidies to production, in what we later call strategic industrial policy). Extending the analysis to the political economy of trade policy formation would reinforce this conclusion since trade activism promotes unproductive rent-seeking activities.

Industrial Policy: Scope and Optimality

We will define industrial policy as the set of government interventions that by way of taxes (or subsidies) and regulations on domestic products or factors of production attempt to modify the allocation of domestic resources that results from the free operation of the market.

This is a very broad definition, which includes measures related to goods and services, as well as taxes and regulations on labour and capital. In principle, it could encompass policy instruments such as agricultural subsidies, accelerated depreciation allowances and financial market regulations.

We will exclude measures directed to primary sectors as well as those related to non-tradable service industries (i.e. housing services, retail trade) although the extent of tradability may be uncertain in some segments (i.e. telecommunication services, wholesale banking).

Similarly, we will exclude the regulations which attempt to alter the geographical allocation of resources (what is usually known as regional policies) and the policies which have a general nature, in that they affect most of the firms in a country to a similar extent. For example, investment tax credits, subsidies for the employment of particular kinds of labour or public investments in the development of communication infrastructure.

Within these limits, industrial policy will cover three types of actions

a) Strategic industrial policies. These are actions which attempt to develop specific industries, strategically supporting domestic firms in international markets where rents can be obtained. This policy may combine trade instruments (such as tariffs) with industrial policy tools (taxes or subsidies on production and consumption).
b) Structural adjustment policies. These policies aim at facilitating the adjustment to structural changes in the economy when the adaptation through market mechanisms is impeded by factor market rigidities and other market imperfections.
c) Horizontal policies that attempt to modify the allocation of resources of some type of industries (or firms) towards specific inputs (R&D investment) or activities (quality improvement, export networks, brand development) because of the existence of production externalities or other kinds of market failure. Policies that support the access to financial instruments of small and medium enterprises (SMEs) would be included under this heading. Note, however, that SME policies are usually targeted to both industrial and non-industrial companies.

We will consider, next, the last two cases, outlining the optimal industrial policy in each circumstance and the motivation for policy intervention, which in general is the correction of some type of market failure (Caves, 1987). The case of strategic industrial policy has already been discussed in the previous section in the context of rent-shifting trade policy and we will come back to it later when we discuss the promotion of infant industries. As for policies which affect the inputs and activities of some firms, we will focus on the case of R&D investment incentives, a widely used industrial policy instrument.

Structural adjustment policies

Adjustment policies are designed to correct market failures that prevent the natural adjustment of industrial sectors through the individual and decentralized decisions of private firms to changing technological and market circumstances. Note that, in principle, this could refer both to emerging and declining industries. In practice, however, market failures related to emerging industries deal with R&D and we will be treating them separately.

We will therefore focus on mature or declining industries where drastic long-term changes are taking place due to either technical innovation or the changing impact of country-specific comparative advantages.

The nature of the market failure may be quite diverse. Some of the most prominent examples include incomplete information on the part of private agents, capital specificity which leads to the consumption of real resources when deploying capital to new activities and induced distortions such as factor price rigidities.[22] In fact, already within the framework of optimal targeting Brecher (1974) considered the role of trade and other policies in the presence of distorted factor prices (sticky wages) and concluded, in the spirit of the generalized theory of distortions, that the optimal policy should target directly the market failure - in this case, the functioning of the labour market. The work by Neary and Mussa confirms this view. They detect market failures which justify intervention, but the optimal measures are part of industrial policy (including subsidies to factors of production), and trade policy is always a second-best instrument. For example, Neary showed that in a specific factor model with rigid real wages, the optimal policy may sometimes require a temporary subsidy on labour employed in the industry. As Lloyd (1987) indicates, this kind of result is useful as a policy guide, but when the market failure is induced by an institutional distortion (wages might be sticky because of the design of the bargaining process), first-best policy requires the direct removal of that distortion.

This type of research provides in principle a substantial basis for active industrial policy in these domains. As usual, a note of caution is needed because the analysis often presumes that either the governments have information which is not available to the private sector, or they know the extent of the distortion, which allows them to optimally implement the corrective policy. Additionally, the framework assumes an altruistic government and one needs to worry about the usual incentives of industries to misrepresent their case for assistance. Overall, however, we may conclude following Caves (op. cit.) that despite those caveats, it is probably wise not to be dogmatic about the general efficiency of private decisions in intersectoral allocation.

Note, finally, that the results that we have reviewed emphasize the efficiency aspects of adapting to structural change and sidestep the income distribution question by assuming the existence of lump-sum taxes that

---

22 See Mussa (1982) and Neary (1982).

may be used to compensate the losers. In reality these taxes are not easily implemented and it is worth considering the optimal policy in its absence. That is, optimal industrial (or trade) policies need to be formulated, taking into account their redistributive impact.

Diamond (1982) explicitly assumes away lump-sum taxes. His results suggest that subsidies to the production of declining industries might be justified on equity grounds. At the same time labour mobility out of these industries needs to be fostered by subsidizing labour. In terms of the actual adjustment of the industry to the changed competitive circumstances, the first kind of subsidy retards exit but it may be counteracted by the effect of the second subsidy.[23]

Research and development

The case for an active industrial policy has traditionally been quite strong in the area of research and development. This is not unrelated to the fact that a substantial body of economic theory appears to show that under some circumstances R&D policy is welfare-enhancing.

The existence of market imperfections in the provision of R&D has been explored in detail. Essentially, the theory emphasizes the public good nature of R&D, which may lead to the provision of insufficient effort in R&D on the part of private firms and to an inefficient pricing of the resulting knowledge. On both accounts public policy may be justified in order to achieve a social optimum.

The basic argument has to do with the degree of appropriability of knowledge.[24] To the extent that the benefits from R&D cannot be fully internalized by the firm (because of imperfect patent protection or other reasons) we are likely to observe an insufficient amount of effort devoted by firms to research and development activities.

At the same time, once knowledge is generated, optimality requires that it is transmitted at the marginal cost of transmission, which is likely to be very low. Higher appropriability, while providing the right incentives to engage in R&D, does not lead to the conditions that facilitate the optimal transmission of research results.

It must be realized, however, that economic theory provides a well-known counter argument to this under-provision thesis. The argument focuses on the impact of rivalry on the incentives to invest in

---

23 See also Brander and Spencer (1994) and other papers in the same issue of the *Journal of International Economics* for more research on optimal trade adjustment assistance.

24 Several detailed accounts are provided elsewhere. See for example Tirole (1988), chapter 10.

R&D. Competition among firms in patent races will lead to excessive R&D spending since each firm disregards the effect of its own spending on the expected returns of its rivals. This is sometimes known as the business-stealing effect.

The welfare analysis of the market provision of R&D is thus inconclusive. Furthermore, even if one accepts that the appropriability effect may dominate the business-stealing effect, the general issue of the optimal policy intervention is still unresolved. The best-known result is due to Spence (1984) who (in a specific setting) argues that subsidizing R&D (which is modelled as lowering production costs) will improve market performance, in particular in the presence of low appropriability. Spence incorporates the business-stealing effect partially to the extent that he considers several market structures and takes into account that, with some of them, too much spending in R&D is needed to achieve a given level of cost reductions.

If the theoretical basis for an active industrial (R&D) policy is weakened when the question is explored in some detail, the issue is even more inconclusive when the empirical evidence is examined.

Empirical research has indeed highlighted that the extent of appropriability is relevant, although its importance appears to vary widely across industries. This is reinforced by empirical evidence indicating that patents are an appropriate tool of protection on a very limited set of industries (see Cohen and Levin, 1989). It seems, however, that there is no clear correlation between the degree of appropriability and the extent of R&D spending undertaken at the industry level.[25]

It seems fair to conclude that the results of theoretical analysis are not robust enough to provide a definite guidance for optimal policy. For that matter, theory has even failed to support detailed empirical analysis of some of the important issues at stake (i.e. the relationship between appropriability and R&D effort). But this may not be all that surprising by the very nature of R&D spillovers, which leave no paper trail and therefore are very difficult to track down. Economic policy has been guided by the presumption that the public good nature of R&D leads to its under-provision and to an incorrect pricing of the knowledge generated. The issue of excessive rivalry and duplication of R&D efforts has been tackled by fostering R&D cooperation among firms, a question which we will discuss later on, as it pertains to the interaction of competition and industrial policy.

---

[25] Cohen and Levin (op. cit., p. 1095). Note, though, that this result is not a direct test of the importance of the appropriability effect.

Competition Policy

Competition policy focuses on the static and dynamic allocation of resources within specific industries or a limited set of related markets.

In many industries the strategic behaviour of firms may lead to market outcomes which differ from the social optimum. Strategic moves by firms can impinge upon the final stage of the competitive process (pricing, production) or affect early stages of competition (i.e. product introduction, R&D spending) and thus alter the structure of the industry.

Thus, competition policy attempts to maximize social welfare either through regulating the conduct of market participants (anti trust or dominant firm regulations), or by direct intervention in the structure of the market (merger regulations).

From a static point of view the question of the optimal competition policy does not seem controversial. The basic issue is the trade-off between the possible efficiency gains from increased firm size and the welfare losses that may arise if a reduction in the number of competitors leads to increased collusion.

However, even within a static setting things get complex, because in most industrial markets firms compete in many dimensions (i.e. service, advertising) and the social optimum is possibly more complicated than what is prescribed by simple marginal cost pricing. Consider, for example, a market with spatial product differentiation. The socially optimal provision of goods is the result of two conflicting tendencies: the fixed costs involved in the supply of each good, and the increased consumer welfare as goods closer to what consumers prefer are being provided. The key issue is, however, that in theory it is unclear whether an invisible hand (free entry) outcome is likely to result in too much or too little product variety as compared with alternative (regulated) market structures. In the free entry equilibrium the non-appropriability of social surplus leads firms to underprovide variety, but this effect is counteracted by a business-stealing effect whereby firms disregard the cost imposed on their competitors by introducing a new variety and diminishing the rivals' market share (see Tirole, op. cit.). On the whole, theoretical analysis offers only partial guidance to antitrust or competition policy.

What complicates matters most, however, is introducing dynamics. Then the optimality of competition policy has to be discussed within the context of the compatibility with the other objectives of industrial policy, an issue which we will develop below.

Policy Conflicts

In this section policy conflicts are discussed at the normative level but also in relation to the kind of policies implemented in practice given the usual political and institutional constraints. As we will see, policy conflicts are widespread because policies have multiple objectives and not only those that would be specified under optimality.

We will offer here a very broad overview, since later on we will focus on the conflicts that arise at the EC level given a) the (statutory) objectives of EC policies; b) the limited set of instruments available; and c) the EC decision-making process.

Trade and competition policy

Some of the conflicts that arise between trade and competition policies are straightforwardly identified from simple economic theory. First of all, the existence of multinational firms operating outside the jurisdiction of individual countries may weaken the effectiveness of competition policy. Second, the implementation of trade policy itself may result in market outcomes which jeopardize the objectives of competition policy. Apart from these theoretical contradictions, however, divergences in the implementation of competition policy have led to an increasing number of policy conflicts.

Consider first the case of firms (or the mergers of firms) which potentially enjoy market power beyond the reach of national jurisdictions. Clearly, unless competition policy is applied under the principle of extra-territoriality, a policy of open trade conflicts with the objectives of competition policy. Several cases are possible. For example, foreign firms might coordinate their sales in the domestic market, or they might merge with the resulting increase in the domestic market share. The domestic competition authorities need to apply competition law beyond their borders (or restrict trade) to limit the increase in market power.

Alternatively, the foreign firm might acquire a domestic rival that serves only the domestic market and enjoy a dominant position in that market with the cumulative share of exports and domestic production. In that instance, competition policy authorities in the two countries may disagree on their assessment of the impact of the merger since they are likely to take into account a different set of interests (see Neven and Siotis, 1993).[26]

Finally, in the two cases that we have considered we have focused on the impact on the domestic market, but clearly the assessment of the consequences of acquisitions or coordination in third (world) markets may also be relevant. Again disagreements on the extent of potential non-competitive behaviour and diverging interests might lead to conflicting competition policies, which may result in trade restraints.

The second illustration of possible policy conflicts is related to the extent to which trade policies have an unwanted impact on domestic competition or are inconsistent with domestic competition policies.

Several conflicts may arise. First of all, it is well known both theoretically and empirically that foreign competition is a significant discipline in non-competitive domestic markets. Under a variety of market structures, it is easy to show that protection policies such as tariffs, quotas or VERs are likely to lead to an increase in the market power of the protected firms.[27] The empirical evidence on the importance of foreign competition to limit the exercise of market power is also abundant for exports markets in general and also for the EC.[28]

Additionally, we have to consider the contradiction between laws relating to unfair trade practices and domestic competition policies. For example, the OECD has indicated that 'in the enforcement of anti-dumping and countervail laws, different standards are applied to import pricing practices than if such practices were examined under competition statutes' (see OECD, 1984). In a recent paper, Hoekman and Mavroidis (1994b) argue that allegations of dumping should first be investigated by competition authorities of the two countries involved. According to these authors, a prerequisite of dumping would be either the existence of anti-competitive practices or government-induced entry barriers in the exporter's home country, or the finding that the importing country's market is competitive, so that introducing trade restrictions could not be protecting oligopoly rents. The authors argue that the unavoidable discrepancies between the different competition authorities

---

26 Barros and Cabral (1994) analyse in detail the conflicts of interest that arise when national competition authorities are concerned solely with domestic welfare: consumers' surplus plus profits earned by domestic firms. See also OECD, 1988.

27 See Chapter 3 of Helpman and Krugman (1989) for a summary of the cases and the basic intuitions.

28 See Schmalensee (1989) for the general result, and Jacquemin and Sapir (1991a) for the case of the Community.

could be resolved within the framework of GATT. We will return to this issue when examining this conflict of policies at the EC level.

Finally, a third area of policy conflict relates to the implementation of competition policies that lead to trade distortions.[29] This includes the treatment of issues such as state aids as well as divergences in the enforcement and nature of antitrust rules (for example, anti trust exemptions for export cartels or for distribution sectors that might restrict access to markets).

Note that this policy conflict is intimately linked to the sort of strategic industrial and trade policies discussed above. The key contentious point is the extent to which policies such as allowing oligopolistic coordination or granting subsidies improve the competitive position in third markets.

According to Hoekman and Mavroidis (1994a) and Jackson (1992), at the international level policy conflicts in this domain can be at least partially handled with the current negotiating and dispute settlements procedures within the GATT.

Trade and industrial policy

In the realm of theory, trade and industrial policy should entail little conflict since the optimal trade policy is usually free trade, and industrial policy is aimed (as a first best) at a well-defined set of market failures.

The conflicts that arise in this domain may be traced to the political economy of trade and industrial policies. That is, trade policy is often used to achieve industrial policy objectives. This is so because of the different public finances implications of both policies. Trade policy raises revenue while industrial policies usually lead to increased spending.

In general, one can also view trade (and industrial) policies as the results of lobbying competition between interest groups (Grossman and Helpman, 1993). In this respect, taxes or regulations on imports involve mostly foreign interest groups which are less well represented in the domestic political process and, therefore, less successful at preserving their interests and limit the use of discriminatory trade policy.

Conflicts arise to the extent that trade measures which might conflict with international trade agreements are used to achieve industrial policy goals. This happens usually when the policies are sectoral (whether aimed at facilitating adjustments or at promoting specific industries), and to a much lesser extent when they are broad-based policies (R&D tax credits, etc.). Support for strategic trade/industrial policy leads to a

---

29 See Chapter 1 of OECD (1984) and Hoekman and Mavroidis (1994a).

conflict with the objective of trade-barrier reduction which is the cornerstone of international trade agreements.

The issues at stake in these policy conflicts mirror those highlighted when discussing strategic trade policy. In fact, a well-known case of policy contradiction is the infant industry argument, which is currently perceived under a new light in part thanks to the theory of strategic trade.

As opposed to the simple rent-shifting argument behind the strategic trade policy considered above, the modern infant-industry argument takes into account that industry support might be worthwhile at the early stages of industry development because of the existence of learning by doing effects.[30]

The traditional infant-industry argument has been based on the existence of market failures such as capital-market imperfections, informational barriers or production externalities. The consideration of learning by doing has usually reinforced the case for industry support if one assumes that governments can pre-commit to a specific policy course.[31] In that case, by supporting the industry at the initial stages, the domestic firms are able to move down the learning curve and beat their rivals in international markets. Similar results are obtained if the industry enjoys static economies of scale - the marginal cost curve is downward sloping - and the industry is protected (for example, through public procurement) at the beginning; or if the economies of scale are dynamic and achieved through investment in R&D (see Krugman, 1990).

The results of the dynamic strategic trade/industrial policy resemble those of the rent-shifting trade policy reviewed above. They provide an attractive depiction of some industrial markets and therefore they pose a more serious potential conflict between interventionist industrial policies and free trade. Nonetheless, they are subject to the same type of criticisms remarked above. In particular, the dangers of retaliation are quite significant since the targeted industries are likely to be objectives of industrial policy in several countries.

Industrial and competition policy

The conflict between industrial and competition policy is apparent even at the theoretical level and it is made even stronger because of the often ill-defined objectives of both policies.

---

30 Alternatively, if R&D competition takes place in stages, R&D support in the early phases of competition may be required.

31 See Leahy and Neary (1994).

As a first example, in theory competition policy might work against industrial policy in R&D-intensive industries if it is the case that large or dominant firms are likely to invest more in R&D than small competitive firms. It is often argued that R&D investments by small firms may be thwarted by the high fixed costs involved. This, of course, will be relevant if we assume that capital markets are imperfect. However, if we leave aside the issue of capital markets, it is not clear that the incentives to innovate are higher for a monopolist than for a perfectly competitive firm. Consider an innovation which reduces (constant) marginal costs. The monopolist stands to gain less than a competitive firm from such an innovation because of the well-known replacement effect (Arrow, 1962). In the absence of perfect price discrimination, the incremental gains from innovation are smaller for monopolists, because they already earn rents and restrict output before innovation.

Note, however, that comparing different market structures may not be the most useful approach. Alternatively, we could consider the possibility of entry. Then the incentives of the monopolist change substantially and lead to a higher R&D effort because of a profit preservation effect which counteracts the replacement effect.[32]

Research joint ventures (RJVs) may be institutional forms that can suitably deal with the contradictions between static (and dynamic) efficiency and appropriability externalities. RJVs allow small firms to undertake R&D investments which otherwise may be beyond their capabilities and may also avoid duplication of R&D. Additionally, RJVs might increase R&D investment by way of internalizing at least part of the appropriability externalities.[33] It is often feared, however, that these gains in efficiency can be counteracted by strategic effects which work in the opposite direction. Competition could be reduced in R&D markets, and the same could happen in output markets. Nonetheless, recent work on this topic shows that cooperation both in R&D and the product market can lead to social welfare improvements. In the presence of substantial spillovers, R&D investments increase and, although output is reduced, the overall welfare effect is positive.[34]

Finally, it is important to note that the conflicts between competition and industrial policy will tend to be widespread if the two policies reflect fundamentally different views of policy-makers on the impact of

---

32 For a summary of these results see Tirole (1988), Chapter 10.

33 See Tirole (op. cit.), Chapter 10, for the basic references.

34 See d'Aspremont and Jacquemin (1988), Suzumura (1992) and Motta (1992).

government intervention in economic performance[35] (i.e. if cooperation among firms and firm size are viewed as sources of competitive advantages in international markets). On the contrary, competition policy will be consistent with industrial policy objectives if competition among firms is perceived as a major force behind industrial competitiveness. However, even within such a free market approach industrial policy measures designed as responses to market failures will conflict with the competition policy objectives in strategic or structural adjustment sectors. Typical examples are exemptions from competition policy that allow firm coordination or state subsidies designed to phase down capacity in mature industries.

The optimal deployment of policies

Overall, theoretical analysis provides some clear principles which should guide the optimal deployment of trade, industrial and competition policies.

Despite recent advances in trade theory in imperfectly competitive markets, free trade appears to be the optimal trade policy in most instances, even if one neglects the political economy and the practical implementation difficulties of undertaking an interventionist strategy. Moreover, protectionist trade policies often contradict competition policy objectives by contributing to non-competitive conduct in domestic markets.

At the normative level, the case for an active industrial policy seems, however, more powerful. Theory shows, nonetheless, the stringent conditions that justify such an activism, pointing out the relevant market failures (i.e. the cases of imperfect sectoral adjustment, R&D investment). In many cases, moreover, theory indicates the second-best nature of industrial policy relative to other more suitable interventions (i.e. labour market reform). Still in other instances, theory clarifies the conflicting tendencies at work (as in the case of the incentives for R&D) thus orienting policy, but falling quite short of providing detailed guidelines.

Additionally, the political economy of industrial and trade policies implies that in practice industrial policy objectives are pursued by trade policy tools. This is, of course, a main source of conflict between industrial policy and the free trade objectives of trade policy.

Finally, competition policy has a clear objective: preserving competitive markets. Theory helps to underline the few exceptions to this rule. They arise precisely because of the complexities of industrial markets,

35 See, for example, Neumann (1988).

especially from a dynamic viewpoint. A relaxation of competition policy may be used as an appropriate tool to guarantee the achievement of industrial policy objectives in industries where dynamic efficiency gains might outweigh short-term static welfare losses arising from reduced competition. This is an example of the inherent tension between industrial and competition policies.

II. TRADE AND INDUSTRIAL POLICIES IN THE EC

The analysis of the consistency of trade and industrial policies in the EC requires a preliminary assessment of EC policy objectives and a discussion of the scope of Community and Member State policies.

The determination of EC policy objectives is, in itself, a complex issue. At the Member State level, policy goals are determined through the political process. It is possible to think in terms of an aggregate social welfare function which policies attempt to maximize or, alternatively, in terms of the different constituencies that politicians attempt to satisfy in order to maximize the probability of reelection.[36] By contrast, EC economic and social objectives have a statutory nature and are more limited in scope than the usual economic policies. Conceptually, one cannot easily think of EC policy-making in terms of maximizing a welfare function, and much less a probability of reelection.

Since the objectives and the scope of policies themselves are substantially limited by the EC statutes, the analysis of potential conflicts between policies requires a clear definition of the goals and instruments included in each policy category.

Finally, given the multinational nature of the Community, the coherence issue relates not only to policies, but also to the question of the level of government where decisions should be taken. Conflicts can arise between actions undertaken by administrations at different layers of government. This has always been an important issue in the Community, but it has become of paramount concern with the establishment of the subsidiarity principle in the EU Treaty.

A related question is that of the decision-making process. Whether it is the Commission or the European Council that adopts and approves policies (and whether the approval takes place with unanimity or qualified (or simple) majority within the Council) turns out to be significant, as these different procedures involve *de facto* that different sets of interests are taken into account in policy implementation. Only in a few cases do

---

36 As in Grossman and Helpman (op. cit.).

the distribution of competences among administrations and the decision-making process involve a federation-like institutional arrangement (see CEPR, 1993).[37]

This section will start by briefly outlining the broad EC policy objectives that are embedded in the Treaties. Later on, we turn to a summarized description of each policy as defined in the Treaties and some European Council statements, focusing on the main instruments available, the assignment of competences and, when appropriate, the design of the decision-making process. Note, however, that we will not perform detailed individual policy assessments, since the focus of the chapter is in the consistency of policies, to be appraised in section III below.

The EC Social and Economic Objectives

The EC has established as one of its main objectives the promotion of 'balanced and sustainable social and economic progress (Article B of the EU Treaty). The Community purports to achieve this broad objective fundamentally by means of three intermediate goals: a) the creation of an area without internal borders; b) strengthening social and economic cohesion and c) the establishment of economic and monetary union (EMU) (Article B of the EU Treaty).

The revised Article 2 of the Treaty provides a detailed description of what balanced and sustainable social and economic progress means. It includes the following: 'a harmonious and balanced development of economic activities, sustainable and non-inflationary growth respecting the environment, a high degree of convergence of economic performance, a high level of employment and social protection, the raising of the standard of living and quality of life, and economic and social cohesion and solidarity among Member States'.

Article G(b) of the EU Treaty, which revises Article 3 of the Rome Treaty, includes a long list of policies which detail the three basic intermediate goals established in Article B and which should be used to achieve the objectives of the Community. These policies range from the

37 The introduction of qualified majority voting by the European Single Act was clearly a move towards the adoption by the Community of a federation structure. However, the federal nature of the Community is rather limited. It is certainly true that the fact that some significant decisions do not require unanimity any more means that some soverelgnty of the Member States has been surrendered. But the institutional design of the Community (there is no clear separation between central and national authorities) and the design of the decision-making process mean that many of the decisions can still be 'controlled' by Member States through the Council. A true federation arises when the Council has delegated powers to the Commission, as in some areas of competition and trade policy.

suppression of border duties to issues such as tourism, energy and civil protection.

Two broad issues have to be raised in terms of the general EC objectives and the deployment of policy tools.

First of all, in terms of the conventional distinction between the allocative and the distribution function of government (see Padoa Schioppa, 1987) it appears that the drafters of both the Rome and the EU Treaty considered that the role of the Community is to provide increased economic performance (an efficiency assignment) while achieving an appropriate territorial balance (a distributive role).

However, it is possible to argue that most of the detailed policies correspond to the intermediate goals of achieving the internal market and EMU, while little attention is paid to the strengthening of economic and social cohesion. Specific policies on this issue are absent and the only reference is included in Article 3(j) where the intermediate goal is simply reasserted. The article gives no further details on the means by which this general objective is to be achieved.

The specific Title in the Treaty that deals with social and economic cohesion (Title XIV) supplies more details. Apart from providing specific funding for this objective, Article 130(b) establishes that 'the formulation and implementation of the Community's policies ... shall take into account the objectives set out in Article 130(a)'. That is, strengthening social and economic cohesion and, in particular, 'reducing the disparities between the levels of development of the various regions'.

As we will see, this provides a major source of inefficiencies in EC policy-making, to the extent that this equity or redistribution mandate constrains the formulation of policies in all domains and gives rise to the inefficient use of policy instruments.

A second issue refers to a certain inconsistency between the intermediate goals by which the Community is to achieve its general objectives, and the set of policies at its disposal as established by the Treaties. Although Article B indicates that the internal market and the EMU are the basic means to achieve the EU economic objectives, the list of policies in Article 3 includes areas which are not mentioned in Article B and which have not been traditional Community policies in the past. In particular, this refers to Article 3(l) the strengthening of the competitiveness of industry, Article 3(m) the support of R&D and Article 3(n) the development of trans-European networks. We will return to this question when discussing industrial policies, since the debate on the scope of EC industrial policy is related to the potentially ambiguous status of this policy in the statutory determination of the EU general social and economic objectives.

EC Trade Policy: Objectives, Main Instruments and Implementation

The general objectives of EC trade policy are the harmonic development of world trade and the reduction of restrictions to international exchanges (Article 110 and also Article 18). The EU Treaty also indicates that the common commercial policy should 'take into account the advantages that the absence of internal barriers offers to EU firms'(Article 110). Arguably, this constitutes a statement which furnishes an additional rationale for the mandate of negotiated tariff reductions.

Nonetheless, a first thing to note is that the objectives of EC trade policy do not correspond to any of the main Community objectives established by the Treaty. The common commercial policy is mentioned in Article 3, but it is possible to argue that it is considered as an EC policy to the extent that supports the accomplishment of the central intermediate goals of the Community (basically the internal market).

Nonetheless, the objective of liberalization of international exchanges has been achieved by the participation of the EC in the GATT and the successive negotiations of tariff reductions. Of course, critics of EC trade policy (see, for example, Winters, 1993) indicate that, from the very beginning, agriculture, steel and textiles were under a different - and substantially restrictive - trade regime. However, it is also clear that the willingness to decrease tariff protection has resulted in the progress experienced in the Uruguay Round where, for example, textiles are being progressively brought into the main GATT procedures.

It is nonetheless true that the EC has developed substantive instruments to take (arguably within the bounds of GATT) what is perceived abroad as a defensive attitude (see Tyson, 1992) in world trade. These instruments include basically Regulation 288/82, which allows quantitative restrictions,[38] the anti-dumping regulation (Regulation 2423/88); and the New Commercial Initiative (Regulation 2641/84), which is an instrument designed to react promptly to foreign trade policy.[39]

---

38 This regulation allows, in principle, unrestricted market access. However, it includes exceptions that allow surveillance measures/quantitative restrictions; and does not cover agriculture, textiles and steel (see CEC, 1993a).

39 This policy measure attempts a) to respond to any illicit commercial practices undertaken by trading partners; and b) to exercise the Community's rights by means of any commercial policy measure compatible with the international obligations of the Union.

With regard to competences, commercial policy is an example of a policy where the Community is obliged to take action. Under some circumstances (for example the Common External Tariff) this implies an exclusive competence to the extent that Member States have been deprived formally of their own competences. Nonetheless, this affects only some domains of commercial policy. Member States have not been deprived of all their competences, particularly in the areas of trade instruments and bilateral international agreements, and in practice competences are shared.[40]

The discussion of EC trade policy should therefore encompass also the trade policies of Member States. Of course, as a substantive part of the internal market objectives, the Treaties establish significant limits on Member States' trade policies, aimed at guaranteeing the maintenance of a free trade area and a uniform trade policy with respect to the rest of the world (Articles 3(a) and 113). However, the fact that Member States have not been formally deprived of all trade competences and the existence of a trade deflection provision in the Treaty (Article 115 which allows the temporary introduction of quantitative restrictions to the movements of goods within the internal market), have meant that, at times, the independent trade policies of Member States have disrupted the uniformity of EC trade policy and the smooth functioning of the internal market.

The possibility of these disruptive activities has been significantly reduced by the EU Treaty (Articles 190(h)-2(b) (see CEC, 1993). We will return to this below.

In terms of the decision-making process, most of trade policy is carried out by the standard decision procedure within the Community: the Commission presents proposals to the Council, which takes decisions on the basis of majority vote. For a few cases, however (anti-dumping cases and safeguard actions), the Council has delegated decision powers to the Commission, although even then the Council has the right ultimately to review the decision (see CEC, 1993) and therefore it is not a complete delegation of powers.

40 For example, a ruling by the European Court of Justice on 15 November 1994 determined that the European Commission and the Member States should share responsibilities for negotiation in certain trade areas, such as transport, services and intellectual property rights (see *Financial Times*, 16 November 1994).

EC Competition Policy: Objectives, Main Instruments and Implementation

Competition policy has always been one of the corner-stones of EC policies. It was already included in the Rome Treaty (the current Article 3(g)) and it has remained unchanged with the Single Act and the EU Treaty. If anything, competition policy has been strengthened, since the new Article 3(a) explicitly states that in pursuing the goals established in Article 2. 'the activities of the Community shall include an economic policy which is conducted in accordance with the principle of free competition'.

The Treaty is not very explicit on the objectives that are assigned to competition policy, although from the relevant articles it appears that the legislators designed competition policy with the basic aim of maintaining a level playing field for all competitors within the single market. Competition policy includes a set of rules that deal with cooperation among firms that may distort competition (Article 85), behaviour of firms that may constitute abuse of dominant position (Article 86) and state aids (Articles 92 to 94). All of them, however, focus on the extent to which the behaviour of firms or governments affects intra-EC trade. Actions that have an effect only within Member States or on third non-EC markets are not tackled by EC competition policy.

The other important piece of EC competition legislation is the merger regulation (Regulation 4064/89). The objective of the regulation is to deal explicitly with all Community size mergers in order to make sure that they do not result in reduced effective competition at the EC level.

Competition policy is an area of policy explicitly assigned to the Community in the Treaty. Obviously this does not mean all competition policy, since non-competitive behaviour that does not restrict intra-EC trade is left to Member States. Otherwise, however, the Community has the obligation to take action and in some cases it has an exclusive competence, since Member States have been deprived of theirs. This is the case of the merger regulation, one of the few areas where the delegation of competences from the Member States to the Community has been made clear and formalized (as noted by CEPR, op. cit., p. 26, this is an unresolved issue in other domains of policy).[41]

[41] Note, however, that the Court of Justice has recently ruled that international agreements on competition policy have to be signed by the Council which puts into question the agreement reached by the Commission with the United States of America in 1991.

Finally, in terms of implementation, competition policy has been delegated to the Commission by the Council (Regulation 17, 1962), with the exception of state aids. This delegation is significant since it implies that the functioning of the Community on this matter comes close to that of a federation. State aids follow the standard procedures (qualified majority voting by the Council on proposals presented by the Commission) according to the details laid down in Article 94.

EC Industrial Policy: Objectives, Main Instruments and Implementation

From the point of view of the broad definition of industrial policy introduced in section I, EC industrial policy comprises some policies related to the completion of the internal market, R&D policies and sector-specific policies.

EC internal market policies have, in general, a scope that goes beyond a strict definition of industrial policy. They comprise a complex set of measures that has as its main objective the removal of barriers to the movement of goods, persons, services and capital as established in Article 7(A) of the Treaty. For example, internal market policies include actions in services such as banking. For the purpose of this chapter, only internal market measures related to public procurement, normalization and intellectual property will be considered as part of industrial policy.

R&D policies are, in principle, horizontal measures that aim to support collaborative research and technology development among EC countries and firms. It could be argued, however, that to the extent that these technologies affect a few specific sectors, we are really confronting sectoral policies of positive adjustment for high-technology industries (see for example the Council Resolution which deals with electronics, information technology, and biotechnology (CEC, 1991).

Finally, sectoral policies refer to actions regarding mature industries such as steel, automobiles or textiles, where governments intervene to prevent market disruptions and to encourage a particular adjustment to changed market (or technological) circumstances.

Historically, Community competences on industry have been constrained to measures related to the internal market, a domain in which the Community has to take action as mandated by the Rome Treaty. Competences have been quite limited with regard to specific sectors, except for steel where the CSCA Treaty equips the Community with ample competences. In this industry the Community is obliged to take action and the competences are exclusive to the extent that certain actions by Member States are ruled out.

The rest of the industries, and in particular high-tech industries, were dealt with by Member States' industrial policies. Nevertheless, some Community programmes for advanced technologies were already started at the beginning of the eighties (ESPRIT, BRITE, BAP).[42] Similarly, intervention in other industries such as textiles and clothing, shipbuilding and automobiles has been substantial, as the Community has attempted to coordinate Member State sectoral adjustment policies.

As we discussed earlier, the Treaty of the European Union has further extended the competences of the Community in what we define as industrial policy. With the European Single Act, R&D policy was already brought into the realm of the competences of the Community (the current articles 130(f)-130(p)). R&D has been explicitly mentioned in Article 3(j) of the EU Treaty.

Similarly, the Treaty states unambiguously that the activities of the Communities 'shall include ... the strengthening of the competitiveness of Community industry' (Article 3(l)). In fact, Article 130 in the new Title XIII devoted to industry endorses the view of industrial policy advanced in earlier Commission documents and Council Resolutions (CEC, 1990, 1991). This policy standpoint has also been developed in the *White Paper on Growth and Unemployment* (CEC, 1993b) and in what is known as the Bangemann Communication (CEC, 1994b).

From these policy statements we may conclude that the Community's approach to industrial policy is based upon an active policy of positive adjustment that attempts to avoid defensive strategies by industries in difficulty. This policy is to be pursued in a context characterized by competitive markets, both within and outside the Community. The competitive domestic environment is to be supplied by an adequate competition policy (with special care of mergers and state aid) and the strengthening of the internal market measures; internationally, by an open trade policy.

Community statements also emphasize that industrial policy has to be deployed within an overall framework of policy that favours industry but is compatible with social and environmental goals. No explicit reference is made, however, to the need to maintain economic cohesion throughout the EC when implementing these policies. This can be inferred, however, from the general objectives of Community policy.

---

42 See Sharp and Pavitt, 1993.

This approach to industrial policy includes some substantive industrial policy measures, as outlined above (internal market, R&D policy and sectoral policies), as well as a set of accompanying policies. Some of the latter clearly fall outside the sphere of industrial policy, and relate to issues such as education, human resources and business services. In a sense this is a set of general infrastructure policy measures which may favour industrial competitiveness (as would be the case with the general tax policy).

Another set of accompanying policies may be closer to what is usually understood as industrial policy. This refers to SME support and the development of trans-European networks. We will, however, not be including these policies in our discussion either, since they are horizontal policies which can effect non-industrial business.

Through Article 130, the EU Treaty opens the door to specific industrial policy measures by the Community in the attempt to strengthen the competitiveness of European industry. But it requires that these initiatives be adopted unanimously by the Council. In the absence of specific measures approved by the Council with this procedure, the new Community industrial policy buttressed by the EU Treaty is limited to: a) the coordination of individual Member State policies; and b) the fact that the Commission is instructed to take industrial policy objectives into account when implementing other policies.

Nonetheless, the other areas of industrial policy have been rather active in recent years. Public procurement and standardization are not explicitly mentioned in the Treaties but both have come to be regarded as key aspects in building the internal market and in the Community policy designed to foster industrial competitiveness (CEC, 1990).

In public procurement this has led to several Directives which should open up public contracts to all Member States on an equal footing and in all industries and services including previously excluded sectors such as telecommunications (Directives 93/4, 93/36, 93/37 and 93/38). In standardization, the new approach based on mutual recognition was started by the single market initiative and has continued to be promoted by the Commission (for example, the Council Resolution of 9/7/92). Of course the promotion of industrial policy through internal market measures has been facilitated by the fact that this is a domain where the Community has the obligation to act and where decisions are adopted by the Council by qualified majority voting.

Article 130(f) of the EU Treaty clearly indicates that the objective of the Community R&D policies is to strengthen the scientific and technological bases of Community industry. This objective is to be achieved by the Community complementing the activities of Member States in a) the promotion of cooperation with and between undertakings, research centres and universities; b) the promotion of cooperation with third countries and international organizations; c) the dissemination and optimization of the results of activities; and d) the stimulation of training and mobility of researchers.

Community R&D policy is to be implemented by means of multiannual framework programmes, which coordinate the different domains of EC activity on R&D support. The multiannual programme is adopted by the Council by unanimity (Article 130(o)), and specific programmes within this general framework are approved by qualified majority (Article 130(i)).

As for sectoral policies, recent statements on industrial policy indicate the desire of the EC to avoid interventionist industry-specific policies that might prevent the positive adjustment of industrial sectors (see CEC, 1990).

In the past, Community adjustment policies have attempted to coordinate the intervention of national industrial policies, to the extent that these interventions could affect negatively the internal market objectives. The results have shown divergent degrees of success since the powers of the Community to intervene differ substantially across industries (see Geroski, 1989; and the literature cited therein). As we will discuss in the next section, the control of state aids constitutes a key area of Community policy to intervene in industrial markets. Additionally, for statutory and political reasons trade policy has been used to achieve industrial policy targets.

III. COHERENCE AND CONFLICT IN EC POLICIES

The conflicts between the different Community policies reviewed in the previous section may have several different roots. First of all, some of the conflicts are inherent in the very nature of the policies and modern industrial markets, and have been highlighted in section I of this Chapter. An obvious example is the contradiction between industrial and competition policy in terms of the efficiency gains associated with increased firm size.

A second source of conflict is the statutory nature of policies within the EC. The aims of policies are usually defined by the fundamental regulations and, furthermore, other policy tools that might be available at the Member State level are absent at the EC level. A clear example is state aid policy, where the EC treaties allow several objectives to be considered apart from the purely internal market objective of levelling the playing field. To the extent that the additional objectives involve the strengthening of economic cohesion, it is possible to argue that this multiplicity of objectives is the result of a weak cohesion policy.

A third reason for conflict has to do with the fact that the policies involved are sometimes defined and implemented at different levels of the administration. This explains, for example, the contradictions between EC competition or trade policy and national industrial policies.

Finally, an ultimate source of conflict arises from the differences between the nature of the integration process that is taking place within the EC, as compared to the international integration process. As we will see, this translates into a conflict between the trade policy of the Community and both competition and industrial policies.

Trade and Competition Policy

As emphasized in the general discussion of policy conflicts, three categories of policy conflict arise between trade and competition policies. All of them have become substantial policy issues at the EC level.

The first conflict refers to the question of the impact on world markets of the activities of conglomerates outside the jurisdiction of antitrust authorities of the different trading partners. From the point of view of EC policy, Jacquemin (1993, p. 94) points out that this issue involves not only the impact of 'external actors and practices on the domestic European market', but also 'the problem of the conduct of European actors in foreign markets'.

According to Jacquemin, an analysis of the application of Article 85 and the EC merger regulation shows a 'trend towards rejection of strict territoriality'. The EC merger regulation takes into account the impact of foreign actors on the EC economy both when assessing market dominance (the case of market definition, for example in the de Havilland acquisition) as well as when determining whether non-EC mergers affect the EC market through the European-based subsidiaries of the merging companies. Similarly, Article 85(1) has been applied to non-EC companies selling in the Community. In both cases, 'jurisdiction is grounded on the territoriality principle while there is an extra-territoriality principle in terms of enforcement'.

In terms of the conduct of EC firms (or governments) in foreign markets, the provisions of EC competition policy imply that competition policy cannot interfere when agreements or concentrations affect third markets, since European competition policy is geared at prohibiting decisions 'which may affect trade between Member Countries and which have as their object or effect the prevention, restriction or distortion of competition within the common market' (Article 85).

However, this question should not be considered independently of a second source of conflict between trade and competition policy. Commercial and competition policy may clash as the result of conflicting anti-trust practices between trading partners. EC competition policy does not interfere in the actions of European firms and governments in third markets, but is aware of the problem, which is tackled together with the impact on the EC market of anti-trust and competition policy practices abroad. To this regard, article 24 of the EC Merger Regulation establishes a reciprocity clause which implies that the EC expects from its trading partners a merger policy treatment 'comparable to that granted by the Community to undertakings' from non-member countries. According to Jacquemin (op.cit.), this implies that the EC should establish negotiation with trading partners whenever mergers of EC firms are blocked abroad not on the basis of actual and potential competition, but on other criteria such as industrial policy.[43]

This is nothing but one instance of the more general issue of conflicting competition policy practices and stances among trading nations. The EU-US agreement on this issue is an important step in the process of convergence of criteria between policies and practices. As we already pointed out it has been proposed that this question be addressed at the Gatt level (see Hoekman and Mavroidis, 1994). However, it is likely to remain unresolved as it involves a much deeper integration between countries than the one that seems to be currently feasible. As Jacquemin puts it, the integration required goes beyond the 'national treatment' principle. To take into account the mutual interests of the trading partners in anti-trust procedures as contemplated in the EU-US agreement, implies an advance in the integration process along the mutual recognition lines, which requires a much deeper sense of trust between countries (Woolcock, 1993). This, at most, can be found between some of the

[43] See also Neven and Siotis (1993) on the type of agreements between different authorities that can be reached and are more appropriate depending on the scope of externalities and the similarity of administrative procedures.

industrialized nations and that is why bilateral treaties are possibly a feasible way to proceed.

The third policy contradiction refers to the extent to which some trade measures may counteract competition policy objectives. The application of anti-dumping policy is possibly the clearest case, but the impact of VER is also worth mentioning. For example, Winters (1992) has shown that VER on footwear in Europe led to reduced competitive pressures and higher prices by the domestic incumbents.

According to some researchers, one of the problems with anti-dumping rules is that they are based on the impact of dumped imports on the domestic industry (the concept of injury), disregarding whether the industry enjoys oligopoly rents and therefore neglecting the pro-competitive effect of imports (see Nicolaides and Van Wijngaarden, 1993). In fact, Nicolaides and Van Wijngaarden (op, cit. table 2) quote official figures that indicate that for many of the EC anti-dumping cases between 1988-1991, dumping margins where lower than the extent of price undercutting of local firms. This would clearly show that in many cases the foreign firms would be able to establish lower prices than domestic firms without having to dump their products in the EC market.

A detailed analysis of the competitive consequences of anti-dumping policies has been conducted by Patrick Messerlin (1990). This author studied two anti-cartel actions where the companies involved had previously benefited from anti-dumping decisions. The author argued that EC firms used anti-dumping law as a means of obtaining a de facto exemption from EC competition law. Messerlin showed that anti-dumping actions where crucial to the survival of the cartels and, moreover, according to his analysis the cartels captured the anti-dumping procedures, both in terms of the definition of the extent of damage and the duration of the penalties.

Trade and industrial policy

Trade and industrial policies in the EC have conflicted to the extent that the absence of a coordinated industrial policy and different levels of decision have resulted in the use of trade policy to achieve industrial policy objectives. This has two aspects. The first is the use of trade policy to undertake sectoral (fundamentally adjustment) policies. The second area of conflict is the extent to which the goal of the internal market, which is a key dimension of the industrial policy of the Community, conflicts with the external trade relations.

A third related issue is the way in which the Community is proceeding through integration, and whether it conflicts with the broader objective of multilateral integration. That is, the question of regionalism vs. multilateralism.

The sectoral use of trade instruments has been highlighted and investigated by many analysts of EC trade policy. For example, Winters (1993) points out that restrictive trade policy has tended to gain ground in industries with weak performance in terms of the world market share of EC producers (mechanical engineering, consumer electronics, machinery, household appliances and motor vehicles). Tyson (1992) stresses also the role of trade and investment policy to promote high technology industries (in particular electronics), by way of discouraging imports using anti-dumping regulations and promoting inward investment by means of local-content requirements.[44]

Trade policy has been used at the EC level as a substitute for an absent industrial policy. In so doing it has not fulfilled its statutory objectives, which should lead to the development of freer trade. Moreover, nor has it fulfilled the industrial policy objectives, since it has not promoted a positive adjustment to changed market conditions and an increasingly competitive environment.

However, even the more competition-oriented policy-makers within the EC have argued that trade policy has basically reacted to unfair international competition, and that, in that respect, it has fulfilled its aim (see, for example, Brittan, 1994). This refers to policies such as anti-dumping, although it is precisely this policy which has been more widely criticized. According to many analysts the design of the anti-dumping process in the EC is severely flawed. In a detailed research, Hindley (1988) shows that the methodology prescribed by EC Council Regulations 2176/84 and 2423/88 is strongly biased against exporters. It relies upon the computation of ex-factory prices where the deductible expenses differ between the domestic and the foreign market. Additionally, when investigations cannot rely upon actual prices, constructed prices are based upon unrealistically high rates of return for domestic sales.

Criticism of the EC anti-dumping procedures are, indeed, widespread. As we saw, some authors argue that it is based on the extent of injury to the domestic firm, not on the relative efficiency of firms (Nicolaides and Van Wijngaarden, 1993). Others complain that the impact on consumers is not taken into consideration (Winters, 1992a); that the policy punishes not only the offending firm but also other exporters (Tyson, 1992) and,

---

44 See also Flam (1994) on this issue for the case of automobiles.

finally, that it is not perceived as a transparent regulation by trading partners (Tyson, op. cit.).

In high-technology industries anti-dumping could, however, be justified from a trade policy (and an industrial policy) viewpoint as a retaliatory move to foreign subsidies. But again, the design of the anti-dumping regulations does not seem to support this view.

Finally, it is possible to defend policies such as VER or safeguard actions such as sectoral adjustment policies on the grounds that the private market adjusts inefficiently slowly to changed market conditions because of market imperfections. However, EC industries that have been protected by VER do not seem to have adjusted successfully (see Winters (1992a) in footwear, and de Melo and Messerlin (1988) and Smith and Venables (1990) in automobiles). This would cast doubt on the efficacy of such a trade policy to achieve the adjustment objective.

A second source of conflict relates to the introduction of protectionist rules in order to preserve the internal market (see Jacquemin and Sapir, 1991b). As a result of the action of domestic pressure groups, some Member States have rejected the acceptance of some imports and preserving the internal market has resulted in an overall trade restriction. O'Cleireacain (1990) and Winters (1993) provide a detailed discussion of the extent to which these internal market breakdowns have continued despite successive drives to complete the internal market.

Winters (1993) has gone even further and argued that 'an organization designed to promote mutual market penetration and whose yard-stick is integration is particularly prone to such protectionist pressures' particularly if policy-makers 'persuade themselves that competition from other EC members is a substitute for that from outside the Community', which is not the case (see Jacquemin and Sapir, 1991a). It is not clear the extent to which Winters substantiates this point. The political economy of protection within a customs union (see de Melo and Panagariya, 1993) provides arguments that may explain the pressure towards more protection, but also a tendency to a more liberal stance. The asymmetry of preferences between the countries comprising the Union may lead to higher demands for protection, as some countries are obliged to accept the protection of some of their partners' industries. However, pooling trade policy may also lead to preference dilution and allow national governments to resist lobbying which on a purely national level might well be successful.

The question of translating Member State protection to EC-wide restrictions is, of course, not unrelated to the possible contradiction between the integration within Europe and the integration of Europe with the rest of the world.

Woolcock (1993) discusses the extent to which the 'acquis communautaire' is compatible with multilateral trade rules. This author reviews the areas of technical standards, public procurement and services-investment. He argues that, on the whole, the integration process within Europe has reinforced the multilateral negotiations. For example, this has been rather clear in the issue of public procurement. However, the basis for integration within Europe has increasingly shifted to mutual recognition and departed from the national treatment approach prevalent in multilateral negotiations.[45] Since these are two fundamentally different procedures to achieve integration, the question arises as to whether they will tend to be compatible in the future. Mutual recognition requires a deep mutual understanding and substantial trust among the countries involved (see Jones, 1993). This is likely to be achieved within some regions in the world, particularly in industrial countries. And the question is whether these advancements will, or will not, favour or not further integration with other areas. As discussed previously with respect to the antitrust policies, there is a risk that the use of reciprocity provisions render these advancements incompatible with the multilateral liberalization process, but bilateral agreements between trading blocs appear to be feasible steps in the right direction.

Industrial and Competition Policy

There are three broad areas of conflict between competition and industrial policy within the European Community. The first refers to the consideration of industrial policy objectives when implementing competition regulations, in particular with regard to mergers. The second has to do with the possible conflicts between Member State aid policies as an instrument of industrial support and the competition rules established in Article 92 of the Treaty. Finally, a third domain of conflict has to do with the cooperation of firms in R&D-intensive industries, and the competitive concerns that this may raise.

According to Jacquemin and Sapir (1991a), the fact that the merger regulation looks at the impact of mergers on effective competition, implies that the 'efficiency defence' is not explicitly taken into account and this reduces the danger of mixing competition and industrial policy.

---

45 Neven (1992) draws attention to the fact that mutual recognition has interacted with competitive deregulation in fostering integration.

This view is only partially shared by the analysis in Neven et al. (1993). According to these authors, most observers agree that the regulation excludes an efficiency defence of mergers, despite the fact that Article 2 refers to the 'development of technical and economic progress provided that it is to consumers' advantage and that does not form an obstacle to competition'. However, Neven et al. (op. cit.) conclude that a close analysis of merger decisions indicates that quite often efficiency criteria have been used in the procedures.

From a general competition point of view, some authors have argued that competition policy may have been applied to different industries to a divergent extent (Holmes and Smith, 1994) as a substitute for industrial policy. This is clearly a misuse of the competition policy instrument in relation to Articles 85 and 86. If the differences relate to state aid, then one could argue that the policies may be consistent provided that it can be shown that granting state aid was justified as a positive policy of sectoral adjustment.

The Community distinguishes between horizontal aid, regional aid and sectoral aid. We are mainly interested in sectoral aid, although horizontal aid includes public enterprises and the so-called rescue and restructuring aid, which could also adversely distort competition. Horizontal aid and regional aid are not considered here, since they are not sector- or firm-specific. However, (horizontal) R&D aid will be discussed below since this is an example of the use of competition policy to achieve an industrial policy objective.

In general terms, sectoral state aids cause a contradiction between competition and other EC policies to the extent that overall EC objectives other than those pursued by competition policy (i.e. levelling the playing ground within the common market) are taken into consideration when appraising state support for industries. For example, when the Commission ties the aid to industries to cohesion objectives (see CEC, 1994a), it risks generating inefficient intervention unless the support is also related to positive geographical externalities.

Community guidelines (for example, in motor vehicles) indicate that sectoral aid can be granted if the aid benefits regional development exceeding 'possible adverse effects on the sector as a whole' (CEC, 1991); and if 'it relates to fundamental rationalization beyond the firm's capacity to finance ... or to products or processes which are genuine innovations from the Community standpoint'. Even 'rescue and restructuring aid' may be allowed if there is 'a Community interest in keeping the firm in business'.

These guidelines follow statutory prescriptions. Article 92 (3)(c) reads that 'aid to facilitate the development of certain economic activities or certain economic areas' may be considered compatible with the common market 'where such aid does not adversely affect trading conditions to an extent contrary to the common interest'. But since they incorporate cohesion and industrial policy objectives into the decision criteria they do not provide effective tools to curb state subsidies and to set a level playing field for EC competitors. The Treaty recognizes that the aid distorts the common market, but the failure to define 'the common interest' may mean that aid will be disbursed to those interest groups with the more powerful pleas.[46] As an alternative, it would be more efficient to strictly eliminate sectoral aid and grant general-purpose (training, infrastructure) support linked not only to the level of development but also to the evolution of indicators such as unemployment, which measure the extent of the local adverse impact of the process of integration.

In fact, the variety of statutory arguments for defending state aid has seriously hampered the efforts to curb state subsidies. The conditions to grant aid should be flexible with regard to general aid and very stringent at the sectoral level.

The Commission's view on aid granted to investment in R&D is also very lenient.[47] Some analysts consider that this lax competition policy is consistent to the extent that the internalization of externalities at the EC level may be forwarded by a coordinated subsidy policy. Sharp (1991) argues that there is a creative tension between the cooperation induced by R&D policies (i.e. in relaxing state aid) and the pro-competition deregulatory forces also set in motion by the internal and external competition that is predicated as a basis of EC industrial policy. As our discussion of trade policy reveals, however, the external pressures sometimes are not all that strong. Some authors want to go even further. N'guyen and Owen (1992) clearly favour a much more active EC policy in technology on the basis of the aforementioned externalities despite the fact that the theoretical basis for intervention on this issue are not very conclusive (see section I and Ulph, 1991)

A related issue is the question of competition policy versus cooperation between firms in R&D-intensive industries. It is possible to argue that the block exemption to Article 85 granted for pre-competitive R&D is undermining competition policy to the extent that it is fostering product

---

[46] Neven (1994) shows that the political economy determinants of state aid explain a substantial amount of state aid in the European Community.

[47] See the Community framework for state aid for research and development (CEC, 1994a).

market coordination and not changing basically the incentives to invest in R&D of private firms. In fact, critics such as Tyson (op. cit.) have seen in this exemption a consistent policy of industrial promotion which uses R&D subsidies together with the instruments of trade and foreign direct investment policy.

Attempts to allow more coordination at the competitive stage on the grounds that Europe fails to adopt innovations should probably be resisted since this would substantially change the likelihood of diminished pressures in the product market given the EC practice on trade policy. That is, stronger coordination should only be allowed if it were guaranteed that the full rigours of international competition would be felt.

CONCLUSIONS

EC Treaties restrict the use of EC policies to the achievement of a pre-established set of objectives and limit also the ability of the EC to act in some areas. Trade and competition policies have well-defined priority objectives: the preservation and encouragement respectively of external and internal competition. But they have to fulfil other competing goals, notably in terms of cohesion and/or industrial competitiveness.

One could argue that this multiplicity of objectives is the result of the limited competences available to the Community. This could reflect a belief that the direct instruments available (structural and cohesion funds) are insufficient for the task assigned to them and that, as a consequence, policies aimed at securing a competitive and integrated market should be tempered by the contradictory goal of maintaining social cohesion. Alternatively, it could be that achieving one goal supports the attainment of the other. For example, the belief that industrial strength is better achieved through vigorous domestic competition and the full exposure to foreign competitors.

The nature of the conflict between trade/competition policies and cohesion policy is clear. Imposing the cohesion restriction might lead to the choice of non-optimal policies in trade and competition, protecting or subsidizing a particular industry on the grounds of cohesion. Nevertheless, the optimality of the free-market adjustment can also be disputed. In the presence of market imperfections (for example, imperfect foresight) and/or externalities (geographically-based pecuniary externalities), adjustment support could be justified on efficiency grounds, without having to resort to distributive considerations which are best left to strict redistribution (cohesion) policies.

However, the difficulty in assessing the extent of those market imperfections and externalities should lead to a cautious policy stance - one that grants support which is limited over time and on the basis of verifiable steps towards adjustment. The policy of the EC on state aid shares in some cases this spirit, but this happens to a much lesser extent in trade policy.

The second main source of policy inconsistency arises between trade/competition policies and the industrial policy of Member States. Although the Community policy is based upon the central idea that the best industrial policy is the promotion of an environment of competition with a large internal market and external pressure, actual policy at the EC and the Member State level has departed from this rule. In some cases, economic theory itself has cast doubt on this principle. In others, policy practice has not followed the statutory objectives.

The theoretical results have influenced the relaxation of EC competition policy with regard to R&D subsidies and R&D cooperation. Even in mergers, policy practice has led to consideration of the efficiency defence. Arguably, this need not be the best policy for R&D. Softening competition policy need not be the optimal reaction to the externalities involved. A better alternative might be to adopt a policy mix that combines stricter competition control with some centralization of technology policies (along the lines of what is argued below for the rest of industrial policy).

Policy practice has departed from the statutory objective in the case of trade not so much as the result of inconclusive theory but of the political economy of EC trade and industrial policies. Indeed, there is a danger that strategic trade theory and other theoretical developments might be used to support protectionist positions. Since this theory is not very conclusive and its optimal implementation is contingent upon many unknown parameters, it seems convenient to design trade policy instruments to avoid its capture by the interested parties. An effort should be made to restrict trade instruments to their proper use under Treaty objectives, and not to use them as instruments of industrial policy. But then, this begs the question of how these industrial policy objectives might be achieved.

Industrial policy is in fact a conflictive area itself, quite apart from its interaction with other policies. Aside from the potential disagreements on the extent of intervention in a centralized nation-state, there is the question of the conflict not between policies at the EC level, but between the policies of different administrations. This is of course very much a political economy issue, tied to the question of subsidiarity and the decision-making process within the EC.

Two basic alternatives are available. The first is to strengthen significantly the decisions in the area of the internal market (state subsidies, procurement, national quantitative restrictions). This would be consistent with competition and industrial policy. However, it would be strongly opposed by powerful Member States' interest groups which could easily find cohesion arguments to support their case. The institutional process by which decisions are taken at the EC prevents at this time the successful adoption of this course of action.

Note, moreover, that further strengthening this integration process need not imply a deterioration of the relations with the rest of the world. Negotiations with third parties would continue on the basis of national treatment, but the EC could present a more homogeneous position. In fact with areas such as the non-EC countries of the OECD a more homogeneous EC policy could make it easier to proceed further, and advance into integration on the basis of EC-style mutual recognition.

The second alternative argues that more centralization is needed in industrial policy. In several industries (whether they are mature industries like automobiles or sunrise industries like telecommunications), Member States' governments intervene (through public procurement, state aid, procrastinating in transposing legislation) to favour the national competitors. In mature industries we confront an exit game with a non-cooperative outcome which is significantly inefficient. In rising industries the subsidizing of entry often leads to a similar result.

Of course, given the institutional nature of the EC and the fact that Member States retain most of their sovereignty and governments are responsible to national electorates, it is not reasonable to expect a non-intervention, free-market outcome. And, arguably, the approximation of such an outcome by means of the strong integration policy advocated above need not be adequate. Simply curbing further state aid will not do the trick since state aid will be assigned mostly as a reaction to the pressure of interest groups and political constituencies.

A more centralized system of industrial policy (with an adequate assignment of competences and a proper design of voting system) is therefore justified in terms of efficiency. It could be the appropriate way to break the current deadlock, where Member States' interference is leading to inefficient outcomes in many industrial markets, and promote the positive adjustment that - in principle - EC industrial policy attempts to achieve.

Of course, favouring and focusing on the achievement of an efficient economic outcome might have its costs in terms of redistribution. To that extent such an industrial policy needs to be complemented by cohesion policy measures which should automatically compensate the losers (through infrastructure and training investment) depending upon the geographical impact of the rationalization that would take place.

Finally, note that centralization of this policy is clearly superior to coordination,[48] given the lack of credibility of the cooperation and the imprecise nature of industrial policy, which makes it harder for the parties to stick to the negotiated agreements. Moreover, undertaking a more active industrial policy would be consistent with the new emphasis given to industrial policy by the EU Treaty. The new Article 3(l) recognizes that the activities of the Community shall include 'the strengthening of Community industry', and the new Title on industry and its Article 130 provide that, with unanimity, the Council may decide 'specific measures in support of action taken in the Member States' to achieve the objectives of industrial policy, and among them, 'speeding up the adjustment of industry to structural changes'. The Community has therefore the instruments to act in a policy area which has thus far enjoyed an uncertain status, but which might be crucial to achieve a more efficient deployment of Community policies.

REFERENCES

Anderson, J.E. (1994), 'The Theory of Protection', in D. Greenaway and L.A. Winters (eds.), *Surveys in International Trade,* London: Basil Blackwell.

Arrow, K. (1962), 'Economic Welfare and the Allocation of Resources for Inventions', in R. Nelson (ed.), *The Rate and Direction of Inventive Activity*, Princeton: Princeton University Press.

d'Aspremont, C. and A. Jacquemin (1988), 'Cooperative and Noncooperative R&D in Duopoly with Spillovers', *American Economic Review* 78,(5), December, pp. 1133-7.

Barros, P. and L. Cabral (1994), 'Merger Policy in Open Economies', *European Economic Review,* 38, pp. 1041-55.

Bhagwati, J. (1971), 'The Generalized Theory of Distortions and Welfare', in J. Bhagwati et al. (eds.), *Trade, Balance of Payments and*

48 See CEPR, 1993, for a discussion of the arguments that favour centralization versus coordination.

Growth: Papers in International Economics in Honor of Charles P. Kindleberger, Amsterdam: North-Holland Publishing Co.

Bourgeois, J.H.J. and P. Demaret (1994) 'The working of the three common policies: a legal analysis', paper presented at the conference, 'E.C. Policies on competition, industry and trade', Louvain-la-Neuve, 27-28 October 1994.

Brander, J. and B. Spencer (1983), 'International R&D Rivalry and Industrial Strategy' *Review of Economic Studies*, 50, pp. 707-22.

Brander, J. and B. Spencer (1994), 'Trade Adjustment Assistance', *Journal of International Economics*, 36, pp. 239-61.

Brecher, R. (1974), 'Optimal Commercial Policy for a Minimum-Wage Economy', *Journal of International Economics*, 4, pp. 139-49.

Brittan, L. (1994), *Europe. The Europe We Need.* London: Hamish Hamilton.

Caves, R. (1987) 'Industrial Policy and Trade Policy: The Connections' in H. Kierzkowski (ed.) *Protection and Competition in International Trade*, London: Basil Blackwell.

CEPR (1993), *Making Sense of Subsidiarity: How Much Centralization for Europe?*, Monitoring European Integration 4, London.

Cohen, W. and R. Levin (1989), 'Empirical Studies of Innovation and Market Structure', in R. Schmalensee and R. Willig (eds.) *Handbook of Industrial Organization*, Vol. 2, Amsterdam: North Holland.

Commission of the EC (1990), 'Industrial Policy in an Open and Competitive Environment' Com (90) 556, 16 November 1990.

Commission of the EC (1991), 'The European Electronics and Information Technology Industry: State of Play, Issues at Stake and Proposals for Action', 3 April 1991.

Commission of the EC (1993a), 'A concise overview of the EC Trade Policy' in *The European Community as a World Trade Partner, European Economy,* 52.

Commission of the EC (1993b), *White Paper on Growth and Employment.* Luxembourg: EC Commission.

Commission of the EC (1994a), 'State aid control in the context of other community policies', *European Economy*, Supplement 4, Recent Economic Trends No.4, April.

Commission of the EC (1994b), 'An Industrial Competitiveness Policy for the European Union' Communication from the European Commission to the Council, Com (94) 319 final, 14 September 1994.

Diamond, P.A. (1982), 'Protection, Trade Adjustment Assistance and Income Distribution', in J. Baghwati (ed.), *Import Competition and Response*, Chicago: University of Chicago Press.
Dixit, A. (1987), 'Strategic Aspects of Trade Policy', in T. Bewley (ed.), *Advances in Economic Theory: Fifth World Congress*, New York: Cambridge University Press, pp.329-62.
Dixit, A. and G. Grossman (1986), 'Targeted Export Promotion with Several Oligopolistic Industries', *Journal of International Economics*, 21, pp. 233-50.
Eaton, J. and G.M. Grossman (1985), 'Tariff as insurance: optimal commercial policy when domestic markets are incomplete', *Canadian Journal of Economics*, XVIII(2) May, pp. 258-72.
Eaton, J. and G.M. Grossman (1986), 'Optimal Trade and Industrial Policy under Oligopoly', *Quarterly Journal of Economics* (2) May, pp.383-406.
Flam, H. (1994), 'EC members fighting about surplus. VERs FDI and Japanese cars', *Journal of International Economics,* 36, pp. 117-31.
Geroski, P. (1989), 'European Industrial Policy and Industrial Policy in Europe', *Oxford Review of Economic Policy*.
Grossman, G. and E. Helpman (1993), 'Protection for Sale', CEPR Discussion Paper No. 827, June.
Helpman, E. and P. Krugman (1985), *Market Structure and Foreign Trade*, Cambridge, Mass.: MIT Press.
Helpman, E. and P. Krugman (1989), *Trade Policy and Market Structure*, Cambridge, Mass.: MIT Press.
Hindley, B. (1988), 'Dumping and Far East Trade of the EC', *The World Economy* , 11(4), pp. 445-463.
Hoekman, B.M. and P.C. Mavroidis (1994a), 'Competition, competition policy and the GATT', *The World Economy*, 17(2), March.
Hoekman, B.M. and P.C. Mavroidis (1994b), 'Antitrust-based Remedies and Dumping in International Trade', Policy Research Working Paper 1347, World Bank, August.
Holmes, P and A. Smith (1994), 'The coherence of EC policies in trade, competition and industry: Car industry case study', paper presented at the conference: 'EC Policies on competition, industry and trade', Louvain-La-Neuve, 27-28 October 1994.
Horstman, I. and J. Markusen (1986), 'Up the average cost curve: inefficient entry and the new protectionism', *Journal of International Economics*, 20, pp. 225-47.

Jackson, J. (1992), 'Statement on Competition and Trade Policy', *Journal of World Trade*, 26, October, pp.111-116.

Jacquemin, A. et al. (1989), 'Horizontal Mergers and Competition Policy in the European Community', *European Economy*, 40.

Jacquemin, A. and A. Sapir (1991a), 'Competition and imports in the European market', in Winters and Venables (eds.) *European Integration: Trade and Industry*, London: Cambridge University Press, CEPR.

Jacquemin, A. and A. Sapir (1991b), 'Europe post-1992: Internal and External Liberalization', *American Economic Review, Papers and Proceedings*, 81(2), pp.166-70.

Jacquemin, A. (1993), 'The International Dimension of European Competition Policy', *Journal of Common Market Studies*, 31(1), March.

Jones, R. (1993), Comment to 'Regionalism versus multilateralism: analytical notes', by P. Krugman in J. De Melo and A. Panagariya (eds.) *New Dimensions in Regional Integration*, London: Cambridge University Press CEPR.

Krishna, K. and M. Thursby (1991), 'Optimal policies with strategic distortions', *Journal of International Economics*, 31, pp. 291-308.

Krugman, P. (1990) *Rethinking International Trade*, Cambridge: MIT Press.

Krugman, P. and M. Obstfeld (1992), *International Economics. Theory and practice*.

Krugman, P. and A. Smith (eds.) (1994), *Empirical Studies of Strategic Trade Policy*, NBER/CEPR Chicago U. Press.

Laussel, D. and C. Montet (1994), 'Strategic Trade Policies' in D. Greenaway and L. A. Winters (eds.), *Surveys in international trade*, London: Basil Blackwell.

Leahy, D. and J.P. Neary (1994), 'Learning-by-doing, pre-commitment and infant industry protection' CEPR Discussion Paper No. 980, July.

Lehner, S and R. Meiklejohn (1991), 'Fair competition in the internal market: Community State aid policy', *European Economy*, 48, September.

Lloyd, P.J. (1987), 'Protection policy and the assignment rule' in H. Kierzkowski (ed.), *Protection and Competition in International Trade*, London: Basil Blackwell.

Maggi, G. (1993), 'Strategic Trade Policies with Uncertainty about the Mode of Inter-firm Competition', CEPR Discussion Paper No. 359, August, Stanford University.

Melo, J. de and P. Messerlin (1988), 'Price, Quality and Welfare Effects of European VERs on Japanese Autos', *European Economic Review*, 32, pp. 1527-46.

Melo, J. de and A. Panagariya (eds.) (1993), *New Dimensions in Regional Integration*, London: Cambridge University Press, CEPR.

Messerlin, P.A. (1989), 'The EC Anti-dumping regulations: A first economic appraisal 1980-1985', *Weltwirtschaftliches Archiv*, 125, pp. 563-587.

Messerlin, P.A. (1990), 'Anti-dumping Regulations or Pro-Cartel Law? The EC Chemical Cases', *The World Economy*, pp. 465-492.

Motta, M. (1992), 'Cooperative R&D and Vertical Product Differentiation', *International Journal of Industrial Organization*, 10, pp. 643-661.

Mussa, M. (1982), 'Government Policies and the Adjustment Process', in J. Bhagwati (ed.), *Import Competition and Response*, Chicago: University of Chicago Press.

N'guyen, G. Dang and R.F. Owen (1992), 'High-tech competition and industrial restructuring in light of the single market', *American Economic Review. Papers and Proceedings*, 82(2), pp. 93-97.

Neary, P. (1982), 'Intersectorial capital mobility, wage stickiness and the case for adjustment assistance', in J. Baghwati (ed.), *Import Competition and Response*, Chicago: University of Chicago Press.

Neumann, M. (1988), 'Industrial Policy and Competition Policy', *European Economic Review*, 34, pp. 562-7.

Neven, D. (1992), 'Regulatory reform in the European Community', *American Economic Review. Papers and Proceedings*, 82(2) pp. 98-103.

Neven, D. (1994), 'The political economy of state aids in the European Community: Some econometric evidence', CEPR Discussion Paper No. 945, April.

Neven, D. and G. Siotis (1993), 'Foreign Direct Investment in the EC: Some Policy Issues', CEPR Discussion Paper No.798, June.

Neven, D. et al. (1993), *Merger in Daylight. The Economics and Politics of European Merger Control*, London: CEPR.

Nicolaides, P. and R. Van Wijngaarden (1993), 'Reform of the Anti-dumping regulations: the Case of the EC', *Journal of World Trade*, 27(3), June, pp. 31-53.

O'Cleireacain, Seamus (1990), 'Europe 1992 and Gaps in the EC's common commercial policy', *Journal of Common Market Studies*,28(3), March, pp. 201-17.

OECD (1984), *Competition and Trade Policies. Their Interaction*, Paris.

OECD (1988), *International Mergers and Competition Policy*, Paris.

Padoa-Schioppa, T. et al. (1987), *Efficiency, Stability and Equity. A strategy for the evolution of the economic system of the European Community,* Oxford: Oxford University Press.

Schmalensee, R. (1989), 'Inter-industry studies of structure and performance', in R. Schmalensee and R. Willig (eds.), *Handbook of Industrial Organization*, vol. 2. Amsterdam: North-Holland.

Sharp, Margaret (1991), 'The Single Market and European Policies for Advanced Technologies', in Christopher Freeman, Margaret Sharp and William Walker (eds.), *Technology and the Future of Europe: Competition and the Global Environment in the 1990s*, London: Pintner.

Sharp, Margaret and K. Pavitt (1993), 'Technology Policy in the 1990s: Old trends and new realities', *Journal of Common Market Studies*, 31(2), June, pp. 129-51.

Smith, A. (1994), 'Imperfect Competition in International Trade', in D. Greenaway and L. A. Winters (eds.), *Surveys in International Trade*, London: Basil Blackwell.

Smith, A. and A. Venables (1990), 'Automobiles', in G. Hufbuaer (ed.), *Europe 1992: An American Perspective,* Washington, DC: Brookings Institution.

Spence, M. (1984), 'Cost reduction, competition and industry performance', in *Econometrica*, 52(1), January, pp. 101-21.

Suzumura, K. (1992), 'Cooperative and Noncooperative R&D in an Oligopoly with Spillovers', *American Economic Review*, 82(5), December, pp. 1307-20.

Tirole, J. (1988), *The Theory of Industrial Organization*, Cambridge, Mass.: MIT Press.

Tyson, L.A. (1992), *Who's bashing whom? Trade conflict in high-technology industries*, Washington DC: Institute for International Economics.

Ulph, D. (1991), 'Technology Policy in the completed European Market', in L.A. Winters and A. Venables (eds.), *European Integration: Trade and Industry*, London: Cambridge University Press, CEPR.

Ulph, D. and L.A. Winters (1994), 'Strategic Manpower Policy and International Trade', in P. Krugman and A. Smith (eds.), *Empirical Studies of Strategic Trade Policy*, Chicago: NBER/CEPR Chicago University Press.

Winters, L.A. (1992a), 'Goals and own goals in European Trade Policy', *World Economy,* 15(5), September, pp. 557-74

Winters, L.A. (1992b), 'Integration, trade policy and European footwear trade', in Winters (ed.), *Trade Flows and Trade Policy after 1992*, Cambridge: Cambridge University Press.

Winters, L.A. (1993), 'The European Community: a case of successful integration?', CEPR Discussion Paper No. 755, January. Published in J. De Melo and A. Panagariya (eds.), *New Dimensions in Regional Integration*, London: Cambridge University Press, CEPR.

Woolcock, S. (1993), 'The European Acquis and multilateral trade rules: are they compatible?', *Journal of Common Market Studies*, 31(4), December, pp.539-58.

Discussion

Didier Laussel and Christian Montet

INTRODUCTION

It is well understood that the relations between trade policy (hereafter TP), industrial policy (IP) and competition policy (CP) depend on the type and level of distortions existing in the economy and of the political economy of state interventions. We recall in this discussion that the more distorted the markets and the more predatory and distortive the actions attempted by national policy-makers, the more one needs a coordination of policies and ultimately supranational institutions to get out of mutually harming equilibria and to restore efficiency. We will see that the current calls for an international harmonization of CP respond both to a need similar to that of a GATT for trade policies, but also contain real dangers of using unfair competition issues to get further protection. Thus, the development of a coordination of policies must be welcomed, but at the same time treated with caution if it is to be truly efficient.

THE IDEAL SCHEME OF TP, IP AND CP

The picture is quite simple in a world of price-taking agents described by competitive general equilibrium theory. There is no need for industrial policy nor competition policy. One may note, however, that even in this wonderful world, trade policy could conflict with competition. The optimal tariff (or optimal tax on exports) argument is precisely about the monopoly or monopsony power that the country could exert as a whole. Individually the domestic producers cannot use any market power but the government may have the power to do so and to improve in this way the terms of trade of its country. Notice that this policy is not mercantilist since it could consist of taxing the exports (in order to increase the export price) while mercantilism encourages exports. However, like mercantilism, the optimal tariff argument is an example of predatory conduct detrimental to foreigners.

Other big countries or smaller countries having monopoly powers in some commodity markets could of course implement their own optimal tariff policies. A prisoner's dilemma would follow. But a good understanding of the repeated game could nevertheless lead to free trade. In the case of a large asymmetry between a big country and small countries or countries having no kind of monopoly powers, the latter would certainly suffer. Clearly, national welfare and international welfare objectives do not coincide and a kind of GATT would certainly be useful in order to preserve competition in this highly idealized world (no antitrust regulation is needed here because the distortion to competition comes only from some countries' trade policies).

The previous story is well known and certainly not very realistic. It is interesting, however, to see how even in this highly idealized world some possible predatory conducts may require an international institution to coordinate and monitor national trade policies.

Of course, the presence of market distortions on the goods and factors markets, such as imperfect competition, external effects, or obstacles to factor mobility, reinforces this argument since it justifies some kind of state intervention and increases the chances and opportunities of predatory behaviour. There is a good theory of optimal targeting of policies in that case (Bhagwati, 1971). Free trade would bring the usual gains augmented by the gains from a more competitive market outcome. Market failures and structural adjustments issues would be treated by industrial policy (which corresponds to the types of actions a) and b) in Gual's definition of IP), while competition policy would fight monopolization, collusion and other anti-competitive practices. Assuming that IP and CP work rather well in each and every country, we would be back to the situation examined above, the optimal tariff being the only cause of concern.

But the equilibrium of national policies here rests on the assumption that each country succeeds in the task of correcting the distortions. Everybody knows that even the best IP and CP available in reality cannot correct all the distortions. Some external effects, market-size effects, lasting effects of historical accidents, and other similar 'imperfections' will inevitably remain. Antitrust authorities cannot track every price-fixing conspiracy or monopolization strategy. Moreover, the persons in charge of the policies will often ignore the optimal actions or simply prefer to implement other policies for pure political reasons.

But as soon as there are rents on some markets abroad, the best policy-mix for one country is not the kind of targeting suggested by Bhagwati. Predatory conduct might become welfare maximizing from each nation's point of view. Once some countries have deviated from the Nash equilibrium of optimal policy-mix, with the result for instance that oligopolistic rents exist in some markets, then the national interest is to implement various types of predatory behaviour. TP, IP and even CP (or the lack of it) can then be combined to perform this task (and some type of targeting of policies is still useful here - see Krishna and Thursby, 1991 and Laussel and Montet, 1988). But once distortions are in the picture, the good old theory warns us about the risks of failure of the international scheme of policies. Not only is a GATT or a WTO then needed, but also a supranational institution (possibly part of the former) which would also check that IP and CP are used for their optimal purpose and not in the pursuit of predatory goals.

LESSONS FROM THE STRATEGIC TRADE POLICY DISCUSSION

Basically the Brander and Spencer model and the related literature on so-called 'strategic trade (and industrial) policy' are examples of the predatory conducts which become optimal from a nationalistic point of view, assuming that sufficiently large distortions persist in the world markets.

It is now well understood that sophisticated governments could use the tools of trade policy (export subsidies, tariffs) or industrial policy (production subsidies, R&D subsidies, capacity expansion subsidies, and so on) to turn the national firms into Stackelberg leaders in the market game, thus increasing their profits. The credibility of government actions is supposed to be greater than that of the firms to implement the irreversible actions required for changing the game outcome. In the end, national welfare increases even if sometimes the domestic consumers lose in the process.

The argument has been extensively discussed. Gual is right in stressing the doubts shared by most economists about these policies. The difficulty of getting the right information about firms' behaviour, the great sensitivity of the results to the evaluation of relevant parameters, as well as the type of game played on the product market, the risk of retaliation and counterproductive tariff or subsidy wars do not argue in favour of the implementations of such policies. Moreover, the few quantifications which have been attempted and the likely evaluations of the amount of rents at stake, seem to imply that the policy is not worth implementing in any case.

This has even led Krugman to write: 'The strategic trade policy argument, then, has not turned out to be a major reason for questioning the academic orthodoxy on free trade - nor is it the kind of intellectual ratification of sophisticated mercantilism that many have supposed' (Krugman, 1992).

However, this kind of rejection of the Brander-Spencer argument could be misleading in different respects. Nobody believes seriously that a team of economists could be able to advise their government on the best means to transform the domestic oligopolies into Stackelberg leaders on the world markets. The politicians would simply not listen in the first place (especially if the economists conclude that the government should tax the exports because the game is Bertrand).

But one must remember that the Brander-Spencer model is just an example of the many various ways by which a government may implement predatory strategies to the detriment of foreigners.

Krugman (1992, 1994) emphasizes that the 'new trade theory' has also revived the interest for the study of the role of external effects in shaping specialization and trade flows. An argument in favour of state intervention similar to the Brander-Spencer model can be devised in this framework. Krugman regrets that it has not yet received the empirical attention needed, and he suspects that the potential gains from an activist policy centred on external effect issues could be many times larger than the eventual gains through rent-shifting policy.

Many other kinds of actions on trade, industry and competitive environment could in principle play the same role and eventually with simpler means and larger effects. Most of these policy schemes involving TP, IP and CP (or rather a lack of them) or mixtures of them may present the same basic drawbacks as the Brander-Spencer argument: difficulty in implementing the best policy, weak gains expected in the end, prisoner's dilemma situation when all countries act, and so on. But once we consider the political economy aspects of these policies, they may perform rather well from a politician's point of view, in terms of probabilities of reelection.

OTHER PREDATORY COMBINATIONS OF TP, IP AND CP

There are a lot of combinations of policies (trade, industrial and competition) which can provide predatory weapons to domestic industries. Various examples are given in all the papers on these issues (Gual; Jacquemin, 1994; Hay, 1993). Lenient competition policies or crude exemptions for particular sectors can help to protect a market from foreign competition, or to invade the foreign markets, or else to win a race abroad, and so on.

All the structures and actions studied in IO can be applied here. We think of such things as: predation, raising rival costs, exclusionary vertical contracts, or overt collusive agreements.

Collusion

Students of IO are familiar with the models of collusive behaviour in repeated non-cooperative games. So far, such models have hardly been evoked in the strategic trade policy literature (one exception is Harris, 1989). It would certainly be interesting to see how governments can interfere in such games.

Among the issues involved are the effects of an activist policy on the likely sharing of profit in the implicit cartel between domestic and foreign firms, as well as the specific problem of the trade-off between producers, gains and consumers' losses.

One knows from IO models that there can be a positive link between tacit collusion and multi-market contacts of firms. The multiplication of contacts between oligopolists on separate markets increases the probability of future meetings and consequently reinforces the credibility of the eventual threats and promises sustaining the tacit agreement. Similarly, the mutual invasion of national markets could reinforce the likelihood of tacit collusion and the problems of profit sharing going with it.

The previous argument can be related to the empirical work on the links between imports and the level of market power in the domestic markets. Generally a positive relation is found between domestic competition and imports. But it may be that in oligopolistic industries with strong entry barriers, low foreign market shares are correlated with low profit margins, while larger market shares facilitate collusion and thus higher profits for domestic firms as well.

Of course this conjecture needs empirical support. Its implications in terms of commercial policy would in any case be complex and ambiguous. Here again the presumption would be in favour of the implementation of an international antitrust policy rather than in favour of triggering dangerous international battles of subsidies and other predatory devices. But the possible incentives that some governments could have to intervene in collusive agreements in favour of their national firms need to be investigated in order to assess the political economy arguments of state interventions.

PREDATORY PRICING

The issue of predatory pricing on international markets is often quoted by managers but rarely discussed in the economic literature (see, however, Elzinga, 1989 and the comments in Ordover and Saloner, 1989). A firm has a predatory pricing strategy when it decides to lose money during a certain period of time by pricing very aggressively, in order to gain more in the future after having thrown the rivals out and obtained a monopolistic position. Although the plausibility of such behaviour is generally acknowledged in the business community, most IO studies have cast serious doubts on its rationality and consequently on its real probability of occurrence. On the other hand, modern research in terms of dynamic games and incomplete information have given some renewed credit to the predatory pricing story. However, it is generally admitted that the conditions of success of such a strategy are rather difficult to find in practice.

But, clearly, governmental support can give to a candidate predator the required credibility. Through a lenient or even non-existent competition policy, a government can let a firm or group of firms (cartel) raise the higher monopolistic rents on the domestic market and finance a predatory pricing campaign abroad. This possibility of international predatory pricing is in fact one case of dumping with a monopolization objective.

When the predator is a cartel of domestic firms, cheating is always possible and rewarding. Monitoring a predator cartel is not as easy as monitoring a 'normal' cartel. In the latter, when a firm cheats there may be a reversion to the non-cooperative price, but in the former prices are supposed to be already low. Does the deviant punition imply a reversion to high prices, forbidding the elimination of the foreign targets? The presence of the government, with its various policy instruments, is certainly a crucial factor here.

Finally, the possibility of international predatory pricing raises a series of questions concerning the rationality of firms and government. One can guess that the logic of government activism may induce firms to implement strategies which would normally be discarded as being irrational. The answers to these questions rest on the development of political economy of international governmental predatory actions. It may appear that this is not very feasible, but the issue needs to be investigated further, especially through empirical studies, again to see if policy-makers have genuine incentives to implement such schemes.

Raising Rivals' Costs and Exclusionary Vertical Arrangements

In an oligopoly, a firm can increase its profits by changing the pattern of relative costs between the competitors. Any action which raises its rivals' costs relative to its own is ultimately profitable, and among the great advantages of this type of behaviour, is the fact that it does not require any sunk investment before getting the rewards (see for instance Salop and Scheffman, 1983, 1987).

At the international level many governmental actions may help the domestic firms to implement such strategies. For instance there may be a legal requirement to use a specific technological network designed in such a way as to penalize foreign firms. One can imagine a lot of similar devices. The general idea is that these possible predatory actions do not require preliminary sunk expenses, in the form of subsidies or strategic investments.

This type of predatory conduct is closely linked to exclusionary vertical arrangements (and in fact can act through them). The government can use a lenient competition policy to let vertical arrangements be organized which block the entry of a foreign rival, like, for example, the organization of a locked distribution channel. In the other direction, the policy-makers can help domestic firms to establish beach-heads abroad, in order to prevent similar foreign actions. Examples of such conducts in real life are certainly not hard to find and document: it is well known that the block exemption of the automobile sector in the EU can be used by car producers to avoid some imports and intermarket arbitrage.

Closely related to this discussion are the vertical structures and arrangements recently introduced in the strategic trade theory literature (see Spencer and Jones, 1992). One could envisage several other transpositions of IO models to the international trade policy area. A good candidate could be the theory of mixed oligopoly which studies how the simultaneous presence of private and public firms in the same oligopolistic market is likely to modify the equilibrium (see for instance De Fraja and Delbono, 1989 or Cremer et al., 1989). It would certainly be interesting to study how the game between oligopolists and governments can be modified by the action of state-owned firms. In any case, there are plenty of examples in the EU of oligopolistic markets further distorted by the actions of several national state-owned 'champions'. The subject is certainly interesting and important on its own from a pure descriptive and empirical point of view.

In all the cases above, the antitrust authorities are supposed to remain passive in the face of the important distortions created. They might be asked to watch the rest of industry in order both to maintain a competitive environment in the 'non-strategic sectors' and to show to foreigners that the country has an active antitrust policy. In most instances industrial policy is also involved in the predatory plan: various subsidies and aids supposed to be required for IP objectives can easily serve as part of the 'war chest' for the predatory plan.

A brief comparison of the cases envisaged above with the Brander-Spencer argument might be useful at this stage. First, one may note that the essence of the arguments is basically the same: in each case the logic of the governmental action lies in taking advantage of the imperfections of competition to favour domestic firms at the expense of foreigners (assuming that the distinction still has meaning). So, in a sense, all the cases envisaged in this section are just other illustrations of strategic trade policy. Also, as the discussion of strategic trade policy has shown, it would not be realistic to expect a guide for policy-makers from the theoretical and empirical developments of the possible strategies mentioned above. One may find the difficulties already mentioned: incomplete information, costly retaliations, ultimate expectation of low welfare gains. And, above all, the predatory nature of such policies is not desirable from a world welfare perspective.

However, the differences in terms of implementation of the policies are certainly important, especially from a political economy point of view. Here is a short list of the main differences.

- First, one may notice that the cases examined in this section are in many respects more straightforward than the original Brander-Spencer argument. The implications of facilitating a collusive agreement, funding a predatory pricing plan, or raising foreign firms' costs are easier to contemplate for a policy-maker than the effects of subsidies on a supposedly Cournot oligopoly, which could well be closer to a Bertrand oligopoly after all.
- All the dynamic links which can turn a temporary blow into a long-run advantage, such as learning effects, switching costs, first-mover advantages in distribution channels, and so on, may often be large enough to justify the kinds of predatory conduct envisaged in this section. It may be that these elements are easier to find in practice (or at least to believe) than the presence of large oligopolistic rents required for launching a Brander-Spencer-type of policy.
- The chances of mistakes are real in all these examples, like in the original Brander-Spencer case, and the welfare trade-offs are hard to evaluate in each and every case. But the profit side of the welfare function may be easier to evaluate in the cases envisaged in this section. This point may be very important for the political economy aspects of the policy, since profits are likely to weight relatively more than consumer surpluses in the politicians' objective function.
- In the cases above, the government does not need to spend money in a strategic investment: it is easier from a public finance perspective to be lenient on an anti-competitive arrangement than to subsidize exports of a big oligopoly.
- The risk of retaliation exists too, but the policy here can be more easily hidden from the foreign government than the Brander-Spencer-type of policy.

To summarize, one can easily find a series of international policies involving TP, IP and CP (or lack of them), which could favour domestic firms at the expense of foreign ones, and eventually maximize national welfare. These policies are just other instances of the strategic trade policy argument, but with attractive features for satisfying interest groups. One can only guess that they are already more common than the usual discussions on strategic trade policy seem to admit. The likelihood of such policies and the eventual popularity of some of their aspects, imply that an international institution should watch for the possible distortions of TP, IP and CP towards predatory objectives.

FLAWS IN REAL POLICIES AND ADVANTAGES OF A SUPRANATIONAL INSTITUTION

We saw in the two previous sections that, at least in theory, TP, IP and CP could well cooperate in order to increase national welfare, eventually at the expense of foreigners' welfare. In reality, policy-makers are neither the benevolent regulators of perfect theory nor the clever manipulators of strategic devices.

The policy-makers try to maximize their election or reelection probabilities. This fundamental objective implies satisfying powerful interest groups, but also keeping an eye on the general interest, or at least the perception that the majority of voters could have of the major decisions.

The relatively young theory of endogenous protection has thrown some light on this problem. Large features of protection are understandable in a median voter model applied to a general equilibrium representation of the economy. It is clear, of course, that the results will depend on the type of GE model used: Hecksher-Ohlin or Ricardo-Viner for instance. Game-theoretical models are also useful here and sophisticated models of the relations between politicians and lobbies have been proposed recently (see Grossman and Helpman, 1994, or Riezman and Wilson, 1993). It is not, however, unfair to say that this theory has not yet come to commonly admitted results as we can find in other parts of trade policy theory.

Industrial policy is also greatly influenced by interest groups. The discussion of IP in terms of political economy arguments parallels that of TP. Even CP is the result of forces different from the simple objective of promoting efficiency: several competition laws are more a defence of small firms against big business than a defence of consumers or an objective of collective welfare, and some sectors are exempted from the most stringent rules. The American experience is a good example of some inconsistencies of the policy and it is certainly the best CP in the world (see White, 1993, which says that competition policy in the US is 'sloppy').

Thus, because of political factors, affecting differently the authorities in charge of TP, IP and CP, these various policies are often internally inconsistent, and contradictory.

Trade policies are generally far from what theory would suggest, not only far from free trade, but also from optimal strategic policy. It is not even certain that the policies implemented are the best for the purpose of maximizing the profits of the more powerful lobbies, simply because mistakes are made, such as bad moves in negotiations, or bad assessments of the amounts at stake.

Industrial policies are also generally far from the optimum, which most of the time should be *laissez-faire* and just maintain a general pro-business environment. Recent history has seen an accumulation of terrible IP, highly costly in terms of efficiency and generating huge losses for tax-payers and consumers.

It is ironic to see how ill-designed and sometimes internally inconsistent IP can turn out to operate against their claimed objectives. Lawrence (1987) notices that France, although 'committed to industrial policy, did not develop major poles of competitiveness' (p. 370). Although highly targeted, the French IP has failed to produce strong trade performances in particular sectors.

By contrast to TP and IP, competition policy is generally conducted by people more independent from lobbying activities, because CP is under the supervision of justice which is in principle independent. However, it remains that CP cannot be done correctly if the conflicts with the other two policies are too strong or if the policies abroad are too anti-competitive. Gual and others (Jacquemin, 1994; Hay, 1993) give excellent examples of impediments to development of correct CP policies in a too distorted environment (both internal and external).

How can national CP authorities seriously fight a price-fixing arrangement if a foreign government (or several of them) is (are) involved in the conspiracy? Also, CP authorities cannot detect and punish each and every collusive agreement. So, foreign competition normally serves as a useful complement. Now, if a domestic cartel can easily develop alliances with producers in neighbouring countries through FDI, joint ventures or mergers, this strategy may be used as a barrier to imports of rival products, thus reinforcing the domestic collusive agreement. Clearly, international cooperation is needed here to supervise the mergers.

More generally, merger policy in each country increasingly has an international dimension at each step of the procedure: definition of the relevant market, measure of ease of entry, potential effects on international collusive agreements, efficiency gains. The definition of the relevant market, which economists have rarely found very enlightening, but which is needed to compute market shares, at least in a preliminary administrative step of the analysis, involves more and more different countries. A major question here is whether all the capacities of the foreign producers must be included in the market. The possibility of a change in trade policy, through a tariff or a quota, makes an enormous difference. So what is needed is not only a collaboration between national CP authorities but also a coordination with the TP authorities of the countries involved. The evaluation of the ease of entry raises the same kind of problem. Is entry from abroad likely and isn't it too contingent on trade policy revisions?

One issue generally studied in the merger investigation is the likelihood of collusion in the relevant market. It is thus useful to have the cooperation of the foreign CP authorities to document eventual past episodes of collusions, which could induce a more cautious attitude towards the planned merger.

At last, CP authorities now tend to pay more attention to the efficiency gains that could be obtained through the merger. An important component of efficiency gains may be the competitive advantage on foreign markets. So a kind of strategic trade policy element may surreptitiously be included as a part of a competition law: the authorities officially assessing the trade-off between some harm to competition at home and a new competitive advantage with respect to foreign rivals. For example, Article 41 of the French law (1986 'ordonnance') suggests taking into account: 'the competitive advantage of enterprises on the international markets'. International cooperation of national authorities may avoid dangerous drifts on this point.

So CP, even one with the best intentions, needs international cooperation in order to be really efficient. One may add that it is also a matter of credibility. If CP is too obviously surrounded by other distortive policies either at home or abroad, its usefulness will soon be put in doubt. Take the case of France where the competition law since 1986 is sensible and where the authorities, especially the 'Conseil de la Concurrence', are playing a key role in diffusing, sometimes through hard penalties, the discipline of competition. It remains true, however, that the major part of the expenses of an average household in France are for commodities and services which are exempt from the toughness of competition. The average budget is spent largely on food (highly protected through the CAP), transport (where cars, airlines, rail are - or were until recently - protected, exempted from major competition rules, or even organized as state monopolies), energy (protected or state monopoly), telecommunications (state monopoly). In general, when the larger companies are allowed monopolies or exemptions, the consumer surplus is seriously harmed. The CP authorities take care of the rest of the economy, but they are sectors relatively less important in terms of inefficiencies. This is in a sense exactly the opposite of what should be done in terms of focus of the CP (see Hay and Morris for instance(1991, pp. 609-10), who argue that 'the policy should be concerned only with those situations where there is evidence of market dominance' and they add that only a few large firms pose the most serious problems).

The credibility of the whole CP, then, may be seriously shaken and one can understand managers of small and medium enterprises who think that CP is only another means for the state to raise taxes on their business.

Now the question is: if actual policies are so flawed, how could international coordination of policies really improve the situation? The answer is that it is the only way to get out of the prisoner's dilemma in which the countries could be trapped with their mutually harming and predatory policies. The experience of the GATT is generally positive in this respect. Countries have moved in the direction of freer trade through a complex process of negotiations on the access of foreigners to each national market. Although sustained by a rather mercantilist idea (it seems in fact that closing the market to foreigners is better and that a country can only offer a concession to enter in exchange for a concession in the other direction), the system has proved able to impose better trade policies on all the participating countries. One can only guess that similar bargaining on IP and CP could force the countries to move towards more sensible policies both internally and from a world welfare perspective.

The EC experience is also a good example of the discipline which policy cooperation imposes on the countries having the worst IP or the more lenient CP. Despite big mistakes in TP and IP (such as the CAP), the general trend has been in favour of freer trade and a view of IP on the average as more business-oriented and competition-oriented than the policies prevailing before in the more interventionist countries.

DESIGNING A COORDINATION OF POLICIES OR A SUPRANATIONAL COMPETITION AUTHORITY

We saw in the previous sections that if all the countries were implementing the targeting of policies as suggested by Bhagwati, there would remain a place for a kind of GATT, in order to avoid optimal tariff wars. But since a Nash equilibrium of optimal policy-mix is not likely to appear spontaneously, one needs a strong WTO, which can take care of TP and the international aspects of IP. We need also a coordination of CP and probably also a supranational competition authority, whether directly within the WTO or out of it.

What is far from clear are the precise tasks of this institution, the extent to which national CP must be harmonized and finally how the international regulation of competition is going to work.

At the very beginning one must note that the best way to operate in favour of competition is to extend still further the freedom of international trade. WTO is needed more for freeing trade first than for a harmonization of national CP.

Also one must be conscious that the forces which now push in favour of international antitrust harmonization are not all going in the right direction. Many proponents of various extensions of CP policies at the international level are begging for disguised protection, following the model of anti-dumping duties. The idea is that many foreign firms are using unfair conditions of production and unfair commercial practices. While this situation may actually be true in certain circumstances, this kind of argument creates a risk of abuse or distortion of the idea of harmonization of CP.

A possible outcome could be a mixing of antitrust issues and comparative advantage issues. We must not forget that the gains from trade come from differences between countries, which may include differences in vertical industrial relations, in the organization of distribution channels, and so on, all elements which can easily be confused with unfair practices. A consequence could be a multiplication of antitrust cases with the only objective of protection against supposedly advantaged foreign firms, again following what happens now with the anti-dumping rules.

The new institution could be at the beginning a centre of coordination of national policies and then evolve towards a more supranational organization. Its tasks should be:

a) to facilitate cooperation on issues which are of common interest among the countries involved;
b) to avoid distortive and predatory uses of CP regulations (or the lack of them in obvious cases of international predatory conducts).

Actions corresponding to a common interest among the countries are relatively easy to implement. The example of the EC competition policy is good in this respect and such seems to be the case of the recent US-EC agreement.

The cases where national interests conflict will of course be more difficult to deal with. The supranational feature of the new organization is important here. However, even the supranational institution will have a hard time getting the information from the countries involved. One must notice here that it is more difficult to see through each national system of competition law than to observe trade policy (although problems of asymmetric information also arise in trade policy cases). Incentives schemes should be designed in order to sustain cooperation, but the design of such schemes needs a lot of work, both from a theoretical and from a practical point of view.

The main advances in international trade negotiations have come through a process of bargaining, where many equilibria were possible and where focal points were obtained by choosing simple rules of symmetry (such as a proportional decrease in tariffs - on this point see McMillan, 1988). But such symmetric 'mutual concessions' are harder to define for competition rules, taking into account all the structural and cultural differences among countries.

Finally, there may be very tough problems of enforcement of decisions. Unlike for trade issues, retaliation and their extent (through a kind of most favoured nation principle) are far from clear for CP. While an obvious punishment in a trade conflict is a threat to reduce trade flows, the reaction to a predatory use of a lenient CP may be hard to define. Should the harmed country develop in turn a symmetric lenient CP? In many cases, this solution does not make much sense. A reply through an action on trade flows is feasible. Indeed that may even be an argument for keeping the conflicts on CP under WTO supervision. But then the danger is a multiplication of trade restrictions brought by disagreements on CP.

Pressures are so strong to use CP issues as new arguments for protection, that the designers of any new scheme of negotiations on these issues must be very cautious about the possible perverse effects of a seemingly good policy.

CONCLUDING REMARKS

Trying to harmonize TP, IP and CP at the international level has now become necessary in an integrated world economy. The main objective should be to improve efficiency both at the national and international levels, by moving towards an equilibrium of policy-mix closer to the ideal of the theory of trade policy in the presence of distortions.

For the European Union, there is the double objective of improving the harmonization of policies among its member countries and of contributing to an extension of the coordination with non-EU countries. On the first issue, a quicker move towards a more integrated competition policy is needed, together with the taming or withdrawal of state aids to national monopolies or oligopolies, and other highly distortive IP. On the second issue, one can only encourage the EU authorities to initiate and support international negotiations, such as the one which led to the EU-US agreement.

The recent proposal by the European Commission (DG III) of 'An Industrial Competitiveness Policy for the European Union' mentions the need for such cooperative policies with the rest of the world. The paper supports efficient changes of policy toward 'more open trade', 'monitoring state aid more rigorously', or 'proposals for the development of rules on competition'. However, the same document contains several points which can only inspire worries about the intended policy. The so-called 'industrial cooperation' which should (according to the document) be encouraged 'to enable industrialists from inside and outside Europe to identify and harness their mutual interests', looks a bit like supporting industrial collusion. The objectives of 'ensuring fair competition' may easily be translated into protection against new NIC or LDC. What we learnt from the political economy of protection gives reasons to worry about the possible drifts of such proposals.

REFERENCES

Bhagwati, J. (1971), 'The generalized theory of distortions and welfare', in Bhagwati et al. (eds.), *Trade, Balance of Payments and Growth*, North-Holland, Amsterdam.

Cremer, H., M. Marchand and J.F. Thisse (1989), 'The public firm as an instrument for regulating an oligopolistic market', *Oxford Economic Papers*, 41.

De Fraja, G. and F. Delbono (1989), 'Alternative strategies of a public enterprise in oligopoly', *Oxford Economic Papers*, 41.

Elzinga, K. (1989), 'Collusive predation', in J. Kwoka and L. White (eds.), *The Antitrust Revolution*, Scott, Foresman & Co, Glenview, Illinois.

Grossman, G. and E. Helpman (1994), 'Protection for sale', forthcoming in the *American Economic Review*.

Harris, R.(1989), 'The new protectionism revisited', *Canadian Journal of Economics*, 22: 751-78.

Hay, D. (1993), 'The assessment: competition policy', *Oxford Review of Economic Policy*, 9: 133-51.

Hay, D. and D.J. Morris (1991), *Industrial Economics and Organization*, 2nd edition, Oxford University Press, Oxford.

Jacquemin, A. (1994), 'Competition policies for a highly integrated economy', in F. Scherer *Competition Policies for an Integrated World Economy*, The Brookings Institution, Washington.

Krishna, K. and M. Thursby (1991), 'Optimal Policies with Strategic Distortions', *Journal of International Economics*, 31: 291-308.

Krugman, P. (1992), 'Does the new trade theory require a new trade policy?', *The World Economy*, 15: 423-42.

Krugman, P. (1994), 'Empirical evidence on the new trade theories: the current state of play', in *New Trade Theories*, CEPR Conference Report,

London.

Laussel, D. and C. Montet (1988), 'On the Hierarchy of Trade and Industrial Policy for Oligopolistic Industries', mimeo, University of Aix-Marseille II, 23 pp.

Lawrence, R. (1987), 'Trade performance as a constraint on European growth', in R. Lawrence and G.L. Schultze, *Barriers to European Growth: A Transatlantic View*, Brookings Institution, Washington.

McMillan, J. (1988), 'A game theoretic view of international trade negotiations: implications for developing countries', in J. Whalley *Developing Countries and the International Trading System,* Macmillan, London.

Ordover, J. and G. Saloner (1989), 'Predation, Monopolization, and Antitrust', in R. Schmalensee and R. Willig, *Handbook of Industrial Organization*, North-Holland, Amsterdam.

Riezman, R. and J.D. Wilson (1993), 'Politics and trade policy', Working Paper 93-08, University of Iowa.

Salop, S. and D. Scheffman (1983), 'Raising rival's costs', *American Economic Review*, 73: 267-71.

Salop, S. and D. Scheffman (1987), 'Cost-raising strategies', *Journal of Industrial Economics*, 36: 19-34.

Spencer, B. and R. Jones (1992), 'Trade and protection in vertically related markets', *Journal of International Economics,* 32: 31-56

White, L. (1993), 'Competition policy in the United States: an overview', *Oxford Review of Economic Policy*, 9: 133-51.

2. The working of EC policies on competition, industry and trade: a legal analysis

Jacques H.J. Bourgeois and Paul Demaret

INTRODUCTION

This chapter analyses the working of EC policies on competition, industry and trade from a legal point of view. It comprises three parts. First, the legal framework inside which the three policies are to be conducted is examined, then selected cases exemplifying the interaction or the lack of interaction between the three policies are presented and discussed. The paper concludes with some recommendations to improve the common working of the three policies at the Community level.

For the purpose of this article, the scope and the content of the three policies is to be understood by reference to the relevant provisions of the EC Treaty, namely Article 85 and seq., Article 130 and Article 113, as construed by the Court of Justice and as implemented by EC secondary legislation.

I. THE LEGAL FRAMEWORK

As understood in this chapter, the legal framework consists of the provisions of the EC Treaty which define the purpose and the content of the three policies, as well as the instruments available for their implementation, together with relevant pieces of secondary legislation adopted by the Community on the basis of the EC Treaty. The legal framework will be analysed from two angles.

First, we will discuss the relationship between the three policies in terms of substance. The two main questions which we will address are:

- whether the EC Treaty, i.e. the Community Economic Constitution,

gives equal weight to each of the three policies;
- whether the Treaty or secondary legislation provides for their common working and if so, how and to what extent.

Second and more briefly, we will look at the relationship between the three policies from an institutional angle and examine:

- what is the respective role assigned by the EC Treaty to the Community institutions and the Member States in the implementation of the policies;
- whether Community measures implementing the respective policies are taken according to similar or different decision-making procedures.

These institutional aspects are not without importance if consistency is to be achieved in the implementation of the three policies.

A. The Relationship Betwenn the Three Policies from the Standpoint of Substantive Law

Hereafter, we will consider what the relationship between the three policies is, first according to the 'general principles' of the EC Treaty, then according to specific provisions of Community law. The main developments will concern industrial policy and its links with the two other policies. It is only since Maastricht that the main Community Treaty mentions industrial policy.

1. The 'principles' underlying the EC Treaty

The common provisions of the Maastricht Treaty, which state in broad terms the objectives of the European Union, do not refer to competition, trade or industrial policy. These three policies appear in Part One ('Principles') of the EC Treaty among the policies and activities of the European Community. Article 3 refers respectively in paragraphs (b), (g) and (l) to 'a common commercial policy', to 'a system ensuring that competition in the internal market is not distorted' and to 'the strengthening of the competitiveness of Community industry'.

Although Article 3 taken in isolation sheds no light on the relationship between the three policies, it does shed some light on the content of 'industrial policy'. Article 3(l) does not use the words 'industrial policy' as such, but instead the words 'the strengthening of the competitiveness of

Community industry'. Such words express the objective which the Treaty assigns to industrial policy. They are meaningful in two ways. First, in keeping with the concept of an internal market, industrial policy should aim at improving the competitiveness of the Community's industry as a whole. Second, industrial policy, even if it implicitly refers to industrial competition from third countries, is not to be equated with protection of the Community's industry, but rather, and more positively, with improving its ability to compete.[1] Article 130, the specific industry provision which is examined *infra*, confirms that view.

Following the Maastricht Treaty, a new provision, Article(3a), which refers to economic and monetary union, was inserted among the introductory provisions of the EC Treaty. Paragraph 1 of Article (3a) provides that the economic policy of the Member States and the Community shall be conducted 'in accordance with the principle of an open market economy with free competition'. This principle is again affirmed in Article 102(a) and in Article 130 of the Treaty.

Taken together Articles 3(g), 3(a), 102(a) and 130 imply that competition policy enjoys a higher status than the two other policies. Admittedly, the principle of free and undistorted competition has essentially a political content. It cannot by itself serve as the basis for the creation of rights and obligations which legal subjects could routinely ask the courts to enforce. Its operative content depends on the specific competition rules provided in Articles 85 to 94 and Community legislation implementing these rules. Nevertheless, the principle of free and undistorted competition as such could influence the interpretation of

1 For a discussion of the link between industrial policy and international competitiveness, see D.B. Audretsch, 'Industrial Policy and Industrial Competitiveness', in Ph. Nicolaides (ed.), *Industrial Policy in the Community: A Necessary Response to Economic Integration?*, Martinus Nijhoff, 1993, 68-105 and M. Bangemann, *Meeting the Global Challenge - Establishing a Successful European Industrial Policy*, Kogan Page, 1992.

Community law[2] when there is an actual conflict between competition policy and, for instance, trade policy measures. We refer here to a conflict between competition policy and trade policy, for in the case of a conflict between competition policy and industrial policy, Article 130 makes clear that industrial policy has to yield.[3]

2. Specific Treaty provisions and secondary legislation

a. Industrial policy

1) The 'constitutional' constraints: the primacy of competition policy and the non-discrimination rule.

As a result of the Maastricht Treaty, a new provision, Article 130, was introduced in the EC Treaty to specifically deal with industrial policy. The most striking feature of Article 130 is that it leaves no doubt as to the prominent position of competition policy. Not only does Article 130 provide that industrial policy measures must comply 'with a system of open and competitive markets' (a reminder of Article(3a) and 102(a), it also stresses, somewhat emphatically, that it may not serve as 'a basis for the introduction by the Community of any measure which could lead to a distortion of competition'. The limit thus set to the possible content of industrial policy measures seems sufficiently precise to be justiciable. The words used refer back to Article 3(g) of the EC Treaty ('a system ensuring that competition in the internal market is not distorted'), a provision which is not precise enough to be legally enforceable. But

---

2 In the past, the Court of Justice did not hesitate to rely on Article 3(f) of the EEC Treaty (now Article 3(g) of the EC Treaty) to supplement or even, according to some authors, to modify the letter of Article 86. See Continental Can, ECJ Feb. 21, 1973, case 6/72, 1973 ECR 244, where the Court said: 'The ... argument that this provision merely contains a general programme devoid of legal effect, ignores the fact that Article 3 considers the pursuit of the objectives which it lays down to be indispensable for the achievement of the Community's tasks. As regards in particular the aim mentioned in (f), the Treaty in several provisions contains more detailed regulations for the interpretation of which this aim is decisive. But if Article 3(f) provides for the institution of a system ensuring that competition in the Common Market is not distorted, then it requires *a fortiori* that competition must not be eliminated. This requirement is so essential that it corresponds to the precept of Article 2 of the Treaty according to which one of the tasks of the Community is "to promote throughout the Community a harmonious development of economic activities". Thus the restraints on competition which the Treaty allows under certain conditions because of the need to harmonise the various objectives of the Treaty, are limited by the requirements of Articles 2 and 3. Going beyond this limit involves the risk that the weakening of competition would conflict with the aims of the Common Market.'

3 Cf. *infra*.

Article 3(g) has received concrete meaning and become enforceable through the rules of competition laid down in Articles 85 to 94, as construed by the Court of Justice and implemented by the Council and the Commission. One may therefore argue that industrial policy measures leading to results inconsistent with competition rules would be invalid under the EC Treaty. In other words, competition rules must be seen as determining the permissible content of industrial policy measures. The extent to which EC competition rules allow the pursuit of the industrial policy objectives listed in Article 130, will be discussed *infra*.

The leading role of competition rules in the industrial policy field is in stark contrast with the limited role given to competition rules in the agricultural sector.[4] This also contrasts with the regime applicable to coal and steel. There, competition rules can in effect be temporarily suspended in times of crisis through the imposition by the High Authority of production quotas and minimum prices respectively on the basis of Articles 58 and 61 of the Coal and Steel Treaty. The fact that the Coal and Steel Treaty permits the conduct of an interventionist industrial policy explains the debate concerning the question of whether it will be renewed or allowed to lapse in 2002. This also helps to explain why, in a series of cases now pending before the Court of First Instance, steel producers make the argument that the Commission should not interpret and implement Article 65 of the Coal and Steel Treaty in the same manner as Article 85 of the EC Treaty, since the former allows a degree of public intervention in the industry.[5] The argument is that the Steel and Coal Treaty competition rules should be construed in the light of the sectoral and interventionist industrial policy permitted under that Treaty. Article 130 of the EC Treaty makes plain that under the latter the reverse should apply: industrial policy measures need to be consistent with competition rules.

The EC Treaty places another 'constitutional constraint' on the conduct of industrial policy. Article 58 of the EC Treaty does not distinguish between companies on the basis of the nationality of the controlling shareholders. Therefore, any company set up in accordance with the laws of a Member State qualifies as a Community undertaking under the EC Treaty and may not be discriminated against. This means that, as the general objective assigned to industrial policy is the strengthening of the competitiveness of the Community's industry, the concept of Community

---

4 See EC Treaty, Article 42, and the recent Banana judgment, ECJ October 5, 1994, Case C-280/93, as yet unreported.

5 See O.J. 1994, C 146/10, 12, 14 and 15.

industry encompasses all firms established in the Community whether controlled by Community or third country interests. All these firms should benefit equally from any industrial policy measure taken by the Community or the Member States.

2) Objectives assigned to industrial policy

According to Article 130, §1, the general purpose of industrial policy is to ensure the competitiveness of the Community's industry, as already mentioned in Article 3(e). That goal is to be achieved through the pursuit of four sub-objectives:

- speeding up the adjustment of industry to structural changes;
- encouraging an environment favourable to undertakings, particularly small and medium-sized undertakings;
- encouraging an environment favourable to cooperation between undertakings;
- fostering better exploitation of the industrial potential of policies of innovation, research and technological development.

As it is readily apparent, the final version of Article 130 does not incorporate the proposals made by some Member States during the Intergovernmental Conference, which would have explicitly linked industrial policy and commercial policy and singled out high-tech industries as deserving special attention or even some measure of trade protection.[6] Some have nevertheless expressed the fear that Article 130 might in some instances be used to implement an interventionist form of industrial policy.[7]

As spelled out in Article 130, both the general and specific objectives of industrial policy seem to have been largely inspired by the Commission Communication of 1990, 'Industrial policy in an open and competitive environment',[8] which received the Council's approval.[9] The 1990 Communication, known as the Bangemann Memorandum, is based on the

---

6 The legislative history of Article 130 was analysed by the late Emanuele Gazzo in Europe, 6-7, 8, 9 and 10 January 1992.

7 See the ninth report (1990/1991) of the German Monopolies Commission, summarized in *Europe*, 7 October 1992. As P. Buigues and A. Sapir ('Community Industrial Policies', in Nicolaides (ed.), op. cit. *supra*, 21 at 33), indicate, Article 130 leaves open the possibility of sectoral measures provided they enhance structural adjustments.

8 COM (90) 556 final.

9 Doc. 10159/90 (Press 198-G), reproduced in Europe Documents, No. 1667, 7 Dec. 1990.

premise that competitiveness and continuous adaptation to industrial change is primarily the responsibility of business firms.[10] In that Communication, the Commission repudiated direct public intervention in industrial sectors, but emphasized the need for a horizontal approach to industrial policy, where the task of public authorities is the creation of a favourable environment for industrial development.[11] [12] In keeping with that approach, the Commission, in a new Communication entitled 'An industrial competitiveness policy for the European Union',[13] now identifies four priorities: the promotion of intangible investment, the development of industrial cooperation, fair competition (internally and externally) and the modernization of the role of the public authorities.

3) Instruments available to the Community for the conduct of industrial policy [14]

Article 130, §3, opens up two different roads for the conduct of industrial policy, one which may be termed the main road, the other which looks like a side road and is rather narrow.

The main road available for the implementation of the industrial policy objectives mentioned in Article 130, §1, is 'through the policies and activities the Community pursues under other provisions of the EC Treaty'. Indeed, the programmes set out by the Commission in its 1990 and 1994 Communications show that in order to achieve these industrial policy objectives resort has to be made, at one point or another, to almost all substantive provisions contained in the EC Treaty: Articles 85 and 86 (competition rules), Articles 92 and 93 (control of state aids), Article 99 (fiscal harmonization), Article 100 a (legislation concerning the internal market), Articles 101 and 102 (state measures resulting in distortion of competition), Articles 112 and 113 (commercial policy), Article 123 (social adaptation to industrial changes), Article 129(b) (trans-European networks), Article 130(a) and seq. (economic and social cohesion), Article

---

10 On this new approach, see Ph. Nicolaides, 'Industrial Policy: the problem of reconciling definitions, intentions and effects', in Nicolaides (ed.), op. cit. *supra*, 1 at 11-14.

11 The European Parliament (see Resolution A3-177/91, O.J. 1991 C 240/213), even though agreeing with the general content of the 1990 Commission Communication, insisted on the need for a more forceful industrial policy, including a more vigorous trade policy.

12 Previous Commission Communications concerning industrial policy are briefly summarized in the opinion of the Economic and Social Committee on the 1990 Communication, see O.J. 1992 C 40/31.

13 COM (94) 319 final.

14 For a review of the budgetary and regulatory instruments of EC industrial policy, see P. Buigues and A. Sapir, op. cit. *supra*, 21-35

130(f) and seq. (research and technological development), Article 130(r) and seq. (environment). This is not surprising. Once the objective ascribed to industrial policy is as general as the strengthening of the competitiveness of the European industry, industrial policy extends its scope to all economic and social aspects of European integration.

If industrial policy should normally be implemented through the instruments available under the EC Treaty for the implementation of other policies, Article 130 also provides for a secondary road. The Community may take specific measures on the basis of Article 130 in order to support action by the Member States. But such specific measures require the Council's unanimity, and not simply a qualified majority as some Member States had wished. Unanimity is the safety catch which other Member States wanted in order to ensure that measures of a protectionist character could not be adopted on the basis of Article 130, without their agreement.

The unanimity required by Article 130 has a rather obvious implication. The pursuit of a sectoral protectionist policy can be more easily attempted through the channel of other Treaty provisions such as Article 113 (which allows the use of trade policy instruments on the basis of qualified or, as will be seen *infra*, even simple majority voting) or Articles 92 and 93 (through possible lax enforcement of the control of state aids by the Commission).

4) Industrial policy in relation to other EC policies

Article 130 calls for the Community to take a more active role with respect to industrial policy. The opening sentence of the third paragraph of Article 130 reads: 'The Community *shall contribute to the achievement of the objectives set out in paragraph 1 through the policies and activities it pursues under other provisions* of this Treaty' (emphasis added).

The language used in Article 130, §3, seems slightly stronger than the language found in Article 128, §4, concerning culture: 'The Community *shall take cultural aspects into account in its action under other provisions of this Treaty'* (emphasis added).

Article 130, §3, ought to be construed as requiring Community institutions to implement other Treaty provisions in the light of industrial policy as defined in Article 130, §1 (see *supra*). However such an obligation which in any event applies within the 'competitive perimeter' also defined in Article 130, is not very precise since the objectives of industrial policy are expressed in broad terms. There is a political obligation for Community institutions to pursue these industrial policy objectives through the implementation of other Treaty provisions, and this is indeed what the Commission proposes in its Communications. But such an obligation cannot be seen as justiciable, if by that one means the possibility given to a person to challenge the legality of a Community measure on the grounds that it was taken in disregard of certain industrial policy objectives. Here it is worth observing that the wording of Article 130, §3, is somewhat weaker than that of Article 130(r), §2, whose last sentence, as modified by the Maastricht Treaty, reads: 'Environmental protection requirements *must be integrated into the definition and implementation of other Community policies*' (emphasis added).

An obligation so phrased could perhaps be subject to judicial review, if not on substantive, at least on procedural grounds. It is submitted that the legality of a measure taken by the Community, for instance in the field of trade, without giving any regard to environmental protection needs, could be challenged before the Court of Justice by a Member State. This can be linked to the fact that environmental protection needs can probably be more easily identified than industrial policy needs, even though the degree of environmental protection to be achieved in a given case may be a matter for debate.

5) Brief assessment of the contribution of the Maastricht Treaty regarding industrial policy

The Treaty of Maastricht puts industrial policy on the EC Treaty map. But the new Article 130 does not really add to the powers the Community already held under the EEC Treaty with respect to industrial policy. Indeed, Article 130 refers in the first place to other provisions of the Treaty for the implementation of industrial policy. That essentially corresponds to the situation which existed under the EEC Treaty. Second, Article 130 allows specific measures to be taken subject to unanimous voting in the Council. But previously, the Community could and did adopt specific industrial policy measures on the basis of Article 235 of the Treaty, which also requires the Council's unanimity.[15]

Since it defines in a positive way the purpose of industrial policy, i.e. the strengthening of competitiveness, and stresses the prominent role of

[15] See for instance Council Decision of 22 July 1993 on an action plan for the introduction of advanced television services in Europe, O.J. L 196/1993; Council Decision of 21 December 1990 concerning the implementation of an action programme to promote the development of the European audiovisual industry (Media) (1991 on 1995), O.J. L 380/90; Council Decision of 27 April 1989 on high-definition television, O.J. L 142/1989.

competition policy, Article 130 seems designed to curtail rather than to enlarge the margin of discretion that Community institutions hold in the conduct of industrial policy. The main significance of Article 130 is that is clearly invites the Community to follow an integrated approach in the implementation of industrial policy.

b. Trade policy

1) The Treaty provisions

Articles 110 to 113[16] do not directly deal with the status of commercial policy *vis-à-vis* industrial policy or competition policy. Nevertheless, these provisions contain references to each of the latter.

Article 110 in its second paragraph states that: 'The common commercial policy shall take into account the favourable effect which the abolition of customs duties between Member States may have *on the increase in the competitive strength* of undertakings in those States' (emphasis added).

As seen *supra*, the increase in the competitive strength of Community undertakings is now the very purpose assigned by the Treaty to industrial policy. Transposed in the internal market context, Article 110 would stand for the proposition that the positive effects resulting from the establishment of the internal market on the competitiveness of the Community's industry should lead to a more liberal trade policy. Of course, as the Court of Justice has ruled,[17] Article 110 is merely a statement of intent, with no binding effect on the Community.

Article 112, §1, provides for the harmonization of national aid schemes for exports to third countries, 'to the extent necessary to ensure that *competition between undertakings of the Community is not distorted'* (emphasis added).

The Treaty thus confirms the functional link which exists between the uniformization of export regimes and undistorted competition in the internal market. But Article 112 too is a mere statement of intent, with no binding effect on the Community legislator. Indeed, export aid schemes, which supposedly were to be harmonized before the end of the transitional period, have not yet been harmonized at the Community level, except to the extent that the Community is party to the OECD arrangement on

[16] Article 115 will not be considered here. With the advent of the internal market and the uniformization of import regimes, resort to Article 115 should cease, with the possible exception in cases where 'regional' safeguard measures are taken.

[17] See Dürbeck, ECJ, May 5, 1981, case No. 112/80, 1981 ECR 1095.

export credits.[18] That situation is, in part, due to the fact that for some Member States export aids schemes remain an instrument of foreign policy. From the standpoint of both competition policy and industrial policy, the Community ought to proceed with the harmonization of export aid schemes on the basis of the trade policy provision, Article 113.[19] In case it were not to do so, Article 101 could be viewed as an alternative. However, one should observe that decisions cannot be more easily taken on the basis of Article 101 than on the basis of Article 113: both require qualified majority voting.

Article 113, the main commercial policy provision, states that the external trade regime should be based on uniform principles with respect to imports and exports and it explicitly mentions 'measures to protect trade such as those to be taken in the event of dumping and subsidies'.

From the standpoint of competition policy and industry policy, it is also quite clear that the uniformization of import regimes is necessary so that firms belonging to a given Community industry are all exposed to a similar degree of competition from outside the Community.[20] Such uniformization is also indispensable if a true internal market is to emerge. As we will see *infra*, import regimes were made (almost) fully uniform only very recently. The difficulties which the Community had to overcome in order to establish common rules on imports illustrate the links between trade policy, industrial policy and competition policy.

2) International law

The Community is bound by GATT. Now that the agreement establishing the WTO has entered into force, the Community has to comply with the various multilateral agreements negotiated during the Uruguay Round, which are destined to liberalize international trade.[21] In several respects, these agreements limit the ability of governments to intervene in favour

---

18 The question of export credits is well analysed in M.-L. Hoube-Masse, '*La CEE et les crédits à l'exportation. L'intégration en question*', Rennes, 1992.

19 The Commission has recently presented a draft directive, see O.J. 1994, C 272/2 and *Europe*, 8 September 1994, p. 10.

20 The influence of imports on competition in the European market is discussed in A. Jacquemin and A. Sapir, '*Competition and imports in the European market*', in L.A. Winters and A. Venables (eds.), *European Integration, Trade and Industry*, London: Cambridge University Press, CEPR 1990, pp. 82-92. See also P.C. Padoa's comments, ibid., 92-5.

21 For the detailed content of these agreements, see P. Demaret, 'Les métamorphoses du GATT: de la Charte de la Havanne à l'Organisation Mondiale du Commerce', *Journal des Tribunaux Droit européen*, 1994, p. 121 and seq. and the articles published in *Revue du Marché unique européen*, 1994, No. 4.

of their domestic industry.

Admittedly, the Uruguay Round negotiations did not result in making significantly more difficult the imposition of anti-dumping duties and the pursuit, through such means, of industrial policy objectives. However, orderly marketing agreements and unilateral trade restrictions which do not conform with Article XIX of GATT of 1947 and the new agreement on safeguards are to be gradually scrapped so that they can be completely eliminated by the end of a transitional period. The extension of a safeguard measure beyond a four-year period is itself subject to the condition that the domestic industry protected by the measure proceeds to adjust to foreign competition. Speeding up the adjustment of industry to structural changes is one of the objectives set by Article 130 to industrial policy. These firm rules have obvious implications for the Community's textile and car industry.[22]

In addition, there is a new agreement on subsidies which provide for much clearer and stricter rules than the Tokyo Round code. The new agreement deals not only with subsidies which directly affect trade (through the boosting of exports or the reduction of imports), but also with subsidies to industrial research and with regional and environmental aids.[23] The European Community (and its Member States) will have to take the new international rules on subsidies into account when they try to achieve industrial policy objectives through the granting and the control of public aids. It should, however, not be too hard for the Community to fulfil its obligations under the agreement on subsidies since the Community exerted a significant influence on the content of that agreement.

The new multilateral rules resulting from the Uruguay Round are not only much more comprehensive than the present GATT rules. They should also be more effective, because of the new rules which will govern the settlement of disputes between members of the WTO. What precedes, however, essentially applies at the international level. The effectiveness of multilateral trade rules within the Community legal order remains

---

22 As the Community invoked the derogations permitted by the General Agreement on Trade in Services, the main provisions of that agreement will not apply to the Community's audiovisual sector. This means that the local content requirement (the European works quota) provided by the TV without Frontiers Directive of 1989 does not have to be eliminated. This could be seen as the implementation by the Community of Article 128, §4 (the 'culture provision' of the EC Treaty) in the external field and as a form of industrial policy in the old sense.

23 In the future aids to the Community's shipyards may have to conform to the new multilateral rules negotiated in the context of the OECD, as indicated in the preamble to Council Directive 94/73, OJ L351/10/1994.

limited as a result of the case law of the Court of Justice. In the recent Banana case,[24] the Court confirmed that GATT rules could neither be invoked by a private complainant, nor by Member States in order to challenge the validity of a Community measure, except if these rules were incorporated into, or specifically referred to by Community secondary legislation.[25]

3) The uniformisation of import regimes and the reform of trade policy instruments

- The completion of the internal market

The manner in which the Community proceeded to subject all imported products to common regimes illustrates the interaction between different policies at the legislative level.[26] At the time the internal market was supposed to be completed, the situation regarding imports was as follows.[27] The importation of products from most third countries was governed by common rules either as a result of autonomous measures taken by the Community or as a result of trade agreements concluded by the latter with third countries. Nevertheless, products imported from a number of third countries (most notably certain imports from current or former state economies as well as Japanese cars) had remained governed by national import rules. Such a situation was obviously inconsistent with the notion of an internal market.[28]

All products imported from third countries are now governed by common rules.[29] But this was achieved only after significant trade-offs were made between internal trade liberalization, external trade protection, industrial policy and competition policy.

- The debate surrounding the reform of trade policy instruments:

---

24 See *supra* note 2.

25 Community legislation implementing the Uruguay Round agreements appears in O.J. L349 of December 31, 1994.

26 For the interaction of the different policies in individual cases, see the second part of the chapter.

27 For a detailed examination of import regimes on the eve of the completion of the internal market, see E. Völker, *Barriers to External and Internal Community*, Amsterdam, 1993, 62-73, 79-81.

28 About 6,000 national quantitative restrictions were still in force at the end of 1993.

29 See Council Regulations No. 517/94, 518/94 and 519/94, O.J. 1994, L67/1, 77 and 89, which were adopted on March 7, 1994.

Some Member States (France, Italy, Spain, Portugal and Greece) wanted to link tightly the uniformisation of import regimes, internal trade liberalization and the granting of new competences to the Court of First Instance in the trade field to the reinforcement of trade policy instruments (safeguard measures, anti-dumping duties, 'new instrument'). They wanted to speed up the adoption of trade protective measures and to give more power to the Commission. The Commission itself submitted to the Council a draft regulation which would have made the Commission responsible for taking final decisions in all matters relating to trade protection, unless overruled by a qualified majority in the Council.[30] Such reform was opposed by the United Kingdom, Germany, The Netherlands, Denmark and Luxemburg, Belgium standing in the middle.[31] The Commission also proposed to give to Community industries the right to lodge complaints with respect to safeguard measures, similar to the right of complaint which exists in dumping cases.[32] This proposal raised the fear that the number of safeguard measures would increase as a result.[33]

Despite the opposition of the United Kingdom, a deal was eventually struck.[34] It provided for the elimination of all remaining national quantitative restrictions and the adoption of new rules on imports.[35] But, in exchange, stricter deadlines were set for the conduct of anti-dumping investigations.[36] Moreover, anti-dumping duties imposed by the Commission now become definitive if confirmed by a simple majority in the Council,[37] instead of by a qualified majority as previously required. The adoption of anti-dumping duties thus can no longer be prevented by a blocking minority in the Council. The new rules are generally seen as making the imposition of anti-dumping duties easier than before. However, such a view in a sense prejudges the Commission's future attitude towards dumping. Indeed, to consider that simple majority voting in the Council will lead to an increase of successful anti-dumping applications rests on the rather intriguing premise that the Commission is

---

30 See O.J. 1992, C 181/9.

31 See *Europe*, 30 December 1992.

32 See O.J. 1993, C 328/8.

33 See *Europe*, 29 and 30 December 1993.

34 See *Europe*, 9 February 1994.

35 See Council Regulations Nos. 517/94, 518/94 and 519/94, O.J. 1994, L 67/1, 77 and 89. Regulation 518/94 has now been replaced by Regulation 3285/94, OJ L 349/53/94.

36 See Council Regulations No. 521/94, O.J. 1994, L 66/, modifying Regulation 2423/88 now replaced by Regulation 3283/94, OJ L 349/1/1994.

37 See Council Regulations No. 522/94, O.J. 1994, L 66/10, modifying Regulation 2423/88 now replaced by Regulation 3283/94, OJ L 349/1/1994.

intrinsically more favourable to trade protection than the Council.

The Community's industry did not receive the right to lodge complaints with respect to safeguards. Moreover, safeguard measures will normally continue to require the consent of a qualified majority of the Member States in order to be adopted by the Council or to remain in force where they are taken by the Commission.[38] More complicated rules apply to the textile sector.[39]

- The 'interests of the Community' and the competition policy factor

That the rationale underlying, respectively, anti-dumping legislation and competition rules differs, is a well-known fact. Anti-dumping legislation provides for measures to counteract price discrimination and sales below cost which would not be unlawful under competition rules. Indeed, the latter prohibit only predatory pricing. This, however, does not mean that anti-dumping legislation should be systematically implemented in a manner which would contradict competition policy rules and objectives.

Community anti-dumping legislation, as well as legislation regarding safeguards, have now for many years included provisions which refer to 'the interests of the Community'. From the standpoint of competition policy, such a reference becomes meaningful only if the Commission or the Council, as the case may be, is obliged to consider separately from the interests of the domestic industry, the interests of consumers and industrial users and more generally the market competitive situation. As argued *infra*,[40] the Community interests should, in our view, be understood as requiring that Community trade measures never result in the elimination of competition in respect of a substantial part of the relevant Community market.

As it stood until the end of 1994, Community anti-dumping legislation provided that definitive duties could be imposed if a Community industry was injured and 'where the interests of the Community so required'.[41] The latter were not precisely defined. The Commission acknowledged that among these interests the most important were 'the interests of the consumers and processors of the imported product and the need to have

---

[38] See Regulation No. 519/94, Articles 14 and 15; Regulation No. 519/94, Articles 15 and 16.

[39] See Regulation No. 517/94, Article 25, paras 3, 4 and 5 which provide for different procedures.

[40] See the developments concerning the limits set by competition rules on the conduct of industrial and trade policy and the second part of this chapter.

[41] See Regulation No. 2423/88, Art. 12§1.

regard to the competitive situation within the Community market'.[42] However, in practice, the interests of consumers and the competition policy factor did not play a significant role in anti-dumping proceedings.[43]

- The new anti-dumping legislation

The new anti-dumping regulation in force since 1 January 1995[44] defines in Article 21 what the Community interest means and describes how it should be assessed.[45] There now is an explicit reference to the interests of users and consumers. In addition, a procedure is established whereby the parties representing all the different economic interests at stake can be heard and can comment on each other's views.[46] Article 21 specifically states that: 'measures, as determined on the basis of the dumping and injury found, may not be applied, where the authorities, on the basis of all the information submitted, can clearly conclude that it is not in the Community interest to apply such measures'.[47]

The new provision should give a stronger voice to consumers and industrial users in anti-dumping proceedings and its implementation could be subject to judicial review in so far as compliance with procedural requirements is concerned. Whether it will bring changes in the material outcome of anti-dumping proceedings is another matter. For reasons stated elsewhere,[48] the injury caused by dumped imports tend to loom larger, in most instances, than the loss which consumers or industrial users may suffer as a result of anti-dumping duties. Moreover, it should be pointed out that the new regulation provides that, in determining where the Community interest lies, special consideration shall be given to the need to eliminate the trade distorting effects of injurious dumping and to restore effective competition.[49] This flies in the face of logic: the analysis of the Community interest comes after dumping and injury findings and the rationale of the regulation is precisely to eliminate the effects of

---

42 On this point, see J. Bourgeois, 'Trade Measures, Competition Policy and the Consumer', in Demaret, Bourgeois and Van Bael (eds.), '*Trade Laws of the European Community and the United States in a Comparative Perspective*', *Story Scientia*, 1992, 227 at 257.

43 For a detailed review of past practice, see J. Bourgeois, op. cit. *supra*, and Van Bael and Bellis, *Anti-Dumping and other Trade Protection Laws of the EEC*, CCH 2d, ed. 1990, §311.

44 Council Regulation No. 3283/94, O.J. L 349/1/1994.

45 Council Regulation No. 3284/94, O.J. L 349/22/1994, which concerns subsidized imports, contains a similar provision.

46 See Article 21§§2 to 5.

47 See Article 21§1.

48 See J. Bourgeois, op. cit. *supra*, at 257-8.

49 See Article 21§1.

dumping and 'to restore effective competition'; the 'Community interest' is a corrective that refers to other interests.

In addition to mentioning the interests of the consumers and the users, which normally benefit from competition between foreign and domestic firms, the new anti-dumping regulation attempts to reconcile trade policy and competition policy in other ways. In two instances, it refers to restrictive trade practices which may occur in the context of dumping. The first relates to injury determination. Among the known factors other than the dumped imports, which the authorities are invited to consider when deciding whether the Community industry is injured as a result of the dumped imports, are 'trade restrictive practices of and competition between the foreign and Community producers'.[50] The second instance concerns price undertakings. These should not be accepted if they were likely to lead to anti-competitive behaviour.[51] In both instances, the language used is not of a mandatory character. In practice, much will hinge upon whether the Commission takes an active role in order to identify possible anti-competitive behaviour in the context of anti-dumping proceedings.[52]

- Safeguard measures

The interests of the Community are also mentioned in the regulations dealing with safeguard measures. But, contrary to what was done in the context of dumping and subsidized imports, the relevant provisions here were not made more explicit when new legislation was adopted at the end of 1994[53] and no explicit reference to competition policy is to be found.

In the context of safeguard measures, the meaning of the concept 'the interests of the Community' varies. At times, the interests of the Community seem to mean something distinct from the interests of the domestic industry which suffers from foreign competition.[54] At times, the interests of the Community appear merely to coincide with the interests of the domestic industry.[55] At times, the 'economic interests' of the

---

50 See Article 3§7. The new regulation concerning subsidized imports contains a similar provision.

51 See Article 8§3 read in combination with the Preamble. The new regulation concerning subsidized imports contains a similar provision.

52 See the third part of this chapter for recommendations in that regard.

53 See Regulation No. 3285/94, O.J. L 349/53/1994, which replaces Regulation No. 518/94.

54 See Regulation No. 3285/94, Article 17 ('where the interests of the Community so require').

55 See Regulation No. 3285/94, Article 16§1 and Regulation No. 519/94, Article 15§1 ('in order to safeguard the interests of the Community').

Community are mentioned as an alternative to the injury requirement.[56]

• The industrial policy factor

The insistence of some Member States that the imposition of trade protective measures be facilitated as a counterpart to the completion of the internal market was inspired by industrial policy motives not devoid of certain protectionist overtones. Since anti-dumping duties can be used, consistently with Article 113 of the EC Treaty, as an industrial policy tool, it is important to stress that they may now be adopted (the Commission willing) with the consent of a simple majority of the Member States. This should be compared with the unanimity required by Article 130 for the adoption of specific measures.[57]

Regulations 518/94 and 519/94 explicitly refer to the industrial policy measures that the Community has taken or might take in order to offset the consequences resulting for certain national industries from elimination of national quantitative restrictions.[58] In the textile sector, together with the adoption of the new import rules, the Council, acting on a Commission proposal, decided to give financial help to Portugal to restructure its textile industry (to the amount of 400 million ECU). Portugal was considered as a special case in view of the importance of the textile sector in its economy. Other Member States made similar aid requests, but without success.[59]

This is an example of a type of complementarity between trade and industrial policies, which in the proper circumstances ought to be followed more frequently by the European Community. There may in fact be more cases in which, with a view to taking account of the needs of EC industries in their competitive relations with outside suppliers, this type of measures, which in the USA are qualified as import adjustment assistance, could be used as an alternative to the classical import restrictions.[60] Such measures should obviously comply with the principles underlying the EC Treaty provisions on state aids.

---

56 See Regulation No. 517/94, Article 11§2 ('or where the economic interests of the Community so requires').

57 See *supra*.

58 The preambles of the two Regulations state that 'the economic and industrial repercussions of their elimination have been or can be taken into account in the Community's horizontal policies for the market concerned'.

59 See *Europe*, 16 December 1993.

60 An illustration of other possible alternative measures is the suggestion aired by some members of the Commission to rely on a form of import adjustment assistance rather than on a genuine quota system of European audiovisual production.

• The EC-Japan car arrangement

Through the Commission, the Community negotiated with Japan an arrangement which defines the acceptable level of car imports from Japan into the Community until 1999. Such an arrangement was indeed indispensable for the completion of the internal market. This arrangement, even more than the autonomous import regimes just discussed, entailed a balancing act between internal trade liberalization, trade protection and competition policy. As indicated in the second section of the chapter, certain features of the arrangement seem to run afoul of Article 85, while others are inconsistent with the concept of an internal market and probably also with Articles 6 and 58 of the EC Treaty combined. The arrangement concerning Japanese cars is the most vivid illustration of the pursuit of a sectoral industrial policy objective through a trade instrument.

c. Competition policy

As indicated above, the EC Treaty recognizes the primacy of competition policy over other EC economic policies in general and over industrial policy in particular. The legal and practical implications of the higher status conferred by the Treaty to competition policy depend on the content given to EC competition rules by the EC Treaty, the Court of Justice, the Community legislator and the Commission. Competition law cannot be examined here in any detail. It is at any rate one of the most developed and most extensively studied areas of Community law. Significant competition cases involving industrial and/or trade policy issues are surveyed in the second section of this chapter.

Hereafter, as part of our examination of the legal framework within which the three policies are to be implemented, only two related questions need to retain our attention. First, do competition rules set precise limits on the conduct of either industrial or trade policy? Second, can industrial or trade policy considerations be taken into account in the conduct of competition policy?

1) Limits set by competition rules on the conduct of industrial and trade policy

There is a first and obvious limit. In order to achieve certain industrial or trade policy objectives, neither the Community nor the Member States may resort to or allow the use of instruments or practices which are forbidden under EC competition rules. For example, the Commission may not induce Community firms and third country competitors to enter into a restrictive trade agreement forbidden under Article 85 by arguing that such an agreement would serve the same ends as a safeguard measure or anti-dumping duty. Nor may the Community or the Member States provide for the setting up of a cartel or permit the flouting of block exemption regulations in order to police or to comply with orderly marketing agreements concluded with a third country. Similarly, a merger which would, on its face, create a dominant position in the meaning of the Merger Regulation cannot be allowed under the pretext that such a merger is needed in order to strengthen the competitiveness of a Community industry.

But, in our view, competition rules set another limit, which could be called the outer limit, on what can be done by the Community under the heading of industrial or trade policy. That limit results from Article 85, §3, Article 86, as construed by the Court of Justice in Continental Can,[61] and the Merger Regulation. Even though Article 85, §3 allows certain restraints on competition, these may never have the effect of 'eliminating competition in respect of a substantial part of the product in question'. In Continental Can, the Court of Justice construed Article 86 in the light of the rule laid down in Article 85, §3(b). The same idea underlies the Merger Regulation which in Article 2, §2, outlaws mergers which 'create or strengthen a dominant position as a result of which effective competition would be significantly impeded in the common market or in a substantial part of it'. That competition may not be restricted beyond a certain point, as determined in Article 85, §3(b), Continental Can and the Merger Regulation, should be the minimal substantive content given to the principle of undistorted competition, which is proclaimed by Articles 3(g) and 130 of the EC Treaty. We submit that the principle according to which competition may not be eliminated in respect of a substantial part of the relevant market is to be viewed as a general principle of Community law and that, as such, it ought to bind Community institutions not only when they apply the competition provisions of the EC Treaty, but also when they take measures implementing other policies.

We would thus suggest that in the conduct of industrial or trade policy, the Community may not take measures whose effect would be to eliminate competition to a significant degree in a substantial part of the internal

---

61 See *supra* note 2.

market. Such a principle has practical implications in those cases where measures taken by the Community are not by themselves technically inconsistent with Articles 85 or 86 or the merger regulation. A possible example arises where a safeguard measure or anti-dumping duties severely reduce foreign competition on a Community market dominated by one or two domestic firms. Such trade policy measures are, in our view, inconsistent with the EC Treaty. Compliance with the principle that competition may not be substantially impeded as a result of measures taken by the Community can be subject to the control of the Court of Justice, in the same way as the implementation of Article 85, §3(b), Article 86 or Article 2, §2 of the Merger Regulation is reviewable by the Court of Justice.

Assuming the primacy of competition rules as construed here, is accepted, there remains ample room for the implementation of trade and industrial policy. Indeed, from a legal point of view, the primacy of competition policy only implies that the Community may not violate its own specific competition rules and that, in addition, it may not take measures whose effect is to significantly distort competition in the internal market. Beyond that, the primacy of competition policy is essentially of a political nature and cannot be translated into sufficiently precise norms of conduct to become operative.

2) Integration of industrial or trade policy objectives in the competition policy field

Within the limits just discussed, industrial and trade policy objectives can be taken into account in the course of implementing competition rules. Actually, competition rules as they stand, represent an essential tool for the conduct of industrial policy as defined in Article 130 of the EC Treaty.[62]

For instance, Article 85, §3 and the system of block exemptions may be used, and have already been used at one time or another, by the Commission in order to promote each of the four sub-objectives assigned to industrial policy by Article 130.[63] In addition, regulations have been adopted to define how competition rules are to be implemented in specific sectors such as insurance, air or maritime transport. In defining such conditions and in particular ceilings of intensity of state aids the Commission is necessarily making industrial policy choices. The

---

[62] The point is stressed in Bangemann, op. cit. *supra*, at 26-37

[63] See *infra* part II.

Commission guidelines concerning the application of competition rules to the telecommunication sector[64] can also be viewed as a kind of industrial policy exercise within the boundaries of competition policy. The same observation applies to the directives concerning the telecommunication sector adopted by the Commission on the basis of Article 90, §3.[65] As these directives are intended to open up national markets, which until recently had remained sheltered from competition, they certainly contribute to the strengthening of the competitiveness of the Community's industry, the main objective of industrial policy. To the extent that industrial policy objectives of a general character, such as those listed in Article 130, play a role in the application of competition rules, the practice of issuing regulations, directives or guidelines ought to be encouraged for the sake of legal security.

The control of state aids by the Commission on the basis of Articles 92 and 93 is another competition policy instrument which can and often does serve as an instrument of industrial policy.

Articles 92, §3(c) and (d) concern respectively aids to facilitate the development of certain economic activities or of certain economic areas and aids to promote culture and heritage conservation. Such aids may be considered to be compatible with the Treaty 'where such aid[s] do not adversely affect trading conditions to an extent contrary to the common interest'. In other words, a balance needs to be struck between a certain degree of distortion of competition and the possible positive effects resulting from the aid. That provision, which has given rise to an extensive case law, reveals somewhat paradoxically, as does Article 85, §3, that if ever industrial policy may lead, consistently with the Treaty, to a certain degree of distortion of competition, it is only on the basis of the Treaty competition rules that such a result can be achieved. In particular cases the granting of state aids may even be needed in order to correct certain market deficiencies, as the EC argued with respect to Airbus in the dispute with the USA. However, as explained above, this distortion of competition may never result in competition being eliminated in a substantial part of the relevant market.

The Commission has issued guidelines or codes where it defines, sometimes with great precision, the conditions which horizontal aids (such as aids to small and medium-sized firms, aids for the protection of the environment and aids to research and development), regional aids or

---

64 See O.J. 1991, C 233/2.

65 See Directive 88/301, O.J. 1988, L 131/73, and Directive 90/388, O.J. 1990, L 192/10, as modified by Directive 94/46, O.J. 1994, L 268/15.

sectoral aids (such as aids to the automobile, the synthetic fibre or the textile industry) have to meet in order to be consistent with Article 92. As industrial policy considerations necessarily influence the attitude of the Commission in the field of state aids, it is again better from the standpoint of legal security that that attitude be known in advance rather than *ex post facto* as a result of individual decisions, which are more easily influenced by political pressure from Member States.

Article 2, §2 of the Merger Regulation adopted in 1989 makes incompatible with the Treaty concentrations with create or strengthen a dominant position as a result of which effective competition would be significantly impeded in the common market or in a substantial part of it. As such, the Merger Regulation does not empower the Commission to clear a concentration which creates a dominant position and significantly impedes effective competition on the grounds that it produces offsetting efficiency gains and that it would reinforce the competitiveness of European firms.[66] When competition is significantly impeded, other economic factors, which can be taken into account in the context of Article 85, §3 (within the limit defined by Article 85, §3(b)), become irrelevant. The comparison between the final version of the Merger Regulation and an earlier draft is revealing in that regard.[67] The lack of an explicit reference to industrial policy considerations, distinct from competition policy considerations, has been criticized by some, including the European Parliament, [68] after the de Havilland decision.[69]

However, the Merger Regulation provides for a full economic assessment of a concentration in order to determine whether it creates or strengthens a dominant position that would significantly impede competition. As pointed out by Ehlermann,[70] the Commission has a margin of discretion when it makes that assessment. Indeed, the regulation allows for some flexibility since it implies that the creation of a dominant position does not automatically result in 'effective competition

66 See A. Jacquemin, 'Horizontal concentration and European merger policy', *European Economic Review* 34, 1990, 539-549 who, however, observed that: 'It is hard to believe that, in practice, such a strict policy will be fully implemented and that the role of potential dynamic efficiency gains will be ignored. A danger is that, instead of an explicit cost-benefit analysis, surreptitious compromises would be sought within the Commission'. Recent merger cases seem to bear out that observation, see *infra*.

67 See A. Pappalardo, 'Le règlement des concentrations', *R.I.D.E.*, 1990, p. 24.

68 See Resolution on the de Havilland affair, O.J. 1991, C 280/140; see also L. Idot et C. Momège, 'Faut-il réviser le règlement sur le contrôle des concentrations? Brefs propos sur l'affaire de Havilland', Ed. Techniques, *Europe*, january 1992, p. 5.

69 O.J. 1991, L 334/2.

70 Deux ans d'application du contrôle des concentrations: bilan et perspectives', *Rev. Marché commun et de l'Union européenne,* 1993, p. 245-7.

being significantly impeded'. The Commission, which is a political body, where votes are taken, has recently made use of that margin of flexibility in the Tubes case.[71]

One should add that the Merger Regulation authorizes the Commission to attach to its decision conditions and obligations which the undertakings concerned have to fulfil if the concentration is to be cleared.[72] There too, the Commission enjoys a degree of discretion which it can use to directly influence the structure of a Community industry.[73] As acknowledged by Ehlermann: 'néanmoins, il faut reconnaître que la pratique des engagements est délicate et que le reproche du 'mécano-industriel' est sérieux'.[74]

B. The Relationship Between the Three Policies from an Institutional Standpoint

In the trade field, the Community is exclusively competent to act, at least with respect to trade in goods. In the competition field, the Community, even though it shares power with the Member States, is the leading actor. Industrial policy is, as Article 130 clearly indicates, a field where Member States and the Community share responsibilities. When the Community is competent, one, two or three institutions, i.e. the Commission, the Council and the Parliament, may intervene, depending on the policy which is implemented and the legal basis to which the implementing measure refers. The plurality of actors raises the question of whether the three policies can be implemented in a consistent manner first by the Community itself, acting alone, and second by the Community and/or the Member States when the latter share powers with the former.

1. The Community Level

At the Community level, the question of consistency arises not only with respect to the implementation of the three policies, but also and more fundamentally with respect to the implementation of industrial policy as such. As we have seen *supra*, under Article 130, industrial policy is to be

---

71 That case is discussed in the second part of the chapter. See also for an application of the failing company defence in the context of mergers, Kali and Salz, O.J. 1994, L 186/38.

72 See Merger Regulation, Article 8, §2.

73 For a recent example, see Kali and Salz, cited *supra*.

74 Cited *supra*, at p. 247. For critical comments regarding the Commission's practice, see I. van Bael, 'Two years of Community Merger Control', in Campbell and Flint (eds.), *1993: The European Market: Myth or Reality*, Kluwer, 1994, 53, at 65-6.

implemented through many different Treaty provisions. Specific measures, based on Article 130 itself, are taken by the Council acting unanimously, the Parliament simply being consulted. Thus, each Member State enjoys a veto power and this may have practical consequence as was shown in the case of HDTV.[75] But as a rule the industrial policy objectives are to be implemented on the basis of a series of other Treaty provisions. If, for example, a measure is based on Article 100 A, the internal market provision, it will require the approval of only a qualified majority of the Member States, but also the approval of the Parliament. It should be observed that the Parliament seems at times favourable to a higher degree of public intervention in industry than the Council (or at least than a blocking minority of Member States in the Council). In the field of research and development, framework programmes are adopted by the Council acting unanimously, with the Parliament's approval, whereas specific programmes are adopted by the Council acting by a qualified majority, the Parliament being merely consulted.[76] Where the pursuit of industrial policy objectives requires the harmonization of national tax laws, the Council act unanimously.[77] Still other decision-making procedures apply to decisions taken in relation to the European Social Fund[78] or to Economic and Social Cohesion.[79]

In the trade policy field, decisions are taken, as seen above, by the Council acting by a qualified majority or, with respect to dumping by a simple majority. The Parliament has a significant role to play only when a trade agreement is sufficiently important to come within the scope of Article 228, §3.

In the competition field, the main and often unique actor is the Commission, as it is specifically entrusted with the task of implementing Article 85 (and most notably Article 85, §3), Article 86, the merger regulation and Articles 92 and 93. Moreover, the Commission possesses autonomous legislative powers under Article 90, §3. It also legislates extensively on the basis of delegation from the Council.

From this brief survey, it clearly emerges that if either industrial policy (seen in isolation) or the three policies are to be implemented by the

---

[75] See Council Decision of July 22, 1993, O.J. 1993, L 196/48, concerning the Community funding needed to facilitate the introduction of HDTV in Europe. That decision, taken before the Maastricht Treaty came into force, was based on Article 235. The United Kingdom, by using its veto power, was able to obtain a sizeable reduction of the funding which had been initially proposed.

[76] See Article 130(i) of the EC Treaty.

[77] See Article 99 (indirect taxes) and Art. 100 (direct taxes).

[78] See Article 125 of the EC Treaty.

[79] See Articles 130(d) and 130(e).

Community with any measure of consistency, the burden is on the shoulders of the Commission. The Commission is always present, whatever the policy implemented or the legal basis used, at least at the proposal stage. The unifying role of the Commission is particularly crucial since the Council, when it does intervene in order to implement the different EC policies, does so in different settings and under the influence of different national ministries. By contrast, the composition of the Commission, which is stable, should help it in the task of developing a consistent approach for the implementation of the three policies. Whether the Commission is always successful in that respect is examined in the second part of this chapter.

2. The Community and the Member States

The question of consistency here mainly concerns the implementation of industrial policy to the extent that it is distinct from trade and competition policy.[80] There is a need for coordination since Member States are responsible for the financing of most measures affecting the Community's industry. Here again the natural coordinator can only be the Commission and the EC Treaty indeed confers that role on the Commission.

The Commission is, under Articles 92 and 93, given the task of controlling state aids. It would of course be advisable that aids granted through the Community structural funds be subject to the same control as state aids under Articles 92 and 93.

Under Article 130, §2 and Article 130(h), the Commission is invited to take any useful initiative to promote the coordination of the action of the Member States and the Community respectively in the industrial and research and development area.

Finally, under Article 169, the Commission may challenge industrial policy measures taken by a Member State in violation of the EC Treaty.

Outside the EC Treaty framework, the Commission is also increasingly

[80] In the trade policy field, the question of consistency arises only in those areas where Member States have not yet relinquished their powers, such as export aid schemes, see *supra*. In the field of competition policy, the question of consistency arises to the extent that national courts are competent to apply Article 85, §1 and that national competition authorities implement competition rules which may differ from EC competition rules. See J. Bourgeois, 'EC Competition Law and Member State Courts', in *1993 Fordham Corporate Law Institute* (B. Hawk ed.) 475 at 494-5 (New York, Transnational Iuris Publications, 1994) and J. Bourgeois, 'Cooperation between National and Community Authorities: a Role for Subsidiarity?' Liège Conference, November 1993, *Le droit communautaire de la concurrence et son influence sur les droits des Etats membres et des Etats tiers* (forthcoming). In the merger field, the question of consistency is also raised by the fact that below a certain threshold national authorities are exclusively competent.

invited, with the approval of the Court of Justice, to coordinate the action of the Member States in differents areas of intergovernmental cooperation, including sometimes cooperation involving third countries. The true limiting factor which the Commission faces in its role of coordinator is its lack of resources.

II. SELECTED CASES

The purpose of this section is to examine, by reviewing a number of selected cases, whether and how the Commission and, as the case may be, the Council take account in practice of the relationships between competition, industrial and trade policy. To have a more complete picture, where appropriate and in so far as the issue of such relationships was put before the Court of Justice and the Court of First Instance of the European Communities, the stance taken by them will also be considered.

The cases are presented under the heading competition or that of trade policy depending on the qualification given by the Commission or as the case may be, by the Council, either expressly or implicitly by relying on the powers conferred in the relevant area to the EC.[81] In some instances the cases are presented under a joint heading where the matter happened to be treated under two distinct policies.

A. Competition Policy Cases

1. Rules applying to undertakings

In relation to industrial policy:

A good starting point is the 1968 Commission Notice on Co-operation Agreements[82] intended to give guidance to industry as to a range of horizontal agreements against which the Commission would not object under Article 85.

The main emphasis lies on research and development agreements, specialization agreements, joint ventures and latterly restructuring

[81] There are no meaningful cases which, up till now, are qualified in legal terms as industrial policy. This does not mean that industrial policy considerations are totally absent in competition policy and in trade policy decisions. Such considerations will be referred to where appropriate.

[82] Commission Notice of 21 July 1968, OJ (1968) C 75/3. See also XXIIIrd Report on Competition Policy (1993), para. 157: 'The Commission considers that, far from being the direct opposite of industrial policy, competition policy is an essential instrument, with clear complementarity between the two policies'

arrangements. Many other types of agreement have subsequently been investigated and cleared.

In respect of production and the introduction of new technology, the Commission's policy is to permit agreements to cooperate in manufacture, or in joint research and development, that seem genuinely likely to lead to better use of resources, such as rationalization of production, the achievement of economies of scale, or the faster, or more effective, development of new products, particularly where the undertakings concerned are likely to be better able to compete with third parties. Thus, even undertakings with a substantial market share or a large turnover may benefit from exemption under Article 85(3). This is likely to be so, particularly, in capital-intensive industries where restructuring[83] or specialization[84] is necessary to remove excess capacity, or in industries where the capital costs[85] or the technical difficulties[86] of developing new products are such that even large undertakings need to cooperate to produce the desired results, particularly bearing in mind that many EC undertakings have not yet attained the scale of their American and Japanese competitors.[87]

The main types of agreements cleared by the Commission under Article 85(3) with the aim of promoting a particular EC industrial policy objective are the following.

- Research and Development Agreements

Given the relatively fewer resources devoted by EC undertakings to R&D compared to Japanese and the US undertakings, and their fragmentation, the Commission is generally prepared to encourage joint ventures which promote R&D. The encouragement of such cooperation now is one of the aims of the Community under Article 130(f) of EC Treaty. Already in 1980 the Commission stated that: 'The introduction of new processes and products on the market stimulates competition within the common market, and helps to strengthen the ability of European industry to compete internationally',[88] after having pointed out in 1984 that its policy is 'to

83 E.g. SYNTHETIC FIBRES, OJ L 207/1984; BPCL-ICI, OJ L 212/1984; ENI-MONTEDISON, OJ L 5/1987; ENICHEM-ICI, OJ L 50/1989.

84 E.g. LIGHTWEIGHT PAPER, OJ L 182/1972.

85 E.g. ROCKWELL-IVECO, OJ L 224/1983; CARBON GAS TECHNOLOGY, OJ L 376/1983; KSB-GOULDS-LOWARA-ITT, OJ L 19/1991.

86 E.g. VACUUM INTERRUPTERS, OJ L 383/1980; GEC-WEIR, OJ L 327/1977; OPTICAL FIBRES, OJ L 236/1986.

87 E.g. ALCATEL ESPACE-ANT, OJ L 32/1990; FORD-VOLKSWAGEN, OJ L 20/1993.

88 XIVth Report on Competition Policy (1985), para. 28.

seek the best possible balance between on the one hand a reinforcement of the competitivity of European industry and on the other hand the maintenance of workable competition'.[89]

The favourable attitude towards restrictive agreements in the field of research and development in particular is reflected in the 1984 Block Exemption Regulation on certain joint research and development agreements[90] and the 1993 block exemption of such agreements for joint ventures to market the products resulting from the joint research and development.[91]

- Specialization agreements

The Commission has stated that: 'Such agreements do ... provide a means of obtaining a specialization which contributes to lower costs by the setting up of long production runs and a better utilization of available production capacity by the concentration of effort on a limited number of products'.[92]

The basis of specialization agreements is the agreed allocation of production between the parties, accompanied by mutual obligations on each party to supply the other exclusively with the products in which it specializes for sale in the territory of the other party. In this way the parties are usually able to rationalize their production and achieve economies of scale while continuing to offer to third parties the same, or a wider, range of products often at more competitive prices. However, co-operation of this kind between enterprises of a certain size restricts competition within the common market.

The essential condition for granting exemption is that the specialization will not compromise the effectiveness of competition in such a way that the parties to the agreement can utilize the savings in costs for their exclusive profit instead of sharing them fairly with customers.

The two main issues for the Commission are whether the advantages of the agreement outweigh the disadvantages and whether the restrictions in the agreement are indispensable to the attainment of its objectives.

Favourable results from the point of view of the economy as a whole can be obtained by means of specialization agreements, especially where such cooperation enables small and medium-sized undertakings to work more rationally and increase the productivity and competitiveness on a larger

89 XIIIrd Report on Competition Policy (1984), para. 42.
90 Regulation 418/, OJ L 53/1995.
91 Regulation 151/93, OJ L 21/1993.
92 Ist Report on Competition Policy (1972), para. 27.

market.

- Restructuring agreements

Certain EC industries are affected by chronic over-capacity as a result of changes in market demand. The Commission considered it as one of its general objectives to enable structural over-capacity to be eliminated so as to allow the industries concerned to recover profitability.[93] The classic illustration of this policy has been the Commission's approval of restructuring agreements in the petrochemical industry and its approval of the Synthetic Fibres and Stichting Baksteen crisis cartels.[94] However, exemption of specific restructuring agreements within an industry subject to serious over-capacity does not give general protection to the industry to indulge in anti-competitive practices.[95]

- Production joint ventures (primarily as regards to high-technology)

In a number of important high-technology sectors EC undertakings are at a substantial technological disadvantage. The Commission has therefore favoured joint ventures between EC undertakings and non-EC undertakings, particularly from the USA and Japan, where the non-EC undertaking transfers important advanced technology. This has been a permanent feature of the EC competition policy beginning with early decisions such as De Laval Stork.[96] However, the increasing recognition of the relative disadvantage of EC undertakings in the high-technology sector has led to an arguably more flexible Commission approach where EC undertakings seek to obtain advanced technology from overseas as in

---

93 XXIst Report on Competition Policy (1992), para. 207 et seq.

94 SYNTHETIC FIBRES, OJ L 207/1984. The Commission also indicated its preparedness to authorize crisis cartels for the zinc smelting industry (Commission Notice ZINC SHUTDOWN AGREEMENT, OJ C 164/1983); however, the zinc producers decided shortly thereafter that a crisis cartel was unnecessary (XIIIth Report on Competition Policy (1984), para. 58); STICHTING BAKSTEEN, OJ L 131/1994.

95 See Commission Decisions: POLYPROPYLENE, OJ L 230, 1986; PVC, OJ L 74/1989; LdPE, OJ L 74/1989. See Bellamy and Child, *Common Market of Competition*, 4th ed. (Sweet & Maxwell, 1993), footnote 14.

96 DE LAVAL-STORK I, OJ L 215/1977.

the Optical Fibres, the Olivetti-Canon and the Olivetti-Digital Decisions.[97]

- Energy Sector

The application of competition rules in this area is relatively new and the issue of priority in any potential policy conflicts between the internal market and the competition rules is only beginning to be addressed.

In its Decision of 22 December 1992 approving the Jahrhundertvertrag, the Commission again confirmed the applicability of competition rules in the energy sector: the energy market must not be excluded from competition and, against the background of further development of the internal market, restrictive measures must be limited to what is necessary to guarantee basic security of supply.[98]

As regards the Nuclear Energy Sector, the Electricity Sector and the Oil Sector in granting exemption under Article 85(3) the Commission has always attached much weight to security and independence of supply.

CASE 1 Becton Dickinson / Cyclopore

Cyclopore is a Belgian-based undertaking with close links to the UCL; it produces membranes based on a patent licence granted by UCL. Becton Dickinson is a US medical supply company which has developed a technique to weld these membranes into tissue culture products.

Under the agreement between these two undertakings Cyclopore grants Becton Dickinson the exclusive worldwide right to manufacture and sell its membranes for as long as Becton Dickinson purchases a minimum quantity, and Becton Dickinson undertakes to purchase exclusively from

97 'The agreements enable several European companies to produce a high-technology product with significant advantages over traditional cables in the Community and promote technical progress in relation to both optical fibres and optical cables. Moreover, the joint venture facilitate a more constant and rapid transfer of Corning's technology that would otherwise be possible. The concurrent introduction of Corning's most up-to-date technology in the common market is essential to enable the European companies to withstand competition from non-Community producers, especially in the USA and Japan, in an area of fast-moving technology. A partial or total divestiture would destroy such benefits for the European companies which would then risk becoming uncompetitive on the EEC and world markets. The joint ventures give rise to important benefits for European industry which can be maintained only by the continued participation of Corning'. OPTICAL FIBRES, OJ L 236/1986, para. 59. Similarly, in OLIVETTI-CANON, OJ L 52/1988, para. 54, the Commission stated: 'It is reasonable to expect that the combination of this technology with that of an also R&D oriented EEC undertaking will contribute to improving the technological patterns of the EEC industry and ultimately its competitivity'.

98 XXIInd Report on Competition Policy (1993), para. 146. See OLIVETTI-DIGITAL, OJ L 309/1994.

Cyclopore all its microporous track-tech membranes for use in tissue culture, while Cyclopore undertakes to supply exclusively Becton Dickinson.

After parties agreed to limit the latter obligation for five years, the Commission issued an Article 85(3) comfort letter.[99] The Commission cited this case as a good example of its approach of authorizing agreements involving a restriction of the parties' freedom of action, if such restriction is necessary in order to achieve technological innovation that is beneficial to all.[100]

In relation to trade policy

There are a number of competition policy decisions addressing trade policy issues raised by the parties concerned. They reject the arguments according to which the parties entered into agreements with foreign competitors to put an end to the latter's dumping practice on the grounds that it is not up to private parties to take trade policy measures.[101]

Other trade policy issues relating to the competitiveness of EC undertakings entering into restrictive agreements or engaged in merger operations are addressed from time to time in competition policy decisions. Strictly speaking, taking account of actual or potential competition from third countries could be considered a competition policy exercise. This is true. Much depends, however, on the conclusion one draws. The conclusion that a merger may be cleared because competition from third countries will ensure that the resulting dominant merged undertaking will not be in a position to engage in price maximization is a competition policy conclusion. The conclusion that a merger must be cleared in order to enhance the competitive position of the EC undertakings that merge is an industrial policy conclusion.

CASE 2 The flat panel display case

The Flat Panel Display B.V. joint venture between Philips (80 per cent), Thomson (10 per cent) and Sagem (10 per cent) was established with a

---

99 XXIIIrd Competition Report (1993), para. 241.

100 XXIIIrd Competition Report (1993), para. 160.

101 Certain of these cases have been reviewed by J.H.J. Bourgeois, 'Competition Policy and Commercial Policy' in M. Maresceau (ed.), *The European Community's commercial Policy after 1992: the Legal Dimension*, 113 at 121-2 (Dordrecht, Martinus Nijhoff, 1993). For a critique see M.C.E.J. Bronckers, 'A Legal Analysis of Protectionist Measures affecting Japanese Imports into the European Community', revisited, in E.L.M. Völker (ed.) *Protectionism and the European Community*, 37 at 81-2 (Kluwer, Deventer 1987).

view to creating the first EC company capable of producing very large-scale series of Liquid Crystal Display screens.

Initially notified under the Merger Control Regulation, the joint venture was examined under Article 85(1) EC. The Commission did not issue a decision but sent a comfort letter to the parties stating that the conditions for the granting of an individual exemption were fulfilled.

The Commission stated that it 'ascertained that the joint venture is going to be means for the parent companies to develop and sustain mass-production in Europe of new high technology products in a field where competition from foreign suppliers (mainly Japan) is strong'.[102]

This is an interesting case particularly in the light of the Commission's stated position on anti-competitive agreements in third countries affecting the position of EC undertakings on the markets of these third countries. Although apparently it does not intend to apply the EC competition rules against restrictive agreements in third countries impeding EC undertakings' access to the markets of these third countries, as the US Department of Justice announced that it would, it criticized such restrictive agreements and stated that it would not sit idly by.[103]

CASE 3 The Tubes case

The creation of a joint venture, DMV, by Mannesman, Vallourec and Ilva to which the stainless steel tube business of the parents were to be transferred was cleared by the Commission under the Merger Control Regulation.[104]

The Commission found that the joint venture would increase the degree of concentration in an already highly concentrated market, the joint market share held by DMV and Sandvik, the other important player on the market, amounting to approximately 70 per cent, with none of the existing competitors holding more than 13 per cent.[105]

The Commission also found that this was a case in which a joint dominant position (DMV and Sandvik) would result, noting that '[t]heir mutual interdependence thus creates a strong common interest and incentive to maximize profits by engaging in anti-competitive parallel behaviour' (para. 129).

Yet the Commission cleared the merger. Ostensibly the grounds for doing so are that it did not create a dominant position 'as a result of which

102 XXIIIrd Competition Report (1993), para. 215.
103 XXIIIrd Competition Report (1993), para. 107.
104 Decision of 31 January 1994 (OJ L 102/1994).
105 Decision, *supra* n. 100, para. 127.

effective competition would be significantly impeded in the common market', the second criterion for assessing mergers. The Commission considered that the entry by Japanese competitors would be sufficient to constrain the behaviour of the two market leaders (DMV and Sandvik) and that it was likely that Eastern European competitors would significantly enter the market in the near future.[106]

However, press reports suggest that the competition analysis in the decision, as drafted by DG IV and submitted to the Commission by Mr Van Miert, concluded that the merger should not be cleared. These same reports indicate that other commissioners took the position that in view of the competition from third country tube manufacturers the merger should be approved. One should think that the competitiveness of the EC industry was the real reason, as the arguments relating to the constraints on the two leaders' behaviour by Japanese and Eastern European competitors do not appear very convincing.

2. Rules on state aids

As indicated in section I of this chapter, Commission decisions declaring state aids 'compatible with the common market' under Article 92, (3)(b) and (c), and (partly) (d) involve industrial policy choices. An analysis of individual cases of state aids with a view to determine complementarities and conflicts with other policies is difficult as a result of three factors.

First, in many cases involving individual state aids the industrial policy or trade policy assessments have been made in advance and in the abstract in the 'frameworks' and 'guidelines' which the Commission issues from time to time defining conditions and 'aid intensity ceilings'.

Second, there is a fairly important number of cases in which Member States fail to properly and timely notify state aids with the result that Commission decisions do not deal with the merits of such State aids.[107]

Third, there are cases in which the Commission has kept silent. A significant example in this respect is Airbus. After having stated in 1973 that 'important projects of common European interest' within the meaning of Article 92 (3)(b) include the manufacture of aircraft and aircraft parts,[108] the Commission has stated very little about state aids to Airbus.

---

106 Decision, *supra* n. 100, paras 131 and 132.

107 In the Boussac judgment of 14 February 1990 (France v. Commission) ECR I-307, the Court of Justice has, however, ruled that state aids which have not been notified are not automatically illegal. After taking interim measures, the Commission may order that such aids be recovered only if it concludes that these aids are inconsistent with Article 92.

108 IInd Report on Competition Policy (1973), para. 100.

In the light of the dispute with the USA this is quite understandable. In addition, as the world market is the relevant geographical market rather than the EC, one could probably argue that state aid to Airbus is beneficial rather than detrimental for competition in view of the competitive structure on the world market of wide-bodied civil aircraft.

CASE 4 R&D support to SGS-Thomson

The French Government's proposed aid towards an R&D programme of SGS-Thomson Microelectronics was submitted to the Commission. SGS-Thompson designed the programme to acquire the key techniques and architectures of semi-conductor products. The total cost of the programme came to ECU 1.261 billion and the French Government intended to award a capital grant of ECU 321 million.

In authorizing this state aid the Commission took account of the EC's current deficit in the output of semi-conductors and of the advisability of strengthening the EC industrial capacity in a sector dominated by Japanese and US manufacturers, SGS-Thomson Microelectronics ranking 13th worldwide in terms of turnover.[109]

This, it is submitted, is a clear case of complementarity of competition, industrial and trade policies.

CASE 5 EUREKA projects

Twenty-nine Commission decisions relating to state aids to EC undertakings participating in EUREKA projects were identified by relying mainly on the RAPID data base. Several of these decisions deal with more than one proposed state aid. They cover a great variety of EUREKA projects from biotechnology to telecommunication, from electronic dictionaries to new materials for car body panels.

These proposed aids could be cleared almost automatically as they met the criteria laid down in, and did not exceed the aid intensity ceilings set by, the Framework for State Aids for R&D.[110]

Some of these state aids were, moreover, qualified as promoting 'the execution of an important project of common European interest' within the meaning of Article 92(3)(b) of the EC Treaty.[111]

For others the Commission expressly referred to the need to ensure the

---

109 Commission press release of 27 July 1994 (IP/94/714).

110 E.g. Italy - Alcatel Italia SpA - Synchronus Digital Hierarchy - press release IP/95/34.

111 E.g. Germany - Jessi Programm - press release IP/94/211.

viability of EC industry in the face of international competition[112] or the aim of improving the competitiveness of EC industry[113] or to the fact that the project 'represented a significant step to create a competitive European supply'.[114]

B. Trade Policy Cases

CASE 1 Anti-dumping measures against calcium metal from China and the Soviet Union

The facts in this case are interesting. They are briefly restated here.[115] Following a complaint from Pechiney, the sole EC producer of calcium metal, the European Commission initiated an anti-dumping proceeding which led in September 1989 to the imposition of definitive anti-dumping duties.[116] Calcium metal is used mainly in the metallurgical industry. There are few producers. One of the importers was Extramet who processes the calcium metal into granules of pure calcium.

In the course of the anti-dumping proceeding, Extramet stated that it started importing calcium metal when Pechiney became unwilling to supply it with calcium metal in sufficient quantities. Extramet claimed that Pechiney did so because it wanted to enter itself into the market of granules of pure calcium. Extramet had lodged a complaint with the French Conseil de la Concurrence alleging that this refusal to supply was an abuse of dominant position within the meaning of Article 86 EEC.

During the anti-dumping proceeding Extramet put forward an argument relating to the EEC competition rules, to which the following reply was given: 'The third argument concerns a claim that the Community producer has suffered self-inflicted injury in refusing to supply calcium metal to the importer, who has begun court proceedings in one Member State against the Community producer alleging abuse of dominant position'.

The Commission notes that the Community producer has denied these allegations and that no final judgment has yet been reached in the Court proceedings in the Member State concerned.

The Commission takes the view that the purpose of anti-dumping

---

[112] E.g. Italy - Computers Integrated Manufacturing for Constructional Steel - press release IP/90/448.

[113] E.g. Italy - Laser Work Station for Surface Treatments - press release IP/90/126.

[114] E.g. Italy - Three Eureka Projects - press release IP/89/220.

[115] For a more complete account see Jacobs AG in his submissions to the CJEC in EXTRAMET INDUSTRIE v. EC Council 67 CMLREP 2 619 (1993).

[116] Regulation 2808/89, OJ L 271/1989.

proceedings is not, and cannot be, to condone or encourage restrictive business practices, and that the initiation of such a proceeding does not therefore deprive an undertaking of its right to initiate proceedings under Articles 85 and 86 EEC, the outcome of which cannot be prejudiced by an anti-dumping investigation. Moreover, if and when an infringement of Articles 85 and 86 is discovered and a decision has been made under Regulation 17, the Commission may review the present anti-dumping proceeding in accordance with Article 14(1) of Regulation 2423/88 (Regulation 2808/85, para. 15).

Extramet subsequently challenged the regulation imposing anti-dumping duties in the Court of Justice. In its submission Jacobs AG addressed the competition argument put forward before the Court of Justice by Extramet and concluded that 'the Council failed to give proper considerations to the question whether the imposition of a duty was consistent with the need to avoid the distortion of competition in the Common market'.[117]

Regretfully the Court of Justice examined only Extramet's submissions that mistakes were made in determining the injury suffered by Pechiney, in particular that Pechiney suffered self-inflicted injury. It allowed this submission and annulled the regulation on this ground.

Following this judgment the investigation was resumed. This investigation resulted in findings of dumping and injury and in the imposition of anti-dumping duties. Not unexpectedly the investigation focused on the issue of whether Pechiney had contributed to its own injury.

The competition aspect was addressed but discarded in the following terms: 'In this context, the Council considered whether the adoption of anti-dumping measures might lead to a situation in which effective competition might be significantly reduced. In view of the fact that supplies were available from the United States of America and Canada, and that the imports from the People's Republic of China and Russia would remain at non-dumped prices, the Council concluded that there was no such danger and that there was need to ensure that the Community industry continued to operate'.[118] This is a far cry from the sort of analysis that the Commission usually carries out under the competition rules on possible 'barriers to entry'.

The end-result is not very satisfactory from a competition law and policy perspective. Had this been a decision under competition rules, conditions would have been laid down and charges imposed.

---

117 EXTRAMET *supra* n. 115 at 670.

118 Regulation 2557/94 (OJ L 270/1994) para. 29.

The Council appeared to be aware of this. It took the unusual step of announcing a review by the Commission after six months 'provided that competition conditions in the sector concerned so require' and of deciding that a review is to be initiated at any rate after one year (para. 31).

CASE 2 Automobiles from Japan

In the arrangement between the Commission and the Japanese government taking the form of parallel statements the Japanese side undertakes to 'monitor' exports from Japan to the EC market in accordance with a forecast level of exports in 1999 (1.23 million), based on the assumption of demand in the EC in 1999 (15.1 million), and to 'monitor' exports to certain individual EC Member States in accordance with specific forecast levels of exports. The EC declared 'that the necessary measures will be taken to ensure that the operation of competition law does not constitute an obstacle to the operation of the cooperative measures on the Japanese side'.[119]

It is obvious why the Japanese side sought assurances in respect of competition policy. In order to comply with the forecasts for individual Member States the Japanese authorities must impose guidelines on the Japanese manufacturers or, as the case may be, the Japanese manufacturers must prevent sales by distributors and dealers of Japanese automobiles from Member States to a Member State with an individual forecast level when that level is exceeded in a given year. Measures taken to that effect by Japanese manufacturers or their distributors and dealers infringe the EC competition rules and, in particular, provisions of the block exemption regulation for the automobile sector.

When the Commission argued in the Council that the arrangement with Japan should be approved by the Council under the EC's trade policy powers or that the Council should enact a proper trade policy regulation, the idea was rejected.[120] So far, to the knowledge of the authors of this chapter, no other measure has been taken to resolve the legal conflict between the arrangement and the EC competition rules.

The Commission's uneasiness in this respect is reflected in the position it defended in the Court of First Instance claiming that the EC-Japan

119 Text reproduced in *1992 Revue du Marché Unique Européen* at 323 (No. 3).

120 In a Resolution of 16 May 1994 (PJ C 149/94) the Council calls upon the Commission to reach a decision quickly on how the Block Exemption Regulation should be applied taking account of "the contribution that the Regulation makes to efficient management of the arrangement between Japan and the European Union on trade in automobiles which should not be weakened in any way" (para. 7)!

agreement was a 'commercial consensus'.[121] This is also reflected in Mr Van Miert's statement in relation to the draft new block exemption on motor vehicles about the EC-Japan agreement 'that we cannot get away from'.[122]

OTHER CASES

There are a number of trade policy cases in which industrial policy issues are treated. In fact, eliminating injury resulting from imports, whether considered 'fair' or 'unfair', could generally be considered as a form of industry policy.

Many anti-dumping regulations consider, either under the 'injury' or the 'Community interest' heading, the argument that the EC industry must be maintained and its competitiveness protected in the face of unfair imports. This has been contested from time to time in the legal literature. The authors of this report do not share the view that it is legally improper for the EC to consider industrial policy issues when adopting trade policy measures. They are of the view that the purpose of anti-dumping and anti-subsidy action is not primarily to counteract dumping and subsidies as such; it is to eliminate injury resulting therefrom. Moreover, measures are subject to the 'Community interest', which is an additional requirement that is separate from the interest to counteract 'unfair trade'. Obviously when safeguard measures are taken it is proper to take account of industrial policy considerations.

This is also the case when legislation is enacted on rates of customs tariffs and on origin rules. However, where the Commission determines in specific cases the origin of products, a legal issue arises, not because of the fact that legislation on rules of origin may not take account of industrial policy concerns but because of the fact that the delegation of powers to the Commission does apparently not allow the Commission to take industrial policy concerns into consideration.[123]

The question arises, however, whether the European Community could still use origin rules as an instrument of industrial policy or even of trade policy in view of the Uruguay Round Agreement on Rules of Origin. Further to this agreement a harmonization programme is set up based on the principle that 'rules of origin should not be used as instruments to

---

121 Judgment of 18 May 1994 (BEUC and NCC v. Commission) 1994 ECR II-289.

122 *Europe* 25 January 1995, p. 25.

123 For an example see CJEC, judgments of 31 January 1979 (YOSHIDA NEDERLAND v. Kamer van Koophandel) 1979 ECR 115 and (YOSHIDA GmbH v. Industries- und Handelskammer) 1979 ECR 151.

pursue trade objectives directly or indirectly' (Article 9(1)(d)).

It should be noted, however, that this agreement does not cover preferential origin rules, such as those that the EC applies to imports from Central European Countries or ACP countries.

C. Competition and Trade Policy Cases

CASE 1 Ballbearings

In its 1974 Franco-Japanese ballbearings decision[124] relating to an infringement of Article 85(1), the Commission found that the agreement between French and Japanese manufacturers designed to bring the prices of Japanese ballbearings imported into France into line with French manufactured ballbearings infringed Article 85(1) of the EEC Treaty. It held that: 'the restriction of competition is especially serious because of the volume of sales on the French ballbearing market, the share of Japanese imports in this market and the position of the undertakings in question on their respective national markets and, for some of them, on the world market in bearings' (para. 35).

The Commission noted that no decision in application of Article 85(3) could be taken since the agreement had not been notified. It added: 'In any case, the Commission does not see how this agreement could produce the favourable results specified in Article 85 (3) and, in particular, allow consumers any benefit' (para. 44).

In 1976 following a complaint from the Committee of the European Bearing Manufacturers' Associations, whose members were the German, British and French Trade Organizations, the Commission initiated an anti-dumping investigation which led in 1977 to the imposition of definitive duties whose application was suspended as the four major Japanese producers had signed an undertaking that they would increase their prices.[125]

The preamble of the regulation imposing the anti-dumping duties states, following the recital finding that the dumped imports were demonstrably the principal cause of the material injury suffered by the EC industry, that: 'Whereas, in the circumstances, the interests of the Community render necessary the imposition of a definitive anti-dumping duty of 15 per cent on imports of ballbearings and tapered roller bearings of Japanese origin and for the definitive collection of the amounts secured by way of

---

124 OJ L 343/1994.

125 OJ L 195/1977.

provisional duty in respect of the four major Japanese producers up to the rate mentioned above'.

CASE 2 Photocopiers

In August 1983, the Commission initiated an anti-dumping investigation[126] against photocopiers from Japan following a complaint lodged by the Committee of European Copier Manufactures consisting of five EC manufacturers representing a major proportion of Community production of the product in question, Olivetti being one of the complainants. One of the Japanese manufacturers mentioned in the complaint and subsequently found to have dumped was Canon. Provisional duties were imposed in 1986, the Commission having found dumping and injury resulting therefrom.[127] Definitive duties were imposed in February 1987 by the Council, who confirmed substantially the Commission's findings.[128]

Among the various findings and statements made by the EC Institutions two deserve to be mentioned in particular.

First, Rank-Xerox's imports from its affiliate Fuji-Xerox which were sold in the EC represented about 7 per cent of Rank-Xerox's total sales in the EC.[129] Moreover, Rank-Xerox imported sub-assemblies and components for the low-volume copiers it assembled. It was found that overall, in the reference period, the value added by Rank-Xerox in the EC in the production of these low-volume copiers was between 20 per cent and 35 per cent.[130]

Second, the Japanese exporters had argued that the EC industry was not competitive as a result of the inferiority of EC manufactured machines. The regulation contains in this respect the following statement: 'Submissions arguing that the high share of the market of Japanese exporters was due to the alleged superiority of Japanese manufactured machines over those produced by Community producers were not supported by convincing evidence except in respect of multiple features. As regards the range of machines, the evidence suggests that the Community producers as a whole manufacture as wide a range in terms of copy speed as that of their competitors. With regard to quality and reliability no evidence was produced that indicated that Community

126 OJ C 194/1985.
127 Regulation 2640/86, OJ L 239/1986.
128 Regulation 535/87, OJ L 54/1987.
129 Regulation 535/87, para. 52.
130 Regulation 535/87, para. 55.

machines as a whole were inferior or required more servicing. Nor was there any indication that Community producers' after-sales service was inferior compared with that of their Japanese competitors' (Regulation 535/87, para. 86).

An issue about which no interested party apparently put forward any argument but which the Commission ought arguably to have addressed was that of the competitive situation resulting from the corporate links between Fuji-Xerox and Rank-Xerox. Imposing anti-dumping duties on imports of photocopiers from Japan, while allowing Rank-Xerox to continue to import sub-assemblies and components from its affiliate Fuji-Xerox without anti-dumping duties, certainly changed the competitive position of the Xerox Group *vis-à-vis* its Japanese competitors on the EC market.

About ten months later, in December 1987, following a notification made to it by the parties, the Commission granted an exemption under Article 85(3) EEC to the Canon/Olivetti joint venture.[131] The Commission described this joint venture as follows: 'The scope of OCI is to develop, design and manufacture copying machine products, laser beam, printer product and facsimile products'.

Among the grounds on which the Commission relied to grant the exemption the following one is particularly noteworthy in the light of its finding on the same element in the anti-dumping investigation: 'The joint venture enables a transfer of the benefit of advanced technology to Olivetti, a Community undertaking, in markets where technology is of crucial importance'.

CASE 3 Soda-Ash

- Anti-dumping measures against soda-ash imports

In 1983, anti-dumping duty was imposed on imports of dense sodium carbonate from the USA and price undertakings from three US companies were accepted.[132] In 1984, anti-dumping proceedings were reopened following a request from the European Council of Chemical Manufacturers Federations; the scope of the existing measures was amended[133] and price undertakings offered by two US companies were accepted.[134]

131 OJ L 52/1988.
132 OJ L 64/1993.
133 OJ L 311/1984.
134 OJ L 206/1984.

In 1988, a review of the existing anti-dumping measures was requested by certain US producers and the EC glass industry which claimed that US exporters were no longer dumping. In March 1989, the Commission initiated a review and investigated whether dumping had occurred between 1 December 1987 and 28 February 1989.

- Competition decisions against soda-ash producers

In March 1989 the Commission carried out investigations under the EC competition rules at the premises of EC producers of soda-ash and opened formal proceedings under these rules in February 1990. On 19 December 1990 it adopted a series of decisions under the EC competition rules.

In one of these decisions it found that two EC producers had participated, since 1 January 1973 until at least the institution of the proceedings, in a concerted practice by which they confined their soda-ash sales in the EC to their respective home markets. The Commission ordered the two producers of soda-ash to cease and desist, and imposed on each of them a fine of ECU 7 million.[135]

In a second and third one of these decisions[136] the Commission found that two EC producers of soda-ash occupied a dominant position in the relevant product and geographic markets (70 per cent, viz. 90 per cent) and that they had abused their dominant position by various measures. The Commission ordered them to cease and desist, and imposed a fine of ECU 20 million, viz 10 million. The Commission found that the measures taken by both EC producers to ensure the continuance of their dominant position were aimed in the first place at direct competition from outside the EC (the United States and Poland). It also found that 'a major plank' of the commercial policy of one of these EC producers was 'to ensure the maintenance of the anti-dumping measures in place against the United States producers of heavy ash as well as the East European light ash suppliers'.

For good measure in another one of these decisions[137] the Commission found that the American Natural Soda-Ash Corporation (ANSAC) (a Webb-Pomerane association) membership agreement and related agreements which ANSAC had notified to it infringed the EC competition rules in so far as they related to the EC market. The European Commission ordered ANSAC and its members to refrain from

---

135 OJ L 152/1991.

136 OJ L 152/1991.

137 OJ L 152/1991.

implementing the agreements in the EC.

- The fate of the anti-dumping measures against soda-ash imports

In the meantime the review proceeding of the existing anti-dumping measures had been going on. On 7 September 1990 the Commission adopted a decision on the matter. It found dumping margins for four US companies ranging from 2.9 per cent to 12.8 per cent. However, it terminated the investigation without imposing anti-dumping measures, having found that the dumping had not caused injury and recognized 'that it has not been established that the expiry of the existing anti-dumping measures would threaten to cause serious injury to the Community industry'.[138]

It took the view that there was no 'threat of injury': the current level of US exports was very low, and the US producers did not have the proper sales structure needed to increase their sales significantly.

Whether the decision to terminate the review without anti-dumping measures being taken resulted from the anti-competitive conduct of the EC soda-ash producers, the role which anti-dumping measures had played in shoring up the dominant position of at least one of them and the subsequent decisions taken against them under the EC competition rules, is a matter for speculation.

Whereas in some of its decisions under the competition rules relating to the soda-ash sector the Commission refers to existing anti-dumping measures, in its decision terminating the review of the existing anti-dumping measures on soda-ash it does not say a word about its findings under the competition rules.[139] On the face of it, the Commission could, as it did, terminate such review a purely on grounds relating to the Anti-dumping Regulation and did not need to refer to competition law policy considerations. But in this case the tension between the two policies was too obvious to be ignored in substance. It is noteworthy in this respect that in its 1993 review of the EC's trade policy, the GATT secretariat commented on this case as follows: 'A recent case in which the EC authorities intervened to restore competitive conditions concerns soda-ash, where domestic producers had sought anti-dumping protection to defend cartel rents against competing imports. The companies involved were convicted under EC competition law and the anti-dumping measures

---

138 OJ L 283/1990.

139 P. Vandoren, "Recent Developments in the Area of the Interface between Anti-dumping and Competition Policy in the EC", (1993) LIEI 21 (No. 1 at 27) finds it surprising that competition considerations were not mentioned in connection with imports from the USA.

repealed in 1990/91'.[140]

This statement has apparently not been contradicted by the Commission in the course of the so-called 'review meetings' conducted in the GATT on the basis of this GATT report containing these comments.

This, however, is not the end of the story. In August 1993 following a new complaint from the European Council of Chemical Manufacturers Federations, the Commission initiated yet again an anti-dumping proceeding relating to soda-ash from the USA.[141] It has been reported that this preliminary investigation is terminated and that draft measures are being considered by the Commission. At the time of writing measures have not been taken.

One will have to wait for the publication of a regulation or a decision to know whether the market has changed much in the meantime. That the share of the EC market taken by US producers has increased would not be surprising. As the abuse of dominant position by some of the major EC players consisted precisely in measures designed to keep the US producers out, stagnating sales by US producers would arguably show that the Commission's decisions under the competition rules did not have any effect whatsoever.

Apparently, there has been not much change in the market structure in the EC, except that ICI reportedly sold its soda-ash division to the main Australian producer of soda-ash. Normally, the new owner of ICI's soda-ash division may be expected to want to protect his investment and to refrain from importing soda-ash from Australia into the EC at low prices.

In addition, the acquisition of substantial production capacities in the US by certain EC producers raises yet another competition issue, that is, whether it is appropriate and wise to allow EC producers to strengthen their position on the US market *vis-à-vis* their competitors by restricting the latter's access to the EC market.[142]

The Commission could, however, once again duck the competition law and policy issue and terminate the investigation without taking anti-dumping measures by relying on the 'Community interest' clause of the Anti-dumping Regulation. In a case such as this there is something to be said for taking account of the interests of the user industry, in particular

---

140 GATT, Trade Policy Review Mechanism, European Communities. Doc. C/RM/S/36A p. XII (19 April 1993).

141 OJ C 213/1993.

142 This sort of situation is described in more detail by J. Temple-Lang, 'Reconciling European Community Antitrust and Antidumping, Transport and Trade Safeguards Policies- Practical Problems', in 1988 Fordham Corporate Law Institute, B. Hawk (ed.) 7-1 at 7-41 (Matthew Bender, New York, 1989).

the glass industry, which offers employment to several times the number of people employed in the soda-ash industry and whose production costs depend significantly on the price of soda-ash.[143]

Be it as it may, under the post-Maastricht rules referred to in section I of this chapter competition policy has been given a more prominent function. Taking anti-dumping measures in a case such as this one would appear on the face of it as highly questionable.

III. RECOMMENDATIONS

While preparing this chapter, the authors wondered whether as lawyers they ought to put forward recommendations on the proper policy mix the EC Institutions should strive for when taking into consideration the three policy areas within the broadly defined legal mandate set out in the 'constitutional' instruments described *supra* (Section I). In the end they decided to refrain from doing so, mainly for two reasons.

First, they were of the view that the policy choices which decisions on the proper policy mix involve are too dependent on the facts of each case and the economic and policy assessment thereof to be capable of being regulated by substantive norms that would be precise enough to be operational and at the same time offer legal certainty, while being sufficiently durable to be predictable.

Second, they considered that, at any rate, while lawyers may assist policy-makers in their decision-making process, they do so in a legal perspective, while the choices to be made in the matter discussed in this paper are essentially policy choices. There are, however, recommendations to be made from a legal perspective. Such recommendations are of a procedural nature.

First Recommendation

From an institutional and organizational point of view the Commission is, as a decision-making body, in a fairly advantageous position. While in other jurisdictions, e.g. in the USA, policy management is spread over different bodies, each responsible for a given area such as antitrust policy, industrial policy and trade policy, the Commission is as a collegiate body in a position to consider at all times the interrelationships between the

143 The situation is complicated further by soda-ash imports from Central and Eastern Europe. These imports have increased from 27,000 tonnes to 162,000 tonnes in 1992 and have replaced West European production (FT 6 July, p. 5).

various policy areas. As the exclusive source of legislative proposals, at least under the EC Treaty, the Commission is also acting as a collegiate body and here as well it is in a position to consider these interrelationships when working out such proposals and to ensure that these interrelationships are considered when its proposals are discussed in the various 'specialized Councils' of the European Union. This requires appropriate internal procedures within the Commission to ensure always that, when a draft decision to be taken within a given policy area is considered, the relationships with other policy areas are taken into account.

There are effectively within the Commission internal procedures requiring the input of 'services associés' and of 'services consultés'. There also are the Chefs' meetings. However, from the cases examined in this report one is bound to conclude at first blush either that these procedures and machinery are inadequate or that they do not function properly.

The first recommendation is thus that the Commission adopt internal procedures ensuring that generally when the responsible DG submits a draft decision, say in the competition area, there is a genuine input of the DGs in charge of say industrial policy and trade policy and conversely.

The objections which are from time to time put forward against this are not convincing.

The first objection has to do with the legal limits on the use of information collected and the rules on professional secrecy. Under the legislation as its stands[144] information collected by the Commission in competition investigations, i.e. in trade policy investigations, may be used only for the purposes of the enforcing competition rules, (trade policy rules) and, as the case may be, only for the purposes of the relevant investigations; moreover, the Commission and its officials may not disclose information acquired through these investigations of the kind covered by the obligation of professional secrecy. This, however, should not impede the Commission and its officials from taking account of the interrelationship between different policy areas when considering measures in a given policy area.[145] The Commission and its officials are not under a legal duty to initiate a competition policy investigation when, in the course of a trade policy investigation, they are made aware of a

144 In the competition policy area: Regulation 17/62, Article 20 and Regulation 4064/89, Article 17; for the anti-dumping and anti-subsidy area: Regulation 2423/88, Article 8(1), now Regulation 3283/1994, Articles 7(1) and 9(4) and Regulation 3284/94, Articles 9(1) and 11(6), both OJ L 349/1994.

145 Acc. Jacobs AG in his submissions in EXTRAMET n. 24 at p. 669.

possible infringement of competition rules, and conversely. The involvement of officials in charge of trade policy when competition policy measures are prepared, and conversely, does consequently not put them in a situation of conflicting duties. In addition, when in a competition case trade policy implications are considered this does not turn a competition case into a trade policy case. The subject matter is and remains enforcement of competition rules.

The second objection concerns the limited scope of the examination of issues relating to a given policy in the framework of an investigation relating to another policy. It has been argued e.g. that the Commission could not investigate fully a competition matter arising in an anti-dumping investigation.[146] However, 'le mieux est l'ennemi du bien': what is required is that the Commission does not disregard considerations of competition policy in an anti-dumping case. To that purpose the Commission does not need to embark on a fully-fledged competition investigation.

The third objection is that in a case pertaining to a given policy area and therefore allocated to the DG in charge of that policy undue consideration would be given to other policies as a result of interference by other DGs. While 'undue consideration' is to be avoided, the present situation in which apparently the Commission's left hand too often ignores what the Commission's right hand is doing is a cure worse than the disease. Moreover, as far as consideration of competition aspects is concerned, the objection has little legal merit in view of the prominence now conferred to competition policy by Article 130 of the EC Treaty.

Second Recommendation

The Commission does not investigate on its own initiative whether possible infringements of competition rules in trade proceedings are involved. Nor does it, as a rule, examine on its own initiative possible competition policy implications of trade policy measures. In competition policy proceedings the Commission follows a similar approach as far as trade policy issues are concerned. In proceedings in both these areas the Commission practice is to leave it to parties to raise issues pertaining to the other policy area.

One of the authors of this chapter has in the past raised doubts about the need of systematic competition impact analyses in anti-dumping case, to the extent that injury determinations are carefully made, the general

---

146 Argument put forward by the defence in EXTRAMET n. 115 at p. 669.

practice to limit anti-dumping duties to what is necessary to remove such injury is followed, the position of the import-using industry is taken into account and, where appropriate, existing measures are reviewed.[147] This author is bound to recognize, however, that these qualifications, while allowing account to be taken of the interests of parties as they are protected by competition rules, do not exclude the risk that competitors of the parties involved in such proceedings may be affected, nor the risk that the exporters and importers refrain from raising competition policy issues in view of a deal they may want to make with the complainant industry. In the final analysis not only the interests of competitors and users are matters of concern but also the maintenance of competition as such.

Thus the Commission ought not to leave it to parties in proceedings in a given policy area to raise issues relating to other policy areas but should examine such issues on its own initiative.

In competition investigations, at least those relating to agreements and concerted practices, this may give rise to a problem, to the extent that examining industrial and trade policy implications would, under the traditional interpretation of Article 85(1) EC, only be relevant for Article 85(3) EC purposes. Under the rules as they stand,[148] Article 85(3) individual exemptions may only be granted in respect of agreements which have been specifically notified for the purpose of seeking an exemption. One could argue, however, that this rule may be set aside in appropriate cases and exemptions thus be granted in the Community interest rather than in the interest of the parties to such agreements.

Third Recommendation

'Justice must not only be done. It must also be seen to be done'.

In trade policy decisions most of the existing legislative instruments require the Commission and, as the case may be, the Council to consider whether the 'Community interest' calls for intervention. The 'Community interest' clauses remain the 'parent pauvre' in trade policy investigations and in the decisions taken following such investigations.[149]

Competition policy decisions, i.e. the formal ones, not the comfort letters, are more explicit and better drafted in this regard if and when they address issues relating to other policies.

---

147 J.H.J. Bourgeois, 'Trade Measures, Competition Policy and the Consumers', in P. Demaret, J. Bourgeois and I. Van Bael (eds.) *Trade Laws of the European Community and the United States in a comparative Perspective* at 241 (Story-Scientia, Brussels, 1992).

148 Regulation 17/62, Articles 4(1), 5(1) and 25.

149 E.g. with respect to consumers' interests, see J.H.J. Bourgeois, *supra* n. 1472 at 258.

The third recommendation is consequently that not only issues relating to the other policies be examined in investigations relating to another policy but also that these issues, their assessment and the conclusion reached be clearly reflected in the text of the decisions.
of the decisions.

Discussion
Pietros Mavroidis

The chapter by Bourgeois and Demaret deals with a very interesting legal question in theory, namely whether a hierarchy exists among the competition, the trade and the industrial policies of the EC. The Maastricht Treaty on the European Union provides the legal background where this alleged hierarchy is examined. It further explores the interplay of the three aforementioned policies so far in the EC practice and advances recommendations that according to the authors would, if adopted, render the interplay between the three policies more functional. The comments that are presented here do not necessarily follow the structure of the chapter. They do capture though, hopefully, its essence.

The first part of the chapter tries to establish a hierarchy among the three different policies.

A blunt statement to the effect that competition policy by definition increases efficiency while the other two do not is incorrect and, rightfully, avoided by the authors. An example could be where competition policy standards are relaxed in a merger situation in order to create national champions. Conversely, full liberal trade policy leads to enhanced competition in the domestic market. It is true, however, that the focus of competition policy is competition, whereas the focus of the other two policies is competitors. To what extent justice is done to the basic aim especially of the competition policy, depends on state practice.

The authors start by a simple factual observation that is, however, crucial for what follows: Article 130 of the Maastricht Treaty put into the frame what previously existed through various instruments: that is, the industrial policy. In the context of the Maastricht Treaty, two ways are provided through which the EU industrial policy can be realized, depending on the nature of the measures that have been planned.

In the case of specific measures, which could in practice be the most usual and, allegedly, the most controversial, the Maastricht Treaty provides for a unanimous decision by the Council following a proposal made by the Commission.

On the surface it seems as if the Maastricht Treaty has added an extra threshold to the existing disciplines of the Treaty of Rome (Article 93), namely the required unanimity by the Council for specific measures to be approved. Article 93 of the Treaty of Rome, however, whereby the Commission enjoys considerable discretion, has been retained in the Maastricht Treaty. Moreover, the argument could be made that Article 93 is a *lex specialis* to Article 130 in that it regulates only one form of intervention for industrial policy purposes, i.e. state aids; consequently, it should prevail. This, in practice, could mean that, with respect to specific measures, the Article 130 disciplines could prove to be a dead letter. The recent experience with approved state aids to national air carriers, where no recourse to the new Article 130 disciplines was made, proves this point.

It is true, however, that with respect to non-specific measures, Article 130 could enhance transparency. Much, however, will depend on the relevant EU practice. Moreover, as the authors rightfully point out, such powers were already within the realm of competence of the relevant Community institutions and found expression in the past through recourse to Article 235 of the Treaty of Rome.

As far as the other two policies are concerned, the state of play has not evolved dramatically with the entry into force of the Maastricht Treaty.

It is in this context that the first part of the chapter deals with the question of hierarchy between the three policies in the system of the Maastricht Treaty. The answer to this question defines what follows in the rest of the chapter:

a) if we can establish a hierarchy beyond any doubt, then our work is substantially facilitated, in the sense that the hierarchically higher norm (in this case, policy) should always be respected;
b) if we cannot, then we should focus on specific instruments that will put into place the objectives sought by the three policies.

The authors conclude that the answer to this question lies somewhere between the two alternatives. It is true that the EC Treaty recognizes the primacy of competition policy over industrial policy. The language of Article 130, however, is already weak (the industrial policy shall be exercised 'in accordance with a system of open and competitive markets').

The authors admit that if this general principle is translated in to operative language two limits will be imposed on the exercise of industrial policy:

a) recourse to instruments which are forbidden under EC competition rules will be prohibited for industrial policy purposes;
b) the exercise of industrial policy should not have the effect of significantly impeding competition.

There is not much that can be said with respect to the first point. With respect to the second point, the authors propose a test similar to that applied in the context of Article 85(3) of the EC Treaty or 2(2) of the Merger Regulation. The criterion proposed is flexible. Inflexible proponents of legal security could arguably refute it on the grounds that it does not establish a clear-cut legal threshold. Flexibility is needed, though, in this field and, consequently, a case-by-case analysis is appropriate.

The main instrument of industrial policy is subsidies. With respect to subsidies the EC is under the international law obligation to abide by the WTO Agreement on Subsidies recently concluded in the context of the Uruguay Round negotiations. One of the novelties of the new agreement is that it distinguishes between actionable and non-actionable subsidies; countervailing duties will be permissible only with respect to the former category. Moreover, the list of prohibited subsidies is enlarged. Actionable subsidies are not necessarily prohibited, since the case could well be that perfectly legal subsidies cause injury to third parties that, in turn, have the right to impose countervailing duties.

What is missing from the text of Article 130 is a Community-wide discipline on subsidies comparable to that in the WTO Agreement, which will be operating at the Community level. This, of course, will be the role that the translation of Article 130 into operative language will be called to play. Here, however, a problem could potentially lie in view of the recent European Court of Justice (ECJ) jurisprudence. In the case of 'Bananas' (C-280/93), decision of the Court of 5 October 1994), quoted by the authors, the ECJ seems to impose stringent conditions with respect to the observance of the GATT/WTO law. One of the major achievements of the Uruguay Round negotiations was the 'automaticity' rule to be applied in the field of Dispute Settlement: all WTO Panel and Appellate Body decisions will be automatically adopted unless there is a 'negative consensus' against them.

Were the EC to implement in good faith its international obligations, it would have to abide by such rulings. Consequently, the only limit to the exercise of its industrial policy, outside those invoked by the authors, will be the WTO case law in the field of subsidies. The recent 'Bananas' jurisprudence seems to condition the respect of the GATT/WTO law on Community action purporting to give effect to obligations undertaken in the GATT/WTO context. Such an approach, if followed literally in the future, could seriously reduce the importance of this extra threshold to the exercise of the EC industrial policy.

The link between competition and trade policy is more problematic. The comments here will focus on the defence mechanisms of the EC trade policy and, especially, anti-dumping mainly for the following two reasons:

a) anti-dumping is the instrument most often used by the EC;
b) one of the results of the Uruguay Round negotiations was the tightening of the Agreement on Safeguards. Moreover, the same agreement outlaws all voluntary export restraints (VERs), allowing the possibility for signatories to notify one VER that will be tolerated for a specific time-limit. This means that with VERs out of place (were the agreement to be implemented in good faith) recourse to anti-dumping could conceivably be more frequent.

At the institutional level, the EC trade policy is delinked from the EC competition policy. One could only speculate about the possible shaping of the EC anti-dumping policy as far as DG IV is the competent authority to investigate. Such a perspective should not sound unrealistic, since it has already been put into practice in other European countries (Poland). This is not the place to argue the pros and the cons of anti-dumping. It is clear that outside predation active anti-dumping policy leads to reduced competition.

The current EC anti-dumping legislation contains a public interest clause: consumers' interests are represented during the investigation process. The same obligation is imposed on investigating authorities with respect to users of the allegedly dumped imports. Moreover, in March 1994 the EC legislation was modified and, as a result, the position of the aforementioned categories was strengthened. The EC system could operate in this context as a cost-benefit analysis: the Commission will have to weigh the interests of the domestic industry seeking protection against the interests of the consumers/users interested in cheap imports. As a result, the investigating authorities will be called to estimate the effect of protection on the whole of the EC economy. The authors correctly state that public interest clauses exist in different Community instruments with different meanings. What has been described above, though, should constitute the essence of the discretion to be exercised.

It is true that the EC legislation has evolved quite substantially in this respect. Public interest clauses were perceived to be a 'dead letter' for some time. Recently, however, two events have changed this perception. In a case concerning imports of gum rosin, the Commission concluded that 'the negative effects of anti-dumping measures would be overwhelmingly disproportionate to the benefits arising from anti-dumping measures in favour of the Community industry' (OJ L 41/54, 12 February 1994). Then came the modifications to the anti-dumping legislation stated above (OJ L 66/7ff., 7 March 1994). The cited passage from the gum rosin case implies the cost-benefit test described above.

Public interest clauses have been included in the Uruguay Round Agreements on Anti-dumping, Subsidies and Safeguards. They are not however, as far-reaching as those inserted in the Community instruments.

The cases selected by the authors illustrate the interplay among the three policies. It becomes obvious to the reader that trade policy instruments have been used to attain industrial policy objectives (this is mainly the case of anti-dumping). It also becomes obvious that competition policy considerations are neglected in the overwhelming majority of cases. One can only wonder at the inconsistencies of the EC bureaucracy (see, for example, the 'Photocopiers' case); such inconsistencies are often the result of non-coordination between the various branches of the EC administration.

The selected cases further show that the multilateral context has been neglected when it could be of considerable help. An example to this effect is provided by the 'Flat Panel Display' case. It is true that there is a limited scope to advance efficiency arguments in the GATT context. However, to the extent that restrictive business practices (RBPs) deny market access possibilities, the GATT legal system can provide an efficient remedy through recourse to the so-called 'non-violation' complaints. In this context, a complaint can be brought to challenge national measures, independently of whether they are consistent or inconsistent with the GATT, if benefits of third contracting parties have been nullified or impaired as a result of the application of these national measures. It is not only the EC, though, that has failed to test the limits of the multilateral system. This point holds for the majority of the contracting parties that on the one hand fail to test the limits of the system but, on the other, continue to load it with extra responsibilities.

The title of the chapter could have been posed in the form of a question: 'EC policies on competition, industry and trade: complementarities or conflicts?' Were the chapter to serve as an answer to this question, the following two basic conclusions could be reached:

a) there is no definitive answer as a matter of principle; one has, therefore, to look at the relevant practice;
b) practice shows that most of the time the interplay of the different policies has led to conflicts.

Economic history teaches that government failures are more important and more frequent than market failures. This does not suggest that all regulation is bad and all deregulation is good. Intervention, though, should be exercised with caution. The authors of this chapter refrain from proposing any substantive recommendations; instead, they advance three procedural recommendations. Procedural recommendations, though, can in practice turn out to be more substantial than substantive ones, especially in the case where considerable discretion is left with the authorities entrusted with the application of the policies. The crux of the three recommendations is two fold: coordination (among the different branches of the EC administration) and transparency (in the exercise of the policies).

Above all, though, it remains to be seen to what extent efficiency will be the guiding light in EC practice in the future. Efficiency is, in principle, the common ground of the three policies. In a rather simplistic way:

- it is the hard core of competition policy where authorities are entrusted with preserving and promoting competition;
- it can enhance competition in domestic markets through active pursuit of free-trade policy;
- intervention meant to correct distortions constitutes efficient industrial policy.

Viewed in this context, the proposals of the authors can make a difference. Transparency will be understood in its widest possible context, i.e. participation of all interested parties in the process. To this effect, public interest clauses could play a role not only in the exercise of trade but also of industrial policy. Adequate motivation of all decisions - a domain where the ECJ case law is particularly rich - is the necessary complement of transparency. When it comes to coordination one can only wonder why a sophisticated bureaucracy like the EC has yet to reach what seems to be the obvious for any efficient administration. As far as the form of coordination is concerned, other contributors to this book have advanced elaborate proposals.

Future experience will show to what extent efficiency arguments will prevail in the EC practice and, consequently, whether the three policies will be exercised in a complementary rather than a conflictual way. The substantive means are there (public interest clauses). The procedural means are hereby proposed. What is missing so far is the political will to proceed in this direction.

PART II

CASE STUDIES

3. Automobile industry

Peter Holmes and Alasdair Smith

INTRODUCTION AND OVERVIEW

In this chapter, we first give an outline of the structure and problems of the European car market. Then we discuss Community policy objectives towards cars, and what should be the correspondence between policy objectives and policy instruments. In practice the policy-making process of the car industry is affected by the multi-level structure of the EU decision-making system. Although policy towards the car industry has displayed a certain coherence at EU level, and has perhaps nudged the sector towards liberalization, current policies are not consistent with either economic efficiency or the principles of the Rome Treaty, and a more appropriate matching of aims and instruments is desirable.

1. THE EUROPEAN CAR MARKET

1.1. Structure and performance

The car industry inevitably attracts attention by policy-makers in view of both its size and its prominence in trade. Although the value added in the automobile and component industry itself is under 2 per cent of EU GNP, car assemblers in the EU were estimated (European Commission, 1994b) to employ around 1.05 million workers in 1993 (down from 1.3 million in 1983, with the larger reductions taking place first in 1983-86 and then in 1991-93). Vehicle assembly accounted for some 3.7 per cent of total EU manufacturing employment in 1992. The components industry employs a further 900,000; and Vigier (1992) estimates that if all suppliers are added in, the sector accounts for a total of 4.5 million workers or about 15 per cent of Community industrial employment.

For many Community Member States the industry has been a major contributor to the balance of payments. The Community still had a surplus by value in motor vehicles of 5.6 bn ECU in 1992, but this surplus has been steadily diminishing during the second half of the 1980s, and has turned into a deficit by volume. The positive aspect of this is that the industry has moved up-market to be able to export cars of higher value added than are imported, but the general picture is one of increasing competitive pressure from the Japanese, and is likely to remain so. The declining competitiveness of EU producers shows up most conspicuously in the rising share of import penetration and local production by Japanese producers, but perhaps the gravest element in the picture is the loss of export markets. Historically, cars were one of the leading exports for France, Germany and the UK, especially to North America. In recent years, however, the ability of EU producers to sell in North America has been severely diminished by the success of Japanese suppliers, and the USA, which accounted for 46.3 per cent of EU motor vehicle exports in 1987, took only 16.9 per cent of 1992 exports. EFTA markets now account for more sales than the USA The past strength of European producers in the North American market was based on sales of luxury cars at premium prices, but this strength has been undermined by the ability of Japanese firms to raise quality standards on mass-produced cars, while at the same time using low-cost 'lean production' methods to reduce the cost of producing luxury cars.

Hourly labour costs which were lower in the EU than the USA for much of the 1980s (but lower still in Japan) are now roughly comparable at about 20 ECU/hr in all three major trading regions. The strength of competitiveness depends therefore on productivity and product quality and innovation.

The research of the International Motor Vehicles Programme (IMVP) (Womack, Jones and Roos, 1990) strongly suggests that the success of the Japanese motor industry has been based on managerial methods rather than on technological superiority in a narrow sense or on other conventional sources of comparative advantage. Key and interlinked areas of Japanese advantage are the control of inventory costs (through 'lean production'), monitoring of quality and reliability, and successful personnel policies. The IMVP research has identified a very large gap between the efficiency levels of Japanese and European producers, with European productivity less than 50 per cent of the Japanese level. American experience in the late 1980s suggests that considerable and rapid progress can be made in catching up with Japanese managerial skills in these areas (though the spur to the American catching up seems to lie more in private competition than in public policy intervention). The statistics in Table 3.1 below show that the Japanese market share in

Western Europe declined in 1994, and some see evidence that the European producers are catching up with Japanese competition (Kevin Done, 'Eyes on the fast lane', *Financial Times*, 31 January, 1995, p. 18).

Table 3.1 shows that six firms account for over 75 per cent of the EU car market. There is much higher concentration within national markets, with sales being concentrated in the principal firms' home markets in most cases. The two French producer groups which have 23 per cent of the EU market take 60 per cent of the French market and over 30 per cent of the Spanish market; Fiat used to have over 60 per cent of the Italian market, though its share has now fallen below 50 per cent; while the UK market is dominated by the US multinationals. The asymmetric pattern of market shares means that some producers are dependent on a limited number of national markets for most of their sales: Fiat makes two-thirds of its Western European car sales in Italy alone; while the two French groups are very dependent on the French and Spanish markets.

Table 3.1: The Western European car market 1993-1994[1]

	Market share 1994	*Market share 1993*	*Growth 1993-4 per cent*
	per cent of total units sold	per cent of total units sold	per cent volume change
Volkswagen group	16.0	16.3	3.8
General Motors	13.1	13.2	5.2
Peugeot Citroen	12.8	12.4	9.7
Ford	11.8	11.6	8.0
Renault	11.0	10.6	9.2
Fiat	10.8	10.4	9.7
BMW (inc Rover)	6.5	6.5	6.5
Mercedes-Benz	3.5	3.2	19.1
Nissan	3.2	3.5	-3.8
Toyota	2.6	2.8	-1.1
Volvo	1.7	1.5	16.7
Mazda	1.5	1.7	-7.6
Honda	1.4	1.4	3.8
Mitsubishi	1.0	1.2	-14.0
Suzuki	0.6	0.8	-20.3
Japanese makes	*10.9*	*12.3*	*-5.8*
TOTAL			5.9

1 *Financial Times*, 13 January, 1995.

The role of multinationals in the car market is at the core of some of the policy issues we discuss in this chapter. Two of the six largest groups are US-owned, and have production bases in several EU countries; VW, Renault and Peugeot all have significant manufacturing presences in the EU outside their 'home' countries; while Nissan has plants in the UK and Spain, Toyota and Honda in the UK, Suzuki in Spain and Hungary, and Mitsubishi in the Netherlands.

1.2. Policy Issues

The fact that the car industry is a creator of demand in the rest of the economy is often cited as a reason why it requires special treatment from public policy, and surely a main source of policy concern about the car industry arises from the conjunction of its sheer importance to the economy and the possibility that its loss of international competitiveness is irreversible. More specific issues might be raised about the importance of the car industry as a demander of high-technology products, giving rise to concerns about market failures in high-technology sectors.

The key industrial policy issue is the productivity gap between the Europeans and the Japanese. Some analysts of the European car industry see its problems as due to the difficulties of adapting to the intensity of competition suddenly faced during the 1980s while others suggest that the problems of the industry are because protectionist policies have minimized incentives to adapt. Another dimension of disagreement is displayed by the contrast between those who argue that the EU industry could never compete with the Japanese without support and those who argue that it could adapt if only it were given the stimulus. There remains heated debate about how far EU firms are inherently weaker than the Japanese. Raymond Lévy of Renault was quoted in the *New York Times* (30 April, 1989) as asserting that new car plants operated by EU firms could produce vehicles with half the manpower of existing plants, implying that it would be economic for EU producers to scrap old plants and compete on equal terms with the Japanese, but that they are constrained from doing so by social and political considerations.

In addition to the specific issues associated with the car industry, more general questions can be asked about the market failures associated with R&D, whose role is important in the car sector.

A number of potential issues are raised by the concentrated market structure displayed in Table 3.1. Concentration *per se* need not be of great concern if there is strong competition from imports, but if the main importers, the Japanese producers, face restraints on European sales, the competition-enhancing role of imports is unlikely to be great. Similarly, if intra-European competition were strong, one might be unconcerned about the high degree of concentration at the national market level, but there is evidence of continuing national market segmentation. There are competition policy questions to ask about the vertical relationships between assemblers and component suppliers, and between assemblers and dealers. In a more competitive structure, it might be argued that such relationships are likely to be efficiency-enhancing; but in concentrated markets, the possibility exists that vertical restraints on competition may be used to buttress monopolistic positions.

Although the industry is one with substantial fixed costs and lumpy investments, it does not seem prone to the cycles of shortage and destructive competition that can arise in industries such as steel and chemicals where the degree of product differentiation is less.

The multinationality of the car producers raises central issues about the nature of public policy. Should there be public concern about a productivity gap between Japanese firms and European firms if Japanese producers located in Europe achieve the same efficiency levels as they do in Japan? Are Ford and General Motors European firms in a way that the Japanese are not and will not become? The answers to these questions may depend on what is the focus of policy concern: if employment is the issue, the nationality of producers is less important than the location of production, while the concerns of technology policy may be more focused on the ownership than the location of producers.

Finally, the centrality of international competition to the development of the European industry raises the question of whether there are roles for trade policy in counteracting unfair international competition or in furthering European interests by intervention in global competition.

1.3. Policy Assignments

In the light of the above discussion, traditional welfare economics might assign the targets of trade, competition and industrial policy *at the EU level* for this sector as shown in Figure 3.1.

The absence of employment or social policy objectives in Figure 3.1 reflects the general presumption among economists that sectoral policies should be directed towards economic efficiency and that social policy considerations and compensation for injury due to economic change ought to be dealt with through the social security system rather than by sector-specific measures. Sector-specific adjustment assistance may sometimes be justifiable, but in general using microeconomic policy instruments for macroeconomic or distributional purposes is likely to lead to a second-best outcome.

Figure 3.1: Optimal allocation of instruments and targets at EU level

Policy	Overall objective	Car sector instrument
Competition	Internal market-wide anti-competitive distortions by EU firms and governments	Monitoring distribution arrangements, regulating mergers, limiting subsidies
Trade	Anti-competitive distortions coming from external firms and governments	Trade barriers, anti-dumping measures
Industrial	Externalities and other internal market imperfections; seeking to help EU firms gain rents	Generic R&D aid; environmental supports; retraining and adjustment measures; 'strategic' rent-capturing subsidies

In practice, as summarized in Figure 3.2, the car industry has been subject to economic intervention for reasons quite other than these and using instruments quite different from those that might be suggested by economic theory. Some of the reasons for this divergence between principles and practice arise from the particularities of the car industry, while in other respects the car market is just a particularly striking illustration of general problems of policy coherence in the EU. First, there is substantial disagreement among the principal actors about how the car industry should be treated, indeed about the objectives of policy. Second, the nature of the Community decision-making process means that there are only imperfect mechanisms for reconciling these divisions of view. Third, the rule-based nature of the Community system means that even if there is a political consensus, this may not be entirely consistent with the legal rules as agreed in the Rome Treaty.

Figure 3.2. Trade, competition and industrial policy in practice in the EU car market

	MEMBER STATES		COMMUNITY	
	Individually	**Ad-hoc cooperation**	**Council**	**Commission**
Competition	National competition authorities		Regulations approved	Block exemption; chooses what to investigate; monitors subsidies
Trade	Pre-1993 VERs; post-1993 national sub-quotas?		**Legal power**, but unable to formalize decision	Post-1991 negotiates VER
Industry	**MAIN ACTORS**	Prometheus, DRIVE	Slow standardization	

2. EU POLICY IN THE CAR MARKET

2.1. Decision-making for the car industry

The principal political actors in this area have been the Member States *qua* national governments who have in many cases had ownership of the car industry and who have been responsible for subsidy policy and for most trade policy measures. But we should also stress the role of firms as political actors. As Gandillot (1992) shows, one of the most important elements in securing acceptance of the policy towards Japan has been the ability of the car producers (excluding Peugeot) in Europe to agree and commit to a common political position through ACEA (the Association of European Automobile Constructors) and negotiate with the Commission. Member governments are ill-placed to oppose policies which they are assured have the support of the European industry.

Partly as result, the Council of Ministers has been less active. Despite the approval given to the communications on the industry the Council has found it very hard to agree new policies and it has tended either to leave matters at national level or to let the Commission take action informally. Joint technology policy has been more vigorous under Eureka than in the Community Framework programmes. If action were proposed, there is major scope for disputes over subsidiarity. Intervention on the grounds of environmental impact has sometimes been motivated not so much by concerns for cross-border pollution as by a wish for a 'level playing field', as in catalytic converters. In addition, the Council has general powers to oversee subsidy decisions which it could use for this sector, but it never has.

The Commission has been obliged to use both informal influence and such direct powers as it has to the limits, to accommodate the pressures from national governments and firms. It appears to have negotiated directly with the industry and sometimes presented the Council or COREPER with a *fait accompli*. It has had to be somewhat creative in its approach to subsidies and to restrictive agreements and it has been forced to undertake unofficial trade negotiations with Japan that have not been formally approved by the Council of Ministers, who seem to prefer a legally and economically ambiguous agreement.

Community policy in general has been a constraint on action by Member States rather than an agreed joint action (as is stressed by Marchipont, 1994). It has been much easier for Member States to agree on what not to do than on what to do. Agreement is possible on what they wish to stop each other doing, for example excessive and self-defeating state subsidies. But the establishment of a common commercial policy in cars awaits at least the year 2000 while a true common market may have to wait till 2005 if the current proposal for a renewal of the 'block exemption' for selective and exclusive dealerships is accepted. Member States have in the past interpreted the idea of subsidiarity so as to leave the main levers of policy in national hands with the Commission acting mostly as monitor and only occasionally as a catalyst. The Maastricht Treaty does not appear to offer much scope for change. It calls for the Commission to assist the Member States to coordinate their individual actions, which is sensible, but unanimity is required for any positive action.

2.2. Rules v. Politics in the Car Industry

A further aspect of the Community decision-making system that affects this sector is that the Community is constrained by complex legal rules and procedures which cannot easily be changed. Competition policy is assigned the task of ensuring free and fair competition. It would require a Treaty amendment for the fairness aspects to be wholly eliminated, or for the competition rules of the Community to provide explicitly that competition should be less intense in the motor industry than in some others, even if the Council agreed that this was desirable in the absence of other policies. In practice, the Commission has been obliged to stretch its discretion to the limits. Industrial policy is inherently restricted because even if the Member States could agree that it would be desirable to spend money on a programme for the car industry, whether to deal with spillover effects or to capture rents in foreign markets, or even to tax polluting vehicles, the Community faces the problem of not having the capacity to raise tax revenue.

Disagreements between Member States on trade policy raise difficulties for the administration of competition policy. If competition policy is applied strictly it may undermine the tacitly agreed trade policies of the Member States. But if competition policy is tailored to meet the needs of trade policy its rule-based character may be undermined.

A further issue highly sensitive in the car industry and where Member States cannot agree firm common rules concerns the 'nationality' of firms. Here a simple interpretation of the Rome Treaty seems to be quite clear: all suppliers of goods located in the EU are to be treated identically. There is no provision for discrimination against foreign affiliates. The Treaty does in fact make indirect reference to the national origins of *goods*: Articles 9 and 10 of the Treaty specify that all goods legally imported and with duty paid must be treated within the common market in the same way as goods produced within the Community. An exception is only permitted under Article 115 where, in the absence of a fully fledged common commercial policy, Member States may be allowed by the Commission to take action against third country goods being imported through another Member State. In the absence of Article 115 measures no such discrimination is allowed. This means that the output of goods from foreign-owned plants in the EU must be treated exactly the same as that of any others irrespective of local content. The authors of the Rome Treaty could not conceive of proposing discrimination against products on the basis of the ownership of their producers. But the existence of a 40-year-old Treaty prohibition on such discrimination is not enough to ensure it will not happen when there is strong political pressure for such discrimination, especially in the case of the car industry as output from foreign-owned EU-located plants gradually replaces a significant part of domestically owned production.

Trade and competition policy merge closely together since any measure designed to restrict total sales of Japanese brands has quite different effects from a measure to restrict imports from Japan. From a legal point of view, once Japanese firms become producers inside the EU any voluntary agreements they make to restrict output become matters for competition policy not trade policy. In the case of competition policy only consumer interests can be taken into account, but there is a strong current of opinion that says trade and industry policy should support producers, especially in the car industry. This debate will not be settled in practice by the Treaty and yet if France and Britain have disputes about whether Nissan cars are to be treated as 'Japanese' or 'British' it means that the essential nature of the European Community as a regime in which economic disputes are settled by law is called into question.

2.3. The Context of EU Policy

This industry exemplifies the issues of policy conflict and incoherence. Individual Member States have for some time had separate national policies for the sector, policies which have differed radically across countries or across time. State ownership has been a widely used option, and most Member States have clung tenaciously to national trade policy regimes long after the common commercial policy was due to come into effect. The location of car plants has been widely used as an instrument of regional policy at various periods and the closure of plants has been a source of regional problems and the motive for regional intervention. Member States have thus revealed a preference for a scale and structure of car industry that is not necessarily the same as that which the market would produce and have taken the decision to regulate the intensity of competition in this sector. On the whole, Member States have opted to sustain a larger motor industry than market forces might have promoted, but policy inevitably must reflect the fact that the objective position of Member States is very different. Some are net importers, some actual or potential net exporters, and one or two have no production of cars at all.

There has not been a true common market in this sector largely due to the inability of Member States to agree on these measures, in particular with respect to external competition. The car industry in Europe has been one of the less integrated industries, with even multinational producers supplying markets locally, many firms relying very heavily on home sales (especially Fiat), and a considerable emphasis on the role of 'national champions'. The 1980s have seen both the rise of the single market and the encroachment of globalized Japanese firms, alongside increasing scepticism about the value of state control and subsidy.

On the central issue of the extent of optimal public intervention, the Commission has clearly taken a position somewhere in the middle which consists of continuing to tolerate and even promote supportive measures for the industry while publicly declaring an intention to remove them. This stance is politically astute and can be economically defended, but has the disadvantage of ambiguity in that economic actors risk being more pre-occupied with sustaining the protective measures than with preparing for the eventual liberalization.

In the area of *trade policy*, in addition to the common external tariff of 10.5 per cent, a number of EU markets have been subject to restrictions on imports of Japanese cars. From 1977 to 1991, the Japanese producers had a voluntary agreement with the UK industry, with the connivance and encouragement of the UK government, to hold their imports to a share of 11 per cent of the UK market. In France, the Japanese import share was fixed at 3 per cent, by an agreement between the French government and the Japanese producers; while in Italy, Spain and Portugal, Japanese car imports were held to even lower levels by quotas. By contrast, Japanese market shares in 1990 were 16 per cent in the essentially unrestricted German market and averaged 24 per cent in the rest of the EU. In 1991, the national restrictions were replaced by the arrangements agreed in a 'consensus' with the Japanese.

Member States have found national trade regimes increasingly unsatisfactory, if only because inward investment can circumvent trade measures and is politically impossible to resist. They have been reluctantly persuaded to accept an EU-wide trade policy in principle, but the problems in achieving agreement on a common trade policy are at the root of the difficulties in that policy which we discuss below.

A key *competition policy* issue has been, and remains, the arrangements for selective and exclusive car dealerships. The EU has given these arrangements 'block exemption' under Article 85 of the Rome Treaty and has to decide whether to renew the exemption after 1995. The link between the block exemption and the trade policy regime is addressed below.

The car market is a paradigmatic case of the links and conflicts between trade policy and competition policy. When Japanese firms face import restrictions, European firms know that an important group of their competitors face limitations on their ability to compete. European firms can then set prices higher than if they had to worry about their Japanese competitors cutting prices to increase sales. Also, the fact that many of the import restrictions are administered by the Japanese industry acts as a barrier to the entry of new Japanese firms. Thus quantitative restrictions on imports have an inherently anti-competitive nature.

Past quantitative restrictions on international trade in cars have all taken very different national forms with different legal implications. It is clear that the Commission has been wary of this minefield. However, as we discuss in detail below, the post-1992 trade regime raises further issues concerning the compatibility of trade policy with EU competition law.

Community-level *industrial policy* has been on a modest scale in the past, mainly confined to a small amount of retraining adjustment assistance and a very small amount of collaborative R&D activity. Womack and Jones (1992) regard the Prometheus and Drive programmes as likely to bring rather modest benefits, and since their results will be available to all suppliers, licensing income would be more important than any direct competitive advantage. The Commission does not formally discriminate against non-EU-owned firms, but support for R&D and for retraining workers from old plants is likely to affect some firms more than others.

European industry seems to have fallen behind on the implementation of new technologies, notably in the production process (rather than lacking innovative components or technologies). The policy adopted has been to allow a lengthy 'breathing space'. The encouragement of Japanese transplants has been something of a by-product. More pro-active policies on the part of the EU are effectively ruled out by the nature of decision-making.

American commentaries (such as Womack and Jones, 1992) have highlighted one positive aspect of EU industrial policy in cars. There appears to be much higher local value added in the EU from Japanese car plants than in the USA. They note (p. 204) that 80 per cent European local content has been aimed at by Japanese firms in the EU but not by those in the USA. They say explanations of this include threats of trade restrictions on components, a naturally strong EU components sector, and the fact that US component producers were more integrated with big assemblers and less attractive partners to the Japanese.

Womack and Jones suggest that the pressure to have high local content may slow down Japanese investment in Europe but they argue that the European components industry is ultimately better placed to respond to the Japanese needs than the US industry, where they note that the components firms are typically larger and further removed from the 'lean' system.[2]

The recent Communication from the Commission to the Council (European Commission, 1994a) proposes an enhancement of the role of Community funding from the regional and social funds. The Communication understandably places a great deal of emphasis on the

---

2 Womack, Jones and Roos (1990), p. 165 note with approval that there are far more independent EC car component supplying firms than in the USA 1,500 major and 10,000 minor against 1,000 and 4,000.

human resources aspects. It is reasonable to suppose that market failures are greatest here. The potential demands of adapting to 'lean production methods' are an obvious candidate for expenditure on Objective 4, assisting workers' adjustment to industrial change. There is a significant element of spillover here. It could be argued that the acquisition of skills required for new methods of production could be profitably funded by firms; but European firms do not offer lifetime contracts and skills acquired with one employer may be used by another. Moreover newer 'lean' production methods, if they are to raise productivity, are certain to lead to major reductions in employment. It seems extremely unlikely that EU or export demand could absorb output levels that would correspond to best-practice Japanese productivity levels from the entire current EU workforce in vehicles. The most striking number is the IMVP's estimate that 16.8 man-hours were required to assemble a vehicle in Japan in 1989 against 36.2 in Europe on average,[3] while Japanese plants in the USA achieve a figure (21.2) close to the level in Japan. Even if one postulates that demand would rise as costs fall there would be no chance of output rising to offer employment to the same workforce if these levels of productivity were achieved. The alternative strategy is to allow wages in the car industry to fall to match relative productivity. The Communication suggests that such a strategy would presumably be unwelcome to the Commission as it would to most Member States.

The Communication also notes the importance of environmental issues. Some of the stated aims would have negative impact on the car industry *per se,* if alternative modes of transport were promoted. On the other hand, the emphasis placed by the Commission on the environmental impact of vehicles is clearly situated in a domain of market failure where there is room for collaboration between and among public and private actors at the broadest European level.

The Community has also made advances in recent years in developing harmonized standards for cars. The Communication notes that from 1 January, 1993, common testing and certification rules were available to firms, and will be compulsory in 1996. It is interesting to remind ourselves that these measures are discussed in the context of the achievement of the single market plan rather than being presented as an element of the industrial policy *per se.* The idiosyncratic national standards have often functioned as a market segmentation device.

---

3 Womack, Jones and Roos (1990, p. 92).

2.4. Subsidies: Industrial Policy v. Competition Policy

EU policy to date has inevitably been more concerned with laying down criteria for defining allowable measures under Article 92 than in defining a positive role for subsidies. Regional policy considerations have played a very important role. In the recent cases involving FIAT in the Mezzogiorno, and Opel and VW in former East Germany, the Commission has applied the principle that an aid is acceptable if it just offsets the cost disadvantages of production in those regions (OJ C37/15, 1993, C43/14 1992 and C68/14 1992). Conventional economic theory would say that aids were justified only to the extent that the cost disadvantage came from some form of market failure or factor price distortion. This is quite different from structural aid to remove the cost disadvantages of disadvantaged regions which reflects an approach based on a 'level playing field' rather than on economic efficiency.

In non-regional cases the Commission, e.g. in Valeo (18th EC Competition Report) has been applying a criterion of whether the aid financed 'straightforward modernisation' or 'the introduction of products or processes which were innovative within the EU at the time of their introduction'. This is a form of implicit industrial policy. From a static efficiency point of view one would indeed query an aid that enabled a single firm to develop a unique advantage. On the other hand it is easy to see why such aids are allowed. In other cases aids are allowed where the Commission approves of a 'restructuring plan'. In the Kléber-Michelin case (18th Report, p. 178) the Commission notes that in approving an aid it 'took account of the fact that' it reduced capacity in a growing market, while shifting production to an area of high unemployment.

In the Rover case (18th Report, p. 180), the Commission, despite criticisms of certain aspects of the aid given to British Aerospace, noted that:

> *Although most of the EC car industry is currently operating at very high levels of capacity, there is a danger of re-emergence of overcapacity in this sector. The planned move by Rover from mass car producer to specialised producer will reduce the danger of aid being used to expand capacity.*

There is an implicit value judgement that the public authorities have a role in determining what is and what is not overcapacity. This has been criticized by J-F. Marchipont (1994).

The point is not to criticize these decisions in themselves, indeed the remarks on Rover, published in 1989 show farsightedness. Rather the cases show that, in the absence of a well-specified industrial policy, competition policy is being called upon to perform tasks far removed from supporting the principles of antitrust and free trade.

2.5. Trade and Competition Issues in Relations With Japan

2.5.1. Competition law and VERs pre-1993

The national trade restrictions which existed before 1993 typically consisted of agreed quantitative restrictions on imports of Japanese cars, and the legal status of most of these agreements was at best unclear. The question arises whether Japanese car firms, by implementing trade restrictions of doubtful legality, are breaking EU competition law. The doctrine is clear that where the Japanese government imposes administrative guidance on car producers, they are legally protected, though in US law this would have to be accompanied by a total absence of any agreement about the allocation of quotas. It is also clear that no violation of competition law exists when a firm is restricting supplies having been directed to do so by competent authorities within the Community.

The problem arises when 'grey' measures from a trade policy point of view are implemented by means of informal guidelines. Hawk (1990, p. 130) suggests there is some legal uncertainty about whether or not firms can be accused of violating EU competition law if they obey an apparently binding instruction by an EU Member State to refuse to sell more than a certain amount or act in an anti-competitive way when the state involved has no authority under the Rome Treaty to act in this way. Marquez-Mendes (1991) points out if there is no compulsion of any kind there can be no defence.

The French administrative quotas pre-1993 were evidently an encroachment on EU external trade jurisdiction, and could be argued to be a violation of Article 113. Unlike the Italian quota case, no formal derogation was given for France and no Article 115 measures could be used. It is difficult for a private party to challenge the French action directly if neither the Commission nor other Member States do so. In this case, neither principal suppliers nor dealers complained. Presumably the rents remaining compensate for the loss of market share (and imply that there is no incentive actually to withdraw from this activity). On the other hand independent and parallel importers have brought a number of cases under competition law against suppliers (Automec, Peugeot-Ecosystem, Asia Motors). The involvement of the government has complicated the issue, but the fact that there are individual economic actors with interests at stake makes it harder for the Courts to dismiss challenges to the Commission's reluctance to intervene. In the Asia Motors case an intermediary asked the Commission to investigate whether quotas for car imports into France were being allocated in a way that violated competition law. The Court of First Instance ruled that the Commission was wrong to dismiss an allegation that recipients of quotas acted illegally when they met to distribute the quotas among themselves (*Financial Times*, 6 July, 1993). Though the Commission decided that the French government's action in ordering the import restrictions meant the firms should not be pursued, the Court decided that this did not absolve the firms from the charge of acting collusively in allocating the quotas. In the Peugeot case the Commission itself criticized Peugeot's refusal to supply an intermediary. The Automec case was also important procedurally, as the CFI upheld the Commission's right to select its priorities in deciding when or whether to investigate a competition case, provided it gave sound reasons.

From 1977 to 1993 the UK had an industry-to-industry VER between the two trade associations, SMMT and JAMA, under which Japanese imports were allowed 11 per cent of the UK car market. This agreement was negotiated by government officials but then 'handed over' to the firms, thereby allowing the British government to claim it was not violating the GATT ban on quantitative restrictions. Its nature probably allowed it to escape the UK competition rules (there was only one UK-based party to the agreement, and the meetings always took place outside the UK), but it was almost certainly a violation of Article 85. In the Franco-Japanese Ballbearings and Aluminium from Eastern Europe cases it has been established that governmental encouragement is not enough to make a private restrictive arrangement legal. The Monopolies and Mergers Commission Report (1992) made it clear that the government knew about the arrangement but had encouraged rather than compelled it, and all the evidence is that the Japanese government did not compel it.

In 1991 this agreement was challenged by the European consumer group BEUC in a complaint to DG-IV. DG-IV in its response appeared to acknowledge the potential violation of EU law but responded that it was not in the Community interest to intervene. The Commission said that since the British government knew about the agreement it should be considered a matter of trade policy. But the Commission and the ECJ have in the past held that anti-competitive behaviour can be legalized only if competent public authorities compel such action. Mere encouragement is not enough. In their evidence to the GATT Trade Policy Reviews of the EU and Japan, the Japanese government denied all knowledge of the deal! There would thus be no easy recourse to a sovereign compulsion defence here. DG-IV's letter concluded that their decision not to act did not constitute a formal opinion on the legality of the situation. BEUC appealed to the Court of First Instance against the Commission's refusal to act.

On 18 May 1994, the Court of First Instance gave judgment in BEUC's favour. It annulled the Commission's letter refusing to open an investigation of the BEUC complaint. It argued that although the Automec case gave the Commission the right to choose its priorities, it had to show adequate reasoning for its actions or inaction, and in this case it had not done so. In particular the CFI said that the existence of the 1991 VER could not be used as evidence for the old agreement having been superseded by a properly based trade policy, since the Commission had argued the 1991 'consensus' was not a trade agreement. BEUC demanded the opening of an investigation. But the Commission responded by interpreting the Court's decision as requiring them to provide fuller justification for their decision and accordingly they contacted SMMT and invited them to provide assurances that no anti-competitive agreement with Japanese firms still applied. This the SMMT gladly did.

This may be the first case in EU legal history where consumers have challenged the legality of protectionist measures using competition law. Since the UK VER has been superseded by the 1991 'consensus', the most interesting questions raised by the case concern the legal status of the consensus rather than the UK VER itself.

2.5.2. The 1991 consensus and its background

In 1991, after long intra-EU negotiations but short negotiations with Japan, a 'consensus' with Japan was announced. The publicly announced policy consisted of two separate statements by Commissioner Andriessen and his Japanese counterpart, Mr Nakao. The Japanese side commits itself to 'monitor' sales of cars to the EU in such a way as to ensure that exports in 1999 are 1.23m. on the basis of a forecast total demand of 15.1m. cars, and to engage in regular consultations with the Community in the meantime. The figures in the press statements cannot be considered anything more than hypothetical scenarios. The meat of the agreement is the commitment to negotiate six-monthly binding quotas. The Japanese statement welcomes the absence of restrictions on investment, but the Commission statement makes no mention of transplants. The Japanese statement specifies import 'forecasts' for 1999 for Spain, Italy, France, Portugal and the UK. The EC undertook to abolish national measures by 1992, not to apply Article 115 to cars any more, to achieve full EC type-approval, and not to ask for any further restrictions after 2000.

The accord was deliberately vague. Vigier (1992) notes that this measure was avowedly a 'grey area' measure under GATT rules, though notified as a special exemption under the Uruguay Round agreement. The Community deliberately refrained from undertaking any formal legislative act to implement the consensus, apparently preferring to let the Japanese side of the 'double-lock' monitoring bear most of the burden. It seems that this was because the Member States could not agree on a form of words acceptable to all of them and to the Japanese, so nothing was put in writing except a commitment that the Commission and MITI would meet every six months to negotiate. GATT authors report the existence of an internal Commission memorandum allocating to EU firms at least two-thirds of any increase in demand and calling on Japan to restrict its exports by two-thirds of any unexpected fall in demand.[4] Renault has argued that the Commission has reneged on its commitments by not seeking to cut imports by a full two-thirds of the unexpected 16 per cent or so downturn in the EU market in 1993[5] even though this would have reduced imports practically to zero.

The great difficulty in securing a common policy on trade in cars before 1991 had led to many issues being resolved implicitly rather than explicitly. For example, because the British and French VERs were not officially recognized trade restrictions, they were not entitled to Article 115 support, and had to be supported by unofficial mechanisms having the same effect as Article 115 border restrictions. Even after 1993 separate national quota regimes exist, enforcement of which requires the Commission to tolerate a segmentation of the common market. Since Article 115 can no longer be used the Community seems likely to be forced to rely on the system of selective distribution arrangements, in a highly flexible interpretation of Article 85(3).

---

4 The GATT Trade Policy Review 1993, para. 363 cites the UK MMC Report as a basis for this. (The Commission has told the GATT Secretariat that sales of transplants are not included in the quotas.)

5 Unpublished presentation to the French Planning Commission.

It can be said that at each successive stage of policy, DG-IV has moved closer to full respect for the underlying principles of competition law. Nevertheless, there have been serious discrepancies between trade policy and competition rules, occasioned by the fact that Member States could not agree on the use of proper legal instruments. Commissioner Bangemann (1992) has himself argued that a purely legalistic approach is not politically sustainable.

The 1991 consensus is said by the Commission to be an informal arrangement. It was not passed as a regulation by the Council of Ministers. The notification to GATT does not in any way give any legal force to the 'non-agreement'. From a GATT point of view the notification reports what has been done, and simply makes it impossible to challenge under GATT law what has been notified: notification does not create any obligations to implement the agreement. The exact legal status of those parts of the consensus not formally reported to GATT remains even more obscure. However, the act of notifying the exemption does have some important economic implications if the mechanism can be put in place to implement it.

2.5.3. Trade Policy v. Competition Policy in the 1991 Consensus

It was clearly politically expedient in 1991 to leave certain problems to be dealt with as they came along, but the need for periodic negotiations between the Commission and the Japanese raises very serious questions about the agreement's effects on competition. It is evident that these negotiations are somewhat more regular than was apparent to outside observers on the publication of the communiqués in 1991. Thus the incentive structure of the 'game' becomes more complex. There are major implications for the EU market in the way that these arrangements with the Japanese will affect competition.

The first big question which arises concerns the treatment of the European output of Japanese carmakers. This was supposed to have been taken into account in the setting of quotas on a once-for-all basis. Commission officials have said that future transplant capacity will not be counted towards quotas, and the Japanese authorities are also adamant that whatever may or may not be in the 1991 accord, they cannot influence foreign direct investment in Europe. The notification to the GATT Secretariat explicitly states that the output from Japanese plants in Europe will have free circulation, and the implication is that divergences of actual transplant output from the forecasts would have no effect on the level of direct imports.

GATT
EC/JAPAN - TRADE IN MOTOR VEHICLES
Joint communication from the European Communities and Japan
16 October 1991

The following joint communication, dated 11 October 1991, has been received from the Permanent Delegation of the Commission of the European Communities and the Permanent Mission of Japan with the request that it be circulated to contracting parties.

1. The EC and Japan wish to inform the CONTRACTING PARTIES to the GATT that, in response to the EC's request for co-operation to achieve the objectives mentioned in 2. below, a mutually acceptable solution has been found through consultations with regard to trade in motor vehicles for the future.
2. The objectives are to achieve, through co-operation between the two parties, the progressive and full liberalization of the EC import régime on motor vehicles with avoidance of market disruption and, through an appropriate transitional period, to facilitate structural adjustments that may be required of EC manufacturers to achieve adequate levels of international competitiveness.
3. The EC has undertaken to ease the levels of national restrictions of any kind on the importation of motor vehicles from Japan, including those measures that can be authorized under Article 115 of the Rome Treaty from now and to abolish them by 1 January 1993 at the latest.
   During the transitional period, which will begin in 1993 and will be fully terminated by 31 December 1999, the Japanese authorities will continue, within the measures of co-operation, to monitor total exports from Japan to the EC and, they will also monitor exports to France, Italy, Portugal, Spain and the United Kingdom, through twice-yearly bilateral consultations on current export trends and future forecasts for the following year.
4. It is confirmed that inward Japanese investment will continue to be free of restrictions and that the products of such enterprises circulate freely within the EC. In addition, measures will be taken by the EC by 1 January 1993 to ensure that type approval can be obtained at the Community level.
5. The exports from Japan in 1999 are forecast at 1.23 million units on the assumption that total demand in the EC would be at 15.1 million vehicles in that year. In the case of the five markets mentioned, the exports from Japan in 1999 are forecast at these levels:

France	150,000
Italy	138,000
Spain	79,000
Portugal	23,000
United Kingdom	190,000

based on the following assumption of demand in that year:

France	2,850,000
Italy	2,600,000
Spain	1,475,000
Portugal	275,000
United Kingdom	2,700,000

6. The coverage of this monitoring is passenger cars, off-road vehicles, light commercial vehicles, light trucks (up to 5 tonnes), and the same vehicles in wholly knocked down form (CKD sets).

Estimates of likely transplant output in 2000, circulated in 1991, varied from the Commission's 1.2 million to 2 million reported by the *Financial Times* to be the UK Department of Trade and Industry estimate. Gandillot (1992) argues that the higher figure is unlikely, but that the Commission's figures excluded some capacity (including vehicles produced by the Volvo-Mitsubishi joint venture in the Netherlands). He suggests that the 1.2 million capacity is likely to be reached in 1995 and would require a holding back of all further Japanese investment if it were to be maintained at this level to the year 2000. Recent developments in both Europe and Japan have made these predictions more uncertain. The still depressed state of the EU car industry and the financial problems of Japanese as well as EU car firms may well do more to restrain investment than public policies. On the other hand, in the wake of the BMW take-over of Rover, Honda has announced plans to increase its capacity in the UK.

Since there are regular quotas to be agreed, the state of the EU car market is bound to be an element in the negotiations, and it is not hard to see that the European capacity of Japanese producers could enter strongly into the determination of the import 'forecasts' without any explicit violation of the European commitment: the terminology of 'forecasts', 'market conditions', and so on, is deliberately flexible. More subtly still, the expectation that foreign direct investment would influence the import quota will itself influence the level of foreign direct investment, irrespective of whether the expectation is justified. Then the import 'forecasts' would mutate into market-sharing agreements. Indeed, it appears that there were private negotiations between the French government and MITI which led to an undertaking by the Japanese to exercise restraint in sales from the UK plants into France, restraint which if it could be formally proved might be inconsistent with Article 85.

If there were any non-voluntary restraints to be placed on Japanese firms' investments in the EU, these would have to come from the EU authorities who lack any formal instrument to do so and who would be opposed by some Member States if they tried to do so. It is unlikely that existing investors, Honda, Nissan or Toyota, would wish to rock the boat. But the new agreement is very different from earlier export cartels, in that it does not simply allow a fixed surplus to be divided up. It actually makes some producers worse off and thus creates a division of interest among Japanese producers. As Table 3.1 shows, the impact of the restrictions seems to have fallen especially severely on those Japanese firms who do not have production facilities in the EU. Between 1993 and 1994 the total of Japanese car sales fell by 5.8 per cent even as total EU demand rose by 5.9 per cent, with the biggest falls concentrating on Mazda, Mitsubishi and Suzuki. These firms, unlike Toyota and Nissan, have very little incentive to adhere to the rules unless firmly constrained by MITI.

The economic costs of the anti-competitive aspects of market-sharing import restrictions were calculated for the European car market by Smith and Venables (1991): they find the costs of European consumers of a VER on Japanese cars exceed the gains to European producers by 5 billion ECU per year, and further that the replacement of a VER by an 'equivalent' tariff would give a net gain of 3.6 billion ECU, so that the greater part of the cost of the VER is the excess cost associated with its anti-competitive effect.

The second key competition-related element in the operation of the consensus is the presence of the block exemption for selective distribution of cars. If this were to be made less accommodating to the carmakers, the national sub-quotas might be harder to enforce. Strong debates have taken place (for example, between BEUC and the Commission) about whether the selective distribution regime really is necessary to control Japanese imports. An argument can be made that it is not necessary. Japanese firms themselves have an incentive at the margin to move cars from less to more constrained markets, but this will be easily monitored and they have very little interest in allowing dealers and other middlemen to undermine the consensus geographical allocation. If Japanese firms are quantity constrained even in less protected markets and are constrained to sell at the same prices to all comers at a given level of distribution, then they have no incentive to promote cross-border trade-deflecting sales, since any sales to intermediaries are at the expense of direct import sales. Thus it may be possible to open up competition within national territories while maintaining the national trade restraints (and given the questions raised by consumer organizations about the quality of service given by tied motor distributors, there do seem to be real doubts as to whether the block exemption is really desirable in its present form). This, of course, is not to say that the national restraints are themselves desirable, just that their existence may not have much impact on the case for keeping or changing the block exemption.

In its proposals for renewal after 1995, the Commission has indicated that the regime may be liberalized, but it will still be kept in place, with the need to support the 1991 consensus being a significant element in its retention: the 1994 Communication states that the Commission was examining the block exemption 'taking account of ... the contribution of the selective and exclusive distribution system to the efficient management of the arrangement between Japan and the EU on trade in automobiles; the efficient management of this arrangement must not be weakened in any way'. The promise to the Japanese that EU competition law would not be permitted to interfere with the operation of the consensus surely means that the Japanese carmakers can use whatever market-segmenting and market-sharing devices are required in order to implement the deal.

2.5.4. The consensus and EU competition law

The consensus has a strange status in trade law. It is like the grin on the Cheshire Cat in *Alice in Wonderland*. A measure has been notified to GATT, but the measure itself does not actually exist. It may well be that a simple administrative act by the Commission executing what is known to be the will of the Council is enough, but if the legal status of the 1991 consensus were cast into doubt under Community law, problems might well arise. The CFI judgment in the BEUC case thus raises problems for the consensus. In its written response to the Juge Rapporteur's questions, the Commission was emphatic that the 1991 consensus did not constitute an 'agreement' with Japan. This point originally made in Pierre Vigier's 1992 article led the Court to conclude that because the agreement was 'purely political' and 'outside the framework of the Common Commercial Policy', the Commission was not in a position to give a firm undertaking to the Court that would guarantee it would not be implemented via anti-competitive business practices. The Court thus indicates that if any party could find a legitimate interest in challenging the agreement, they might succeed. This could take the form of a challenge by a producer whose market share was being cut back, or a complaint by consumers, whose rights were effectively widened by this judgment. It might simply mean that a smaller Japanese producer could seek a way round the agreement (for example, by importing cars from elsewhere in Asia).

There were potential problems for the EU in the new consensus even before the new judgment. First, the implementation of the agreement will require the attribution of specific quotas to specific firms. The Asia Motors judgment, and US jurisprudence, implies that if this is done as a cooperative arrangement among firms, there is breach of antitrust principles. The fact that the 'consensus' is a trade restriction notified to GATT might seem to imply that firms restricting sales in the EU market as a result of it could claim that they are implementing trade policy, not operating a cartel. There is little doubt that if the Japanese government gave very specific instructions to individual firms with no concertation among the firms themselves, these firms would have a sovereign immunity defence. The Japanese government should be aware of this and should be expected to use administrative guidance of a form that would avoid antitrust problems. It is not altogether clear what form these instructions actually take, however. It seems very likely that there will be communications among firms, bringing the Asia Motors case into play. Moreover, the Japanese authorities are increasingly drawing attention to the conflict between requiring them to enforce their own antitrust laws and asking them to enforce export cartels. A recent study group reporting to the Japan Fair Trade Commission (Goto et al., 1993) stated that 'VERs have a significant effect on competition in both importing and exporting countries and international competition' (p. 17).

Second, once the global quotas are allocated among firms, there is the question of how the national sub-quotas are to be enforced, an issue which Mattoo and Mavroidis (1993) see as problematic.[6] They note that there are no actually agreed national sub-quotas but merely 'non-binding national forecasts'. They argue that these could not be used as a basis for a refusal to sell. In the Peugeot-EcoSystem case the Commission and the ECJ condemned Peugeot's attempts to stop EcoSystem from engaging in arbitrage between high and low price markets. They use the Commission's decision in this case to argue that it would be legally indefensible for a Japanese producer to use the national market forecasts in order to refuse to supply an intermediary who wished to engage in intra-EU arbitrage. They argue that any intermediary wanting to move cars in such a way could not legally be refused supplies by a firm acting on the basis of the national forecasts.

They first draw attention to a certain legal fragility of the consensus itself, suggesting that until the Uruguay Round was concluded *all* VERs were GATT-illegal and that EU law recognizes the rules of GATT when they are explicit.[7] This is because the GATT Secretariat views all VERs as violations of the ban on quantitative restrictions on either imports or exports (Article XIII); the new safeguard provisions in the Uruguay

---

6 Mattoo and Mavroides are at the GATT Secretariat, but their paper has the usual disclaimer that it represents the views of the authors not of the Secretariat.

7 Marquez-Mendez (1991, p. 183) notes that in the US *Consumers Union* case the consumer challenged the procedural basis on which the President had negotiated the VRA on steel. In the end the Courts decided that there had been no procedural defect, but if there had been, the firms could have found themselves liable for antitrust violations. The ECJ has recently been very anxious to ensure that Community actions have respected due process. If the consensus appears in any way not to have respected the processes of Article 113, it is quite possible that consumer groups will challenge it.

Round agreement alters these rules and allows for notified exceptions, of which the car VER is the one chosen by the EU. They point out that the consensus is specifically notified to GATT as a VER for the whole EU.

But even if this issue can be evaded, they go on to note that the published text of the consensus states that these forecasts are not binding. This implies that if intermediaries or consumer groups challenged the implementation of the consensus, either because of collusion between firms or because of vertical restraints on distribution, then the national forecasts could not be used to justify such measures on the grounds that they are a legally solid part of *EU* trade policy. So could a firm[8] cite these as a justification of a refusal to sell? Mattoo and Mavroidis say:

> *If the consistency of national forecasts with the EEC law were to be examined, one would be confronted with a situation in which non-binding promises would be offered as an excuse for contravening well established principles of EEC law. We can thus safely conclude that the existence of national forecasts cannot be used as a legally valid excuse for violations of the EEC competition law.*[9]

If indeed the block exemption alone is not enough to allow firms to segment markets as they wish, it is clear that for a watertight sovereign immunity defence firms would have to show that the actions they were undertaking were required of them by Japanese trade policy. They would have to show that MITI really had given very specific binding instructions to the firms without any concertation among the firms on the market shares. Marquez-Mendez (1991, p. 190) points out that the 1981 USA-Japanese VER was implemented in such a way as try to avoid the appearance of any antitrust violation. But he argues that there is still the possibility of legal challenge. Informal administrative guidance backed by the threat of legislation is not actually the same as a legal requirement. This point has been debated in US legal circles but it appears not to have been tested in the courts. Moreover if the legal requirement is to act in a monopolistic or cartellistic way so as to benefit the firms, he suggests that their potential involvement in soliciting such instructions should be investigated.

Given their knowledge of the US requirements for the 1981 VER, it seems likely that the Japanese authorities can provide sovereign immunity

---

8 It would be conceivable for a case to be brought on whereby MITI's orders did not yet go as far as to specify to the last detail the required conduct. It would be a major undertaking for anyone to disprove a claim by the Japanese firms that they had been given such instructions.

9 Mattoo and Mavroidis (1993), p.21.

for their firms. It is an ironic lesson from this analysis that Mr Andriessen's promise that EU competition law would not be allowed to interfere with the workings of the consensus may be inadequate: the Community has to rely on the Japanese to enforce cartel behaviour on its own firms. The lax enforcement of competition law in Japan has been one of the EU and US complaints in the past, though under external pressure Japan is acting somewhat more vigorously and some officials recognize dangers in anti-competitive conduct. (See Sanekata, 1992 and Goto, 1993).

Mattoo and Mavroidis speculate that the renewal of the block exemption may well be part of the incentive for the Japanese firms to comply with the deal rather than a mechanism for its implementation. They raise the possibility that Japanese firms prefer a segmented quota to a global EU quota, because the ability to engage in intra-EU price discrimination actually generates more profit for Japan than totally free unsegmented trade would. This is not altogether convincing as the existence of national quotas creates more uncertainties for Japanese firms than a single quota negotiated with Brussels. But such questions about who gets the benefits from the renewal of the block exemption further call its desirability into question. If the main beneficiaries could be shown to be the producers and the stated reasoning for introducing is a trade measure that does not exist, there would be grounds for a legal challenge to the new block exemption. This said, however, the likelihood of a legal challenge which reached a decision before the year 2000 is remote. Realistically, the EU-Japan consensus is unlikely to be wholly undermined by competition law challenges. The Court of Justice is naturally reluctant to overthrow decisions clearly endorsed by the Council of Ministers, but the Court has been increasingly anxious to ensure that competition and trade policies have no *vice de forme*. The risk is perhaps that the subtleties needed to legalize measures that are in some way 'grey' may have adverse spillover effects on to other aspects of international competition law and the credibility of the EU commitment to the rigorous application of its own rules. The Community clearly needs to find a way of incorporating the consensus into its own legislative rules. With the notification to GATT it seems difficult to suppose that a legal device could not be found. The problem would seem, however, to be political rather than legal. Once on paper the consensus would have to be made quite explicit or the mechanisms for the exercise of discretion would have to be spelled out, for example under the New Commercial Instrument. Unless it does this it would be quite possible for an importer to challenge the validity of any *de facto* restrictions at the EU end. To prevent such a challenge succeeding, the Council would have to empower the Commission to enforce import restrictions.

Finally, it is questionable whether the implementation of the 1991 consensus is a legitimate reason under Article 85(3) for the renewal of the block exemption, as the Treaty refers to the need for consumers to receive a fair share of the benefits of an exempt arrangement, while the 1991 consensus aims to protect producers and surely harms consumers.

2.5.5. Policy after 2000

The Commission proposes to renew the block exemption until 2005, and has promised not to ask for restraint by Japan after 2000. But the Commission cannot make a binding promise to Japan not to introduce safeguard or anti-dumping measures after 2000. Under the Uruguay Round agreement on safeguards, each signatory must transform all VERs into GATT compatible measures, but with one exception being allowed.[10] The EU chose to exempt the deal on cars, to run until 2000. The Uruguay Round agreement widens the class of acceptable safeguard actions. Broadly speaking, measures (which must be justified by evidence of injury or threat of injury) must be terminated after four years in the case of discriminatory quota measures, but non-discriminatory measures can be extended for another four years if the circumstances justify it. Thus, after 2000 it would be possible for the Community to introduce new safeguard measures against Japan for up to eight years, provided that the quotas were allocated in a way that could be said to be non-discriminatory![11] The merest indication in one month's trade figures that exports were surging once the quotas had been removed could justify safeguard action.

Clearly the Commission would prefer veiled threats to actual action. It may well not ask the Japanese to monitor exports but, subject to the procedural rules of GATT, the Community can use or tacitly threaten the use of safeguards or anti-dumping measures after 2000. These procedural rules would require the Commission to give more attention to due process than it has done in the past. It has been argued inside the Commission that the current semi-legal position is a powerful brake on protectionist

---

10 There has been some dispute if this means the EU can claim one or as many as its Member States plus one!

11 The USA might complain about this but only a small amount of ingenuity would be required to set quotas in such a way that they were binding on Japanese exports but effectively non-binding on imports of US origin, probably also by Japanese brands.

measures because they rely on the Japanese to enforce them and if this were no longer possible a majority would have to be found in the Council to re-introduce measures. On the other hand if the current quotas were legalized by the Council it would, it is argued, be harder to get rid of them.

2.5.6. Competition inside Japan

Competition policy in cars within Japan has become a political concern in the USA, and the EU authorities may find an interest in addressing it too. The international dimension arises when it is suspected that the Japanese market is insufficiently competitive. Given the number of Japanese producers it has rarely been suggested that the production sector is not competitive, but in the course of the SII initiative arguments have, however, been made that the distribution system excludes foreign cars, and thus new entry, allowing at least in principle for the possibility of collusion on prices. Ruigrok et al. (1991) argue that the control by manufacturers of the distribution system has been a powerful barrier to entry in the past.

Entry barriers have not been undermined by the marketing practices of Western producers. Most US car firms have used Japanese producers as their agents in Japan. Many European cars went through a single dealer, Yanase, said to have practised a policy of high margins and low sales (the problem of double monopoly). Recently EU sellers have begun to re-negotiate distribution arrangements, sometimes independently, sometimes with firms normally considered their main rivals in Europe. The alliance between VW and Toyota under which Toyota will market cars in Japan is interesting. Toyota has explained it in terms of filling a gap in its model range. While this is almost certainly welcome in terms of trade targets, it raises questions from the point of view of competition on a global level. VW is linked with some activities in the EU with Toyota. Meanwhile Honda sells Chrysler models, Mazda sells Ford, Citroen and Lancia and Mitsubishi markets Mercedes-Benz.

Recent information from the Japan Fair Trade Commission and data on car imports from Japan suggests that the Japanese market may be loosening up somewhat. The first four months of 1994 are reported (*Financial Times*, 24 May, 1994) to have seen a 28 per cent year on year rise in passenger car imports. This may well be connected to price cuts by importers. The *Financial Times* reports 7 per cent price cuts by BMW, while the JFTC reports that Chrysler in 1993 reduced the price of a certain Cherokee model from 5.35 million yen to 3.7 million yen. Nonetheless, it remains the case that the Japanese prices of European cars are higher than the prices of the same cars in Europe, while the price relativities of Japanese cars go the other way.

There is clearly room for attention to be paid to the extent to which the high prices in the Japanese market are due to exclusionary practices by keiretsus and how far they are due to undynamic behaviour by foreign firms. At the same time, solving the former problem by alliances between European and Japanese firms raises other competition questions. But a European Commission which is encouraging market-sharing behaviour by Japanese firms in the European car market may not be well placed to pursue such issues. In any case, it is quite evident that EU policy towards Japanese cars is motivated overwhelmingly by the industrial policy concern of how to help European carmakers compete with the Japanese rather than by competition policy concerns about 'unfair' trade from Japan.

2.6. Trade Policy in the Eastern European Car Market

Interesting interactions between trade policy and competition policy in the car sector have surfaced in post-1989 Eastern Europe, specifically in Poland and the Czech Republic.

Skoda, based in the Czech Republic, produced 188,000 cars in 1989, 110,000 in 1991 and 96,500 in 1992.[12] In April 1991, VW took a controlling interest in Skoda (starting at 30 per cent but due to rise to 70 per cent by 1995). In 1993, VW-Skoda had almost 80 per cent of the Czechoslovak new car market. The long-run plan is for output to rise to 440,000 units by the mid-1990s, of which a substantial proportion would be exported. The import duty on cars is 14.5 per cent for EU-produced cars and 19 per cent for other imports, plus a further import surcharge of 10 per cent which is due to be abolished soon. The import duty was raised to this level as part of the Skoda privatization deal with VW (EBRD, 1994, p. 138). The Europe Agreement with Czechoslovakia involves the EU eliminating its tariff in five steps between 1992 and 1996 and expanding by 20 per cent per year its tariff-free quota; while Czechoslovakia is to eliminate its tariff over a longer period. The timetable for EU tariff removal was cut from five to three years at the Copenhagen summit in June 1993.

---

12 We are grateful to Joshua Charap for advice on this case.

Skoda has naturally attracted the attention of the Czech and Slovak competition authorities ('VW's £3.3bn joint venture with Skoda invalid, says Czech anti-monopoly office', *Guardian*, 7 March, 1992, p. 35). For the Czechs and Slovaks the question is whether the high market shares of Skoda in their domestic markets implies that it has undue market power. The answer to this question turns on whether the tariff is at an appropriate level. If the tariff is higher than necessary to make VW-Skoda marginally competitive with other European producers, then competitors will find it unprofitable to enter the Czech and Slovak markets and VW-Skoda will be able to exploit its market power. If, however, the tariff is nicely judged just to allow VW-Skoda to compete, then it will not have excessive market power. Needless to say, it is not easy to see how governments can make such nice judgements about the appropriate levels of protection.

In Poland, the two existing car plants were taken over by Fiat and GM in 1991. Fiat's initial capacity at FSM is 160,000 cars per year, planned to rise to 240,000; while GM's operation at the FSO plant is at the more modest capacity of 30,000-50,000 cars. It is expected that around half of this output might be exported to the EU. Fiat's initial proposal was to take control of both FSM and FSO (possibly conditionally on formal exclusion of Japanese imports from the Polish market), but it was reported (*Financial Times*, 12 October 1991, p. 12) that this was turned down by the Polish government on competition grounds.

Poland raised its tariff on car imports in 1992 from 15 per cent to 35 per cent, and, as in the Skoda case, it would be surprising if the views of potential foreign investors in the Polish car industry had not played a large role in the decision to set the tariff at this high level. Under the provisions of the Europe Agreement, the tariff on EU cars will be gradually eliminated over a ten-year period. There is also a 30,000 tariff-free quota for imports from the EU. Although there has been a substantial flow of imports of second-hand cars into Poland, the number of imports of new cars was less than 30,000 in 1992 (Christopher Bobinski, 'West hides behind Polish tariffs', *Financial Times*, 6 March, 1992, p. 2) so that the tariff-free quota for the EU effectively excludes non-EU cars from the Polish market. In turn, the EU is to liberalize access to Polish cars in rather similar terms to those agreed with Czechoslovakia.

The figures on output and sales point to one important aspect of the East European markets discussed in more detail by Vigier (1992): even when these markets grow substantially in the future they are still small relative to the minimum efficient scale of production in motor cars, normally thought to be around 200,000 units per year; so the expected future capacity of the CEE car producers can only be economic on the basis of a substantial fraction of output being exported.

Although the details of the Polish case are quite different from that of Skoda, some rather similar issues arise. The key element in this case is the quota of 30,000 EU-produced cars given tariff-free access to the Polish market. Initially, GM had asked for 40 per cent of this quota in return for a \$75m. investment in FSO. But since a tariff-free quota in the presence of a 35 per cent duty might represent some \$3,000 per duty-free car imported, or a total of \$36m. on 12,000 cars per year, the Polish government rightly felt that this would involve an excessive investment incentive for GM, and proposed to divide the quota equally between Fiat, GM and VW, all three of whom had investment plans in Poland. In turn, this proposal raised objections from the EU, especially from the French producers who felt that the allocation of the quota was unfair, and according to Vigier (1992) the matter was not resolved until 3 November 1992 when it was agreed that the quotas would be allocated on a first-come first-served basis.

There are several levels at which the EU has interests in the interaction between trade policy, competition policy and industrial policy in Poland and the Czech Republic. The allocation of the tariff-free quota in Poland raised issues of fairness between EU producers, and since the Polish market is large and the tariff high, the financial privileges are substantial. A little more remotely, one could ask questions about the fairness of the processes by which the foreign investment decisions were made, though there have been no suggestions of unfairness. The potential exists for the privileged positions of particular producers in these markets to have undesirable spillover effects on competition in the EU market, though given how small all of the Eastern European markets are, it is implausible that such effects could be significant.

The major interest of the EU in policy in the car market in Poland and the Czech Republic is that these economies are becoming part of the wider European economy, already having free trade with the EU, moving towards incorporation in the single market, and possible full membership of the Union. From this perspective, the use of tariff protection as an investment incentive raises issues of indirect state aid to industry. Article 92 aims to curb excessive and distorting state aids; the European car market is evidently becoming a genuinely Europe-wide market with, for example, Skoda being only one part of a VW enterprise that stretches as far as Spain; so the potentially distorting effects of state aid have to be discussed on a Europe-wide level rather than on an EU-only basis.

Further, as the Central and Eastern European countries seek to harmonize their competition policy with EU competition rules as required by the Europe agreements, the issues of interactions between competition policy and trade and industrial policy will have to be addressed by them as much as by existing EU members.

Indeed, it is notable how the policy interactions in the car market in Poland and the Czech Republic mirror the interactions in the EU market. Industrial policy objectives are being furthered not by industrial policy itself, but by trade policy, and we see a very striking example in the anti-competitive effects of poorly designed trade policy. The main costs are, of course, being borne by the Polish and Czech consumers who are effectively being taxed to pay for state aids to foreign investors in the car industry.

3. CONCLUSIONS

The operation of the three policies in the EU car market is far from the ideal assignment set out at the start of this chapter. There is little apparent justification for active trade policy, since evidence of distortions spilling from foreign markets into the EU is scant. The concentrated structure of the EU car market and the continued evidence of national market segmentation suggest important roles for competition policy, which should be oriented in a pro-competitive direction and in support of the development of a truly single market. The single most important issue for the future of the EU car market is, however, industrial and technological - whether European producers will be able to catch up with best Japanese practice. This is primarily a matter for the producers themselves, but with supporting roles from public policy to keep up competitive pressure, to limit the protective and distorting effects of excessive state aids, and to support R&D. In practice, trade policy is the main instrument of public policy, it operates in a way that has severe anti-competitive effects, competition policy is slanted towards the support of trade policy, and industrial policy takes a back seat.

There are likely to be serious economic costs to the mis-assignment of policies. In particular, there are large costs to consumers from the anti-competitive effects of market-sharing arrangements promoted under the umbrella of trade policy and from policy on the block exemption being determined by the needs of the 'consensus' rather than by economic objectives.

Problems are also created by the fact that the Community's two main policies in the car sector have very doubtful legal validity. The 1991 consensus has no legal basis at all, and its operation rests solely on the attractiveness to the Japanese of compliance. The prominence given to the consensus in the case for renewing the block exemption casts doubt on the legal validity of the renewal. This state of affairs is unsatisfactory. Legal uncertainty has economic consequences, even if incumbents in the car industry are sufficiently well informed politically to be able to deduce what procedures will be used to determine trade policy after 2000. The attractiveness of different kinds of investment depends on post-2000 trade policy, and on whether or not pressure really is being put on Japanese firms to limit their investment in Europe. The stance of policy may not be the main determinant of the fate of the industry, but public policy is important, and uncertainty about public policy is costly.

It would seem highly desirable that the existing trade arrangement with Japan be put on a proper legal basis in such a way that economic actors, including purchasers, can know exactly what rights and obligations it creates. After the year 2000, any trade policy measure should be undertaken with full respect for the rules of the WTO (which do allow safeguard action) and Article 113. Renewal of the block exemption after 2000 should be determined strictly on competition and single-market grounds. This would not tie the Community to a dogmatically free-trade position, but would simply require that any departures from it were properly justified. The restructuring of EU producers in response to Japanese success in producing in Europe shows that competition does have healthy effects on the European industry, which is not a lame duck, and that promoting competition is not simply a matter of advantaging consumers at the expense of producers.

If for social and other industrial reasons free trade is judged unwise, then trade policy measures should be explicit, and industrial policy rather than competition policy should be used to accompany it. If there are genuine industrial policy cases for intervention this should be done directly, with funding especially for cooperative programmes on environmental questions where spillover effects are relevant in two senses: new technologies are generic and there are real cross-border environmental effects. Other policy measures that deserve attention are adjustment assistance and also support for closer cooperation between manufacturers and suppliers, as both the French government and the Commission have proposed. It would not seem feasible or desirable for very large additional sums to be spent from the Community budget on the industry, but there is ample scope for the Commission to offer its services as a co-ordinator and catalyst for projects at a national level that could be complementary.

The curious story we have identified in the car industry is not typical of other sectors: part of the issue is precisely that the Community chose to give this industry special status in the Uruguay Round. But the fact that *in this case* the Community authorities proved unable to form a concerted policy except one which involved undermining the Treaty principles, could send the wrong message to other sectors. It may well be that the gradual liberalization of this sector was the best achievable in practice, but if the Community's competition policy and if the procedural obstacles to protectionist pressures are to be credible, the Community must avoid letting its policy in the car market set bad precedents.

REFERENCES

Bangemann, M. (1992), *Meeting the Global Challenge*, Kogan Page.

European Bank for Reconstruction and Development (1994), *Transition Report*, London.

European Commission (1972), 'Opinion relating to certain imports into the Community of Japanese products covered by the Treaty of Rome', OJ C111/13.

European Commission, (1994a), 'Communication to the Council on the Automobile Industry in Europe', March 1994.

European Commission, (1994b), 'Panorama of EU Industry 94'.

Gandillot, T. (1992), *La dernière bataille de l'automobile Européenne*, Fayard.

Goto, A. et al. (1993), 'Import-Export Restrictions and Competition Policy', Report of a Study Group of the Japan Fair Trade Commission.

Harrison, G. (1992), *The EC Japan Car VER*, Congressional Research Services, Washington DC.

Hawk, B. (1990), *International Anti-trust*, Prentice Hall.

Japan Fair Trade Commission (1993), *Survey of Distribution of Passenger Cars*, Tokyo.

Marchipont, J.-F. (1994), 'La stratégie industrielle de l'union Européenne pendant et après l'achèvement du marché unique', doctoral dissertation, University of Nancy-II, publication forthcoming.

Marquez-Mendez, J. (1991), *Anti-Trust in a World of Interrelated Economies*, Brussels: University of Brussels Press.

Mattoo, A. and Mavroidis, P. (1993) 'The EC-Japan Consensus on cars: trade and competition policy trade offs', GATT, *The World Economy*.

Monopolies and Mergers Commission (1992), *Report on New Cars*, HMSO, Cmd 1808.

Ruigrok, W., van Tulder, R. and Baven, G. (1991), *Cars and Complexes*, FAST/MONITOR, FOP 285.

Sanekata, H. (1992), 'Competition Policy and Trade Friction in Japan', University of Hokkaido, mimeo.

Smith, A. and Venables, A.J. (1991), 'Counting the costs of VERs in the European Car Market', in Elhanan Helpman and Assaf Razin (eds.) *International Trade and Trade Policy*, Cambridge, Mass.: MIT Press, pp. 187-220.

Vigier, P. (1992), 'La politique communautaire de l'automobile', *Revue du Marché Unique Européen* 2 and 3, 73-112 and 73-126.

Womack, J.P. and Jones, D.T. (1992), 'European Automotive Policy' in Harrison, *Europe and the US: Competition and Cooperation in the 1990s*, US House of Representatives.

Womack, J.P., Jones, D.T. and Roos, D. (1990, *The Machine that Changed the World*, Maxwell Macmillan.

Discussion
Patrick A. Messerlin

INTRODUCTION

The chapter written by Peter Holmes and Alasdair Smith is an indepth analysis of all the forces which were (and still are) at work in the EC car industry riddled with EC (and national) competition, industrial and trade policies. The chapter puts forward three major results.

First, the car sector is a good example of an industry where trade policy has been used as a substitute for industrial policy in an environment of global business. In a very convincing manner, Holmes and Smith show that in such an environment 'trade policy casts its net too wide, while competition policy is somewhat circumscribed'.

This demonstration of how trade policy worked against competition is indeed very welcome. It should warn us about a currently frequent illusion among decision-makers and economists: to substitute competition policy to trade instruments, such as VERs or anti-dumping actions (instead of maintaining a strong pressure in favour of eliminating trade barriers). Building on an abundant literature, Holmes and Smith have no difficulties showing how competition policy can easily be captured by trade interests when it is put in the forefront of the policy. The best example is the 'block exemption' from competition rules granted to the car industry through the arrangements for selective and exclusive dealerships. Holmes and Smith note *en passant* the crucial fact that such an evolution distorts not only the level and structure of competition in the importing country (the EC), but also in the exporting country (Japan in this case).

After this very useful demonstration, can one accept without reservation their assertion (when discussing subsidies in the car sector) 'in the absence of a well specified industrial policy, competition policy is being called upon to perform tasks far removed from supporting the principles of antitrust and free trade'? It is not certain (even if one ignores that European industrial policies of the last three decades have never been in practice 'well specified' and that they have been light-years away from what economists would suggest as optimal in their models). This hesitation derives from the fact that it is debatable that the goals of competition policy are exclusively antitrust and free trade. This ambiguity of competition policy is well underlined by Mavroidis and van Siclen (1994) who show that, for instance, competition policy is not necessarily free trade oriented if free-trade is understood as aiming at eliminating all barriers to trade.

The second major point made by Holmes and Smith is as follows: the analysis of the pre-1993 national VERs and the post-1993 EC VERs underline the division of interests among Japanese firms which run facilities in the EC and those which do not. At a result, the chapter shifts from a perspective where globalization of business is taken as exogeneous to a perspective where it is endogenous. Indeed, powerful trade instruments generate this globalization and make it endogenous: firms threatened by severe protection invest in the large closing economies when they can. Nowadays, trade officials (and sometimes economists) often tend to perceive foreign direct investments as a case of complex 'strategic' games. A look at facts and events suggests an alternative (maybe naive) vision. What is at stake is a more traditional, purely competitive, reaction: whoever can invest in the large closing economy does, and whoever cannot will exit from the world market of this product sooner or later. And, foreign firms do so not necessarily by competing with the domestic firms, but by competing between themselves, as amply demonstrated by the sequence of EC anti-dumping and anti-circumvention cases. In other words, trade instruments are so powerful that firms are 'location-taker'.

This second major point of the Holmes and Smith's chapter suggests two additional developments. First, another (and maybe better) explanation of the endogeneity of foreign direct investment is an approach in terms of 'raising rivals' costs': the domestic firm hopes to raise rivals' costs while keeping them in the market as 'marginal' firms eager to keep prices high so that, despite its relative inefficiency, it can survive and even enjoy rents. Second, the car case (in this respect, it is close to the pharmaceutical case) raises the question of defining the 'national' interests and shows how this question opposes the three policies examined. Competition policy is not interested in principle in this question. Industrial policy defines national interests by the 'nationality' of the producers, either in terms of jobs (the traditional approach) or in terms of capital ownership (a more recent approach which may prove a new way of using competition policy for other purposes than protecting competition). Lastly, trade policy defines national interests by the nationality of the traded 'products' though it tries to expand this definition to a definition of the nationality of firms through *ad hoc* rules of origin or through a wide definition of similar products.

The last main point of the Holmes and Smith's chapter concerns the likely impact of increased integration of the Central European Countries (CECs) in an EC (and Japanese) car industry(ies) marked by such a long history of binding VERs, ambiguous subsidies and 'reversed' competition policy. The chapter begins to underline the dramatic mistakes made by the CECs when designing their car policy: giving up tariff revenues to one or two EC carmakers, not necessarily among the most efficient, favouring non-competitive domestic markets, leaving at bay efficient competitors (the Japanese or Korean firms), etc. The chapter provides a striking illustration of all these problems by looking at the Czech and Polish car industries. Then, the chapter examines how the EC and the CECs could jointly improve their situation: it shows that free access to EC markets should be allowed for CEC car producers. Indeed, it will be interesting to see whether CECs' mistakes will not trigger future intra-EC disputes in the form of safeguards or anti-dumping actions lodged by EC carmakers against EC carmakers exporting from the CECs.

The reviewed points do not do full justice to the Holmes and Smith chapter. Many other discussions are interesting as well. In particular, there is a detailed discussion of the legal - past and more importantly future - aspects flowing from the conflicts between trade and competition policies which shows how this theme will come back, again and again, on the agenda of the Court of Justice in the forthcoming years.

REFERENCE

Mavroidis, P. and S. van Siclen (1994), 'Competition disputes in the WTO?', mimeo, OECD.

4. Chemical fibres industry

Elisabeth De Ghellinck and Christian Huveneers

INTRODUCTION

The objective of the following research is to identify the ways in which competition, industrial and trade policies in the chemical fibre industry complement or contradict each other.

We will attempt to answer the following question: has the chemical fibres industry been characterized by efficient allocation of market mechanisms since the seventies? In other words, has current excess capacity been caused by distortions in the market mechanism, due to state participation, subsidies and barriers to trade, so that privatization and removal of trade barriers would level the playing field? Or is the excess capacity caused by some inherent characteristics of the sector such as economies of scale, capital intensity, lumpiness of investments, high exit costs, and so on?

Depending on the answer, one would have complementarities or tensions (even inconsistencies) between those three microeconomic policies. We try to clarify our analysis by examining the relationships between the policies according to a scheme proposed by A. Jacquemin:[1] Figure 4.1 on page 167 gives the 2 times 2 relationship between competition and industrial policies and Figure 4.2 gives the 3 times 3 relationship, i.e. by considering competition and industrial policies as determinants of trade policy.

Industrial policy is defined as the set of government interventions which by way of taxes (or subsidies) and regulations on domestic products or production factors, attempt to modify the allocation of domestic resources that results from the free operation of the market.

1 A. Jacquemin, 'The Interaction between Competition, Industrial and Trade Policy in the EC - An Economist's view', in *Doing Business in an integrated Europe - The impact of EC Law & Policy*, *Financial Times* Conferences, 13 and 14 May 1992, Brussels.

We start with the 2 times 2 relationship between competition and industrial policies (Figure 4.1). If market mechanisms lead to an efficient allocation at the *European* level, the degree of intervention in the industrial policy should be low (cases A and C in Figure 4.1).

Figure 4.1: Relationships between competition policy (CP) and industrial policy (IP)

CP ⇓ Degree of severity	LOW	HIGH
HIGH	A Strong rules of the game enforcing and supplementing market mechanisms	B Mix of actions leading to tensions and contradictions between excessive competition and excessive interventions
LOW	C Lax policies leaving industry to the 'natural' selection mechanisms of the market	D Interventionist, and elective actions based on strong government-business relationships

Degree of interventionism ⇒IP

Figure 4.2: Competition (CP) and industrial (IP) policies as determinants of trade policy

CP ⇓ Degree of severity	LOW	HIGH
HIGH	A Open trade policy based on low external and internal barriers; efforts to establish world-wide control of restrictive practices	B Strong domestic competition policy coupled with a relatively protective external trade policy
LOW	C Passive adaptation to international division of labour and submission to multinationals' strategies	D Internal interventionism including discrimination against foreign firms; protectionism affecting external trade and mitigating internal competition

Degree of interventionism ⇒IP

Case A would be a good case of complementarity: severe competition policy (prohibiting cartels and taking a strong view on concentrated undertakings like joint ventures and acquisitions) and market-oriented industrial policies (privatization, dismantling subsidies, no government intervention) are complementary. In that case A, the Single European Market (which sharply increases competition) would remove segmentation between national markets and eliminate the least efficient plants.

Case C (lax competition policies leave the fibres industry to the 'natural' selection of the market) would also be a case of 2 times 2 consistency: governments' competition and industrial policies would lead to a *laissez-faire* situation. We shall argue that cases A and C are not plausible for the fibres industry because the industry is not at all left to natural selection mechanisms.

If market mechanisms do not lead to efficient allocation at European level, there is a case for a high degree of interventionism. The 2 times 2 relationship between competition and industrial policy is then represented by cases B and D in Figure 4.1.

As we shall see, this is the case of the European chemical fibre industry: there is interventionism of industrial policy towards the fibre industry at EU level via the Code on State Aid.

We now turn to the 3 times 3 relationship (competition and industrial policies as determinants of trade policy). If market mechanisms lead to efficient allocation, not only at European level but also at the level of the relations of the EU to the rest of the world (i.e. in a world of free markets and free trade, the exploitation of the given comparative advantages leads to efficient production and trade flows beneficial to all consumers), then a free-market external trade policy (low Common External Tariff, Generalized Systems of Preferences, implementation of the Uruguay Round and so on) would also complement competition and industrial policy. This is represented by cases A and C in Figure 4.2.

If market mechanisms lead to efficient allocation in Europe but if free trade with the rest of the world is disruptive for the European fibres market, then there would be scope for a relatively protective external trade policy coupled with a strong EU competition policy (case B in Figure 4.2).

If market mechanisms do not lead to efficient allocation in Europe and if free trade is disruptive (e.g. government intervention and agreement among producers lead to production or capacity quotas and prices above their competitive level on world markets), we then have case D in Figure

4.2 (internal interventionism coupled with protectionism affecting external trade and consequently alleviating internal competition).

If we go beyond the evolution of the fibres sector since the mid-seventies and look at the future of the sector's features, we must ask whether there will be a growing competitivity gap between the European Union and low-cost countries.

Output of fibres in South-East Asia is increasing. There producers benefit not only from low costs but also from a domestic market (use of fibres by the local textile industry). In the future, the same trend could occur in other textile-producing countries such as the Mediterranean ones.

If there is such a growing discrepancy between Europe and the rest of the world, there will be a tendency towards an 'interventionist' external trade policy (cases B or D in Figure 4.2).

We will first focus on the situation of the market for chemical fibres in Europe during the seventies. One basic question is: have some characteristics of the sector led to excess capacity? Which characteristics of the chemical fibres sector justify a specific industrial policy, i.e. the Code on State Aid to the man-made fibres industry?

This issue is addressed in section 2. Section 1 gives the general sectoral outline.

I. GENERAL SECTORAL OUTLINE

1. Basic Definitions

There are two categories of man-made fibres: synthetic fibres made from oil and gas and cellulosic fibres (artificial fibres, mainly rayon) made from renewable raw materials (cellulose from wood pulp, for example).

There has been a dramatic increase in the share of synthetics to total fibres production at the expense of cellulosics since 1970: in 1970, cellulosic fibres accounted for 43 per cent and synthetics for 57 per cent of the total world production of 8.4 million tons. In 1992, with total world production of 20.2 million tons, the share of synthetics amounted to 85 per cent (see Graph 4.1). Synthetics are themselves divided into two types according to their shape: filament (yarns) and staple (fibres *sensu stricto*).[2] The world production of synthetics is fairly balanced between those two categories.

---

2 Staples often have the same characteristics as natural fibres.

Graph 4.1 : Breakdown of world production of man-made fibres

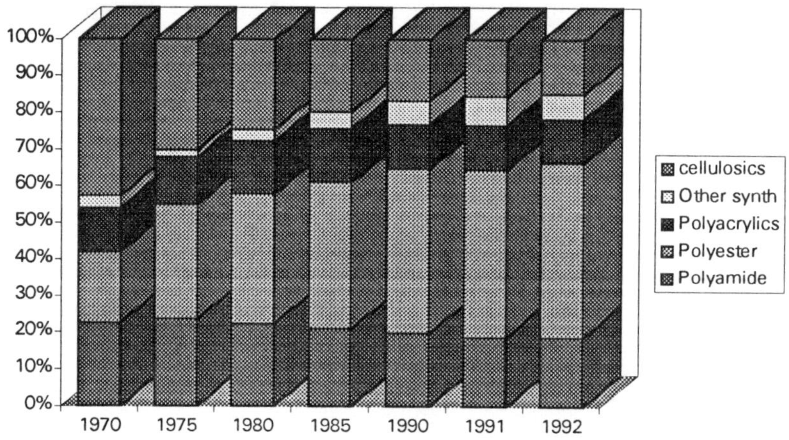

Source: AKZO.

2. Geographical Breakdown of World Production of Man-made Fibres

Table 4.1 reveals that the increase in production is in Asian countries, especially from the South-East (Taiwan, South Korea, China, India, Indonesia). This points to a comprehensive relocation of the whole Japanese chain of fibre production.

Table 4.1: Evolution between 1981 and 1982 of synthetic fibre production.

	Production of synthetic yarn		Production of synthetic staple and tow	
	1981	1992	1981	1992
World	4,883	8,292	6,218	8,920
EC-12	788	1,030	1,164	1,690
West Europe	979	1,282	1,537	2,022
USA	1,439	1,759	1,901	1,871
Japan	621	719	748	730
Taiwan	296	1,151	289	892
South Korea	284	819	329	637
China	55	617	292	956
India	51	322	40	216
Indonesia	46	205	55	163

Source: CIRFS.

As a result, Taiwan, South Korea and China now account for 25 per cent of world production of man-made fibres, as compared with 19 per cent for the USA, 18 per cent for Western Europe and 9 per cent for Japan.

Graph 4.2 shows a clear trend in the geographical breakdown of world production of man-made fibres: between 1970 and the 1990s, production has been stable in the three large industrialized regions (Western Europe, Japan, USA) while it has expanded significantly in the rest of the world.

Graph 4.2 World production of man-made fibres (in million tons)

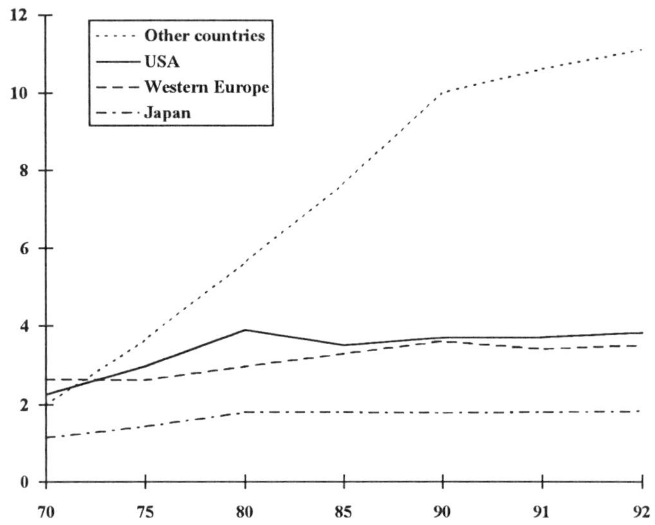

3. Growth Prospects and Price Elasticity of Aggregate Demand: Sectoral Breakdown of the use of Fibres

Table 4.2 shows that the major demand for synthetic fibres comes from the textile and clothing industry. The other main uses are home furnishing (especially carpets) and industrial (filtration, conveyor belts, tyres, and so on).

Table 4.2: Breakdown between fibres in the main end-uses in the EC (%)

	SYNTHETIC		CELLULOSIC		COTTON		WOOL	
	1986	**1991**	**1986**	**1991**	**1986**	**1991**	**1986**	**1991**
apparel	47	45	9	10	30	31	13	14
carpets	82	87	1	1	1	1	16	11
other[3]	41	46	13	9	42	41	4	3
tyres	39	45	60	53	1	2	-	-
other[4]	54	62	21	20	23	18	1	1

It also reveals the extent of substitution between man-made and natural fibres:

- in the 'apparel' sector, the share of man-made fibres is stable at 55 per cent;
- in the categories 'Carpets' and 'Other industrial uses', the share of synthetic fibres is still increasing;
- in the tyres sector, there are still prospects for substitution between synthetic and cellulosic fibres: in the EU market, the share of cellulosics is still high (53 per cent in 1991) while cellulosics are almost not used in the US and Japanese markets for tyres.

Table 4.3 compares the EU market with the US market using a sectoral breakdown according to the end-uses of each type of fibre.

Table 4.3: Comparison between EC (1986) and USA (1988) of the breakdown between end-uses (%).

	SYNTHETIC		CELLULOSIC		COTTON		WOOL	
	US	EC	US	EC	US	EC	US	EC
apparel	27	47	47	41	64	55	72	70
carpets	36	20	-	1	-	1	11	19
other[5]	10	17	22	24	28	33	10	9
tyres	4	1	1	10	-	-	-	-
other[6]	24	14	30	24	8	11	6	2
	100	100	100	100	100	100	100	100

There are two striking differences:

3 Other home furniture.
4 Other industrial uses.
5 Other home furniture.
6 Other industrial uses.

- the sector 'Other industrial uses' is more important in the USA (it accounts for 24 per cent of the use of synthetics and 30 per cent of the use of cellulosics) as compared with the EU;
- in the US market for synthetics, the carpet segment is more important than apparel; it is the opposite for the EU market, where apparel still represents 47 per cent of the use of synthetics.

These breakdowns provide important observations on the growth prospects and the price elasticity of demand (see Table 4.4).

In the apparel sector, demand is more volatile than in the carpet sector (fashion changes every six months as compared with several years for carpets). It is also subject to more international competition (transport costs of knitted fabrics are very low whilst carpets are more costly to transport). Producers of fibres for apparel are also more vulnerable to substitution between fibres. They can nevertheless impede the substitution but only through a costly technical support for their customers, thereby creating transfer costs for apparel plants which switch from one fibre to another.

Producers of fibres for carpets may enjoy a lower price elasticity of their fibres thanks to the necessarily close relations between carpet producers and their fibres' seller (flexibility and continuity of supply of fibres, quality control) and the scope for product innovation (e.g. improving the fibre's performances in resistance, in hiding the dirt, and so on).

The producers of fibres for the sector 'Industrial uses' may also enjoy a relatively low price elasticity of demand.

The ease of substitution between products of competing fibres makers also depends on the buyer's stage of the production process: the more downstream is the buyer's production process, the less easy it is to switch from one fibre to another, i.e. the narrower the end-use market is.

Table 4.4: Comparison between the fibres'main end-uses markets

End-use	Apparel	Carpets	Industry
Major type of fibre	PES PA	PA PP	PP
Price-elasticity	High	Medium	Low
Indirect import competition	Low transport cost of final product (textile, a labor-intensive industry)	High transport cost of final product, which is capital-intensive	Relatively low
Product substitution and volatility of demand	Variable, could be high between synthetics and natural fibres and within fibres	Medium term only but important between fibres[7] and within fibres	More limited
Product innovation	Not propietary quickly imitated even from high-fashioned clothing to mass market	Could be significant for some market segments (contract market)	Important and protected by patent
STRATEGY FROM VOLUME TOWARDS MORE SPECIALIZED PRODUCT			

4. Trade Flows

An analysis of trade flows (see Table 4.5) shows that the synthetic fibres sector appears to be under growing pressure from external trade competition:

- the rate of extra-EC exports (i.e. the ratio of extra-EC exports to production) of synthetic staples declined from 31 per cent in 1988 to 6 per cent in 1992;
- the rate of extra-EC imports (i.e. the ratio of extra-EC imports to consumption) of synthetic yarns is significant: it was about 20 per cent between 1988 and 1991. It was about 13 per cent for synthetic staples;
- the European Community suffers from a trade deficit in synthetic yarns while the USA and Japan still enjoy a trade surplus.

7 PES can only be dyed before texturization, whereas PAM can be dyed during the process of texturization. As a result, carpet makers need less inventories and enjoy more flexibility with PAM fibres than with PES ones. PPP fibres have been gaining shares at the expense of PAM in the low end and middle range of the carpet market, due to lower prices.

Table 4.5: EC trade flows in the synthetic fibre sector

Synthetic yarns in the EC

	1988	1989	1990	1991	1992	US92	Jn92	Taiwan92
Xex-EC	180,331	149,785	133,640	146,004	200,531	140,117	90,764	442,612
Mex-EC	180,876	219,725	242,241	229,825	256,365	65,755	61,012	na
prod	962,000	1017,000	1025,000	1075,900	1029,900			
cons	923,300	1000,100	1052,200	1049,500				
M/cons	0.195902	0.219	0.230	0.218				
X/prod	0.187454	0.147	0.130	0.135	0.194			
Xec-Mec	-545	-69,940	-108,601	-83,821	-55,834	74,362	29,752	
Xue-Mue					-15,996			

Source: CIRFS

Synthetic staples in the EC

	1988	1989	1990	1991	1992	US92	Jn92	Taiwan92
Xex-EC	469,932	362,544	206,397	118,967	107,668	115,220	293,721	382,767
Mex-EC	174,096	164,038	175,064	178,857	180,686	171,657	17,662	na
prod	1515,700	1558,600	1692,000	1724,000	1689,600			
cons	1373,400	1368,500	1377,300	1418,200				
M/cons	0.1267	0.119	0.127	0.126				
X/prod	0.3100	0.232	0.121	0.069	0.063			
Xec-Mec	295,836	198,506	31,333	-59,890	-73,018	-56,437	276,059	
Xue-Mue					-70,524			

Source: CIRFS

Among the trading partners of the EC, EFTA countries and the USA are still important: for synthetic yarns, they account for 25 per cent of EC exports and 47 per cent of EC imports; for synthetic staples, they account for 21 per cent of exports and 31 per cent of imports.

NICs such as Turkey and Taiwan appear as significant exporters to the EC. Taiwan in particular is an impressive exporter: Taiwan's exports in 1992 represented 2.2 times the volume of EC synthetic yarns exports and 3.5 times the volume of EC synthetic staples exports.

South American producers do not appear to be heavy exporters of man-made fibres to the EC market. Eastern European producers cater for only 3.3 per cent of Western European consumption (in 1992), because of lower product quality.[8]

5. Production Costs and Factor Intensities

The structure of production costs is approximately as follows:

- raw materials: 50 to 60 per cent of total unit costs;
- fixed costs: 25 to 35 per cent;
- labour costs: 12 to 15 per cent.

In view of the importance of raw materials costs, European synthetics producers suffer from some cost disadvantage: synthetics industry uses about 7.5 per cent of the whole petrochemical production and the European petrochemical industry is burdened by overcapacity and feedstock prices which are higher than in the USA. European petrochemicals now get some protection from the Common External Tariff. At the same time, both the USA and the European petrochemical industry are engaged in dumping, selling to East Asian markets at marginal costs, in order to increase their degree of capacity utilization (DUC). As a result, the European synthetic fibre industry pays higher prices for its petrochemical inputs than its competitors.

The figures on the structure of production costs also reflect the high capital intensity and the low labour intensity of the production process, specifically in the first stage (polymerization) and the second stage (actual production through extrusion) of the process. The third stage is the textile process (treatment of the filaments by cutting, twisting, and so on) and is more labour intensive than the first and second stages.

Though less capital intensive than the petrochemical industry, chemical fibre production processes are characterized by the importance of fixed costs so that, as we shall stress below, the degree of capacity utilization is crucial in determining profitability.

---

8 'The prices of fibres which are produced in Central and Eastern European countries are considerably lower than the prices in Western Europe and the custom duties are low (6.4 per cent in 1992, with a 1 per cent yearly decline). In spite of those lower prices, Western fibres using firms do not buy much in Central and Eastern Europe, from fears of meeting acute problems of quality, safety and deliveries. The benefits derived from the use of low quality threads would be more than offset by the stoppage of machinery.' (Case Rhône-Poulenc/SNIA, no. IV/M355).

Even more importantly, there is a sharp difference in factor intensities as compared with the main downstream industry, i.e. textile and apparel.

The textile industry, being labour intensive, is now undergoing structural relocalization, due to increased penetration into the EC market of imported textile and clothing.

Henceforth, on top of direct extra-EC imports of fibres, the European fibres industry is exposed to rising indirect imports: the technology of man-made fibres is easily transferable and huge investments in fibre production capacity are being undertaken in textile-producing countries, especially in South East Asia.

The exposure to indirect imports seems unavoidable, even though the polymerization and the production of synthetics is capital intensive.[9]

High fixed investments costs and low marginal costs may also make the synthetic fibre industry prone to dumping: producers of fibres try to increase the degree of capacity utilization by selling abroad at prices close to marginal costs, especially when they benefit from protection of their domestic market (e.g. Indian producers of synthetics may enjoy a domestic price three times as high as the export price at which they sell on the EC market).

The implications for the EC external trade policy are clear: the inducement to engage in dumping and protectionism in non-EC markets calls for some active anti-dumping policy.

II. SITUATION OF THE MARKET IN THE SEVENTIES: WHY HAS A SPECIFIC CODE BEEN ESTABLISHED FOR THE MAN-MADE FIBRES INDUSTRY?

We have chosen three complementary views in order to select the relevant industrial characteristics which enable that question to be addressed.

1. Two features which characterize the structural environment of the firms and consequently determine their corporate strategies: first, the advantage of being a leader (or of having a large market share) on its market; second, the scope for product differentiation.[10]

---

9 'The ready transportability of intermediates, raw polymer and unprocessed fibres indicates the potential to exploit international differences in labour costs through the geographic segmentation of the production processes. Relative labour costs determine the location of textile processing operations due to the near unitary scale economies involved and the lower cost of transporting downstream intermediate products' (Read, 1986, p. 215).

10 Boston Consulting Group, M. Porter, P. Buigues, 1985.

2. Features which are relevant for the Structure - Conduct - Performance (S-C-P) of the sector and consequently for the degree of intervention of industrial policy: to what extent do the features of the market lead to an efficient (or inefficient) allocation?

   The most important Performance variables are the degree of capacity utilization (DUC) and the profitability. The DUC reflects the efficiency of resource allocation as far as it reflects the extent of adjustment of capacity to market demand. Profitability may reflect either Efficiency (minimization of costs in the set up of the plants, high degree of capacity utilization in existing plants) or Strategies (exploitation of market power through barriers to entry, concentration, product differentiation, and so on).

   Those two dimensions of Performance (DUC and profitability) will determine, in our view, the desirable degree of intervention of Industrial Policy: acceptable levels of DUC and profitability allow for a low degree of intervention; very low levels of DUC and profitability call for a high degree of intervention. As underlined hereafter, low levels of DUC will also induce producers to resort to dumping.

3. Features which are relevant for the degree of severity of the competition policy:

   - are there large benefits from big size, cooperative agreements and are the negative effects from reduced competition small, so that competition policy should favourably consider mergers, acquisitions and cooperative agreements?
   - or are there large losses from reduced competition and small gains from big size and cooperative agreements?

1. Structural Environment and Corporate Strategies

The two features which determine the structural environment are the following:

- is there some scope for product differentiation or are products homogeneous?
- are there advantages from being a leader or having a large market share resulting from economies of scale, economies of scope, learning by doing?

Those two features determine four types of structural environment and corporate strategies: fragmented, quit ('impasse'), specialized and volume (see Table 4.6).[11]

We shall assume that the structural environment of 'volume' applies to chemical fibres: output is homogeneous or slightly differentiated (so that price is an important variable when buyers have to decide from whom to purchase) and there are economies of scale.

We shall now turn to each of those factors.

Table 4.6: Structural environment and corporate strategies

Matrix describing the competitive environment			
		competitive advantage from leadership position	
		weak	strong
scope for product differentiation	high	fragmented house building, repair	specialized pharmaceuticals, software, luxury cars
	low	quit ('impasse') steel, shipyards paper	volume airplane, tyre, custom cars, components, white and brown goods

1.1. Output is homogeneous or only slightly differentiated across producers

We consider synthetics as being a homogeneous or slightly differentiated product. As we have seen above, it is not a 'commodity' like petrochemicals: producers of synthetics can change the physical characteristics of their fibre so as to improve their performance or make them adequately suitable for the mix between man-made and natural fibres. This differentiation between producers applies specifically to the end-uses carpets and industrial uses.

---

11 Table 4.6 is extracted from P. Buigues and A. Jacquemin, '1992: quelles stratégies pour les entreprises européennes', *Revue française de gestion*, No.69, June/July/August 1988.

1.2. Advantages stemming from large size and market share

1.2.1. Static scale economies

In the Cecchini Report, the empirical work of Pratten used the economists' method of cost disadvantage ratio. According to this study, the cost disadvantage ratio at half the minimal optimal scale lies between 3 and 12 per cent.

1.2.2. Dynamic scale economies: the learning curve

The learning curve (or 'experience curve') presupposes that the firm which has the greatest cumulative production experience will enjoy a cost advantage over its rivals (and may be able to deter the entry of new producers) so that there is an incentive to gain market share during the early growth phase of a market.

The cost advantages given by the learning curve and the incentive to gain market share are, however, conditional upon some conditions.

- Learning must remain proprietary. This condition is fulfilled in the case of chemicals (Mansfield).[12] But even in petrochemicals and synthetics, a substantial leakage ultimately occurs, e.g. through licensing.
- The learning curve argument applies particularly well to homogeneous products, where production cost advantages are more important, than for markedly differentiated products.

Though few researchers have tried to assess empirically the magnitude of competitive advantages derived from the learning curve, we identified a study made by Shaw and Shaw (1984).[13] They computed market shares over time for European producers of three synthetic fibres (acrylic, nylon and polyester). They concluded that 'early entrants who established major market shares early in the growth phase of the product life cycle were able to maintain that leadership nearly twenty years later ... not only did almost all of the late entrants fail to achieve significant market shares, but

12 E. Mansfield, 'How rapidly does new industrial technology leak out ?', *The Journal of Industrial Economics*, XXXIV, December 1985, pp. 217-23.

13 R.W. Shaw and S.A. Shaw, 'Late entry, market shares and competitive survival: the case of synthetic fibres', *Managerial and Decision Economics*, 5, 1984, pp. 72-9.

in the difficult market conditions between 1974 and 1981 they provided seven out nine market withdrawals'.

This conclusion is not surprising: estimates of learning curves for chemical processing industries (i.e. a sample of industries which is wider than the synthetics sector) concluded that the expected difference in unit cost between a new firm, five years after entry into the market, and an 'average' incumbent firm, amounts to 55 per cent (i.e. the unit cost of the 'new' firm is on average 1.55 times higher than the unit cost of the already established firm).

1.3. Economies of scope

In theory, economies of scope are primarily related to equipments due in the case of joint-product processes (e.g. in the polyester production process, polymerization gives rise to both polyester for fibres and to PET).

In practice, for about 15 years there has been a tendency towards the specialization of plants. This would stem from the fact that, according to industry sources, (i) there is a low degree of substitutability of equipment between the different fibres;[14] (ii) economies of scope hardly exist in developing and marketing different fibres.

Whereas there is little substitution, as regards supply, *between* fibres, there seems to be a high substitutability *within* each fibre.[15]

2. Features Which are Relevant for the S-C-P (Structure-Conduct-Performance) in the Synthetic Fibres Sector

2.1. Structure

2.1.1. Concentration

It is an oligopolistic supply structure: in the mid-seventies, ten firms controlled over 90 per cent of *world* output capacity of synthetics. Although the distribution among these firms varied between the products

---

14 However, some opposite statements were made by the Commission in specific instances. E.g. in the decision relating to the acquisition of Nordfaser by Rhône-Poulenc (RP) and SNIA: 'RP and SNIA, which have interest only in the polyamide activities of Nordfaser, will convert, in the short run, the polyester capacity into polyamide capacity. Such a conversion ... can easily be realized without substantial additional investments' (case no. IV/M.399).

15 This is stated by the Commission in a decision on State aid to Abingdon Carpet (Aid C 42/93, Decision of 16.3.94).

(acrylic, nylon, polyester, polypropylene), the four largest firms controlled more than half of the total capacity in each case: 56.5 per cent for acrylic, 63 per cent for nylon, 71.5 per cent for polyester.

The major explanation for this high concentration is the Relative Market Size (RMS), i.e. the ratio of Minimal Optimal Scale (MOS) to the absolute market size (RMS = MOS/apparent consumption). According to Pratten, MOS lies between 40 per cent and 125 per cent of the production of chemical fibres in the UK and between 16 per cent and 23 per cent of the production in the EEC. Therefore there is a natural oligopoly at the EC level, and even a natural monopoly for the production of some fibres, at national level.

2.1.2. Sunk costs and barriers to exit

The fixed investment costs of a plant are mainly unrecoverable (only equipment may be sold) so that shutting down a plant is costly. A rough estimate of the capital investment cost of a new plant in the mid-seventies is 50 million ECU (the latest new plant established in Europe, by Allied Signal, for the production of high tenacity polyester filament yarn amounted to an investment cost of 135 million ECU).

This creates a barrier to exit. Indeed, the model proposed by Lippman and Rumelt assumes that increases in fixed plant cost will reduce the probability of exit (even if that proposition was not confirmed empirically in a later study by Liebermann).[16]

At this stage, we submit that synthetics in the EC are characterized by high barriers to exit and that 'hit and run' entries (as assumed by the theory of contestable markets) are not very plausible.

Most important, the barriers to exit erected by high fixed plant costs were reinforced by *institutional factors*: national subsidies policies and state participation, especially in Italy, Spain and Eastern Germany.

The degree of vertical integration may also act as a barrier to exit: vertically integrated petrochemical processes utilize joint inputs and generate joint outputs: there exist strict complementarities in the production of the different outputs, so that it is difficult for a producer to stop the production of, e.g., synthetic fibres. It also seems difficult to convert the capital equipment to alternative uses.

---

16 S.A. Lippman and R.P. Rumelt, 'Uncertain imitability: an analysis of interfirm differences in efficiency under competition', *Bell Journal of Economics*, 13, Autumn 1982, pp. 418-38. M.B. Liebermann, 'The Learning Curve, Technology Barriers to Entry, and Competitive Survival in the Chemical Processing Industry', *Strategic Management Journal*, 10(5), pp. 431-47.

In the nylon market, the two leading producers, holding together around two-thirds of the EU market, are completely vertically integrated. Furthermore, more than 86 per cent of the production of nylon salt, a raw material used for the production of nylon 6.6 is internally used (Decision Rhône-Poulenc/SNIA, Case no.IV/M399); in acetate, 83 per cent of flake production worldwide is used by the flake producers for their in-house activity (Decision Courtaulds/SNIA, Case no.IV/M113).

2.1.3. Barriers to entry

a) Economies of scale

The most convenient model to study the barriers to entry resulting from economies of scale is the old model of Sylos-Labini, Bain and Modigliani (SBM model). The model points to three features to evaluate the height of these barriers to entry: (i) the larger the *cost disadvantage ratio* (*CDR*) and (ii) the *relative market size* (*RMS*, i.e. the ratio of minimum optimal scale to absolute market size), the higher are the barriers to entry; (iii) the lower the *price elasticity of demand* (in absolute value), the more effective barriers to entry are related to economies of scale.

The CDR has already been given above: the static CDR (measured along the long-run unit cost curve at half the MOS) lies between 3 per cent and 12 per cent depending on the product; and the dynamic CDR (measured along the learning curve) amounts to approximately 1.55.

The RMS will be higher the smaller the absolute market size, i.e. the more downstream the buyer's stage of production process is (cf. section 1).

As regards the *price elasticity of demand,* it is certainly not equivalent to zero. Price changes can bring about substitution between fibres or increase the share of synthetics in the mix of man-made and natural fibres (like cotton). But we have seen that fibre producers may eventually reduce the price-elasticity of demand through a close relationship with their customers.

b) Growth of demand

Low growth of demand leaves less room for new capacities set up by entrants on the European market, thereby reinforcing barriers to entry.

The man-made fibres industry is a mature industry characterized by low demand growth prospects: the income elasticity of the demand for clothing and textiles is low. The fibre industry also suffered in the recent past from the recession observed in the main users' sectors: textiles, housing and home furnishing and automotive industries.

It is also well known that the rapid growth phase of synthetics came to a halt after 1975. Key factors were world recessions and price rises after each oil shock; changes in fashion from synthetic fibres back to natural fibres; and increasing competition from outside Western Europe.

As already seen, competition from outside Europe brings about gloomy prospects as regards long-term growth: demand for EU-made fibres should decline because of indirect imports of fibres through imports of textiles. Most textile producers outside the EU will have to resort increasingly to their own indigenous sources of chemical fibres. The diffusion of technology is rapid and the cost of licensing foreign technology represents only between 1 and 5 per cent of the total cost of fibres manufacturing.

c) Degree of Capacity Utilization (DUC)

Low DUCs increase barriers to entry as the incumbent firms can increase output at any time to prevent new entries. Even more than that, in the fibres sector, low DUCs go hand in hand with low prices: it is a competitive market where players are price takers so that excess supply results in low DUCs and low prices.

DUC for synthetics as a whole was well above 80 per cent until 1973; it went down between 62 per cent and 75 per cent between 1975 and 1982, stayed above 80 per cent for the rest of the eighties and dropped down to 75 per cent in 1992 (source: CIRFS).

Thus, barriers to entry were high during the seventies.

d) Time-lag for setting up new production facilities

The time-lag for a complete production process is two to three years. This seems high enough to prevent hit and run entries! However, entry into texturization activity by textile or carpet producers seems to be relatively easy.[17] Upstream integration of these producers could form a fringe of potential competitors, pushing the price down.

[17] Whilst the requirements in financial capital are rather high, the technologies which are used are relatively simple and fairly well mastered so that it is possible to buy 'turnkey' texturization production lines or even medium-sized factories (capacities of 5 KT) to make polyamide yarn (Case no. V/M.399, Decision of 3.2.1994).

e) Lumpiness of investment

High (new plant) lumpiness heightens barriers to entry. Lumpiness is of course related to high fixed plant costs and RMS (relative market size): if the CDR is high, any replacement or new investment must be made in a capacity close to the minimal optimal size (MOS).

The average size of existing plants in the EU is still lower than in the USA and in the Far East, so that any new plant in Europe should be even larger than the existing ones.

f) Rate of diffusion of technology

The less proprietary a technology is, and the higher the rate of diffusion, the lower are the barriers to entry related to learning experience.

The academic literature (Mansfield, Stobaugh) and interviews show that the rate of diffusion for synthetics is high and therefore lowers the barrier to entry. This view was shared by the European Commission in its decision on the acquisition of Nordfaser by Rhône-Poulenc and SNIA.[18]

Moreover, such a mature industry is not tremendously innovative (see Table 4.4).

2.2. Conduct and Performance: tendency to accumulate overcapacity

The tendency to accumulate overcapacity may be primarily related to three factors.

2.2.1. Barriers to entry and to exit

As seen above, barriers to exit due to sunk costs do not allow for to be shut plants down in case of overcapacity. Those economic barriers to exit are subsequently reinforced by institutional ones, i.e. state aid and state participation.

In particular, the huge investment made by Italian firms led to a substantial increase in output capacity during the second half of the seventies.

---

18 'Those innovations are most often not patented and are imitated by the competitors only a few months after being launched.' (Case no. IV/M 399, Decision of 3.2.1994).

2.2.2. The shape of unit costs functions

The shape of the unit cost function depends on the structure of total costs: if fixed costs represent a large share of total costs, the short-term unit cost function (i.e. the unit cost function for a given, installed capacity) will have a steep (negative) slope, reflecting the fact that fixed costs have to be spread over large quantities.

Specifically, each plant has to reach a high degree of capacity utilization (DUC) to cover fixed costs and, if the DUC decreases, the increase in unit cost will be high.

This applies to synthetic fibres: it is a capital-intensive process (especially the polymerization phase). The required DUC, at the prevailing selling prices, allowing total costs to be covered is said to obey the 'rule of thumb' of 85 per cent.[19]

Needless to say, such a shape of the short-term unit cost will reinforce the corporate strategies of volume: synthetics producers are not only induced to accumulate large capacities and market shares (in view of economies of scale) but also, once capacities have been set up, they are liable to expand their sales volume (to increase the DUC) by lowering their prices and profit margins.

2.2.3. Lumpiness in investment decisions and wrong evaluation of demand

As we have seen above, investments for capacity replacement and expansion are lumpy in the sense that, in view of economies of scale, any new capacity must be as close as possible to the MOS. In view of those jumps in productive capacity, combined with the long delay between the decision to invest and the start of the production and in the presence of demand shocks, there will be a tendency to build up excess capacity.[20]

Demand shocks stemmed from different factors:

- business cycle fluctuations;

---

19 This rule of thumb appears in a decision of the Commission: 'the extent of capacities to be cut was determined by the rule that a production facility is profitable at a rate of utilization of capacity of at least 85 per cent' (O.J. 85/L/207/19). In an anti-dumping case, it is even stated that: 'the Community producers [who] consider at present a target of 90 per cent as necessary for achieving a reasonable profitability' (O.J. 87/L/103/38).

20 This has been more formally analysed in the following references:

- A. Manne, 'Investments for Capacity Expansion', Cambridge, Mass., MIT., 1967.
- F. Scherer, A. Beckenstein, E. Kaufer, R. Murphy and F. Bougeon-Maassen, '*The Economics of Multi-Plant Operation : an International Comparison study*', Cambridge, Mass., 1975.

- unanticipated sluggishness of demand trends after 1975;
- uncertainties in the substitution between man-made and natural fibres due to changes in fashion or to changes in relative prices (changes in feedstocks prices).

We shall now turn to the behavioural implications of this tendency to overcapacity.

2.3. Possible conducts in view of the tendency to accumulate excess capacity

We shall distinguish four possible conducts, identified by our review of the literature, when there is such a tendency to accumulate overcapacity for homogeneous or slightly differentiated products.[21]

1. Capacity investments at sub-optimal scale.
2. Tendency to price wars, with prices close to marginal costs (Bertrand equilibrium).
3. Tendency to a Cournot-Nash equilibrium through some quantity-setting.
4. Some agreement among producers to reduce capacity (with possibly some degree of government intervention).
5. Mergers and acquisitions.

1. Investments at suboptimal scale are likely if there is some feeling of oligopolistic interdependence. This case was studied by Scherer et al. (1975): the oligopolistic interdependence is strong enough to prevent price wars and cut-throat competition, but horizontal concentration is not high enough (and feeling of interdependence is not tight enough) to set up a formal agreement on capacities and production quotas. This outcome of investments in plants at suboptimal scale is, in our view, reinforced when cost conditions are symmetrical: every competitor realizes that he will not be able to be more cost efficient than his competitors by setting up new and larger capacities.

2. Price wars, with a tendency towards a Bertrand equilibrium, with prices close to marginal costs, are likely to occur when producers are eager to increase their DUC (in view of the shape of their short-run

---

21 C. Huveneers, 'Les interventions de l'Etat respectent-elles le système concurrentiel?', *Reflets et Perspectives de la Vie Economique*, Tome XVIII, 1979, no. 3.

unit cost curve) by increasing their market share and decreasing their prices.

On the other hand, a learning process may develop among producers: in a framework of a 'repeated game', they can realize that their strategy of volume to increase the DUC only leads to price wars (and price wars do not allow an increase in the total demand of the product if the price elasticity of demand is low).

One factor could counteract such a learning process: fibre producers have, as in the steel industry, rather large geographical markets (the cost of shipping fibres over long distances is not as high as for cement, for example) so that each producer may hope to increase his market share on the world market at the expense of competitors.[22]

The deteriorating effect on profitability of such an outcome is larger, if the price elasticity of demand is lower: when there is an excess capacity, the lower the price elasticity of demand in absolute value, the larger should be the decline in price necessary to increase sales and DUC.

3. There could be a tendency towards a Cournot-Nash equilibrium, leading to smaller output and higher prices than in a Bertrand equilibrium, if there is a learning process in the game among producers: firms are able to learn from their experience of possible price wars and refrain from increasing their market shares. In other words, they set quantities which are lower than in the Bertrand outcome, even if that quantity-setting does not allow them to raise their DUC.

   This outcome is even more likely when firms take a long-term perspective of the competitive process and when there is a time-lag for the building of new equipment: the quantity-setting by a firm is, in the long run, a decision related to capacity.[23]

   This outcome is, for example, typical for the cement industry.

---

22 Cost asymmetries among producers reinforce, in my view, the likelihood of triggering-off such an outcome, but interviews suggest that such cost asymmetries are not important in the man-made fibres.

23 A model was developed in the literature: Kreps and Sheinkman show that, in a two-period game, the final outcome is a Cournot equilibrium when two producers independently choose their capacity in the first period and engage in price competition "à la Bertrand" in the second period of the game. The intuition behind this result is the fact that the decision related to capacity in the first period creates a constraint on capacity during the second period, so that the condition required for a Bertrand equilibrium is not fulfilled. That model was very recently extended from the case of homogeneous products to the case of product differentiation (Wauthy, 1994).

4. Another plausible outcome is an agreement among producers on capacities, with some government intervention. This has been observed in the man-made fibres industry with the introduction of rationalization cartels and the Code on State Aid.

   The necessity and plausibility of this outcome for the steel industry and synthetics[24] is developed in Huveneers (1979).

   The outcome for man-made fibres will be thoroughly described in the next section. It was facilitated by a high horizontal concentration and a feeling of interdependence among European producers, at least by the feeling that their common interest was to reduce their capacities.

5. Production rationalization can also be achieved through voluntary exit of the weaker players or mergers and acquisitions followed by capacity reductions and upgrading of facilities. Mergers and acquisitions ease the restructuring process by reducing the number of players - and hence the risk of free-riding behaviour disturbing a rationalization process - and by allowing each firm more easily to achieve the MOS. Examples of such strategies in the man-made fibres industry are the following:

   a) Withdrawals by closure: exit of Fabelta and SIR; exit of Hoechst and Monsanto from the PA market; exit of Bayer from the PES market; exit of Snia Viscosa from the PES staple market; exit of Courtaulds from the PA market; exit of Rhône-Poulenc and Du Pont from the acrylic market).

   b) Withdrawals by cession:

   - Dow Chemicals sold off its holding in Dow-Badische to BASF in 1978;
   - Hercules withdrew from a fibre joint venture it had set up with Hoechst in 1970, in order to focus on the production of intermediates;
   - Akzo sold its interest in Cyanenka, Spanish acrylic fibre producer, in 1984;
   - ICI sold its worldwide polyamide activities to Du Pont in 1993;
   - Nordfaser was sold by Nobel to Rhône-Poulenc/SNIA in 1994.

---

24 The text eventually gives the economic justification of the policy of Commissioner E. Davignon towards those two sectors.

c) Mergers and joint ventures:

- 1991: Courtaulds/SNIA; JV in the sector of acetate filament yarn (Novaceta); it has been approved by the Commission (Decision no.IV/M113 of 19.12.91).
- 1992: Rhône-Poulenc/SNIA; JV in the sector of non-textile uses of polyamide (Novalis); it has been approved (by Decision no.IV/M206 of 10.08.92).
- 1993: Rhône-Poulenc/SNIA; JV in the sector of textile polyamide yarn activities for the whole Western European market (Nylstar); it has been approved (by Decision no.IV/M355 of 8.09.93).
- 1993: Courtaulds/Hoechst; merger of viscose and acrylic staple activities on the Western European market.

d) Exchange of businesses in order to increase specialization:

- SNIA/ENICHEM swap allowing Enichem to specialize on petrochemicals Snia on the downstream part of the petrochemical production chain.

At this point, it is important to raise the issue of the interaction between those strategies of producers in Europe and the degree of severity of the EC competition policy.

3. The degree of severity of Competition policy for man-made fibres industry

In order to identify the features which are relevant for the degree of severity of competition policy, we shall use the scheme presented in Jacquemin, Buigues and Ilzkowitz.[25]

Four features are identified.

- Growth in demand: low growth calls for a more restrictive view on mergers.
- Imports: high rates of imports or imports threats allow for a more flexible view on competition policy, as the producers' behaviour will be strongly disciplined by import competition. In the Courtaulds/SNIA case, this argument of import discipline has been used to accept a market share for the new entity as high as 65 per

25 *Economie Européenne*, no. 40, May 1989.

cent on the WE acetate market. For man-made fibres, in general, the rate of extra-EC imports in 1988 lay between 13 per cent for synthetic staples and 20 per cent for synthetic yarns, as compared with an average of 14.1 per cent for all EC industries.

- Economies of scale give rise to gains resulting from rationalization and a higher concentration. For the fibre industry, as explained previously, they are substantial.
- Technological content: though there are few technological breakthroughs in this industry, the technological content is high enough to ensure a greater efficiency through the rationalization of plants.

One may conclude that merger policy should not constitute an obstacle to the ongoing process of rationalization: the risks resulting from agreements and from a high horizontal concentration stem from the low growth of demand, but these risks may be compensated by import competition.

There could even be gains from high concentration due to economies of scale.

Some preliminary conclusions on the interaction between industrial, competition and trade policies.

We shall refer again to the Figures 4.1 and 4.2.

The tendency to persistent overcapacities, together with barriers to exit, calls for an active industrial policy: these are the cases B or D in Figure 4.1.

There could be friction between such an active industrial policy and a highly severe competition policy (case B of Figure 4.1): as we shall explain in section III, such a tension was materialized by a conflict between DGIII (Industry Directorate) and DGIV (Competition Directorate) in 1978, and even by a conflict within DGIV.

Fortunately, a lower degree of severity in the competition policy, especially concerning concentration, could be allowed for by high import competition, i.e. such a permissive concentration policy would be subject to the constraint of an open external trade policy.

We shall see in section IV that this tends indeed to be the case.

This argument pleads in favour of case D in Figure 4.1.

III. INDUSTRIAL AND COMPETITION POLICY MEASURES

EC industrial policy on man-made fibres is typically a sector-specific policy for a mature industry, where government intervenes to encourage adjustment to changed market conditions and to coordinate Member States' policies (Gual, 1994, pp. 28-9).

1. The Conflict Between DGIV and DGIII on Crisis Cartel-type Agreements

A first attempt to introduce a crisis cartel was made in October 1972 by PES fibre producers. DGIV was not in favour of this agreement because not only was production rationalized and investments coordinated but so were production policies and sales; the parties withdrew their notification before any decision was taken by the Commission.

A second attempt to introduce a crisis cartel-type agreement was made in July 1978. Eleven European producers notified an agreement covering six major fibres - PA textile and carpet yarns and fibres; PES textile yarns and fibres and acrylic fibres - in order to achieve a 13 per cent orderly reduction of the output capacity. According to Shaw and Shaw (1983), the two American firms active on the EC market, Monsanto and Du Pont, which were excluded from the agreement because of the US antitrust laws, were stated to be in favour of such a measure.

Again, DGIV challenged the agreement since it included production quotas. However, the agreement was not formally rejected as negotiations started between DGIV and the notifying parties in search of a modified version of the agreement that could be deemed compatible with Article 85. The parties proposed a first amendment replacing production and sales quotas with a commitment by non-Italian producers to buy from Italian producers. A second amendment cancelling this commitment and asking for a 6-month extension of the initial validity of the notified agreement - until 30 June 1982 - was submitted at the end of 1981, in order to enable the companies to prepare and notify a new agreement. In the meantime, the 1978 agreement had been implemented and had led to a reduction of about 20 per cent of the 1977 capacity by the end of 1981.

The third agreement, notified in November 1982, amended in March 1983 and July 1983, was finally accepted by DGIV in August 1984. The aim of the agreement was to achieve an 85 per cent degree of capacity utilization. As sales have in 1981 amounted to 1,373,000 tonnes and demand was forecast to remain at that level during the period 82-86, the parties were expected to achieve a total output capacity of 1,640,000 tonnes in 1986, that is a reduction of 354,000 tonnes (57,000 tonnes in textile PA yarn, 42,000 tonnes in carpet PA yarn, 61,500 tonnes in textile PES yarn, 33,000 tonnes in PA staple, 71,500 tonnes in PES staple and

89,000 tonnes in acrylic staple). The major part of the agreed reductions was realised in 1982 and 1983, with the exception of acrylic fibres for which a reduction of 75,000 tonnes was expected in 1984 and 1985.

2. The Code: Origin and Evolution

Whilst excess capacity, low prices and losses compelled firms to rationalize their output capacity, plant closures were opposed, in several countries, by trade unions and national governments. Furthermore, not only did state assistance maintain the operation of inefficient plants, but it was also used to create new capacities.

The evolution between the different versions of the rationalization agreement reveals the role played by the massive investment programme of Italian firms. Even if the other European producers would have been ready to reduce their own capacity, the planned Italian capacities, heavily subsidized by the government, would have counteracted their own move and led to sustained excess capacity, depressed prices and losses. Hence, parallel to the discussions relative to the compatibility of a crisis cartel-type agreement with Article 85, the Commission decided in July 1977 to introduce a systematic control on state aid to the fibre industry.

The original Code

By a letter (dated 19 July 1977) and a memorandum setting out certain details concerning the practical arrangements (29 May 1978), the Commission requested that the Member States refrain from making any new decisions to grant aid which would lead to an increase in production capacity for a two-years period. This decision applied to investment projects in respect of man-made fibres of all kind, with particular reference to acrylic fibres, PES fibres and PA fibres for use in the manufacture of textile and in other industries.[26] Any plans to implement aid schemes in the fibre industry had to be notified even if the investment was not intended to increase existing productive capacity. Furthermore, the Commission asked the European Investment Bank not to grant any new loans to finance capacity increases. The Commission would continue to give sympathetic consideration exclusively to proposals to grant aid for the purpose of solving serious social or regional problems. Acceptable aid would speed up or facilitate the process of reconversion away from

---

[26] The Dutch version is even more explicit: 'betreffende alle soorten kunstvezels ... welke zowel voor de vervaardiging van textiel als *voor industrieel gebruik* bestemd zijn'.

synthetic fibres into other activities or restructuring leading to capacity reductions.

According to this memorandum, the ban on aids to finance capacity increases applied to the whole man-made fibre sector, whatever the type of fibre (synthetic or cellulosic) or the end-use (textile or industrial) considered.

The evolution of the Code

Since July 1977, the validity of the Code has been regularly extended over time, even when the degree of capacity utilization did improve over the period considered, as between 1985 and 1989. The usual argument in favour of such an extension of validity is that 'even if excess capacity has been reduced, disequilibrium between supply and demand persists'. The most recent version dates from 30 December 1992 and will be valid until 31 December 1994.

Details on the types of fibres covered by the Code are progressively and explicitly being introduced.

Even if the memorandum specifies that the whole man-made fibre sector is subject to the Code, a review of the major decisions by the Commission concerning state aid proposals notified by national governments reveals a large discrepancy. Only the fibre segments covered by the 1984 crisis cartel agreement (acrylic, polyamide and polyester yarns and staples for textile uses) deemed to be subject to the Code.

A reference to polypropylene appeared for the first time in the 1985 version.[27] On the other hand, a notified aid to Du Pont for aramid fibres was accepted in 1992 on the assumption that this type of fibre is not covered by the Code. Texturization activities are specified in the 1987 version[28] and polymerization activities in the December 1992 version.

Explicit reference to all end-uses is made in the 1989 version, following the European Court decision requiring the Commission to take a new decision concerning an aid awarded by the French government to Allied

[27] Degrees of capacity utilization in the production of polypropylene yarn were systematically under 64 per cent over the 1968-83 period but achieved 81 per cent in 1984 and 87 per cent in 1985. In the staple segment, DUCs evolved between 71 per cent and 76 per cent over the 1978-82 period, increasing to 86 per cent in 1983 and 83 per cent in 1983 and 1984. Furthermore, growth prospects for polypropylene were fairly good.

[28] Following the argument stated in a decision concerning an aid proposal to a German producer of PAM yarns: 'it has to be noted that the 'texturization' processing stage cannot logically be separated from the actual production of the yarn as it is only after texturizing - which in most firms is a fully integrated production stage - that most yarns are sold on the market for the purpose of textile utilization' (O.J. 85/L/181/42).

Signal. The Commission considered that, due to the nature of the product - the aid was granted for a new facility for the production of high tenacity polyester filament yarn, to be used in tyre production - it was outside the scope of the Code.[29] CIRFS, on the basis of the 1978 memorandum, argued, on the contrary, that all end-uses fall under the scope of the Code.[30]

Another significant evolution over time concerns the conditions notified aids must fulfil in order to be accepted. Before the December 1992 version, the major restriction was that the investment should not lead to a net increase in the productive capacity of synthetic fibre. From January 1993, a significant reduction in the productive capacities of the aid's beneficiary became the necessary condition in order to obtain a positive appraisal of any investment aid proposal. The extent of reduction required is evaluated according to the amount of aid, the volume and localization of the investment and the evolution of the average degree of capacity utilization.

Comments on the implementation of the Code

- Cellulosic fibres still seem to fall outside the scope, contrary to the 1978 memorandum.
- The Code has become increasingly technical (reference to decitex, to texturization, polymerization, and so on) and hence sector specific. This increases the need for close contacts between producers or producers' representatives (CIRFS) and the Commission. This contradicts the evolution towards a horizontal approach in the field of industrial policy.
- Some doubts (internal DGIV tensions or between DGIII and DGIV?) on the efficiency of the Code seem to have emerged in the latest version.[31]
- Restricted diffusion in the seventies of the letter to governments and of the memorandum, and restricted diffusion of some of the Commission's decisions on aid proposals (e.g. Filature du Hainaut, Hoechst Guben,

[29] According to the Commission: 'as the very existence of the Code is based on the excess capacity in the sector, the scope of the Code is limited to those fibres which are used in a market with excess capacity, i.e. the textile market, and its scope does not extend to fibres for industrial use' (93/C/205/06, dated 10.09.93).

[30] The aid to Crimpfil LTD for industrial use fibres was approved on the same basis (Press release dated 6.06.91 concerning state aid N 448/90). The aid has been attacked before the European Court of Justice.

[31] 'As the main reason for the code is the situation in the synthetic fibres market, the Commission may, before 31 December 1994, abolish the code or review it with a view to adapting it to changes in that market' (O.J., 92/C/346/02, dated 30.12.1992).

mentioned in the Allied Signal case) generated confusion about the aims and scope of the Code. This has created legal insecurity and generated a feeling of subjectivity in the implementation by the Commission.

3. The Merger Regulation

Since the implementation of the Merger Regulation in September 1990, five cases of concentration in the man-made fibre industry have been notified. One case - the Courtaulds/SNIA case (no. IV/M113, dated 19.12.1991) - concerns the acetate yarn market; the four others - Rhône-Poulenc/SNIA (case no. IV/M206, dated 10.08.1992), Du Pont/ICI (case no. IV/M214, dated 13.01.1993), Rhône-Poulenc/SNIA (case no. IV/M355, dated 08.09.1993) and Rhône-Poulenc-SNIA/Nordfaser (case no. IV/M399, dated 03.02.1994) - deal with the PA market.

In all these cases, the transfer by the parties of their interests to a joint venture or the acquisition by one party of the other party's interests led to very significant market shares after the concentration.

In the acetate market, Novaceta, the Courtaulds/SNIA joint venture, achieved 65 per cent of the West European market; in the PA market, Novalis, the Rhône-Poulenc/SNIA joint venture active on the non-textile yarn market, recorded between 40 and 50 per cent of the EC nonwovens PA fibres market; Nylstar, the Rhône-Poulenc/SNIA joint venture active on the textile PA yarn market, emerged, after the acquisition of Nordfaser, with a 40-45 per cent share of the West European market. Du Pont's market share, after the acquisition of ICI nylon interests was about 24 per cent of the textile PA yarn market and about 43 per cent of the carpet PA market. Despite these significant increases in concentration, the Commission decided not to oppose the notified operations.

In the case of the acetate market, the Commission argued that, despite its high market share, Novacetate would not be able to effectively restrain competition because it would be subject to the threat of potential competitive pressures, particularly from imports (which amounted to only 16 per cent of EC domestic consumption), but also from product substitution and new market entrants (upstream producers integrating backwards or producers of new microfibres). One element which appears to have played a significant role in the Commission's decision is the fact that the European producers suffer from a cost disadvantage as compared with their American competitors.

In the case of the PA market, the threat of direct import competition is deemed to be low, particularly in the carpet market, where long-lasting relations between supplier and client are prevalent. On the other hand, product substitution (mainly to PP in the carpet market and to PES in the textile market) and new market entrants (textile or carpet producers integrating upwards) would exert sufficient indirect competitive pressure.

The comparison of the Du Pont/ICI case with the Rhône-Poulenc cases shows that, despite similar market structures resulting from these concentration operations (characterized by a market share between 40 and 45 per cent for the leader and between 20 and 25 per cent for the next competitor), the Commission's evaluation of the impact of the concentration on competition is much more cautious in the Du Pont/ICI case than in the Rhône-Poulenc/SNIA cases. Specific features of these respective market segments - higher price elasticity of demand resulting from indirect import competition and volatility of demand in the textile uses - explain this difference. It is worth stressing that, in evaluating the potential for the new entity to effectively restrain competition, the Commission takes not only the market share on the relevant geographical market but also the market share on the world market. When Du Pont, leader on the world market, becomes, through the acquisition of ICI's nylon interests, the leader on the West European market, the Commission fears that this increase in market share will considerably reduce the competitive incentive to develop new products. The positive decision was hence subject to a commitment made by Du Pont to let a third party have access to some productive capacity, research facilities and licences.

4. Efficiency of the Competition and Industrial Policy Measures

Table 4.7 compares the rationalization agreements, the Code on State Aids and the Merger Regulation as instruments of the restructuring process in a mature industry. It shows that, depending among others on the time period available and the structure of supply in the industry, the efficiency of these measure will vary.

Table 4.7: Comparison between the efficiency of the rationalization agreements, the Code and the Merger Regulation in speeding up the restructuring process of the industry.

Rationalization cartels	**Code**	**Merger Regulation**
Short- to medium-term effects	Medium- to long- term effects	Short-term effects
Global approach	Case-by-case approach limited to aided investments	Case-by-case
Concerted restructuring involving major players	Favours strategic reorganization by big firms already in the market	Concerted restructuring by some players favours strategic reorganization (by pooling or by exit) among big firms
Ex-post control by cartel members	Limited *ex-post* control	No *ex-post* control if unconditional positive decision

How far have these measures been able to favour the structural adjustment of the industry?

a) Crisis Cartel Agreement

According to Shaw and Shaw (1983, p. 165),

> The first period from 1975 until 1979-1980, which included the Davignon Plan cartel, consisted of the virtual freezing of market shares of most firms and the preservation of both weak competitors and some uneconomic plants. Indeed the main changes were in the improved market shares of the four main Italian companies taken together despite their relative inefficiency and continuing state of near financial collapse. These results are consistent with the predictions for a cartel where the weak companies are protected by state aid.
>
> The second period from 1979-1980 until the end of 1981 covered the period after the formal abandonment of the cartel. In this period, the rationalization pattern followed closely on predictions based on the operation of the competitive process. Many small and uneconomic plants were closed and weaker competitors in each of the three synthetic fibres were forced out of the market. The exceptions to this pattern were mainly Italian companies dependent on state aid for their survival and development. In addition, most competitors chose to withdraw from their weaker market areas and concentrate their efforts on narrower product ranges.

b) The Code on State Aids

- Has a medium- to long-term potential efficiency since it applies only to new investment proposals and excluded schemes, such as the Italian ones, that were already in progress.
- Favours strategic reorganization by big multi-plant firms already active in the market at the expense of new entrants and small (single plant) existing firms. Existing firms are able to maintain their access to state aid since the closure of inefficient plants allows them to meet the condition of no increase in their net capacity. New entrants, on the other hand, have to rely on their own financial means.
- Focuses on only one criterion, namely degree of capacity utilization,[32] and considers each fibre separately. In fact fibres are in competition with each other in some cases. For example, Allied Signal argued that PES is in competition with rayon for tyres.
- Provides neither formal *ex-post* controls of the announced capacity reductions nor tight recovery procedures for illegal aid. The Deggendorf case (O.J. 91/L/215/16, 92/L/183/36, 93/C/172/2) shows how difficult it is for the Commission to get back the payment.

c) The Merger Regulation

Major changes in the pattern of product sources through mergers and acquisitions have occurred in the nylon industry. Remaining firms are long-term committed players with large enough financial resources to accept short-term restructuring costs and write-offs in order to better exploit economies of scale. These firms have R&D resources which allow them to compete by innovation. Competitive pressure from product substitutes and/or from direct and indirect import competition is deemed to be high enough to prevent these leaders from effectively restraining competition on the West European market. A similar restructuring process is expected for the textile polyester filaments as the number of producers involved in the West European market is still high (7 producers controlling 70 per cent of installed capacity as compared with 4 producers controlling 87 per cent of capacity in the USA) and capacity increases in East Asian countries are in process.

---

[32] The analysis of the Japanese policy against the synthetic fibre sector, presented in Ozawa (1980) confirms that several instruments had to be used in order to solve the problem of excess capacity.

IV. COMMERCIAL POLICY MEASURES

1. Tariffs and GSP

The Common External Tariff on man-made fibres lies between 5 and 9 per cent and will be reduced to 4 per cent by the Uruguay Round. However, Turkey, a large exporter to the EU, is exempted from the Common External Tariff.

The Generalized System of Preferences (GSP)[33] gives exporting countries a preferential access to the European market. Indonesia, India, Mexico and (to a minor extent) South Korea are among the beneficiaries of GSP.

Indirect imports of fibres through imports of textile and clothing into the EU also benefit from the GSP. Some large textile producers like Morocco and Romania receive preferential treatment.

The Central European countries benefit from European Agreements which provide for the gradual establishment of free trade with the European Union.

Those agreements include a standstill clause and thus do not allow for introducing new trade restricting measures. However, if exceptional circumstances would require such measures, the rules for introducing them are set out in the agreements. They concern among others the protection of sectors in restructuring or facing serious difficulties and anti-dumping measures.

2. The Multi Fibre Agreement (MFA)

The MFA has only an indirect impact on synthetic fibres by influencing the extent of extra-EU imports of textile and clothing. Direct imports of synthetic fibres are not subject to any restriction of trade under the MFA, with the minor exceptions of the remaining state trading countries, i.e. China and North Korea.[34]

However, as long as synthetic fibres are not integrated in the GATT agreement, the European Union can use a specific safeguard clause of the textile agreement rather than the general safeguard clause of Article 19 of GATT. That indirect impact may be strong: Graph 4.3[35] clearly shows

33 The GSP has been modified in 1995.

34 Moreover, as long as synthetics are not integrated in the GATT agreement, the Community can use a specific safeguard clause of the textile agreement, instead of a general safeguard clause of Article 19 of GATT.

35 Taken from the *Panorama of EC Industry*, 1994, p. 6-64.

that the consumption of man-made fibres follows the pattern of the textile consumption in the EC.

Graph 4.3 - Comparison between growth of apparent consumption of man-made fibres and of textiles in the EC

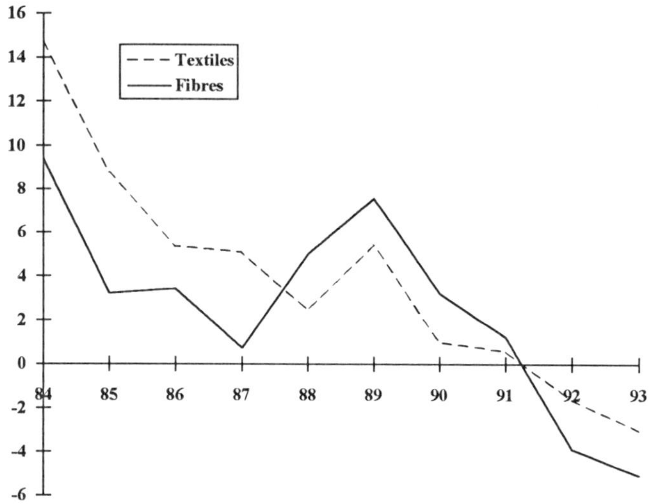

Source : *Panorama of EC Industry*, 1994, p. 6-64.

We have seen that the textile and clothing industry is prone to relocalization in order to take advantage of differences in labour costs.

In that respect, MFA could have resulted in the expansion of production in the NICs, aided by integrated corporate operations facilitating intra-firm trade in unprocessed fibres, raw polymer and fibre intermediates.[36]

This tendency can only be reinforced by the Uruguay Round results: importing countries will have to integrate textile products, step by step, into the GATT and, if quotas continue to exist, they will have to be increased.

36 This analysis is from Read (1986).

3. Anti-dumping and the Relationship Between External Trade and Competition Policies on Man-made Fibres.

We have seen that the synthetic fibre industry is prone to dumping. Due to the shape of the short-run unit cost curve (large fixed costs), the strategy of 'Volume' will induce producers, burdened by excess capacity, to sell abroad at export prices close to marginal cost.

The rationale behind anti-dumping duties (ADD) is the model of the discriminating monopoly: dumping implies price discrimination with protection of the domestic market of the exporter (if there were no protection of the domestic market, there would be parallel re-imports).

From that point of view, the anti-dumping procedure is just an external trade policy measure against imports at less than the normal value, when those imports cause injury to producers in the importing countries. However, in some cases, the complaining firms may be part of the same industrial group as the fibres exporters accused of dumping!

Digging further into cases of ADD in man-made fibres, some issues of possible conflict with competition policies are raised. We rely on two cases.

1. Case against the imports of acrylic fibres from Israel, Romania, Turkey and Mexico in 1984 (Decision: O.J. 86/L/272 of 24.09.86), after that anti-dumping duties (ADD) had been imposed since 1981 on imports of acrylic fibres from the USA.
2. Case against the imports of some polyester yarns from Taiwan, South Korea, Mexico and Turkey.

These cases reveal that the level of some fibres' prices on the European market is higher than on foreign markets.

In both reported anti-dumping cases, the market share of the foreign exporters accused of dumping had remained tiny (about 5 per cent in the first case and 13 per cent in the second case). Despite those modest figures, the Commission decided that EU producers might be negatively affected, because the lower import price could bring down the selling price for the whole European market. This confirms the high substitution in fibres demand - particularly for apparel - between sellers.

Though we have seen that higher European prices could be partly justified by a cost disadvantage (as compared with American competitors), one might fear that policies also played their part. Higher European prices might be somehow related to the industrial policy on man-made fibres (Code on State Aid and Agreement among Producers to Reduce Capacities). We may say that this interventionist industrial policy has induced a relatively protective anti-dumping policy (in Annex 4.1, we give the list, in chronological order, of the main decisions relating to the fibre industry; we look, in particular, at the successive steps in the adoption of the Code and in anti-dumping cases).

The protective anti-dumping policy helps to maintain the higher level of fibres prices, sustains the incentive for new investments and inflates the input costs of downstream users, thereby reinforcing the relocalization outside Europe of textile and apparel producers.

The technical aspects of anti-dumping procedures also raise interesting comparisons with the competition policy and the Code on fibres, especially as regards the definition of the relevant market:

- for anti-dumping, when one has to determine whether there is some prejudice for the domestic (import-competing) producers, the definition of 'similar products' is very narrow. Otherwise, it would be very difficult to find and prove any damage;
- the Code uses a broader concept: as seen above, the Code considers that there is a high substitutability *within* each fibre on the supply side;
- the concepts used by DGIV (substitute products, relevant market) are also broader than the concept of similar products used in anti-dumping.

As a matter of fact, the man-made fibres industry does not lend itself to such a comparative analysis, because most anti-dumping cases are on polyester, whereas, during the 1990-94 period, merger and joint venture cases concerned the nylon market.

NORMATIVE CONCLUSIONS AND PROPOSITIONS FOR A MORE EFFECTIVE INTERVENTION BY THE EUROPEAN COMMUNITY

1. Conclusions on the Evaluation of Community Policies on Fibres

Intervention by the European Community on man-made fibres is centred on a sector-specific adjustment policy for a mature industry: the rationalization cartel and the Code are typically vertical industrial policies.

Our conclusions on the interactions (convergence or divergence) between all the microeconomic instruments (industrial, competition and trade measures) may be summarized as follows:

1. As regards the convergence between the European and the national levels, the Code gives a coherence between the goal of European industrial policy (to facilitate the adjustment of the European fibres industry) and that of national aid policies (especially those state aids which maintained inefficient plants or even created new capacities in depressed areas and 'glamorous' industries).

   In that respect, the Community's intervention to coordinate Member-States' (regional and sectoral) aid policies has been successful during the eighties and has reached its primary goal: it was, after all, the massive Member States' aid until the seventies which made necessary the Code at European level.

2. The adaptation of the fibres industry through pure market mechanisms was impeded by the tendency to excess capacity (tendency resulting from the characteristics studied in section II) and from high barriers to exit. The rationalization cartel was opposed by the competition rule on cartels (Article 85 of the Treaty of Rome) and only had short- to medium-term effects on the structural adjustment. However, the Code on Aid may have had some long-term effect. Moreover, the Code was complemented by a pro-merger policy which has supported increased specialization by big producers (the supply of man-made fibres is now European Union-wide), ever since 1990.

   On the whole, the concerted policy of capacity reduction may boast effectiveness as compared with a pure *laissez-faire* situation.

3. The Code has had an adverse effect on entry conditions by focusing exclusively on the criterion of degree of capacity utilization: the Code went as far as to authorize only those state subsidies designed to phase down capacity. By so doing, the Code favoured strategic reorganization by (large) multi-plant firms already in the market (even in traditional market segments like apparel) and created barriers to entry (especially in depressed, aided regions) for new, single-plant firms. This is an example of conflict between industrial policy measures and the competition policy objectives in a mature industry (Gual, 1994, p. 20).

   Another example of the possible bias in a sector undergoing such a structural adjustment is the pro-merger policy: all submitted mergers and joint ventures were accepted, whatever the market shares achieved by the big European firms on their internal market, because extra-EU competition was thought sufficient to prevent any dominant position.

The only case where restrictive conditions were attached to the merger is the Du Pont/ICI case, because Du Pont - a non-European firm - has a large market share outside the European market.

4. The Code also raises issues of adverse relationships, even conflict, with trade policy. Following Gual (1994, p. 24), trade policy should be geared towards external liberalization as a consequence of the internal market so that the general objectives of EU trade policy are the development of world trade and the reduction of restrictions on international exchanges.

   Arguably, anti-dumping duties (ADD) may be presented as safeguards against trade distortions from dumping and state aid in exporting countries like India, Turkey, and so on.

   However, higher European prices for fibres, possibly brought about by the concerted cuts in capacity and the barriers to entry resulting from the Code, have been maintained in some cases by the imposition of ADD: as we have explained before, ADDs are imposed, at least in part, in view of industrial policy considerations. The Commission considers that, even if extra-EU import shares remain low, their impact on the price of fibres in the European market, and hence on the profitability of European producers, would prevent those European producers from reaping the benefits of the restructuring process initiated by the Code. Furthermore, amongst the criteria used by the Commission to evaluate the damage, the evolution of the European capacity and the DUC are taken into account.

   Clearly, the fibres producers' interests get the priority over the interests of downstream users and final consumers. As a result, anti-dumping policy reinforces the Code's effects of maintaining higher prices and large capacities in traditional market segments(apparel).

2. Why Such a Vertical (Sector Specific) Approach for Fibres?: the Comparison with Petrochemicals

We have seen that the Code on fibres has grown more and more sector specific over time. Some fear that the so-called temporary measures of the Code will in fact be taken for ever.

In view of the drawbacks of the Code on competition and external trade liberalization, one may also raise the question: why such a specific Code for man-made fibres and not for other similarly mature sectors like petrochemicals?

A. There are indeed several similarities with petrochemicals

- Both sectors are capital intensive with economies of scale.
- Both sectors are oligopolistic and, most strikingly, some big players are the same (Hoechst, Bayer, Enichem, ICI).
- There has been the same tendency to accumulate excess capacity (in particular, barriers to exit are high in both sectors).

In petrochemicals, the cost of shutting plants is even larger because of stronger inter-industry linkages and joined production processes, while fibres producers can (to some extent) engage in vertical disintegration (fibres producers can buy petrochemical inputs on the spot market and can enjoy some inputs substitution).

It is therefore not surprising that the European petrochemical producers tried to set up the same kind of rationalization cartel as the fibres industry. However, unlike fibres producers, they could not strike any formal rationalization cartel, nor did they get any compulsory Code on aid. Instead, as shown by Grant (1991), the restructuring of the petrochemical industry was achieved by a combination of actions:

- associative action by the organization of petrochemical producers contributed to a clear view of the scope and nature of the problem;
- EC Commission action ruled out both a rationalization cartel and national aid subsidy schemes; it favoured, however, collective action by the industry itself;
- *bilateral* agreements of companies to specialize led to swaps of plants and the subsequent closure of the least efficient plants. This was the dominant form of restructuring.

In terms of economic analysis, there are structural and behavioural factors which explain the difference in restructuring process between the two industries.

B. Structural differences between fibres and petrochemicals

Petrochemicals could pass on increases in unit cost and in raw material prices into their selling prices.

This contrasts with the weak position of textile fibre producers (and textile fibres make up about 50 per cent of man-made fibres!), which have been unable to roll input price increases over on to their downstream buyers because they are vulnerable to relocalization outside Europe.

This is important in view of the strong cyclical fluctuations of prices of those raw materials (the input prices are strongly cyclical because they are derived from oil and gas and are inputs for various user sectors).

As a result, fibres producers have been unable to compensate for the losses incurred during cyclical downturns by profits in booming periods.

Furthermore, European fibres producers face tougher competition on the extra-EU export market than petrochemical producers.

C. Behavioural differences between fibres and petrochemicals: the conditions of success of rationalization cartels

There are two behavioural reasons why *multilateral* agreements to cut capacity could be reached in the fibres industry, whereas the petrochemical industry's restructuring was achieved through *bilateral* agreements.

First, in spite of the associative action by the organization of petrochemical producers, there was no consensus on the future of the petrochemical industry: the upsurge in demand in 1993 may have convinced some players to keep their level of existing capacity (as Glais's contribution shows, the same has just happened in the steel industry). In contrast, all big players in the fibres sector had, as early as the mid-seventies, the same (gloomy) view on the future of their industry.

Second, there has been inequality amongst petrochemical producers' distribution of the costs of closing excess capacity. When there is such an inequality, with cost asymmetries (i.e. weaker players have higher relative costs of keeping plants), strong producers are liable to expect the forced, voluntary exit of those weaker players. An agreement on reducing capacities for *all* firms will be difficult to reach because some important firms will have the tendency to rely on the natural selection mechanism of the market.

In other words, strong players, having lower marginal costs of production but relatively high costs of exit (because of large sunk investment costs and vertical integration of joined output), will not agree to cut capacity.

In contrast, fibres producers met the conditions of success of a multilateral rationalization cartel. Players in the fibres industry have been increasingly 'equal': for all of them, the high cost of exit might have been larger than the cost of keeping alive money-losing plants so that there have been few incentives to exit and the cost of postponing any reduction in capacity has been high. As soon as all fibres producers recognized the situation (and they did as early as 1972), they were able to reach an agreement (with the helping hand, at the end of the seventies, of the EC Commissioner responsible for Industry, who could carry the firms over the barriers to exit).

3. Horizontal or Vertical Industrial Policy?

DGIII now rejects the Code on fibres on the ground of its horizontal approach of industrial policy (for the definition, see e.g. Gual, 1994, p. 9).

If such a *horizontal approach* was taken, one might wonder which characteristics should be taken into account to determine the firms and the activities which would be targeted for industrial action.

Possible criteria would be, for example:

- the capital intensity and the shape of the short-term unit cost curve;
- the lumpiness of investments for capacity expansion and the shape of the long-term unit cost curve;
- the importance of value-added or of gross profits in total turnover;
- the degree of maturity of demand and the innovative character of the product.

Those criteria are diverse and even mutually exclusive.

Moreover, our analysis shows that a rather positive attitude towards the kind of rationalization agreement reached by the fibres producers is supported by characteristics of the industry:

- it displays economies of scale and is capital intensive;
- it is more and more a natural oligopoly with large players of more or less equal strength;
- the incentives to exit are weak and the cost of postponing reduction of capacity is high, i.e. there is a growing long term commitment of large players to stay in the market, with a possible learning process (from a dynamic, multiperiod game) to avoid price wars (this learning process has already happened in the cement industry, for example).

If the *vertical, sectoral approach* is kept, we formulate the following normative propositions to have a policy mix better adapted to market structures and industry characteristics.

4. Normative propositions for the EEC policy towards man-made fibres industry

A. The Code should not be kept for ever

- Part of the excess capacity in the seventies was created by massive State subsidies (especially by Italy). A tough application of competition policy (Art. 92 of the Treaty of Rome) could curb politically-biased State aid.
- A permanent Code would, as we have seen, make more difficult new entries and intensification of price competition when the degree of utilization of capacity goes down.

It would also discriminate between incumbent firms depending on whether (i) they produce man-made fibres from within the scope of the Code or not; and (ii) they are located in aided areas or not.

- The Code, by focusing exclusively on excess capacity and DUC, is a reason why European producers are still too much engaged in traditional market segments.
- The rationalization process has happened and the supply of man-made fibres is now European-wide (though, Du Pont and Rhône-Poulenc have just notified a joint venture for the production of adipic acid, an intermediate product for nylon).

Thus, for PES (textile filament), the six large producers account for 70 per cent of the market. For PA (carpet), the four largest producers have 79 per cent of the Western European market (the corresponding figure for the USA is 87 per cent).

B. Normative propositions for the improvement of the Code

- The implementation of the Code should be more transparent.
- The motivation of the extension of the validity of the Code should be based not only on the degree of capacity utilization of the incumbent firms but also on a more general assessment of the situation in the

sector (growth of the product markets, innovations). That assessment should be based on information gathered through anti-dumping, state aid and merger cases.

- Policy-makers should distinguish carefully between the economic consequences of the Code (medium- and long-term effects) and of crisis cartel-type agreements (short-term effects). The comparison with the steel industry is very relevant.
- The treatment of the individual cases should be based on the general objectives assigned to the intervention in the sector so that the Code, if prolonged, would not amount to a protection of incumbent multi-plant firms.
- The competition policy could be kept positive towards mergers and joint ventures if, as the Bangemann communication states, those operations lead to cuts in capacities in sectors with high costs of exit.

REFERENCES

Boston Consulting Group (1985), *Strategic Study of the Machine Tool Industry*, European Commission, Brussels.

Boyer, M. and A. Jacquemin (1985), 'Organizational choices for efficiency and market power', *Economics Letters*, No.1.

Buigues, P. (1985), *Prospective et compétitivité*, MacGraw-Hill, Paris.

Buigues, P. et A. Jacquemin (1988), '1992: quelles stratégies pour les entreprises européennes', *Revue française de gestion*, No.69, June/July/August.

Commission des Communautés Européennes (1994), *Une politique de compétitivité industrielle pour l'Union Européenne*, Communication de la Commission au Conseil, au Parlement Européen, au Comité Economique et Social et au Comité des Régions, COM (94) 319, 14 September, Brussels.

Commission des Communautés Européennes (1994), *Panorama de l'Industrie Communautaire*, Bruxelles.

Grant, W. (1991), 'The overcapacity crisis in the West European Petrochemical industry', in A. Martinelli (ed.), *International Markets and Global Firms*, Sage.

Huveneers, C.(1979), 'Les interventions de l'Etat respectent-elles le système concurrentiel?', *Reflets et Perspectives de la Vie Economique*, XVIII (3).

Jacquemin, A., P. Buigues and F. Ilzkowitz (1989), 'Concentration horizontale, fusions et politique de concurrence dans la Communauté Européenne', *Economie Européenne*, No.40, May.

Jacquemin, A. (1992), 'The Interaction between Competition, Industrial and Trade Policy in the EC - An Economist's view', in *Doing Business in an integrated Europe - The impact of EC Law & Policy, Financial Times* Conferences, 13 and 14 May, Brussels.

Kreps, D.M. and J. Scheinkman (1983), 'Quantity precommitment and Bertrand competition yield Cournot outcomes', *Rand Journal of Economics*, 17, pp.618-38.

Liebermann, M.B. (1989), 'The Learning Curve, Technology Barriers to Entry, and Competitive Survival in the Chemical Processing Industry', *Strategic Management Journal*, 10(5), pp. 431-47.

Lippman, S.A. and R.P. Rumelt (1982), 'Uncertain imitability: an analysis of interfirm differences in efficiency under competition', *Bell Journal of Economics*, 13, Autumn, pp. 418-38.

Manne, A. (1967), *Investments for Capacity Expansion*, MIT, Cambridge, Mass.

Mansfield, E. (1985), 'How rapidly does new industrial technology leak out ?', *The Journal of Industrial Economics*, XXXIV, December, pp. 217-23.

Ozawa, T. (1980), 'Government Control over Technology Acquisition and Firms' Entry into New Sectors: the experience of Japan's synthetic fibre industry', *Cambridge Journal of Economics*, 4, pp. 133-46.

Read, R. (1986): 'The Synthetic Fibre Industry: Innovation, Integration and Market Structure', in M. Casson et al., *Multinationals and World Trade*, Allen & Unwin.

Shaw, R.W. and S.A. Shaw (1983), 'Excess Capacity and Rationalization in the West European Synthetic Fibres Industry', *Journal of Industrial Economics*, 32(2), pp. 149-66.

Shaw, R.W. and S.A. Shaw (1984), 'Late entry, market shares and competitive survival: the case of synthetic fibres', *Managerial and Decision Economics*, 5, pp. 72-9.

Scherer, F, A. Beckenstein, E. Kaufer, R. Murphy and F. Bougeon-Maassen, (1975), *The Economics of Multi-Plant Operation: an International Comparison study*, Cambridge, Mass.

Wauthy, X. (1994), 'Capacity precommitment, battle for market shares and product differentiation', Discussion Paper IRES (UCL), No.8, Louvain-la-Neuve.

Zachmann, J. (1994), *Contrôle des concentrations*, Librairie Générale de Droit et de Jurisprudence, February, 457 pages.

ANNEX 4.1: MAIN DECISIONS RELATING TO THE FIBRE SECTOR

1972:	notification of a rationalization agreement between PES producers Second Report on Competition Policy,no.31
July 1977:	letter to the Member States asking for a ban on aid leading to capacity increases in the man-made fibre sector Seventh Report on Competition Policy,no.204
May 1978:	Memorandum setting out details concerning the Code
July 1978:	notification of a rationalization agreement between synthetic fibre producers Eighth Report on Competition Policy,no.42
July 1979:	extension of the validity of the Code for a 2 year period Ninth Report on Competition Policy,no.172
August 1984:	the rationalization agreement between synthetic fibre producers notified on 10.11.82 is declared to be compatible with Article 85. 84/L/207/17
May 1985:	anti-dumping complaint against acrylic fibre imports from Israel, Mexico, Romania and Turkey final decision: 86/L/272/29
July 1985:	extension for a two year period of the validity of the Code + inclusion of polypropylene 85/C/171/3
December 1985:	anti-dumping complaint against PES fibre imports from DDR, Romania, Turkey and Yugoslavia final decision: 87/L/103/38
May 1987:	anti-dumping complaint against PES yarns imports from Mexico, Taiwan, South Korea and Turkey final decision: 88/L/347/10 anti-dumping complaint against PES fibre imports from USA, Mexico, Romania, Taiwan, Turkey and Yugoslavia final decision: 88/L/348/49
July 1987:	extension for a two year period of the validity of the Code + inclusion of texturization activities 87/C/183/4
June 1988:	anti-subsidies complaint against PES fibre imports from Turkey final decision: 91/L/272/3
June 1989:	aid awarded by the French government to Allied Signal, concerning an investment in high tenacity PES yarn for use in tyres production 93/C/215/06
July 1989:	extension for a two year period of the validity of the Code + inclusion of 'all end-uses' 89/C/173/5
July 1991:	extension for a one year period of the validity of the Code 91/C/186/4

December 1991:	constitution of a joint venture (Novaceta) between Courtaulds and SNIA in the acetate filament sector Decision no.IV/M113, dated 19.12.91
July 1992:	extension for a 6 months period of the validity of the Code 92/C/179/3
August 1992:	constitution of a joint venture (Novalis) between RP and SNIA in the carpet and non-wovens PA segment Decision no.IV/M206, dated 10.08.92
December 1992:	extension for a two year period of the validity of the Code + a significant reduction of the capacity becomes a necessary condition for a positive appraisal of an aid + inclusion of polymerization activities 92/C/346/2
January 1993:	acquisition by Du Pont of ICI worldwide activities in the PA sector Decision no.IV/M214, dated 13.01.93
November 1993:	constitution of a joint venture (Nylstar) between RP and SNIA in the PA textile segment Decision no.IV/M355, dated 08.09.93
February 1994:	joint acquisition by RP and SNIA of Nordfaser, active in the textile PA sector - Decision no.IV/M399, dated 3.2.94

Discussion

Colin M. Purvis

INTRODUCTION

In discussing the chapter which has just been presented, I must stress first of all that I am doing so as someone who is actively involved, on a day-to-day basis, in the man-made fibres industry. CIRFS, as you have heard, is the representative body for the West European man-made fibres industry and, as its Director General, I have a particular responsibility for dealing on its behalf with the Commission and other European Union bodies. It must therefore be understood that I am not a neutral party. However, for the purposes of this discussion, I am not here to promote CIRFS' views but to comment, as a practical participant, on the issues that have been raised.

Before I do so, a little background may be helpful. The man-made fibres sector is a modestly sized component of the European Union's industrial structure, with sales last year of 10 billion ECU and a volume output of 3 million tonnes. As an employer, it is relatively small - about 65,000 employees in the present Union, although each production site individually may have considerable local importance. Up until 20 years ago, however, it had a significance in policy-making by governments and the European authorities out of all relation to its size. It was a boom sector, at the forefront of technology, with demand growing by 10 to 15 per cent a year. Governments were falling over one another both to encourage indigenous companies to expand, and to attract inward investment. Then, 20 years ago, the industry moved with surprising rapidity from boom to maturity - some of the rapidity being due to the huge increase in raw material prices linked to the first oil crisis. Demand growth fell to 2 to 3 per cent a year on average with, in some years, an actual decline. Some of the consequences of this boom and bust phase are still with us today.

However, my remarks will concentrate on a more recent period and the way in which, in our experience, the complementarities and conflicts in Community policies outlined in the de Ghellinck/Huveneers chapter are currently being felt.

THE PROBLEM OF OVER-CAPACITY

It is undeniable, looking at the experience of the man-made fibres sector, that there are features within it conducive to the build-up and maintenance of excess capacity. On this, I am in complete agreement with the chapter which has just been presented. From an empirical standpoint, I would place particular weight on the following factors:

(i) Sunk Costs and Barriers to Exit

This has been well demonstrated by Mme de Ghellinck and M. Huveneers. An exit from the sector means writing off a huge amount of capital investment, a step which most companies are reluctant to take. Firms are thus prepared to accept, for extended periods, modest profitability or modest losses, and even to put in incremental investment to maintain competitiveness when, on the face of it, the funds could earn a better return in other activities.

There is one additional barrier to exit to which I would also draw attention: the burden of social costs in the event of closure. There are arguably companies in countries where these costs are particularly high, which cannot afford to exit the sector and which therefore struggle on in a triumph of hope over experience.

(ii) A Static or Declining Textile Market

The textile and apparel industry remains the largest single user, by far, of man-made yarns and fibres in Europe. As the chapter points out, apparel in particular is a labour-intensive process, and an inevitable process of delocalisation to low labour-cost countries is under way. That is not to say that the apparel industry will disappear in Western Europe, even after the final disappearance of the Muld Fibre Arrangement in 2005, but the process of contraction is set to continue. It is not clear whether market growth in carpets, home textile, non-spun and technical uses will be enough to counteract this decline.

(iii) Ease of Entry

I would place less stress on barriers to entry than do Mme de Ghellinck and M. Huveneers. Indeed, entry becomes increasingly easy in some respects with technology internationally available, through a small group of specialist equipment suppliers and contractors. This may not have encouraged entirely new entrants to the European market, but it has encouraged new capacity to be installed by carpet and, to a lesser extent, textile producers through a process of backward integration. This new capacity, with a captive market, has worsened over-capacity in some market segments.

(iv) Government intervention

Despite the existence of the framework controlling aids to the synthetic fibres sector, governments have continued to aid firms in the sector - in some cases, by breaking the Code's prohibition on assisting increases in capacity and then ignoring Commission and even Court requirements that such subsidies be reclaimed; in many cases, by giving assistance for modernization and restructuring, undoubtedly in some cases with hidden increases in capacity; and by rescue aids, preventing the reduction of over-capacity by disappearance of the weakest players. There have also been periods when the Community was careless enough to allow a gap between different periods of validity of the discipline, of which some Member States took advantage to rush through large subsidies.

THE RELATIONSHIP BETWEEN COMPETITION AND INDUSTRIAL POLICIES

In this situation, the relationship between the Community's competition and industrial policies is of great importance to the industry's future. From the industry's point of view, we strongly favour market solutions - but it is clear that a considerable degree of Community intervention is required to promote these.

From the side of competition policy, the industry has mixed but on the whole positive experience. It is clear, as is pointed out in the chapter under discussion, that structural features tend not only to build up over-capacity but also to encourage too many players to remain in the market, each operating on a suboptimal scale. Market pressures - and the market for fibres is essentially a global one - have pushed producers in several sectors to do something about this - by mergers, takeovers and joint ventures. Thus, in acrylics, a declining market, there are three main players in Western Europe; in polyamide, there are two or three, excluding the captive production of downstream processors; in viscose, also in long-term decline, there are three or four. In these areas, the approach of the Commission has been relatively constructive, accepting the logic of market pressures for concentration while endeavouring to ensure that competition remains vigorous. Certainly its approach has been much more satisfactory than that of some national merger authorities, which persisted in looking at competition purely on a national basis long after it was clear that there was no longer national market segmentation in fibres in the Community.

One major sector remains where substantial rationalization is necessary: polyester, the largest single part of the fibres industry. Polyester production in Europe is greatly weakened by its fragmentation. I hope and expect that, before long, we shall see the formation of groups with the resources and confidence needed to remove excess capacity and to concentrate production into world-scale plants. In what I hope is the unlikely event of Community competition policy preventing such a development, I fear that West European production of polyester, certainly for textile uses, would enter a sharp decline.

There is no doubt that this process of rationalization has been greatly assisted by the existence of the Community discipline prohibiting aids for increases in synthetic fibres capacity. Without it, I question whether companies would have had the courage necessary to invest in restructuring and modernization. The industry thus strongly supports this measure of Community intervention, whose purpose paradoxically is to prevent excessive interventionism by public authorities. I therefore strongly endorse the complementarity of the Community's market-based approach to merger policy, and its intervention in the form of the subsidies discipline.

There is, of course, a potential conflict within industrial policy itself between the Commission's preference for horizontal measures, applying to all sectors, and the existence of sectoral disciplines. From the point of view of logic, a horizontal approach has a lot to commend it. CIRFS could have no reason to object to a horizontal framework of state aids whose consequences were at least as effective as our sectoral discipline in preventing distortions of competition. But that condition of effectiveness is a difficult one to fulfil. Many years ago, the European Community agreed that, in some regions, subsidies of up to 75 per cent of investment cost could be given. In our industry, that would equate to a subsidy of up to 25 per cent - using the cost structure included in the chapter under discussion - on operating costs. A normal margin on sales is far lower, say 5 to 10 per cent. Existing rules, in the absence of the discipline, could thus distort competition to a very considerable extent. It is difficult to see how any horizontal discipline on state aids can be successful unless this 75 per cent permitted subsidy level is substantially reduced. But is it likely that Member States, or indeed the Commission's Regional Affairs, Directorate General, will agree to such a reduction?

Nonetheless, CIRFS has an open mind. It has examined the current chapter suggesting a framework for capital-intensive projects before coming, reluctantly, to the conclusion that it could not form an effective alternative to our sectoral code. We are willing to work with the Commission on alternative horizontal scenarios, but we should be clear that any horizontal alternative which is not at least as effective in curbing distortions of competition as the present synthetic fibres framework would be disastrous for our sector.

THE LINK TO TRADE POLICY

I turn now to the relationship of Community trade policy to competition and industrial policies.

Mme de Ghellinck and M. Huveneers rightly identify dumping as a feature to which the sector is prone, because of its high fixed costs. They also, rightly, identify the main problem countries in dumping as those whose tightly protected home markets give a sufficient level of domestic profitability to allow them to export at marginal cost. To this must be added the problem of countries whose foreign exchange controls provide an incentive to export even at a loss to acquire foreign exchange - often disappearing into hard currency bank accounts rather than being repatriated - and the continued existence in some countries of state trading regimes.

CIRFS' experience of the Community's anti-dumping policies is mixed. We have never put forward a case without the strongest possible evidence both of dumping and of resulting injury to the Community industry. All of our cases have been accepted for investigation, and positive findings have followed in most cases. We currently have two cases with the Commission undergoing investigation, and in a third case a review of an existing duty is under way. However, the procedures are unwieldy, and virtually unusable by CIRFS' downstream customers in the textile and apparel industry because of the large number of firms involved. CIRFS welcomes the tighter time limits for investigation agreed last year, and now incorporated in the draft Uruguay Round implementing legislation. However, we worry about the scope for future blockage of justified action arising from the 'Community interest' criterion and - a new factor - the specific mention in the new legislation of consumer interests.

Experience of other Community trade policy measures is, it has to be said, much less satisfactory. All too often, trade policy is linked not to industrial or to competition policy, but to foreign policy objectives of Member State governments. Let me give some examples.

(i) Uruguay Round tariff negotiations

There was a shared objective between CIRFS and the Commission for international harmonization of tariffs on fibres, textiles and clothing. The results achieved in obtaining tariff reduction offers by other countries were, to say the least, disappointing; nonetheless, the European Union went ahead with its offer to reduce tariffs to 4 per cent, giving the European fibres industry the lowest level of tariff protection of any major producing country, while still leaving it with substantial tariff barriers impeding its exports. There was certainly no thought given to industrial logic.

(ii) Tariff preferences

For many years, the benefit of the Community's GSP offer on man-made fibres has gone almost exclusively to countries which are already highly competitive in the sector - South Korea, Thailand, Malaysia, India, for example. The Community industry has thus lost the little tariff protection it enjoys, while the poorest countries which genuinely need the help of tariff preferences have failed to benefit. The Community's new proposals to reform GSP are a welcome injection both of industrial logic and of genuine concern for developing economies - but will the Member States approve them?

(iii) The new commercial instrument

The Community's new commercial instrument was introduced in 1984 to give the Community a new arm to combat unfair trade, but has been little used. A recent CIRFS case shows why. Turkey imposed duties on our fibre exports from Europe of up to 25 per cent, which are clearly in breach of the Ankara Agreement. The Commission, after consulting Member States, accepted our argument that the duties were illegal, but decided that no action was necessary, in the light of Customs Union negotiations and some modest reductions in the extent of the illicit dudes. Thus, despite a clear-cut legal basis for our complaint, injury to European industry is permitted to continue. I stress that the case was not a demand for protection but an attempt to assert our rights in an overseas market. To my mind, this refusal to act is in conflict with the Community's industry policy, and indeed with its trade policy's support for open markets.

Conflict between the two policies also arises when Member States put the priority on defending narrow national trade interests rather than those of the Community. A case in point is European policy on Outward Processing - the export of Community semi-finished textiles to a nearby lower labour-cost area, typically Eastern Europe, for manufacture into apparel and re-import. This is clearly a desirable alternative to goods made 100 per cent abroad, since it preserves capital- and knowledge-intensive manufacturing processes in Western Europe, and has therefore been strongly advocated by CIRFS. And yet, Member States have found it impossible for the past two years to agree regulations to allow further development of this trade, because each has been fearful of upsetting vested interests in its own country. CIRFS can only regard this as a shocking abdication of responsibility by Member States. In short, in trade policy, I see less complementarity than conflict with other Community priorities.

CONCLUSION

Let me conclude by stressing the importance which I attach, as an industrial representative, to the theme of this book. The competitiveness of European industry, as the Commission's recent paper on the subject underlined, is fundamental to the health of the European Union's economy. While I would certainly not attempt to argue that the interests of industry should invariably be the driving force of EU decisions, they require and deserve a high priority. In particular, I would argue that the highest possible degree of complementarity between policies affecting industry, and the lowest possible degree of conflict, must be the aim of the European and Member State authorities, if industry is to flourish and waste of resources to be avoided.

The chapter prepared by Mme de Ghellinck and M. Huveneers plays a useful part in pointing out where and why, in the man-made fibres sector, complementarity rather than conflict, or vice versa, appear. In these remarks, I have tried to illustrate the same theme, with concrete examples drawn from CIRFS' own experience. I do not expect that, today or tomorrow, we shall find magic answers enabling the European Union painlessly to resolve policy conflicts. I trust, however, that increased awareness of the issues involved, and their importance, will underlay future policy-making in the Union.

5. Steel Industry

Michel Glais

INTRODUCTION

Today it is widely accepted that the interventionist sectoral policies adopted during the last twenty years by the Member States and by the Community itself have not generally succeeded in bringing about the structural changes needed to recreate the conditions for a satisfactory measure of international competitiveness in the sectors concerned.

Rethinking industrial policy by integrating it into an open and competitive environment, as the Community authorities hope to do, means choosing new forms of intervention which are more horizontal and broadly intersectoral in nature.[1] In this context, the steel industry is cited as the prime example of an activity where sectoral policy has shown its limitations and shortcomings. Despite the substantial aid granted to firms in the industry, the restructuring process is far from complete since there is still ample excess capacity. In addition, continuing intervention in support of the industry is clearly at odds with the creation of an open and competitive environment. Even though these criticisms are justified at the moment, it should not be forgotten that the steel industry remains a very special sector, in the first place because of its quite specific structural characteristics (section I). It is impossible to make an objective and dispassionate assessment of the forms of intervention applied in this sector during the last thirty years without taking into account the historical and institutional background (in particular, the provisions of the ECSC Treaty). It was very much because of these circumstances that the restructuring process was relatively slow in getting under way; however, the results of Community intervention are, in fact, less disappointing than a superficial analysis would tend to suggest (section II). No objections can be raised regarding the choice made in favour of the primacy of competition policy. Even so, given the still very salient structural

[1] For an analysis of the objectives of the Community's industrial policy, see M. Bangemann, 1992; P. Buigues and A. Sapir, 1993; A. Jacquemin and J.-F. Marchipont, 1993; A. Jacquemin and A. Sapir, 1991.

characteristics of the industry, it must be possible for such a choice to dovetail harmoniously with a number of other aspects of Community policy, and in particular the need to open up the common market in steel, primarily to firms in the countries of Eastern Europe (section III).

I. THE STEEL INDUSTRY: AN INDUSTRIAL CONFIGURATION WHICH IS DIFFICULT TO RENDER 'FEASIBLE' WITHIN THE MEANING OF MODERN MARKET ANALYSIS

The steel market is at present characterized by two main production methods. Now a mature process, oxygen steel-making technology displays a number of characteristics not conducive to market conditions that would allow supply and demand to adapt smoothly. However, the technology of the electric arc furnace, which experts think likely to dominate within twenty years, could make the steel industry no longer appear like a sector that is so difficult to manage according to the classic rules of market forces alone.

A Dominant Technology Making it Difficult for Supply to Adjust Flexibly to Demand

Oxygen steel-making technology is still the predominant technology in use (accounting for some 70 per cent of steel production in the EC). It is a highly capital-intensive process relying on the integration of a series of specific assets located according to the typology proposed by O.E. Williamson.[2]

This production method, based on the transformation of blast-furnace pig iron into liquid steel using oxygen converter technology, allows very large capacity plants (2-10 million tonnes of crude steel annually) producing high-quality steel to be built, the representative unit being some 4 million tonnes thanks to the integration of a blast furnace with two 300-tonne converters. The most productive integrated plants were built in coastal areas where, with prime access to raw materials, they had lower transport costs than the longer-established plants situated inland (close to coal mines or iron-ore mines or in areas close to centres of consumption). However, there is no doubt that oxygen steel plants are economically fragile. Faced with inescapable technological constraints in the shape of significant indivisibilities in their production function and high investment costs, their

2 Site specificity refers to the need for assets to be complementary and to be linked together in a production process requiring plant facilities to be located very close to each other for technical reasons or because of storage and transport problems.

managers had to choose the optimal size of such plants on the basis of forecasts that, of necessity, covered fairly long periods of time.

Since steel is an intermediate product, the demand for it is derived, in the Marshallian sense, from demand for the final products which it goes into producing. In the long run, this demand has a relatively high price-elasticity in so far as: (1) the demand for certain final products also has a relatively high price-elasticity; (2) the cost of steel represents a large proportion of their production costs; and (3) in certain activities, steel faces competition from substitutes. In the short run, however, price-elasticity is low. As suppliers to industrial sectors affected by major fluctuations in demand, Community steel producers can no longer rely on a substantial increase in aggregate demand for steel in the years ahead because of: (a) the productivity gains made in the last ten to fifteen years, a particular feature of which has been the reduction in the quantities of crude steel used in the manufacture of finished products; (b) the increase in production capacity in the newly industrialized countries and in the developing countries, which are now offering final products of acceptable quality (in particular, long products) at competitive prices; (c) competition from other materials (aluminium, plastic) despite strong resistance from steel (which recently has even regained market shares in some cases).

Against this background, the high level of fixed costs and the existence of substantial technical indivisibilities make it difficult to achieve financial equilibrium in the case of integrated steel plants operated at below 75-80 per cent of capacity. It is not surprising, then, to see them regularly run up operating losses when their traditional clients are having to come to terms with cyclical falls in activity. In addition, the difficulties of managing integrated steel plants are all the more severe in that, given the long-term trends in aggregate demand, Community supply is characterized by substantial excess capacity.

Thus, according to the Baumol-Panzar-Willig analysis, the configuration of the Community steel industry is not a 'feasible configuration' whereby a group of firms operating on a given market at least cover their costs at the equilibrium price.[3] Most integrated steel plants in the Community have suffered substantial losses over the last two years as a result of the recent marked increase in the production-cost differentials between the main suppliers. While a number of groups such as British Steel and Usinor-Sacilor have been able to rationalize operations and reduce costs through fundamental restructuring, others are grappling with difficulties which are all the more daunting in that they were very late in embarking

---

3 For a group of m firms selling quantities $Q1......Qm$ at price P, it is essential that $j=1^{m}$ Qj $= Q(P)$, where $P(Q_j)C(Q_j)0$ and $j = 1......m$.

on the inevitable process of closing unprofitable production capacity. German steel makers, once held up as a shining example of how to achieve excellent productivity, have also seen their position eroded as their control over costs has weakened.

Table 5.1: Average unit costs (in US$) on one tonne of flat product (cold-rolled) produced in oxygen steel plants

	1984	1985	1986	1987	1988	1989	1990	1991	1992	1993
F	418.7	393.1	451.0	450.1	440.2	447.4	513.5	505.6	546.3	524.2
G	357.5	343.5	419.9	472.3	476.2	462.8	543.2	547.4	587.3	565.1

F: France
G: Germany

In theory, a return to a more 'feasible' configuration could certainly be achieved by closing unproductive plants or installations through natural selection dictated by the market. Unfortunately, the technology of integrated steel plants is not characterized solely by indivisibilities and high fixed costs; it is also highly labour intensive. Thus, even today, the impact of such closures on employment, which is also highly concentrated geographically, hardly allows us to rely entirely on such a drastic method of regulation since it is difficult for Member States' governments to reject appeals for help.

The Irresistible Rise of Electric Furnace Technology

First used in Italy, where there are no deposits of coal or iron ore, electric furnace technology was for a long time the 'poor cousin' of the pig-iron technique. Since it obviates the need to invest in a blast furnace and coke oven, this method of producing crude steel could be used in small production units (mini steel plants), often with a capacity of less than 200 000 tonnes/year, but only the simplest final products could be made (reinforcing bars, light and medium sections). Built in Italy on the outskirts of large cities, these numerous mini steel plants (whose investment cost towards the end of the 1970s was US$500-700 per tonne of capacity, three times cheaper than investment in an integrated oxygen plant) were operated as family businesses and during the period 1950-70 became a sort of 'hypermarket' for the simplest products, which were used practically *in situ*. Some of them, however, although still managed informally, were absorbed in the 1970s into larger financial conglomerates (such as the Riva group, whose annual total production soon exceeded 3.5 million tonnes) that were capable of extending their geographical customer base and branching into exports.

Electric furnace technology spread rapidly in the newly industrialized countries and in the developing countries as well as in many industrialized countries. In the United States it rapidly carved out a substantial market share because of the lack of competitiveness and the obsolescence of the large, integrated plants. Since the beginning of the 1990s, with a production capacity of 25 million tonnes, the sixty or so mini steel plants have accounted for more than 30 per cent of the supply of steel in the United States. Some of them, such as Nucor (4 million tonnes), North Star Steel (2.8 million tonnes) and North Western Steel and Wire (2.4 million tonnes), are regarded as increasingly dangerous competitors for traditional steel plants. In addition to their low construction cost (currently some US$200-300 per tonne of capacity) for plant sizes much larger than in the past (the plants being built now are capable of producing over 1 million tonnes/year), these mini-plants have three advantages over traditional technology: (a) labour costs are 40-50 per cent lower (in 1990 US $ 50 per tonne produced compared with US$125 for a traditional steel plant); (b) lower maintenance and modernization costs (50-100 per cent lower than for large, integrated steel plants); (c) high degree of flexibility, which since 1987 has enabled them to continue to run on average at over 80 per cent of capacity. Even though, in the sector for the simplest long products, the growth in the sales of mini steel plants has now slowed considerably, some of them, such as Nucor, have begun to compete with oxygen plants in what was until the end of the 1980s the latter's special preserve, namely flat products, thanks to combined use of electric furnace and thin-slab casting technology, which makes it possible to dispense with hot rolling.

Europe is well on the way to adopting this new technology. Thus, after installing its first electric furnace, Arbed plans to construct a second and will very shortly be shutting down its last blast furnace. The restructuring of the Spanish group CSI is planned along similar lines. It is thought that Usinor and Thyssen are also ready to go down this road following their joint research into this process. For them, the move to the industrial phase would simply be a question of strategic choice. According to the German SMS, which constructs Nucor's thin-slab plants, there are today some 200 such projects throughout the world.

In the opinion of a number of experts, the arrival of this new technological combination should benefit existing steel plants rather than new competitors in view of the relatively high investment cost for mini steel plants which are not part of a large group. However, its spread would depend on the solution found to the problem of the supply of scrap iron, whose price is one of the essential components of the cost price of products manufactured using electric furnaces. The often erratic movement in the price of scrap iron is a barrier to its widespread use. The market for scrap iron operates on a day-to-day basis, with contracts being negotiated more often than not on a monthly basis, whereas steel producers tend to conclude annual contracts with their customers (the car industry, for example). The price of scrap iron can, therefore, fluctuate considerably. Thus, between November / December 1992 and February / March 1993, it rose by almost 60 per cent because of increased demand from the countries in the Middle East and Far East, which obtain some of their supplies on foreign markets, and in particular Europe (recently, Italy actually requested the Community authorities to set export quotas for scrap iron on the basis of Article 59 of the ECSC Treaty).

Table 5.2: Production of crude steel by method of production (m.tonnes)

1990	Classic process	Electric arc furnace
EC of which	94,355	42,498
Belgium	10,374	1,041
France	13,614	5,401
Germany	31,328	7,106
Italy	11,200	14,310
Luxembourg	3,560	-
Netherlands	5,180	232
Portugal	337	409
Spain	5,593	7,342
United Kingdom	13,169	4,672
Greece	-	1,050
Ireland	-	326
Denmark	-	610
Other PECO	14,515	9,008
Turkey	3,762	4,955
United States	53,028	32,701
Japan	75,640	34,691
ex Soviet Union	54,365	20,130
Brazil	15,214	4,896
Australia	6,134	532
South Africa	5,473	3,034
India	6,173	4,114
South Korea	15,937	7,188
Taiwan	5,627	4,042

Source: IISI

In the United States too, where it is thought that flat products could be the source of substantial earnings for mini thin-slab steel plants, future users of scrap iron will be faced with major difficulties in managing supplies and a number of firms are already starting to introduce recycling-and-return programmes for new scrap obtained from their customers.

II. FIFTEEN YEARS OF COMMUNITY INTERVENTION IN THE STEEL INDUSTRY (1980-94)

The key role played by the Community authorities in restructuring and modernizing this sector of activity cannot be understood and assessed without a brief look at the doctrinal bases which inspired the fathers of the ECSC Treaty and at its main provisions. Shaped by political and geostrategic factors, these provisions were also strongly influenced by a purposive philosophy of economic action that was merely confirmed by the teachings of the Keynesian model, which had largely held sway until the early 1980s. It is not surprising, therefore, that the Community authorities were heavily involved in the 'management' of the steel industry when the persistent imbalance between supply and demand was judged to be intolerable towards the end of the 1970s. Since the beginning of the 1990s, however, there has been a much clearer shift towards a form of regulation where market forces are supposed to play a key role. The Community authorities' stated objective of treating the steel industry like any other economic sector is explained by the spread of liberal ideas but also by the changing structures in the steel industry and by the application of technologies that are much more conducive to market-based regulation. The chronic excess of production capacity in the steel industry also prompted the Community authorities to pay particular attention to the regulation of trade in these products with countries outside the Community.

The interventionist philosophy of the ECSC Treaty[4]

The provisions of the ECSC Treaty were, of course, heavily influenced by the acknowledged special features of the steel industry and by the lessons that could be drawn from its historical development. At the time the Treaty was adopted, it seemed accepted wisdom that the self-regulation mechanisms, justifiably regarded as one of the features of the superiority of the free-enterprise system over any other form of economic organization, were operating in a far from satisfactory manner in a sector such as the steel industry. The history of the European market for the

---

4 For an interesting survey of the history of the steel industry and of the foundations of ECSC Treaty, see Rieben, H. (1954): *Des ententes des maitres de forges au plan Schuman*, Ambily, Les Presses de Savoie.

products concerned showed that this sector was at all times prey to two dangers. With adherence to an unadulterated *laissez-faire* approach there was a risk of cut-throat competition, while suppliers might also seek to avert this risk by organizing a market cartel.

In the first case, as the former minister A. Phillip[5] noted at the time, *laissez-faire* would lead to total price chaos, plant closures and perhaps an economic crisis similar to that of 1929. In the second case, it is the very efficiency of the market that would be affected since any cartel would inevitably result in prices being set too high and production levels too low. In the view of the promoters of the ECSC Treaty, only a supranational organization capable of coordinating the trade would be able to lead the steel industry towards a situation of equilibrium that accorded with optimization of economic welfare by achieving three objectives: (a) harmonization of individual interests, (b) promotion of technical progress, and (c) organization, by way of an anti-cyclical policy, of effective measures to combat the particularly harmful effects of cyclical fluctuations on such a sector.

Thus, the ambition of the founding fathers of the ECSC Treaty was to take advantage of supranational interventionism in order to channel, if necessary, national and individual self-interest, while at the same time not forgoing the benefits of competition. Article 2(2) of the Treaty makes this absolutely clear: 'The Community shall progressively bring about conditions which will of themselves ensure the most rational distribution of production at the highest possible level of productivity, while safeguarding continuity of employment and taking care not to provoke fundamental and persistent disturbances in the economies of Member States'. By advocating the development of semi-automatic functioning, the Schuman plan showed its intention of creating a form of intervention capable of combining freedom and authority in a judicious balance. The provisions of the Treaty are a perfect reflection of this twofold objective.

1. The option of establishing a system of production quotas in the event of a manifest crisis (Article 58(1)), accompanied if necessary by the fixing of minimum prices within the common market (Article 61(b)), constitutes one of the provisions which most clearly highlights this desire to intervene in market regulation within a general framework of surveillance based on information which firms were required to supply, the aim being to ensure better transparency of the conditions prevailing on the markets concerned. As with what was later to be

5 French O.J. 26 July 1950 no. 90 A.N., p 5939.

French indicative planning (in terms of value), the High Authority was also required to draw up programmes indicating foreseeable developments in production, consumption, exports and imports, these being akin to generalized market surveys intended to act as a guide for firms in making their strategic choices. Such studies were also supposed to fulfil the stated ambition of creating conditions for ensuring the semi-automatic functioning of the steel market by long-term planning of manufacture (Article 46(3)) and the possibility of monitoring the expansion of productive capacity, an important element in the range of interventionist instruments available to the High Authority. Even though every investment programme had to be notified to it for an opinion, the implications of this provision could seem limited since, in the event of an unfavourable opinion, the operation could still be carried out where it was financed from the firm's own capital, i.e. without any subsidies or aid.

2. Competition was, for its part, safeguarded by way of provisions customarily adopted by most of the countries which applied competition rules at that time: prohibition of discriminatory practices, predatory strategies aimed at acquiring a monopoly position (Article 60) and agreements tending directly or indirectly to prevent, restrict or distort normal competition (Article 65). When the Treaty was drawn up, control of concentrations (Article 66) was one of the most innovative measures in its competition armoury in terms of both the general philosophy of the text and its practical arrangements. Most industrialized countries (apart from the United States) had not reached such an advanced stage in the monitoring of the competition process. At the time, the prior authorization mechanism, which required *ex ante* notification of merger plans, represented a genuine innovation which would be introduced into US law only 25 years later. It is also worth noting that Article 66(2) seemed to opt at that early stage for the adoption of what would be described today as a 'competition assessment' of the planned transaction. The assessment carried out by the High Authority seemed to deal only with the planned transaction's expected effects on competition in the relevant market, with scant attention being paid to considerations of its impact on economic progress.

Lastly, the provisions of the ECSC Treaty even took into account the impact of the effects of wage differentials on the prices of steel products. Thus, pursuant to Article 68(1), the High Authority was entitled to make recommendations where prices which it considered to be 'abnormally low' were the result of wages set by certain firms or certain government decisions at abnormally low levels compared with the wage level in the same area.

Substantial Involvement by the Community Authorities (1980-88)

At the beginning of the 1980s, the effects of the recession on the world steel market were felt all the more strongly since production capacity had increased sharply in the euphoric climate of the first thirty years of the post-war period. At the time, there were three possible scenarios for the European steel industry: (a) its virtual disappearance in the long run, which would deprive the Community of one of the strategic links in a production system creating high value-added products; (b) even fiercer competition between European suppliers in the wake of massive intervention by the Member States; and (c) a private cartel system organized between the main operators, with the resulting increases in the price of steel permanently penalizing steel users.

Thus, given the very special features of the European market, Community intervention was inevitable and indispensable. Faithful to the principles which had governed the drafting of the ECSC Treaty, the Community authorities have therefore endeavoured over the last fifteen years to develop an original policy, albeit one difficult to apply, consisting in preserving some freedom of initiative for the players within a tighter overall framework. The clearly stated objective was a gradual move - dictated by the need to take account of the social cost involved - towards reducing and modernizing production capacity. However, while the fundamental rationality of such a project could not be challenged, nobody could claim that the objectives would be easily achieved.

How could the authorities obtain the full support of firms whose financial situations and market positions at the time were very different, some were facing structural deficits, while others were able to cover their production costs more fully? How could certain Member States be convinced not to rush systematically to the assistance of their national steel industry, being as it was a symbol of industrial might but also the provider of many jobs concentrated in certain geographical areas? How could such modernization and restructuring be accomplished smoothly if the undertakings involved did not have sufficient financing capacity or equity capital? Towards the end of the 1970s, a period still very much marked by the optimism in which Western economies had indulged for thirty glorious years, painful surgical measures were scarcely being advocated by many politicians and economic decision-makers. As in the past, the recession affecting the European steel industry was often still regarded as being temporary; the recovery was supposed to arrive as part of a trend which some people still considered favourable to demand growth. The Community authorities, therefore, were obliged to act tactfully and to vary their tactics by combining persuasion, incentives and more authoritarian intervention. However, since the objectives of restructuring and modernization could be achieved only if the main suppliers had sufficient finance available, action had to be taken to restore cash flow while allowing intervention by Member States, intervention that was clearly indispensable in view of the necessary financing requirements. And so, it is with this in mind that the two main facets of Community intervention during the first half of the 1980s need to be analysed: the introduction of a quota system and the adoption of a special Code for State aid to the steel industry.

Noting that the average capacity utilization rate of Community steel firms had declined to below 60 per cent and that prices had fallen by 13 per cent during the first few months of 1980 while production costs had risen by 5 per cent, the Commission declared a 'manifest crisis' in accordance with Article 58 of the ECSC Treaty and imposed a system of quarterly quotas on firms. This 'public cartelization' of the Community steel market was supposed to operate in the same way as a private cartel in that various rules ensured adherence to the market shares fixed: checks on the veracity of information notified, system of fines for firms exceeding their quotas, tightening of compliance with the requirement to publish price lists and conditions of sale in order to avoid any free-rider phenomena. Initially intended to cover a limited period ending on 30 June 1981 (ECSC Decision No.2794/80 of 31 October 1980), the quota system was renewed and extended to a wider range of products (Decisions Nos 1831/81 of 24 June 1981, 2804/81 of 23 September 1981, 2177/83 of 28 October 1983, 234/84 of 31 August 1984, etc.).

Given the scale and duration of the crisis, this quota system was even accompanied, with effect from December 1983, by measures to fix minimum prices since the tariffs for some steel products no longer corresponded to the guide prices published by the Commission. These minimum prices prohibited any discounts (except for activity discounts for steel stockholders published in the price lists) and took account of exchange-rate fluctuations in order to maintain a uniform price level in the common market.

Although these measures made a real contribution to the recovery in prices and margins of Community steel firms, they were still insufficient to ensure the balanced financing of the planned restructuring operations.

With an injection of public funds being inevitable, there was therefore a need to monitor this type of aid since subsidies or aid granted by the Member States had until then been prohibited by Article 4(c) of the ECSC Treaty. The Steel Aid Code adopted by Decision No 2320/81/ECSC allowed the binding Treaty provisions to be sidestepped provided that 'systematic and specific' restructuring plans financed by contributions from the Member States were accompanied by reductions in production capacity. However, this access by steel firms to public financing was authorized for only a limited period (until the end of 1985). At the same time, and so as to allow more rapid removal of the constraints on the development of new economic activities in certain zones adversely affected by the restructuring of the steel industry, an amendment to Regulation (EEC) No. 2616/80 instituting a Community regional development measure adjusted the arrangements for the specific measures to be taken in certain specified areas.

Admittedly, the package of measures adopted for these two main aspects of Community policy between 1981 and 1985 gave rise to many problems of practical application given the cumbersome and complex nature of some of the provisions and in view of the objections raised by some of the firms concerned. It is true that the obligation on the High Authority to determine quotas 'on an equitable basis' (Article 58(2)) was bound to pose serious problems of interpretation. What should be the equitable reference basis for calculating the quotas for each firm involved: the level of production achieved during a particular reference period or the actual level of production capacity? The Community authorities were criticized for deciding to base their method of calculation on the first criterion and for increasing the reference production of firms which, during the period under consideration, had recorded an average rate of capacity utilization at least 10 per cent below the average rate of utilization of the same plant by other Community firms during the same period. A number of operators took the view that the authorities should have made a greater effort to take into account the actual level of production capacity when quotas were introduced, and it is no doubt true that the provisions adopted have had the effect of protecting more particularly those firms that were the least well placed from a competitive angle.[6] The Commission was also criticized for not having taken account of the effects of subsidies granted to certain firms by their national authorities. In the opinion of some operators, it should have allocated higher quotas to firms not in

6 Even though we cannot ignore the fact that the Community authorities had none the less attempted to ensure that the quota system did not jeopardize the effects of the restructuring carried through successfully by some of the firms concerned.

receipt of subsidies or, better still, should have reduced the production quotas of subsidized firms. When challenged before the Court of Justice, the system devised by the Commission was none the less judged to be in conformity with the Treaty. The Court held that the system of allocating quotas was consistent with the objective of spreading in the most equitable manner possible the reductions required by the economic situation and that the aim of Article 58 was not to guarantee undertakings a minimum level of employment proportionate to their capacity (Case 119/81 Klöckner Werke v Commission [1982] ECR, at 2650, paragraph 13). The second ground referred to was also rejected because Article 58 of the ECSC Treaty could not be relied on in the matter of subsidies granted to the steel industry in certain Member States.

Of course, it is difficult to establish the exact scope of this first wave of measures adopted mainly between 1980 and 1986 and to give them full credit for having achieved substantial reductions in production capacities for steel products. The objective in 1982 was to achieve, in an initial stage, a reduction of 30-35 million tonnes of hot-rolling capacity. The actual reduction by the beginning of 1986 was 32 million tonnes and there is no doubt that the constant pressure exerted by the Commission on the Member States, together with the above measures, played a decisive role in this first success, which was doubtless insufficient since it had been established from the outset that the aggregate surplus capacity was in the region of 50 million tonnes but which represented a very creditable achievement in view of the political and social obstacles prevailing at the time (Soenens).[7] On the other hand, many operators had striven during this period to rationalize their production and distribution operations (e.g. strengthening of distribution networks at British Steel; rationalization of activities at Cockerill-Sambre and Usinor-Sacilor as part of their respective concentration programmes).

After a brief period of euphoria linked to the upturn in world demand in 1988 and 1989, which enabled Community operators to return to profit levels not seen since 1974 and therefore made it possible to dismantle the quota system (in January 1988 for wire rod and merchant bars, then in June for flat products, heavy plate and beams), new difficulties began to emerge in 1990.

There are a number of reasons for the new crisis in the European steel industry. Alongside a further reduction in demand, there has been a sharp rise in world supply over the last ten years, in particular because of the construction of new production capacity in the newly industrialized

---

7 For an analysis of the policy pursued during the 1980s, see F.S. Benyon; P. Genevaz; G. Klepper; A. Remy; G. Vanderseypen.

countries and the developing countries. The position of Community producers, who still had extremely high excess capacity at the end of the 1980s, has been further exacerbated by four new phenomena: (a) growing protectionism in the United States, a major traditional customer of European steel producers; (b) the inflow of steel from the countries of Eastern Europe; (c) excess production capacity in Spain; and (d) the problem of restructuring the steel industry in the former East Germany (in particular Eko Stahl).

A New Policy More Closely Based on Control of Aid and Market Forces

The collapse of steel prices on the Community market (30 per cent fall between 1990 and 1992) prompted the Community authorities to take a fresh interest in the difficulties of the European steel industry. However, their margin of manoeuvre had narrowed considerably for both internal and external reasons. As a result, the introduction of a system of production quotas, although called for by some operators, was neither desirable nor likely.

First, even though the steel industry was regarded as having special structural features, it could hardly be exempted from the deliberately liberal stance of the Community's economic policy. Second, the introduction of quotas would have met with uncompromising opposition from a number of Member States and from those firms which had made the effort to undertake fundamental restructuring. A much more conciliatory attitude than previously towards aid from Member States was also necessary in view of the hardening of the US position on steel imports from third countries since the price of such steel could be regarded as being artificially reduced by similar aid. Lastly, closure of the European steel market to products from the countries of Eastern Europe was inconceivable, if only for geostrategic reasons.

The new strategy adopted by the Community authorities was to make European operators face up to their responsibilities while offering them appropriate incentives to undertake further restructuring. The indispensable review carried out by F. Braun in cooperation with the main operators came to the conclusion that excess production capacities amounted to more than 30 million tonnes for crude steel (and to 19-26 million tonnes for hot-rolled products). In addition to the completed or highly probable capacity closures estimated at 8.5 million tonnes for crude steel and 6.6 million tonnes for hot-rolled steel, it was felt at the time that a substantial effort still had to be made (17.3 million tonnes of capacity reductions for crude steel and 11.3 million tonnes for hot-rolled products). The cost of such restructuring was put at ECU 6 billion (ECU 2.5 billion in the form of social aid, the remainder serving to finance the industrial costs of reducing capacity).

Table 5.3: Commission proposal concerning aid to be granted to six undertakings required to reduce their production capacities in the hot-rolled sector.

Firm	Total amount of aid (ECU million)	Capacity reductions (millions of tonnes)	Amount of aid per tonne (ECU)
CSI(1)	2,816.8	2.300	1,225
Sidenor	515.0	0.439	1,173
Sew Freital	140.0	0.160	875
Eko-Stahl (2)	427.9	0.462	926
Ilva (3)	2,585.0	2.000	1,292
Siderurgica Nacional	306.9	0.140	2,188

Notes

(1) Further requirements : CSI withdrawal from Sestao plant. Closure of the hot-rolling mill at Ansio. Financial charges not to fall below those of competitors.

(2) Further requirement: aid must not represent more than 3,5 per cent of turnover in financial charges.

(3) Further requirements: repayment of part of the aid if privatization brings in sums higher than forecast. Financial charges of the firms taking over from Ilva must not be lower than those of competitors.

Source : European Commission.

Additional Community aid in support of social measures accompanied a more original financing method devised by producers, who would bear the cost of these capacity reductions. The Community authorities also agreed to the creation of three economic interest groupings to facilitate the closure of 10.5 million tonnes of capacity (6 million tonnes of flat products, 2 million tonnes of plate, and 2.5 million tonnes of heavy sections). The financial mechanism, which was funded by operators who did not reduce their capacity, was supposed to be supplemented by ECSC loans of ECU 1 billion that would be subsequently repaid by restoring profit margins following the reductions in supply. In a bid to avert any possible slide towards a future private cartelization of the steel market, the Commission made its agreement conditional on a ban on exchanges of information (or unilateral statements) by those taking part in this financing pool regarding prices, capacity utilization rates and production levels (Decision of 21 December 1993).

The hoped-for implementation of this plan by the end of 1993 had to be postponed, however, because it proved impossible to reach agreement in three cases relating to applications for state aid in connection with restructuring in the Spanish (SIDENOR and CSI groups), Italian (Ilva) and former East German (Eko Stahl) steel industries. Under the new steel aid code (Decision No. 3855/91/ECSC of 27 December 1991), the only social aid allowed is aid likely to promote a potential plant closure and aid for financing the permanent cessation of all activities of the least competitive firms. Any other form of operating or investment aid is prohibited. Lastly, any intervention whatsoever by the Member States in the capital of public or private firms (acquisition of shareholdings, injection of capital, reduced-interest loans, etc.) must be subject to Community monitoring and is acceptable only in so far as the Member State is behaving as a private investor wishing to protect his capital. The planned projects (totalling just under FF50 billion), which derogated completely from these rules, were therefore bound to be challenged by the unsubsidized firms, their main criticism being the insufficient capacity reductions planned in exchange for the aid requested. The anger of unsubsidized suppliers was also aroused by the announcement of projects to bail out, with the aid of funds from certain German Länder, companies such as Klöckner and Saarstahl, whose policy of knock-down prices is hardly welcomed by their competitors.[8] Showing great patience the European authorities had twice accepted a postponement of the deadline in order to let the producers finalize the targeted cutbacks in capacities. But, at the end of October 1994, they were led to give up the restructuring plan, only 11 million out of the 19 million tonnes of capacity cuts demanded in hot rolling having been reached. This failure was not surprising. It is often observed that in a line of business such as steel, the good resolutions disappear as soon as the producers 'smell' a positive reversal of the demand. The feeling that 1994 would be the beginning of a steady market recovery sounded the knell for the last step of the restructuring plan. Therefore, the 'accompanying measures' (social aids, quarterly production guidelines) have been given up.

Difficult Regulation of Trade in Steel Products with Certain Third Countries

The various measures adopted within the Community to reduce excess production capacity were bound to affect trade flows between the Community and third countries. The desired price rises (achieved in certain years) on the Community market were, in the first place, to whet

---

8 Following the abortive sale to Riva, the Treuhandanstalt covered Eko Stahl's losses (DM15.6 million) and guaranteed its borrowing. The Commission threatened to oppose the purchase of the German firm by Cockerill-Sambre if the level of state aid was not reduced.

the appetites of foreign exporters. Moreover, the acceptance, on certain conditions, of aid for restructuring provided by the Member States to their firms in difficulties was bound to trigger retaliatory measures by countries, such as the United States, that were structural importers. Like most other industrialized countries, the Community has adopted rules allowing it, in accordance with its international commitments, to intervene to provide effective protection for its steel firms in the event of foreign exporters adopting unfair practices. The Community Anti-dumping Regulation (EEC) No. 2423/88[9] is thus one of the classic instruments available to the Community without derogating from the GATT agreements.

Even though the Community has not failed to use this instrument during the past fifteen years, it has not used it too systematically, preferring, it seems, to negotiate with the foreign firms concerned or with their governments. Embroiled for many years in a more or less simmering conflict with US producers, the concern of Community steel firms has also increased since the political changes in Central and Eastern Europe. Politically and economically desirable, the opening-up to steel products from eastern Europe to the European Economic Area can become a reality only on condition that the countries in transition to a market economy make an effort to reduce their vast excess production capacity, but also that the United States does not substantially reduce access to its territory for Community steel products.

Legal Instruments Protecting the Community Steel Market

Article 74 of the ECSC Treaty empowered the European authorities to take protective measures against products that were being dumped or where some of the products were imported in 'relatively increased quantities and under such conditions that these imports caused or threatened to cause serious injury to production within the common market of like or directly competing products'.

The structural characteristics of the global steel industry (substantial excess production capacity, large proportion of production supplied for many years by state-trading countries which are now in transition to the market economy) was bound to encourage Community producers to refer cases to the Commission on the basis of the anti-dumping Regulation. According to a study published by the European Parliament, some 14 per cent of proceedings initiated by the Commission between 1981 and 1991

[9] Supplementing and strengthening Regulations (EEC) Nos 2176/84 (OJ No. L 201, 30.7.84) and 1761/87 (OJ No. L 167, 26.6.87).

concerned the steel sector, which was in third place in the order of sectors concerned by anti-dumping procedures (and in second place position in 1986 and 1991). Analysis of complaints filed with the competition authorities reveals that as soon as the existence of a manifest crisis was declared, foreign exporters were criticized more for selling their products at prices below those of Community producers than for having offered them at prices below those on their domestic markets.

> The complaint alleges furthermore that the prices at which these imports (iron or steel coils) are being sold in the Community are significantly below the price level which would permit the Community producers to cover their costs, forcing them either to lose sales or to reduce prices to levels competitive with those of the imported products. ... This undercutting prevents the European producers from obtaining even the basic price and jeopardizes the equilibrium of the whole price system, both in so far as it concerns the European producers and the producers in those other supplying countries which have concluded arrangements with respect to trade in steel products. (Complaint against producers of steel plate in Canada and Latin America, OJ No. C 304 of 20 November 1982).

This analysis also reveals that, in the absence of sufficiently reliable references concerning the prices charged on exporters' domestic markets, recourse to the solution of 'constructed value' has often been judged necessary and, hence, it has often proved difficult to calculate dumping margins. In the steel sector, it is not all that easy to demonstrate beyond all doubt that an 'export price to the Community is less than the normal value of the like product' (Article 2 of Regulation (EEC) No. 2423/88). If the solution which consists in referring to the price actually paid (or to pay) during normal transactions for the like product intended for consumption in the country of export or of origin is the most in keeping with the spirit of the provisions of the Anti-dumping Regulations, experience shows that it is not often possible to refer to such a price. Failing other similar solutions (e.g. representative export prices to a third country, prices set or costs incurred by other producers in the country of origin), the competition authorities then have to rely on the results of a very delicate exercise, namely the calculation of a 'constructed value, determined by adding cost of production and a reasonable margin of profit' (Article 2(b)(ii) of Regulation (EEC) No. 2423/88). The difficulty of such a procedure may then be illustrated by analysing the recitals of Regulation (EEC) No. 3296/92 imposing a provisional anti-dumping duty on imports of certain seamless pipes and tubes, of iron or non-alloy steel, originating in a number of countries of Eastern Europe.[10]

At the time the procedure was initiated (end of 1991), these countries could not be considered as being subject to market forces and normal values of the products concerned had to be established in a country with a market economy. The cost and wage structures of countries such as Austria, Finland, Japan, Norway and Sweden (whose markets for the products in question were judged to be representative) proved too different from those of the countries concerned by the procedure to be reasonably used as the basis for a calculation of a constructed value. Despite the similarity between the manufacturing processes, the scale of production and the low labour and energy costs, Brazil too was rejected as a reference because of the distorting effects of its high rate of inflation. The Commission then sought to use as a basis the prices actually paid (or to be paid) in the Community for like products, adjusted to include a 'reasonable' margin of profit (most Community producers were selling at a loss). However, it had to abandon such a reference basis since it would have meant highlighting excessive dumping margins for the exporting countries in question. Thus, the initial proposal from the appellant firms was taken up again; the normal values of the product concerned could be established for the four countries on the basis of prices observed on the domestic market of Croatia!

Lastly, analysis of Community case-law on the application of the Anti-dumping Regulation reveals that in many cases the introduction of provisional duties rapidly prompted the foreign firms concerned to give undertakings to the EC on quantities and prices. Thus, from 1978, and more particularly during the period when the Community steel industry was declared to be in a state of manifest crisis, foreign exporters were generally offered the possibility of submitting to a general monitoring system under which they agreed to comply with certain 'basis' prices established by reference to production costs of the most efficient firms operating under normal market conditions (these 'basis' prices could also be used as a benchmark when fixing any anti-dumping duties). During the 1980s, wider-ranging trade agreements were negotiated between the Community and a large number of countries.[11] The objective of such arrangements is to better ensure equilibrium on the markets concerned thanks to 'quantitative restraints, a reasonable distribution of imports over time, by region and by product, and the observance of arrangement prices which are closely linked to the internal price regulations which bind the

---

[10] Hungary, Czechoslovakia, Poland, Republic of Croatia.

[11] The EFTA countries, Brazil, South Korea, and the countries of Central Europe (Hungary, Czechoslovakia, Poland, Bulgaria, Romania).

industry and steel merchants in the Community.' (OJ L No. 254 of 6 September 1986, p. 20).

Subject, therefore, to the 'triple clause' under which there has to be a balanced distribution of exports over the whole year, the whole range of products and between the different countries of the common market, it seems that the degree to which the quantitative arrangements are binding has varied from year to year. Thus, for a number of years they have not been fully utilized. However, it is true that the undertakings obtained on prices had been negotiated at a sufficiently high level to stem the flow of exports to the Community. In exchange for these quantitative restrictions, the signatory countries to these bilateral agreements were offered a number of advantages such as the non-application of basis prices, the lifting of temporary anti-dumping measures, the possibility of setting their prices at levels slightly above those of Community producers (on average some 6 per cent and 4 per cent higher for certain types of steel according to Zhen Kun Wang and Winters (1993).

However, the undertakings given by foreign producers and accepted by the Commission have had to be closely monitored, leading even to the introduction of new provisional duties in the event of breach of agreements.[12] The risk of foreign exporters adopting free-riding practices was all the greater since gathering evidence for anti-dumping proceedings has always been a lengthy procedure and the information concerning actual flows of imports was not always accurate. It is hardly surprising, therefore, that the Commission recently learned the lessons of past experience and proposed an amendment to the regulations in order to allow complaints to be examined more rapidly (in less than a month) and temporary, then definitive duties to be imposed within 9 and 12-15 months respectively (Regulation (EC) No. 521/94 of 7 March 1994, OJ No. L 66 of 10 May 1994).

However, efficient application of these regulations and, more generally, measures intended to ensure a better balance between supply and demand on the steel market made it necessary to improve the information on trade flows between the Community and third countries. A recent Commission recommendation on a priori monitoring of imports of certain steel products (Recommendation No. 85/94/ECSC of 19 January 1994, OJ No. L 17 of 20 January 1994) has therefore been followed by a decision introducing a posteriori monitoring (Decision No. 176/94/ECSC of

[12] See, for example, Decisions Nos 229/882/ECSC, OJ No. L 23, 28.1.1988; 2131/88/ECSC, OJ No. L 188, 19.7.1988 on the infringement of undertakings by Yugoslavian exporters of iron or steel sheets and plates.

28 January 1994, OJ No. L 24 of 29 January 1994).[13]

III. DELICATE MANAGEMENT OF TRADE FLOWS WITH THE UNITED STATES AND THE COUNTRIES OF EASTERN EUROPE

Relations between European and US steel producers, which have been difficult since the early 1970s, have been marked by sudden increases in tension since 1992 as a result of both the effects of the recession and the loss of competitiveness of integrated US producers. Subject for several years to pressure from many competitive foreign producers, the major players on the US steel market have also lost considerable market shares (some 16 per cent according to certain studies) to domestic mini steel plants.

Trade relations between the Community and the United States are, as far as steel is concerned, governed by arrangements which prompted the Europeans to limit their exports.[14] Initially presented in the form of unilateral undertakings, the system became genuinely contractual from 1985. Intended to end in October 1989, it was to be extended by two and a half years. However, during the last two years, foreign producers (European, Japanese and others) have been subject to an intense campaign of complaints whose effects have already been clearly felt; the American Trade Department has not hesitated to impose provisional duties at often high rates.[15] Although it has lost almost 50 per cent of the proceedings initiated against European firms, US industrialists have on every occasion appealed against the decisions of the International Trade Commission and brought new proceedings[16] despite the protests of Community firms who strictly enforced their undertakings on voluntary export restrictions between 1982 and 1992 (during the last three years of that period, only 70 per cent of the quotas allocated were used). In addition, according to a

---

[13] Under the first text, the Member States are required to notify the Commission, within the first ten days of each month, of the tonnage and values (in ECU) for which import documents or licences were issued during the preceding month. The second text provides for notification of the imports registered during the last month but one preceding the month in question.

[14] Regulation (EEC) No. 2870/92, OJ No. L 307, 1.11.1982, as amended by Regulations (EEC) Nos 2190/83, and 2150/84, OJ No. L 202, 31.7.1984.

[15] Thus, in January 1993, these duties were on average 27% on sheet steel and other products imported from nineteen foreign countries (see Annex Table 5.1 for detailed figures).

[16] Between March and April 1992, fifteen anti-dumping complaints were lodged against imports of long products. Sixty-two investigations were opened in the United States (23 against the EC) in 1991-92. Conversely, the Commission has not opened any proceedings against the United States since 1989.

survey carried out by the ITC during the first quarter of 1993, the price variable was often not the decisive factor in the choice of US buyers for foreign products. European firms' success is explained rather by the acknowledged quality of their products. The survey also established that the prices of foreign products are often higher than those of US steel producers.

Since Europeans and Americans had not been able to conclude a sectoral agreement before 15 December 1993, the dispute could not be settled under the Uruguay Round. Today, the main stumbling block to the conclusion of a durable and multilateral agreement is more particularly the problem of aid to firms and the introduction of an 'anti-harassment' mechanism to filter anti-dumping complaints and eliminate very quickly those which are not well-founded. With regard to the first point, the Community knows that its trading partners will not accept its general steel aid code.[17] However, the compromise proposed on the basis of the Dunkel provisions authorizing aid for R&D, environmental protection and regional development seemed even in May of last year to have been rejected by the Americans. (On the other hand, their position would perhaps appear to be less entrenched with regard to social aid.)

The Community authorities have also had to make allowances in the architecture of their steel policy for the effects of the political changes in the countries of Central and Eastern Europe. The opening-up of the European economic area to steel products from the countries of the former socialist Eastern bloc is a political and economic necessity and the first tangible evidence was the signature of interim agreements providing for the gradual reduction of customs duties (which were low in any case) by 1996 and the immediate removal of quantitative restrictions on imports. However, the recession, which was to have a considerable effect on the world steel industry, and the existence in the countries of Eastern Europe of production capacity much higher than the local capacity for consumption was bound to encourage exporters in these countries to seek sharp increases in their sales to EC countries.

As revealed by the statistics on the issue of import licences for steel from the countries of Eastern Europe, it was becoming difficult for the Community authorities not to take measures to restrain the flow of steel

---

[17] So as not to provoke too strong a reaction from the United States following the decision by the Council of Ministers (Industry) to authorize the payment of more than ECU 50 billion in aid to a number of Community firms, the four countries concerned (Germany, Italy, Spain, Portugal) agreed to abide by voluntary restraints on their sales to the United States for three to five years, quantitative undertakings being reinforced by the acceptance of price thresholds.

products from that region.

The introduction of safeguard measures (provided for in the association agreements with the countries of Eastern Europe in the event of exceptional circumstances or in order to avoid developments adversely affecting the functioning of the common market) was also strongly called for by producers in Eurofer and by the ECSC Consultative Committee. After reiterating its concern that the implementation of interim association agreements would lead to an abrupt increase in the level of Community steel imports from the countries of Central and Eastern Europe under conditions incompatible with the rules of international trade (OJ No. C 197 of 26 July 1991; OJ No. C 80 of 31 March 1992, p. 2), the Consultative Committee stepped up pressure in a Resolution (steel imports from countries of Central and Eastern Europe (PECO), OJ No. C 121 of 1 May 1993[18]) which highlighted the need to organize *a priori* and *a posteriori* surveillance of imports of steel products into the Community (obtained in 1994 - see previous paragraph), to publish periodically updated import reference prices and to negotiate tariff quotas with the main producers in Central Europe.

Table 5.4: Licences granted by country (tonnes of crude steel)

	March 1991	March 1992
Germany	117,000	250,000
Italy	36,000	84,000
France	121,000	58,000
Benelux	7,000	20,000
Spain	13,000	24,000
Imports into Germany of welded tubes originating in Czechoslovakia increased by 420 per cent between the beginning of 1991 and 1992. Imports of welded pipes rose by 672 per cent (3125 tonnes to 23,000 tonnes).		
Exports of magnetic sheet originating in the countries of the CIS to the EC in 1991: 300,000 tonnes; in 1993: 900,000 tonnes.		

[18] The Committee observed that whereas Community steel consumption fell in 1992, steel imports from the five PECO countries rose from 2.2 million tonnes in 1991 to 3.3 million tonnes in 1992 (and those from the CIS rose from 1.1 to 1.4 million tonnes). It stated that these imports were one of the causes for the drop in prices for steel in the Community and, noting the closed US market, was concerned about the repercussions of these two phenomena on the European steel industry.

As early as 1992, therefore, Community authorities fixed import quotas for certain products[19] (Decision of 28 December 1992, OJ of 31 December 1992). Thus, in relation to the former Czechoslovakia, an arrangement was negotiated for 1993. In return for accepting an increase in its exports of only 20 per cent in relation to the 1991 figures, the EC terminated the proceedings initiated in respect of tubes and agreed not to introduce new anti-dumping measures. Apart from the particular case of exports to the new German Länder not subject to duties and quotas,[20] a global quota of 320,000 tonnes (including 200,000 tonnes of flat products) was to be granted in 1993 to the republics of the former Soviet Union, and increased by 3 per cent for 1994.[21] However, all these measures did not cause Community steel producers to let down their guard completely. Thus, in August 1994, Eurofer was about to bring a complaint against a number of Hungarian and Czech exporters, who were accused of selling their products with dumping margins of 35 per cent and 50 per cent, and of setting prices 40-50 per cent below those of Community producers (see *Metal Bulletin* of 4 August 1994, p. 21).

ASSESSMENT AND PROSPECTS

At first sight, the outcome of Community intervention in the steel sector may appear somewhat disappointing since, after more than fifteen years of repeated efforts, there is still considerable excess capacity. Does such an observation sound the death knell for sectoral interventionist policies? Should the matching of supply and demand have been deliberately left to the free interplay of market forces alone?

It seems reasonable, however, to answer these two questions in the negative even though those rejecting the need for any form of public intervention have grown in number in recent years. Indeed, for all that, the shift in Community policy in favour of solutions essentially based on free competition need not necessarily lead to a rejection of all forms of

---

[19] Coils, heavy plate, beams, wire rod. Quotas were set on an annual basis, the quantities allowed during the first four months could not exceed one third of the quota authorized and those for delivery during the first eight months could not exceed two thirds of the quota.

[20] See, for example, OJ No. L 32, 5.2.1994, p. 41.

[21] However, the fixing of quotas raised some problems. The United Kingdom, for its part, had advocated a global increase of 25% for 1994 whereas a number of Member States had preferred the status quo. Eurofer and the major European steel producers were particularly concerned that the Community authorities were going to negotiate with the Russian authorities a cooperation and partnership agreement that could transform the current quota system into a voluntary restraint agreement, which they thought would be ineffective. Accordingly, they are calling for a double control (export licence and import licence) and price monitoring.

intervention. First, at the internal level, Community industrial policy will no doubt have to move fundamentally towards the adoption of horizontal measures capable of creating the conditions for a technological environment conducive to the promotion of technical progress. The steel industry remains a sector where product innovation is continuous. Second, at the external level, the conditions that favour the organization of progressively more liberalized trade flows with the most industrialized countries (in particular the United States) and with the countries of Eastern Europe and the developing countries have yet to be established.

Greater Consistency Between Industrial Policy and Competition Policy

In view of its special structural features, the steel industry is the prime example of an economic activity in which a policy of non-intervention would have been inconceivable given the politically unacceptable social cost that would have resulted if reliance had been placed exclusively on market forces.

If industrial policy has to be regarded as essentially a supply-side policy (De Bandt, 1993), then Community intervention in the steel industry is indeed the result of such a policy and cannot be considered to be at odds with competition policy. As Schumpeter himself stressed, the phenomenon of creative destruction, which lies at the very heart of the competitive process, does not mean that adaptation costs cannot be smoothed out. The Court of Justice has aptly recalled on several occasions that the principle of free trade should not be regarded as being absolute but may be subject to certain restrictions justified by the objectives pursued in the general interest by the Community.[22] A number of the operators who today sometimes sharply criticize current Community policy too often in the past feigned ignorance of the fact that they would no longer participate in this sector of activity if the restructuring policy pursued by the Commission since the end of the 1970s had put an end to all forms of subsidy or equity participation in

---

22 In its first annual report on competition policy, the Commission had also clearly stated its philosophy: 'Even though the operation of market forces is an irreplaceable factor for progress and the most appropriate means of ensuring the best possible distribution of production factors, situations can nevertheless arise when this in itself is not enough to obtain the required results without too much delay and intolerable social tension. When the decisions of the enterprises themselves do not make it possible for the necessary changes to be made at an acceptable cost in social terms, then recourse to relatively short-term and limited intervention is necessary in order to direct such decisions towards an optimal economic and social result.'

firms in difficulties.

Adjustments to supply and demand are one of the tasks that market forces are supposed to fulfil best. However, it is true that the competitive process often produces its beneficial effects only in the long run. Adjustment processes are by no means immediate where excess production capacities are the result of firms whose technological processes are characterized by relatively substantial indivisibilities. In this case, capacity reductions are piecemeal rather than incremental and are often accompanied in the short run by negative effects on employment that are judged to be politically unacceptable. Thus, granting aid for restructuring and retraining is justified as a means of alleviating the pain of the process of creative destruction which drives the long-term functioning of markets. It is therefore as part of this philosophy of public intervention that the Commission intended to establish its role of referee anxious to give formal recognition to the efforts by national authorities to contribute to the reorganization of certain industrial sectors and the minimization of the social cost, but also to prevent the change in the natural flows of intra-Community trade from being too noticeable.

Thus, in order to be credited with positive effects and qualify under Article 92(3), aid for restructuring must be reflected by substantial reductions in the production capacities of firms receiving aid. In the Commission's own words: 'in restoring the viability of the undertakings, the aid should not preserve the status quo or postpone decisions or changes which are inevitable' (Decision concerning aid provided by France to certain primary processing steel undertakings, OJ No. L 47 of 23 February 1990, p. 33). In addition, the reduction must, first, have been the result of a voluntary decision by the firm concerned and not the direct and immediate consequence of the fall in demand and, second, the reduction in capacity must be irreversible. Lastly, over the years the Commission has endeavoured to establish more fully that aid is strictly proportional to the effort made and to the requirements arising from the retraining and employment protection measures provided for in the restructuring plan.[23]

Taking a firmer stance on state aid, the competition authorities should, therefore, first press ahead with developing a constructive policy towards

[23] Thus, it has refused to approve certain 'bridging costs' incurred in respect of the wages of the employees covered by the various social measures and calculated between the time when the social plan was adopted and the time when it actually entered into force. It was impossible to check whether the employees concerned did or did not during that period contribute to the productive activity of the undertaking. Contributing to the cost of such wages would have entailed the risk of covering the operating costs of such undertakings through state aid (OJ No. L 47, 23.2.1990, p. 34).

cooperation projects whose effects are clearly beneficial to the promotion of economic efficiency. They have recently approved a number of important specialization and joint selling agreements: specialization between ARBED and Cockerill Sambre (1984) and between ARBED and Unimétal (1991) in long products; joint selling of beams by ARBED and Usinor (1991), concentration between these two firms of certain production and distribution activities involving these products (1993), identical agreement between Ensidesa and Aristrain (1993), etc.

Second, in so far as it will become less and less frequent for capacity reductions to be achieved through state aid, it is clear that the process of concentration between operators on the market will have to be speeded up[24] since the actual economies of scale in the sector require plants to operate at levels close to their optimal levels of capacity. However, it is not evident that the Community Merger Control Regulation and the accompanying 'competition assessment' technique promote regroupings of firms on what is already an oligopolistic market. The recent 'Mannesmann/Vallourec/Ilva' case of concentration on the market for seamless stainless steel tubes is a perfect example of the difficulty that sometimes arises when the long-term objectives of industrial policy have to be reconciled with those of competition policy, which, in the case of concentrations, seeks to oppose regroupings likely to create or to strengthen dominant positions on the relevant market. Even though, in this case, the Commission gave the go-ahead for the planned joint venture between the three firms in question at just the right time, the final decision threatened to be a negative one. A majority of the Advisory Committee on Concentrations had, in fact, voted against the plan, and the favourable decision was carried with a very small majority within the Commission. It is true that the creation of this concentrative joint venture was such as to alter considerably the conditions of supply on the relevant market. With a share of the Community market estimated at 36 per cent, the new entity was to be faced with only one other operator of similar size (Sandvik with a market share of 33 per cent), the remaining demand being shared between a number of smaller firms the largest of which held only 13 per cent of the market. This was, therefore, an identical problem to that in the Nestlé-Perrier case, i.e. there was a risk of creating a joint dominant position between the two leading operators which apparently loomed especially large as the price-elasticity of demand on the market is low, the

---

24 In its Resolution 92/C 161/03, the ECSC Consultative Committee took the view that industrial regroupings should be facilitated and encouraged since concentration levels in the steel industry remain lower than those of its international competitors, the main industrial sectors with which it has to compete, and its customers.

products are very homogeneous, there is a high degree of price transparency and, so it would appear, none of the groups concerned 'would enjoy a significant structural cost advantage to offset the substantial gains that would result from engaging in anti-competitive parallel behaviour' (see above Decision, paragraph 79). And so, it was by taking account of a sufficient degree of 'contestability' on the market, if not at the time then at least in the near future, that a positive decision was finally taken.[25] Indeed, a substantial increase in prices on the Community market would be likely to accelerate the entry of competitors from Japan and the countries of Eastern Europe.

This case is therefore fully representative of the problems which may arise in the years ahead on the markets for crude steel and for the more elaborate products manufactured using crude steel. On markets with the above structural features, the risks of collusion or concerted policies are very real. For all that, should an attempt be made to eliminate these risks by way of structural intervention designed to restrict concentrations, at the risk of delaying the necessary supply-side adaptations? Would it not be better to promote efficiency and encourage regroupings by using a method of analysis based more on an economic, as opposed to a competition assessment, while adopting a much stricter policy towards concerted behaviour between operators?

The tough line taken at the same time by the Commission in imposing fines of more than ECU 100,000 million on concerted practices between beam producers (OJ No. L 116 of 16 February 1994) may suggest a preference for the second strategy. The anti-competitive nature of the practices identified was unambiguous (exchange of detailed information, individual market-sharing agreements, price setting) although it is not clear that the restrictive practices had always been strictly adhered to or had produced extremely predatory effects in terms of efficiency. The large number of participants (19 producers) doubtless explains the difficulties encountered in cartelizing the sector and in the free-rider strategies sometimes adopted by certain operators. A reduction in the number of suppliers would certainly facilitate coordination and further accentuate the risks of anti-competitive practices. A more stringent competition policy will therefore be needed as steel markets become more

[25] The European Commission has also approved of the planned link-up of Krupp/Thyssen and AST in the flat-rolled stainless sector. The new entity will hold an important share (about 40%) ot the European market. But in spite of the protests of some competitors (notably Ugine), the European authorities have taken into account the important cut in the number of EU stainless flat-rolled mills this operation would imply. The main steel traders have also welcomed this plan without any real criticisms. In their opinion this link-up will not avoid a future slump in the prices.

concentrated. The task of the competition authorities is then likely to be complicated by the very high degree of price transparency, buttressed as it will be by Article 60(2) of the ECSC Treaty, which stipulates that the price lists and conditions of sale applied by firms within the common market must be made public. In addition, the steel industry will always be subject to cyclical fluctuations in supply. Under these circumstances, the question is how to interpret the announcements of price increases made by certain operators after the general price level has fallen sharply in the trough of the economic cycle (Glais, 1993)? In the absence of any explicit concerted behaviour, should they be considered as invitations of an anti-competitive nature designed to restore above-normal prices?

Nowadays, many industrial economists stress that the role of competition authorities is not to force undertakings to choose a 'price equals marginal cost' pricing policy. Indeed, the best these authorities can hope for is that an oligopolistic market reaches a perfect Nash equilibrium.[26] In this case, exchanges of information on future prices, e.g. by unilateral announcements, may sometimes make it easier to attain a new price equilibrium provided that market conditions change in the same way for all participants. Although the possibility cannot be discounted that an announcement of future prices might be the vehicle for an attempt at collusion, the fact cannot be ignored either that a firm making such an announcement considers, if anything, that the market equilibrium conditions are changing and would like to see his competitors confirm or deny his view. There is thus a very fine dividing line between acceptable and unlawful information practices although experience has shown that restrictive agreements are rarely confined to such practices and that really effective collusive coordination requires the participants to come to a much more explicit agreement, in particular to operate a market-sharing arrangement between themselves. Be that as it may, market surveillance must clearly become even more systematic in the years ahead. The competition authorities will therefore have to continue to denounce all collusive practices between the main suppliers and will also have to ensure that open-market traders are a sufficient factor in challenging the producers' oligopoly (Phlips, 1987).

Thus, over a period yet to be determined but which can be estimated at fifteen or so years, the objective of creating a situation conducive to the attainment of a viable equilibrium configuration will require, in particular on the market for crude steel, an increase in concentration between firms,

---

26 A collection of strategies adopted by the participants in a market corresponds to a Nash equilibrium when none of them considers that it can obtain an additional gain by a unilateral change of strategy.

many of which will continue using the oxygen steel-making technology. The structural characteristics of this technology (technical indivisibilities, high fixed costs) require a supply configuration where only a small number of suppliers will be able to maintain a presence on the market. It is only at the end of this transitional period that the more widespread adoption of electric furnace technology should make supply more flexible. Even though efficient market management necessarily involves more systematic intervention under the competition policy, it will also require a market that becomes more contested as a policy of opening up the Common Market for steel to foreign competitors is pursued.

In Search of Better Linkage Between Competition Policy and Foreign Trade

Two main criticisms are levelled at the EC's commercial policy, and they are particularly relevant when it comes to judging the effects of this policy on the functioning of a market where supply has structural characteristics similar to those of steel products.

The first criticism concerns the method of calculation used by the Community authorities under Council Regulation (EEC) No 2423/88 on protection against dumped or subsidized imports from countries not members of the EC. However, when it comes to making a more specific judgement on the coherence of the different elements of Community policy, the most fundamental criticisms concern the negative effects on competition which may be exerted by the procedure for examining anti-dumping cases and the voluntary restraint undertakings most frequently given (or negotiated) in the event of provisional or definitive duties being imposed.

A comparison between the export price and the normal value constitutes the central element of anti-dumping policy. With regard to its effects on the functioning of competition on a market such as the steel market, the criticisms levelled at the method of calculation used by the competition authorities concern the method of establishing the reference 'constructed values' and the dumping margins (Hindley, 1988; Hoeckmann and Mavroidis,1994; Kulms, 1990).[27]

In the case of the steel industry, the basis of comparison is a constructed value. Now, however much care the Community authorities take in devising the most objective possible reference basis, it is clear that such a method tends, by its very nature, to favour the use of a cost structure that is closer to that of Community firms than that of firms situated in countries with a lower level of development. It is even more difficult to establish a constructed value where a 'reasonable' margin of profit has to be added to these costs.[28] Indeed, such a method leads, in the final analysis, to excessive erosion of the potential comparative advantages available to foreign firms established in countries where wage costs are lower than in the EC. Since the price variable is relatively important in competition between products that are very similar, the constructed value method can therefore penalize the competitiveness of foreign suppliers of steel products to a considerable degree.

Second, dumping margins are established on the basis of a comparison between the normal value of the product concerned and the export prices actually paid in specific transactions. Thus, dumping margins arise where every one of those export prices is below the normal value. On the other hand, the positive differences between export prices and reference prices are not taken into account, to the advantage of the exporter, by deducting them from dumping margins in the reverse situation. All sales made at an export price higher than the reference price are therefore treated as if they had been made at that price and no account is taken of 'negative dumping margins' (Hindley, 1988, pp. 42 et seq.). It is therefore clear that in sectors where there is considerable dispersion of prices (in particular where sales are very sensitive to the economic cycle), such a procedure has the effect of artificially inflating dumping margins.

---

27 Harsh criticism has also been levelled at the way in which dumping margins are sometimes defined where foreign products are sold through distribution companies partially or wholly owned by third-country exporters. Using a simple numerical example, Hindley has shown that the method of adjusting prices provided for by Article 2(10) of the Anti-dumping Regulation (where there is an association or a compensation arrangement between the exporter and the importer) can lead to exporters being put at a disadvantage by overestimating the dumping margins or even by highlighting dumping which does not actually exist. However, the problem raised by Hindley essentially arises in the case of trade relations with countries such as Japan where distribution costs are high but clearly marginal in the case of the distribution of steel products.

28 How should the concept of "reasonable margin of profit" be defined? Should it be the minimum return on sums invested in the production process (as it were, covering simple depreciation on the basis of a risk-free interest rate) or should an element of return for commercial and financial risk be added?

The nature of the theoretical criticisms levelled at measures to regulate trade between a particular economic area and third countries is well known. From a very general point of view, such measures are, of course, criticized for reducing the economic welfare of buyers who no longer enjoy the best products at the best prices, and for artificially allowing inefficient operators to survive and therefore to obstruct the mechanism for optimal allocation of productive resources. More specifically, however, the adoption of anti-dumping measures or undertakings on voluntary restrictions on exports, which are often used in the steel sector by foreign firms (or negotiated by their governments), are clearly at odds with a number of the basic principles of competition policy.

Such undertakings form part of the sequences of strategic games characterized first by the formulation of complaints against exporters supposedly offering their products at prices which breach the rules of fair competition. Concerned to nip in the bud any risk of triggering a procedure involving high anti-dumping duties, operators offer (or are asked to offer) a compromise solution. The introduction of such a sequence implies, first, that exchanges of very detailed information on both sides (appellant and defendant) become widespread. Is there any need to stress the very uncomfortable situation of the competition authorities in the importing economic area? Can they credibly criticize the firms under their supervision for having exchanged, purely within the economic area concerned, detailed information on production costs and prices and accept a group complaint against foreign exporters which could only be justified on the basis of such an exchange? For their part, have the foreign producers any solution other than to agree to propose to their opposite numbers a common and acceptable solution?

It is clear that in a sector such as the steel industry, whose characteristics are very conducive to the conclusion of restrictive agreements (low price-elasticity of market demand, technical indivisibilities, high fixed costs, cyclical fluctuations in demand, small number of large suppliers, etc.), the Anti-dumping Regulation and the practice of voluntary quantitative restrictions offer a comfortable home for the negotiation of agreements allowing the parties to reach a satisfactory equilibrium in a game where the only losers will be the final consumers. It is true that the foreign exporters who are party to the agreement often come off quite well. Supposing that they see the mathematical probability of their profits reducing (which, moreover, is not always the case, given the low price-elasticity of demand), they enjoy, on the other hand, a reduction in their variances, since this type of agreement or commitment has the effect of smoothing out the effects of cyclical market fluctuations (Jones, 1984).

Thus, it is understandable that such an assurance cannot be neglected by foreign steel producers, all the more anxious to cover their fixed costs because they are grappling with considerable excess production capacity and local demand depressed by a world recession and the difficulties of transition to a market economy.

Domestic producers in the economic area concerned would undoubtedly prefer more rigid formulae, for example import quotas that are more easily monitored by using import *and export licences*,[29] to voluntary restrictions which are more difficult to manage because of insufficiently precise statistics that give foreign exporters room to play the strategy of the 'free rider'. None the less, as the objective remains the search for a 'meeting point' within the meaning of the analysis by T.C. Chelling, the formula of voluntary restrictions is not so unfavourable to Community producers. Against such a background, a recovery of demand following a cyclical upturn leads to an increase in prices on the Community market. Once the ceiling of quantitative undertakings given by trading partners had been exhausted, Community oligopolists would be the only ones able to exploit the remaining internal demand and to raise their prices (Mucchielli, 1991) as part of a pattern of parallel behaviour that would be all the more likely to emerge since the steel industry's ability to generate profits must be restored.

At the theoretical level, it is therefore clear and hardly open to question that the quantitative restrictions on imports as negotiated by the Community authorities in a sector such as the steel industry produce side-effects which reduce both the credibility and the effectiveness of the provisions adopted by the Community competition authorities under Article 85 of the EEC Treaty. In a series of remarkable studies, P. Messerlin (1990) sought to illustrate this analysis empirically and demonstrate, in particular using the case of basic chemicals, that: (1) industries managed by cartels[30] are those which obtain the highest number of temporary anti-dumping measures (followed by undertakings on restrictions); (2) the fact of obtaining the imposition of anti-dumping duties enables the effect and robustness of the agreement to be increased. Indeed, although substantial fines have been imposed on participants in an anti-competitive agreement, there are apparently cases where the gains resulting from the adoption of anti-dumping measures and the subsequent

[29] As we have already seen, this is what Eurofer is calling for in the future negotiations with the countries of the CIS.

[30] He based this value judgement on a number of decisions given by the Commission under Article 85.

offer of quantitative restrictions have been much higher[31] (see also Stegemann, 1990). In so far as such a policy would be likely to reduce the incentive for an industrial sector to proceed rapidly to supply adjustments which were none the less necessary, Messerlin adds that anti-dumping procedures should be subordinate to the competition rules laid down by the Treaty of Rome.

With regard to the steel sector, the basic question, however, is whether it is actually possible to suddenly remove all protective measures from the Community market. A number of British studies seem to show that too 'cautious' an approach should be rejected since an opening-up of the market without any specific restriction on imports (essentially of long products) from the countries of Eastern Europe would exert only minimal pressure on the profits of Community producers and would improve economic efficiency, in particular the consumer's surplus in respect of the products concerned. These studies also stress, no doubt rightly so, that the necessary restructuring both in the East and the West could be carried through within the context of a pan-European steel sector provided that the rationalization operations were along strictly market lines (the East supplying long products, the Community flat products) (Wang and Winters, 1993). This hypothesis, based on the findings of an econometric simulation of very high quality, is an attractive one and perfectly consistent with the theoretical teachings of international trade. However, does it take enough account of the differing positions of Community producers? It should not be forgotten that some of them, in particular those situated in the regions of the former East Germany and in the southern countries of the Community, generate a large proportion of their turnover from long products. It is by no means clear, therefore, that the solution advocated by Wang and Winters pays enough attention to the political risk of some Member States intervening again to support their firms most affected by competition from long products originating in the countries of the former socialist bloc, thus delaying implementation of the final element of the Braun plan.

Although they have reduced their supply substantially in the last four or five years,[32] these countries still have considerable production capacity and output, particularly since the previous economic system did not encourage them in any way to economize on steel. In the 1980s, per capita steel consumption in Eastern Europe was 100 kg. higher than in Western Europe. In 1992, however, consumption was on average only

---

[31] However, the very high fines recently imposed on the parties to an agreement on the market for beams undermine the substance of this criticism.

[32] E.g. a 40% reduction in the case of the CIS.

half what it had been in 1987.[33] It is not surprising therefore that many large firms located in these countries are seeking at all costs to maintain a minimum capacity utilization rate (in 1993, 19 firms from Central and Eastern Europe were still producing more than 2.5 million tonnes each, and some, such as Magnitogorsk and Cherepovest, exceeded 8.5 million tonnes). The opening-up of the Community to production from these countries was quite genuine, however, even if since 1993 measures have been taken to control the flood of steel products from some of them. The need for such measures can scarcely be challenged, given the sharp rise in imports of such products and the growing pressure from US producers on their government to impose even harsher restrictions on access by the Europeans to North American markets.

Table 5.5: Production of crude steel

10^3 tonnes	1986	1987	1988	1989	1990	1991	1992	1993 (est.)
Bulgaria	2,898	3,044	2,880	2,899	2,184	1,615	1,552	1,941
Hungary	3,716	3,622	3,582	3,315	2,823	1,931	1,533	1,736
Poland	17,144	17,145	16,873	15,094	13,597	10,403	9,835	9,937
Romania	14,276	14,962	14,314	14,415	9,761	7,116	5,376	5,446
Czechoslov.	15,112	15,416	15,379	15,466	14,877	12,071		
Czech Rep.							7,282	6,769
Slovakia							3,848	3,970
Former GDR	7,967	8,243	8,133	7,829	5,566	3,392	2,983	3,144
Total, eastern Europe	61,213	65,532	61,261	59,130	48,887	33,152	29,140	29,799
Former USSR	16,0537	161,874	163,037	160,096	154,414			
Russia						77,076	67,003	58,236
Ukraine						44,992	41,759	30,537
All CIS						129,615	116,172	94,391
All of former USSR						132,839	117,953	95,739

Source : IISI.

Table 5.6: Consumption of finished steel-based products

Million tonnes	1992	Forecasts, 2000
Central Europe	13.6	17.5
Russia	42	41.5
Ukraine	22.3	20.7
Community	101.5	105.5
EFTA	10	10.5

Source : W.S. Atkins, reproduced in *Metal Bulletin*, 25/8/1994.

33 In Hungary, per capita consumption fell from 274.5 kg. in 1987 to 107.6 kg. in 1992, and in Poland, over the same period, from 316.5 kg. to 112.5 kg. (Source: *Metal Bulletin*, 25 August 1994, p. 17).

It is in fact impossible to separate the search for an optimum solution for the trade relations between the Community and the countries in the former socialist bloc from that for relations between the Community and the USA, the leading customer of European steel firms. The Community authorities and European steel firms have to manage a portfolio of very symmetrical commitments with these two large partners (Community quantitative restrictions *vis-à-vis* the United States, commitments in the opposite direction by the Eastern European countries *vis-à-vis* the Community) and must ensure that the Community's balance in value terms of trade in steel products with these third countries does not change too markedly.

Thus, by acceding to the wish of the main Community operators that the common market should be opened up to imports from the Eastern European countries only gradually but nevertheless substantially, the Community authorities are in a good position to get them to accept the necessary capacity reductions without, however, having to depart too much from the principle of opening up the Common Market to foreign trade. If the restructuring and capacity reduction process takes too long to achieve, it will still be possible to brandish the threat of a relaxation of the safeguard measures. Such an eventuality is all the more credible since the European executive is divided (as we have seen in connection with the renegotiation of the agreements with the Czech Republic and Slovakia) between those advocating the primacy of competition policy in the strict sense of the term and those more concerned with ensuring a smooth restructuring of the Community steel industry.[34]

CONCLUSIONS

Public intervention in the Community steel industry has a long history, and in no other sector has the involvement both of the Member States and of the Commission been so great. The supervision of the steel industry has managed to appear therefore as a very unusual exception to the principles of economic freedom and non-interventionism which were to guide the construction of the Common Market.

Community policy towards this industry cannot be assessed

34 The first group, wanting to increase contestability on the Community steel market, declared themselves in favour of adjusting the quotas to be offered until 1995 on the basis of deliveries made in 1992 on the grounds that the quantities at stake represented only a very low percentage of the Community market. The second group wished to base themselves on what they regarded as the more "normal" figures relating to the quotas set for 1991 and to offer progressive annual quotas.

dispassionately, however, if one forgets to take into account three fundamental data: (i) the specifics of the ECSC Treaty, (ii) the special structural characteristics of the supply and demand for steel products and (iii) the effects of the enlargement of the Community and even more recently of German unification. Loaded with symbols and emotional memories, the steel industry could not, for many years, be treated like any other industry. When the existence of excess supply capacity became worrying, the solution of resorting simply to market forces to restore the balance between supply and demand could not be employed for overriding social and regional-development reasons. The involvement of the Community authorities reached its climax in the first half of the 1980s, a period in which the industry was run as a veritable public cartel (quotas, minimum prices, hunt for any free-riding practices). During this period, it is undeniable that only very little scope could be given to regulating the market through the free play of private initiative. In such a context, it has been possible generally to regard the few judgments given against undertakings convicted of concerted practices (e.g. the cast iron and steel rolls case, OJ No. L 317 of 15/11/1983) as customs clearance operations in disguise.[35]

Invoking the lessons of traditional microeconomic analysis and the efficiency gains lost when competition authorities are too laxist with collusive practices, some observers regret that this policy had been applied too long. However, they pretend to ignore that these lessons do not grant sufficient importance to the value placed on 'time' in the analysis. On the contrary, it is legitimate to argue that, marked by the memory of thirty years of post-war growth, people were not ready to accept sudden changes yet. Clearly, a forced march towards a rapid but even more drastic restructuring would have met with inescapable political opposition.

The very heavy penalties imposed in 1994 on Community beam producers and the annoucement (in December) of investigations launched against eight suppliers of large diameter welded pipes (some of them already implicated in the beam cartel) suspected of illegal collusion in their sales to oil and gas industries, are evidence of the credibility of the new policy adopted. If the main objective remains the reduction of production capacity, it must be pursued in strict compliance with the competition rules. This constraint is proving particularly necessary since

---

[35] In the case referred to, the Commission, taking both the financial situation and the restructuring needs of the undertakings concerned into account, was to judge that the Community's objectives would not be better served if heavy fines were inflicted and imposed fairly symbolic penalties on them.

the steel industry can be restructured efficiently only at the cost of growing concentration between a small number of operators.[36] In 1994, the Commission has been able to apply the Merger Regulations with a clever flexibility and not to prohibit some operations wholly acceptable from an efficiency point of view but leading to some market shares which could be qualified as dominant in other lines of business. The spirit of such a policy must be pursued in the next years. But, the necessary compatibility between these two parts of this new policy demands that the European authorities make sure that the contestability of the EU market should be improved and national aids more controlled.

The now stricter application of the competition rules in an industry such as steel, which for many years to come will remain propitious to the emergence of parallel behaviour, particularly when prices are concerned, needs a greater access to the market for foreign producers and specifically for those settled in Eastern Europe. Even today, the contestability of this market is probably too limited by the provisions of a commercial policy which, moreover, is not totally consistent with the common competition policy.

It has been shown that both the architecture of the anti-dumping policy and protective provisions such as quotas or voluntary quantitative restrictions on exports are likely to produce secondary effects which will increase the risks of collusive behaviour or, at least, make it more difficult for each producer to behave independently. It is therefore necessary, first of all, to amend certain provisions in the Anti-dumping Regulation so that the initiation of a procedure does not result essentially in concerted complaints from several suppliers. The search for greater contestability on the Community steel market also involves amending one method of calculating the anti-dumping margins which currently gives too much protection to Community firms. To determine the 'normal' value of a product imported from abroad, it would be appropriate, it seems, to refer more systematically to the selling prices on the exporter's domestic market and much less to the result of calculating the 'constructed' value. As many economists claim, it would also be fair to compare the normal value of the product in question with an average value for the export prices, thus taking into account any 'negative' dumping margins. Lastly, while it is hardly possible in the near future to do away with all measures of quantitative protection, one should probably not be overcautious in the negotiations to be conducted with third countries and in particular with the

---

36 The growth of the number of cooperation agreements to promote economic progress must also be encouraged; 30-40% of the flat steels used currently did not indeed exist five years ago.

countries of Central and Eastern Europe.

The failure of the restructuring plan being admitted, the Commission threatened that it might lift the quotas. But such a threat was not really credible, the Commission having no power to withdraw them without unanimous approval of the twelve governments. On the contrary, following the intense lobbying by steel producers, EU ministers have decided to prolong the quotas on East European steel imports. These quantitative restrictions have only been adjusted upwards for certain countries (a little increase for Czech Republic and Slovakia, a more important one for some countries of the remote Soviet Union). In order to enforce its new competition policy and to fight against price collusions the Commission must have some credible threats at its disposal. To give it the power to remove quickly some quotas (or to adjust them upwards) without the unanimous consent of the governments would be a move go in the right direction. In a much broader policy towards the Eastern countries one could also advise favouring the productions of the newly privatized firms.

Politics is the art of the possible and, on the whole, community intervention in the steel industry has obviously followed this maxim while never completely abandoning the ultimate objective, which is to organize the conditions that will enable it to function in a really competitive manner.

REFERENCES

Bangemann, M. (1992), 'Pour une politique industrielle européenne'. *Revue du Marché Commun et de l'Union Européenne*, No. 358.

Benyon, F.S. (1983), 'La Communauté et l'industrie sidérurgique dans les années quatre vingts'. *Revue du Marché Commun*, No. 269.

Buigues, P. and Sapir, A. (1993), 'Les politiques industrielles de la Communauté au carrefour des conflits', *Revue d'Economie Industrielle*, No. 63.

De Bandt, J. (1993), 'Politiques industrielles et de la concurrence: quelles priorités, quelles combinaisons?, *Revue d'Economie Industrielle*, No. 63.

Ehlermann, C.D. (1993), 'Politique actuelle de la Commission en matière de concurrence', *Revue du Marché Commun et de l'Union Européenne*, No. 371.

Genevaz, P. (1985), 'Sidérurgie: l'après crise en Europe', *30 jours d'Europe. Problèmes Economiques*,No. 1935.

Glais, M. (1993a), 'Analyse économique des ententes illicites soumises à l'appréciation des autorités concurrentielles françaises et communautaires', *Revue d'Economie Industrielle*, No. 63.
Glais, M. (1993b), 'La jurisprudence de la Commission des Communautés vis-à-vis des aides accordées à leurs entreprises par les Etats membres', *Revue d'Economie Industrielle*, No. 64.
Hindley, B. (1988), 'Dumping and Far East trade of the EC', *The World Economy*,11.
Hoekman, B.M. and Mavroidis, C. (1994), 'Competition, Competition Policy and the GATT', *The World Economy*, 17.
Jacquemin, A. and Marchipont, J.-F. (1993), 'Nouveaux enjeux pour la politique industrielle', *Revue d'Economie Politique*, January-February.
Jacquemin, A. and Sapir, A. (1991), 'Europe post-1992: internal and external liberalization', *American Economic Review*, Papers and Proceedings, May.
Jones, K. (1984), 'The political economy of volontary export restraint agreements', *Kyklos*, 37.
Keeling, B. (1982), 'La crise de l'acier en Europe occidentale', *EFTA Bulletin* reprinted in *Problèmes Economiques*; No. 1802.
Klepper, G. 'The steel and metal industry', in the *European Challenge*, Harvester Wheatsheaft.
Kulms, R. (1990), 'Competition , Trade Policy and Competition Policy in the EEC: the example of antidumping', *Common Market Law Review*, No. 27.
Lindert, P.H. (1989), 'Economie Internationale', *Economica.*
Messerlin, P.A. (1989), 'The antidumping regulations: a first economic appraisal 1980-85', *Weltwirtschaftliches archiv*, 125.
Messerlin, P.A. (1990), 'Antidumping regulations or pro-cartels law? the EC chemical cases', *The World Economy.*
Mucchielli, J.C. (1991), 'Relations économiques internationales', *Hachette Supérieure.*
Phlips, L. (1987), 'Information and collusion' in Hay and Vickers (eds.), *The economics of market dominance*, Blackwell.
Phlips, L. (1993), 'Paralélisme de comportement et pratiques concertées', *Revue d'Economie Industrielle*, No.63.
Remy, A. (1988), 'La sidérurgie' in *Stratégie et Compétitivité dans l'industrie mondiale*, Cpe/Economica.
Remy, A., De Sa, P. and Marquez, I. (1990), 'Sidérurgie: consolidation en europe' in *Marché unique, marché multiple*, Cpe /Economica.
Rugman, A. and Gestrin, M. (1991), 'EC antidumping laws as a barrier to trade', *European Management Journal*, 9(4).

Rieben, H. (1954): *Des ententes des maitres de forges au plan Schuman,* Ambily, Les Presses de Savoie.

Schelling, T.C. (1960), *The strategy of conflict*, Harvard University Press.

Soenens, J. (1986), 'La politique sidérurgique communautaire 1980-85: bilan économique et perspectives', *Revue du Marché Commun*, No. 297.

Stegemann, K. (1990), 'EC anti-dumping policy: are price undertakings a legal substitute for illegal price fixing?', *Weltwirtschaftliches archiv*, 126.

Vanderseypen, G. (1984), 'La restructuration de la sidérurgie européenne: une oeuvre en voie d'achèvement?', *Revue du Marché Commun*, September/October.

Winters, A. (1992), 'Goals and own goals in European trade policy', *World Economy*, 15.

Zhen Kun Wang and Winters, L.A. (1993), 'EC imports from Eastern Europe: iron and steel', European Bank-Working Paper, No. 9.

Discussion
Fernand Braun

INTRODUCTION

In November 1992, Mr Fernand Braun, former Director-General for Industry at the European Commission, was asked by Vice-President Bangemann to prepare a report on the state of the Steel Industry in Europe.

The Braun Report, presented to Vice-President Bangemann in January 1993, was based on interviews with some 70 steel companies. The following text presents revisited conclusions of the Braun Report in the light of the results of the 1993-94 restructuring plan.

CHRONOLOGY

The Council of Industry Minister's Meeting of 25 February 1993

Mr Braun's findings, as described in his report of 29 January 1993, inspired to an important extent the Commission's proposals for the Council's meeting on 25 February 1993, and the measures implemented as a result of that meeting. The approach decided on 25 February 1993 was based on a parallel action, namely:

- on the part of ***industry***, the *definition of a sufficient and precise capacity reduction **plan** before **30 September 1993***, to be carried out before the end of 1995;[1]

- on the part of the ***Community***, the adoption of ***accompanying measures, in principle for a three-year period***, meant to facilitate the task of industry.

[1] The minimum closures requested by the Commission were 19 million tonnes, whereas Mr Braun's survey had identified closure intentions for 6.6 million tonnes of capacity as sufficiently firm (categories A and B) and a further 11 million tonnes as potential, i.e. depending on financing conditions.

The *accompanying measures*, which were immediately implemented, but of which the Council as well as the Commission always emphasized the ***conditional link*** *with the implementing of restructuring*, were primarily in four areas.

Social support[2]

In accordance with its intention declared since November 1992, the Commission increased since 1993 its participation, within the framework of the ECSC budget, in the social costs for the workers affected by the reductions in capacity to 9,000 ECU per head; the amount of this extraordinary expenditure from the Community budget could increase by 240 million ECU over three years.

Stabilization of the market

In order to support the necessary steel price recovery and to restore the financial balance of the sector, without which it would be unable to face the social and industrial costs of restructuring, the Commission started publishing indicative quarterly sales guidelines under Article 46 ECSC.[3] Companies were informed in good time of the market prospects, so that they could individually take the guidelines into account when planning their commercial strategy. The majority of companies conformed to it, which contributed to the control of supply and allowed prices to recover.

External measure

Disturbance of the internal restructuring process in the Community steel industry caused by the disorder of the international markets had to be avoided. Thus, multilateral initiatives (essentially the negotiation on a 'Multilateral Steel Agreement' drawing up individual rules for the steel trade in addition to the rules of GATT) as well as bilateral or specific trade measures were taken. The latter involved more particularly the fixing of basic import prices (the purpose of which was to identify the likeliness of dumping) and some bilateral arrangements. In practice, however, the Commission had to negotiate bilateral arrangements only with the Czech and Slovak Republics, which were already confronted with a commercial

2 Modalities of the social measures were described in the information note COM(93)178 of 28 April 1993 from the Commission to the Member States.

3 For the modalities of the system of market guidelines, see the relevant communication in the OJ C83 of 24.3.1993.

safeguard measure since 1992, and incidentally with certain ex-USSR Republics.

Competition

In addition to the implementation of state aid control intended for certain *public sector companies*, the Commission declared its willingness to approve, under Article 53(a) of the ECSC Treaty,[4] agreements for voluntary closures of capacity, by means of a financial compensation to closing companies on behalf of the remaining partners to the agreements. The Commission, for its part, was ready to facilitate the achievement of the aims of these agreements by the granting of loans under Article 54 ECSC. In this way, the companies not receiving state aid (commonly designated as *'private companies'*) did have the potential support of a kind of 'rationalization cartel' allowing the joint financing of the reduction of the supply of the products which concerned them.

Promising Restructuring Initiatives By Private Companies

Following the Council's request to the industry to elaborate a restructuring plan, EUROFER presented to the Commission, at the beginning of 1993, the first draft financial agreements to be concluded in the form of 'European Economic Interest Groupings', which required authorization by the Commission under Articles 53(a) and 65 of the ECSC Treaty, and a prior opinion of the Council. Due to the fact that Eurofer was presenting a precise and ambitious target of 10.5 million tonnes of capacities to be closed under this formula, the impression prevailed at that time that financial negotiations were already under way within Eurofer in order to achieve the withdrawal from the market of some of its member-companies who were facing difficulties (a major one being Klöckner).

A positive opinion to the aforesaid agreements under Article 53(a) ECSC was not delivered by the Council until 21 September 1993, when it implicitly admitted that the Commission could facilitate the financing of such arrangements with ECSC loans.

Nevertheless, the discussions on state aid reported below created a climate which caused industry to become increasingly inactive as far as the materialization of the objectives of those financial agreements were concerned. Therefore, the Council of 21 September 1993 launched a call to

4 Article 53(a): 'The Commission can ... authorize ... all financial mechanisms, common to several companies, that it recognizes necessary."

the 'private companies' to notify closure projects 'without further delay', but at that time the initial deadline of 30 September 1993 had already expired.

Numerous State Aid Cases

The contribution of the state-aided companies to the restructuring effort dominated the scene during the whole 1993. After having rejected the initial aid requests for the Spanish public steel company CSI and for EKO-Stahl, which would allow for capacity increases, the Commission had to cope with a new important case introduced in spring 1993, namely the privatization plan of the Italian public holding IRI. This privatisation involved the steel producer ILVA, which had benefited from government aid in 1989 through the holding FINSIDER.

In the case of ILVA, the Commission had to cope with the rigid attitude of the Italian Government, which disputed the public character of the operation and therefore the principle that the aid in question had to be sanctioned by closures. It was only at the Council Meeting on Industry of 21 September 1993 that Italy made its position more flexible. Since in the meantime there were *as many as six*[5] aid cases to be approved unanimously by the Council under Article 95 of the ECSC Treaty (because they did not fit within the State Aid Code provisions) the Council could not reach a 'package' agreement on the state aid cases (of a total value of 6.7 billion ECU) until *17 December 1993*.

The 'Wait and See' Attitude on Behalf of the 'Private' Companies

Throughout the dealings concerning the state-aided companies, which lasted until the end of 1993, *the restructuring of the remaining companies not receiving aid was virtually stopped* (except for some cases of companies forced to restructuring or closure by the market).

Many private companies were, in fact, claiming that the conditions imposed by the Council and by the Commission[6] on the state-aided companies were unfair and that, in this situation, it was impossible for them, *vis-à-vis* their labour force and/or with respect to their shareholders, to defend any closure decisions on their own part: reference was made, in

5 Namely the two Spanish aid requests for Sidenor and for CSI (plan reformulated and reintroduced by the Spanish government), the two German cases Freital and EKO (also a rearranged plan), the Italian case ILVA, as well as the case concerning the Portuguese public-sector company Siderurgia Nacional.

6 Subsequently, applications for annulment of the decisions adopted by the Commission under Article 95 ECSC in accordance with the agreement of the Council were actually introduced by a number of companies.

particular, to the implicit authorisation given to EKO and to CSI to invest in two new flat product facilities. In the same spirit, the Commission was confronted with excessive expectations on the part of these companies, who looked to the Commission, in its role of creditor involved in the receivership procedure concerning the company Klöckner, to subordinate its agreement with this legal settlement to a maximum of closures on the part of that company.

Already at the Council meeting on 22 June 1994, the Commission reported that the Article 53(a) agreements seemed increasingly lacking in substance because the German company Klöckner, the disappearance of which seemed to have been one of the objectives pursued by these agreements, was about to be taken over by the ARBED group after a rescue operation on the part of the regional government of Bremen.

All this occurred against the background of an ever-improving business context. It became undeniably clear that during 1994 no new important closure was decided in the private sector. The Commission could therefore only note in its final assessment,[7] addressed to the Council at its meeting on 8 November 1994, that the industry had definitely failed in its restructuring attempts. Consequently, political coherence and industrial logic forced the Commission to propose the withdrawal of the accompanying measures, except for the social measures, for which budget resources had already been earmarked before, as well as for the external measures which fell within the competence of the Council.

The Council did not depart basically from this analysis, in the absence of a consensus among the Member States, and thereby marked the *end of the restructuring plan one year before its normal conclusion.*

Moderate Results Have Nevertheless Been Achieved

Despite the premature ending of the restructuring process, the results obtained up to the Autumn of 1994 and as summarized in the appended Annex Table 5.1 appear, at first glance, appreciable.

The *closure commitments which were finally announced as of October 1994* amounted to about 11 million tonnes[8] of rolled products, composed of 5.7 million tonnes of flat products and 5 million tonnes of long products

---

7 Communication COM(94)466 of 25.10.1994 to the Council and to the EP ('Community steel restructuring: assessment and conclusions').

8 This relates to net closures, taking into account the moderating effect of the capacity extension of 0.6 million tonnes resulting from the draft Commission decision establishing the conditions of sale of EKO-Stahl by the Treuhandanstalt to Cockerill-Sambre. That decision allowed a gradual capacity increase of 0.9 million tonnes provided that compensatory closures of 0.3 million tonnes are performed elsewhere.

(including the implications of the EKO-Stahl restructuring)[9], as well as an amount of 0.5 million tonnes not yet specified.[10] To this figure, one could always reasonably add an amount of 5 million tonnes of closures which could be implemented under the Italian law on dismantling and which are supposed to affect the sub-sector of the long products.

The nearly 16 million tonnes of hot rolling capacity thus defined do not remain far from the target of 19 million tonnes of closures judged necessary since 1992 by the Commission as a strict minimum.

A major *nuance must, however, be added to this observation.* This concerns the *way in which these closures were obtained.* Whereas, following the conclusions of the Council of 25 February 1993, it fell to industry to define the closures, it is noteworthy that *the majority of the closures were connected directly or indirectly with government aid notified essentially during 1993.* This even applies to the closures awaited under the Italian law on dismantling, which originated after the failure, at the beginning of 1993, of a restructuring plan which was set up by the Italian private companies grouped in the association Federacciai. Regarding the 'private' closures as such, they hardly exceed the number of closures which were already identified in early 1993 by Mr Braun as sufficiently firm (categories A and B), and which are therefore mainly the result of decisions or projects under consideration before 1993 (cf. Annex Table 5.1).

The Restructuring Policy was Conducted Without Interference With Overall Market Principles

In the normal course of events, the ECSC Treaty expires in the year 2002. As early as 1991, the Commission and the Council agreed on an approach for phasing out the ECSC Treaty, which would affect in particular the financial instruments of the ECSC. The restructuring policy and the financing of the social measures did not prevent the Community from pursuing this policy of 'phasing out', which means, for instance, the progressive abandoning of the ECSC levy on production of coal and steel.

Through its 'soft' intervention in the market by means of the quarterly production and sales guidelines according to Article 46 ECSC, the Commission contributed to a rapid reversal of the depressed market conditions; thus, no real thought was given, either by industry or by the Commission, to the possible reintroduction of compulsory market management on the basis of Article 58 ECSC. Also, the external

9 Cf. communication from the Commission to the Council concerning the state aid N572/94.

10 The latter capacity remains to be given by the new owner of ILVA's assets, after its privatization which has to intervene in principle before the end of 1994 under the Commission's decision on aid for ILVA.

commercial measures remained confined to a limited number of agreements with countries in Central and Eastern Europe.

The number of state aid cases which were, after all, limited in number could all be handled according to the principle of 'closure for aid'. Moreover, the risk of recurrence of state aid is reduced because the companies concerned are largely privatized as a result of the Council decisions of 17 December 1993.

Perspectives

The present outlook indicates a demand for *flat products* which is comparable to the situation of 1991, the year preceding the recession. Capacities are fairly well loaded, order books are replenished, and prices have continued to increase over the last few months in a quite substantial way, enabling most companies to make profits at the end of 1994 and to project quite important benefits for the fiscal year 1995. The question therefore arises whether there could have been any reason to push the restructuring further. As far as *flat products* are concerned, one should recall that the 'European Economic Interest Groupings' created in 1994 by Eurofer companies had considered a target of capacity reduction in flat products of around 8 million tonnes.

In a cyclical industry like steel, another recession is bound to occur in the foreseeable future, and most steel producers accept that the structural adjustments not made during the last recession will be called for during the next one. The next restructuring, for long products as well as for flat products, will not be allowed to proceed with subsidies from Member States, be it for the proclaimed opposition by Council or Commission members to any such interventions, or simply because Member States, for budgetary reasons, will not accept having to make new financial contributions.

The ongoing privatizations of hitherto state-owned companies, and the process of mergers recently observed and which may not have come to an end, should allow companies to make the necessary adjustments, on a company by company basis, without further recourse to mechanisms as suggested in the Braun Report and accepted by the Commission.

Annex: Table 5.1: Restructuring results 1993-1994 (in million tonnes of capacity

			Achieved capacity reductions				
Product group	Estimated excess capacity (a)	TOTAL	State-aided companies (b)	Italian law (c)	'Private' companies (d)	(for the record) private closures in the Braun Report (e)	Remaining excess capacity (approx.)
Hot rolled flat	5.5	5.7	3.8	-	1.9	(1.7)	-
Hot rolled long	13.5	10	1.1	5	3.9	(3.1)	3.5
Total hot rolled	19	16.2	5.4*	5	5.8	(4.8)	3
Crude steel	33	18	2	5	11	(6.5)	15

Notes:

(a) According to the optimistic scenario calculated by the Commission services. A less optimistic scenario, which would have resulted in a hot-rolling capacity surplus of 26 million tonnes, underpins the final comments made under 'Perspectives'.

(b) CSI and Sidenor (E), Freital (D), ILVA (I) and Siderurgia Nacional (P), as well as EKO-Stahl following the takeover scheme involving Cockerill-Sambre.

(c) Italian law on dismantling.

(d) Companies not included in the two previous groups.

(e) By way of comparison are listed the closure intentions declared by the same companies during the survey made by Mr Braun, and which were classified in the report of 29 January 1993 under categories A and B (excluding CSI and Sidenor).

* including 0.5 million tonnes to be defined by the new owner of ILVA, once privatized.

Source: various communications from the Commission to the Council.

6. Telecommunication services

Dominique Foray, Pauline Rutsaert and Luc Soete

INTRODUCTION

Competition, trade and industry policies all serve to achieve the objectives of the European Union as laid down in the Treaty of Rome, the Single European Act and the Maastricht Treaty. However, they feature different objectives and determine specific action spaces. It is thus useful to start the analysis by concisely stating the objectives of each of these three EU policies as applicable to the high-tech sector in general and the telecommunications services sector in particular.

As for any other economic sector, EU competition policy aims at ensuring that competition in the Union is not distorted, that is, to eliminate existing anti-competitive distortions and to prevent potential anti-competitive situations from emerging. For high-tech sectors this means intense efforts, especially in monitoring and disciplining state aids and public procurement as well as a careful examination of mergers and joint ventures taking into account the rapid pace of technological progress and potential consequences for competition. These competition policy objectives refer to the EU as a single market.

The objectives of the EU commercial policy are twofold. On the one hand the EU seeks the abolition of all tariff and non-tariff obstacles to the free movement of goods, capital, persons and services among the EU Member States. On the other hand it promotes, and participates in, the development of world trade and the lowering of trade barriers. Given the intensification of foreign competition, the shortening of product life cycles, and the increasing costs of developing new products and processes in high-tech sectors, the EU aims at ensuring a minimum level of trade fairness and at supporting high-tech firms through the implementation of strategic actions, the promotion of European norms and the constitution of entities of a critical, minimum size. In this case, trade policies reveal the EU as an agent in world competition.

The industrial policy of the EU has been given an explicit status and content only recently, supplementing competition and integration policies and recommending an active intervention whenever Member States' policies are ineffective or harmful to other Member States. The high-tech sectors often represent areas in which the EU runs *de facto* an active EU industrial policy. The reason lies in the idiosyncratic features of that sector, which commend cross-border strategies: importance of R&D investments, international size of networks, need for compatibility of standards and convergence of technology know-how among various industries in the high-tech sector. The high-tech sector industrial policy follows two main lines of action. First, it tries to create the necessary conditions to exploit the sector's positive externalities (for example, by setting up an information infrastructure and network, by encouraging researcher mobility and by launching R&D cooperation programmes). Second, it seeks to maintain and develop technological diversity. This set of measures emphasizes the EU as a system of innovation.

Since the three policies under review are influenced by different objectives and refer to three distinct dimensions of the EU, it is expected that the various ways through which they are implemented may at times reinforce each other and at other times conflict with each other. In our investigation of the coherence among these three policies in the high-tech sector, we begin with a general analysis of the compatibilities and conflicts among the three policies, paying especial attention to specific aspects of the high-tech sector (section A). Then we explore in detail the case of the telecommunications services sector: first, we depict the sector in terms of structure, conduct and performances (section B); second, we describe the evolution of the EU trade, competition and industry policies concerning the telecommunications services sector (section C); finally, we analyse the coherence and conflicts existing among these policies (section D).

A. Analysis of Compatibilities and Conflicts among the Three Policies When Applied to the High-Tech Sector

To inquire into the issue of coherence among the competition, trade and industry policies in the high-tech sector may be done by answering the question: 'What are the factors in this sector which prevent the three action spaces corresponding to the three policies from necessarily and precisely overlapping?'. One way to handle this query is to distinguish three pairs of policies and to analyse each of them separately. In this section, such an analysis will be made in general terms.

Coherence Between Industry and Trade Policies

Various externalities affect the high-tech sectors. The main sources of externalities are found at the R&D level (knowledge and technological spillovers) and at the systems and networks operation level (where interoperability and interconnection matter).

The main clash between industry and trade policies is due to their treatment of different externalities. Indeed, any high-tech generation process produces potentially two types of externalities. Negative externalities basically result from the possibility of appropriating the benefits of being first. Thus they appear in the circumstances defined by the 'innovative race' and 'winner-take-all' principles. Under certain assumptions, at the moment of the discovery, any agent who does not win the race will discard all resources (competencies, instruments) allocated to this specific project. Such races are very common in the high-tech sectors where the flow of innovations is usually continuous. Conditions of negative strategic externalities can conduct to both situations of over-investment (commons effect) and under-investment (public good effect) in research. Positive externalities derive from knowledge interactions driven by the properties of infinite expansibility (non-rivalry) and cumulativeness. These suggest that the more is invented the easier it becomes to invent still more, provided of course that the conditions of wider distribution, and timely, inexpensive access to new findings are fulfilled.[1] The difficulty is that the two types of externalities are not mutually exclusive (David and Foray, 1995). Indeed any process of knowledge generation - either 'scientific' or 'technological' - can generate potentially both types of externalities.

Whether the generation of knowledge is perceived as generating negative or positive externalities is thus a crucial point, influencing the design of the institutions, behaviours, norms of competition and cooperation, in the field of trade and technology policies. In general, industrial policy is viewed as oriented towards the management of systems which are

---

1 There has been a recent resurgence of the view that in the realm of knowledge production positive externalities dominate. See Romer's emphasis upon the so-called 'non-rival' character of ideas; see Scotchmer's work, emphasizing the cumulative nature of inventive activity; and see David's (1993) attention to the impediments that intellectual property protection poses for further innovation, based on the related notion that a major use of new knowledge is as an input into further production of knowledge.

perceived as 'rich-in-positive externalities' whereas trade policy appears to be more focused on the *perception* of strategic negative externalities that are present in the system.[2] Consequently, the policy responses to the perception of the system - as one that requires special incentives to reduce negative externalities (trade policy perception) or to fully realize the potential of positive externalities (industrial policy perception - are obviously difficult to harmonize.[3] Indeed, these two types of externalities refer to different analytical levels and can be characterized by different incentive structures.

On the one hand, numerous industry policy measures target a socially optimal exploitation of the positive externalities arising during the process of research and development of new products and new processes. These types of technology-cum-industry policy measures reflect a logic of openness in the sense that they attempt to enlarge the space and manners in which spillovers can be exploited in a welfare-improving way. On the other hand, several trade policy measures aim at lessening the welfare-reducing consequences of the negative externalities characterizing that same process. These measures reveal more a logic of closeness by which European high-tech sector firms would be partially and/or temporarily protected from the technological leads and market moves from foreign firms. The goal of such a limited protection is to allow the European firms to adjust their marketing strategies and complete their R&D projects in order to be better able to face foreign competition.

It is worth observing that the policy response chosen by each of these policies often leads to a confirmation of the perception that caused the intervention and a strengthening of the elements originally present in the system. Typically, the trade policy response to the perception of the system - as one that requires special incentives to reduce negative externalities - involves the provision of strong protection for innovators, impeding the rapid disclosure of information. Similarly, under the industrial policy's perception of a system 'rich-in-positive learning externalities', obstacles to information dissemination due to intellectual property rights and appropriation by secrecy are to be replaced with devices for coordinating the actions of innovative agents. For example, the intellectual property systems are to be valued because of their

---

2 Notice that competition policy-makers can be viewed as 'agnostic' with respect to the question of the nature of externalities which matter in high tech industries.

3 This section draws upon the Report 'Accessing and expanding the science and technology knowledge base' (DSTI/STP/TIP(94)4) prepared by Paul A. David and D. Foray in the context of the OECD project on national innovation systems.

disclosure features and need not be used in ways that impede the pooling of knowledge.

The confrontation between the open logic and the closed logic shows in various situations. One of them is the issue of participation of foreign firms to European programmes, such as those promoting R&D cooperation or organizing the setting up of standards and norms. Advocates of active and strategic trade policy measures argue that non-EU firms be kept out of these programmes. Among the justifications for such a stand, explicit reasons relate to the wish to keep EU public funding benefiting EU firms and agents and to the possibility of developing a competitive advantage in that way. But there are also hidden motivations, such as the hope that outcomes of these European programs become a source of non-tariff barriers. In the meantime, industry policy would recommend that these firms be part of these programmes. Grounds for such a recommendation are, for example, that some valuable foreign knowledge might spill over to the European firms during the working sessions of these programmes and that European standards should be chosen so as to minimize the risk of incompatibilities with foreign standards which might lead to costly standard wars. The present situation in the high-tech sector seems to reflect various degrees of accommodation of this open versus closed conflict. In some areas, proponents of open dominate; in some others, a closed strategy is preferred. Another situation in which open and closed logics differ is that of technology transfer. Industry policy in the high-tech sector - which often takes the form of technology policy - seeks to maximize the diffusion of knowledge and technology know-how given the relatively low transfer cost compared to the production costs. It thus encourages transfer of know-how. At the same time, some of these transfers of technology towards foreign firms are actively regulated by trade policy interventions and systematic technology transfers from abroad appear to be sub optimal and poorly managed at the EU level.

Beyond compatibilities and conflicts, it is important to observe the trend towards the convergence of trade and technology-cum-industry policies in the high-tech sector. This convergence results from the vanishing of boundaries between the two types of policies. Two factors are identified as its cause: the increased global interdependence in economic and technological spheres and the growing involvement by governments in policies to promote innovation and technological advances. An interesting consequence of this phenomena is the use of some trade measures to palliate certain failures of technology policy, and vice versa the use of industry policies as a response to trade policy deficiencies. Typical examples are VERs in the former case and technical standards in the latter case.

Coherence Between Competition and Trade Policies

With regard to the EU competition and trade policies in the high-tech sector, an important issue is the conflict between the primarily static approach of the antitrust law and the predominantly dynamic approach of the evolution of comparative and competitive advantages in a sector featuring quick technological change. It is often characterized by a trade-off between the intensity of short-run competition and the maintenance of competitiveness in the medium and long run. The thorough study of this trade-off is typically a crucial part of the assessment of the desirability of state aids, mergers and take-overs in the high-tech sector.

Such an evaluation work is very difficult because it is hard to predict the impact of these actions on potential competition and on the evolution of the trade pattern. The reason for this difficulty lies in the characteristics of the high-tech sector: short product life cycle, convergence of technologies among previously distinct industries, importance of standards and norms given the role of networks, prohibitive R&D investments. The combination of these factors may drastically alter the market structure of the high-tech sector in a short period of time. Consequently, the market structure of today may only tell very little about, and is no guarantee of, that of tomorrow. In the face of this uncertainty created by successive and overlapping technological change, there exist two certainties: to fail the technical mastering of one product stage can be fatal to the survival of an industry and to keep up with all needed techniques requires abundant financial resources. This is so because of the tremendous cumulative learning taking place during the production and marketing of that product and because of the scale and complexity of innovative projects in the high-tech sector.

Massive state and R&D aids may be necessary to restore and/or maintain the competitiveness of a high-tech industry while, at the same time, they may be unwanted because they deeply distort the market of that industry. Mergers and take-overs may cause a realization of scale economies necessary to remain competitive as well as provoke an increase in market power susceptible to ease anti-competitive strategies. Thus, trade policy-makers might seek to tolerate massive state aids in targeted industries and to sponsor the occurring of some mergers or take-overs whereas authorities in charge of competition policy might try to prevent them from taking place.

Trade and competition policies show another aspect of inconsistency when some trade measures create an environment propitious to the development of anti-competitive behaviours or when they strengthen industry concentration by lowering the impact of foreign competition. Indeed some procedures, such as those by which VERs and anti-dumping actions can be initiated (e.g., major firms gather and make a case against unfair trade from a foreign importing country), are argued to be stimulative of inter-firm collaboration as a safeguard against competition. In the same way foreign producers may collude in the bargaining of VERs with EU agents in a way that may reduce competition in the EU. Moreover the adequacy and the extent of protection of already highly concentrated industries might need to be questioned. The reason is that an increased protection of a domestic, concentrated industry has not yet been proved to be sufficient to restore incentives for innovation by domestic incumbents and/or entry by domestic entrants.

Still another kind of conflict between trade and competition policies concerns small and medium firms. Trade policy measures which aim to create entities of a critical size in which economies of scale can be achieved are likely to be detrimental to the viability of most smaller enterprises. As a result, they are likely to oppose that objective of the competition policy.

However, it is obvious that many trade and competition measures are compatible. This occurs often when both sorts of measures target the success of higher levels of competition. For example, the lowering of tariff and non-tariff barriers stimulates the free circulation of goods and so increases competition. This augmented competition is likely to be in turn an effective means of reducing the efficiency of anti-competitive practices, such as cartel behaviours. Another example is the opening up of public procurement markets which is expected to simultaneously serve trade policy objectives. Restrictive public procurement policies distort competition but also fragment markets according to national territories hindering trade. The opening up of public procurement will thus imply a reduction of anti-competitive practices as well as a liberalization of the trade in that market.

It is worth noticing that what seems at first to be a seed of conflict between trade and competition policies may turn out to be a source of compatibility. This will occur when some trade policy measure implemented to keep some domestic industry abreast with foreign competitors reveals itself in the long run as an effective mean of maintaining some degree of competition at the world level. The initial fear of an immediate reduction of competition as a result of the trade measure might be more than compensated by the relief brought by the existence of some competition between the preserved domestic industry and a foreign industry that has become extremely concentrated.

Coherence Between Competition and Industry Policies

The principal clash between competition and industry policies arises around the issue of inter-firm agreements. The EU antitrust law is strict *vis-à-vis* inter-firm agreements: it seeks to prevent the formation of any such agreement which is likely to generate anti-competitive practices or a reduction of competition and to dismantle any of them which show welfare-reducing effects. The EU industry policy considers inter-firm agreements in the high-tech sector as an efficient way to internalize the positive technological externalities associated with knowledge production, to reduce wasteful duplication of R&D investments, to improve the diffusion of new knowledge, and to optimize the selection of standards and norms. Indeed the high-tech sector faces fast technological progress. Consequently firms should be given the chance to adjust to and participate in this technological change at low costs and in a manner that maximizes resource allocation. The management of these opposing views on the desirability of inter-firm agreements has led to a compromise: inter-firm R&D cooperative agreements are exempted from notification requirement (1968 Notice on cooperation between enterprises relating only to R&D) and those R&D cooperative agreements which also include joint exploitation of the results also benefit from such an exemption provided that certain conditions are satisfied (1985 block exemption Regulation on R&D agreements). Further effective flexibility *vis-à-vis* the European antitrust law, which has materialized as the Eureka program, has promoted inter-firm agreements which strive to develop and commercialize new products and processes.

A grey area between competition and industry policies appears concerning small and medium firms. On the one hand, compatibility exists to some extent. Competition policy cares about the viability of small and medium-sized enterprises and industry policy encourages these same firms to participate in EC-sponsored R&D programmes. Through these encouragements policy-makers in charge of industrial matters, besides their wish to see these firms get a fair share from the EC measures, may hope to achieve and/or maintain a greater technological diversity. Indeed it is generally agreed that small and medium enterprises in the high-tech sector are often innovative, a source of dynamism and creativity complementary to the financial power and infrastructure strength of large firms. On the other hand, a conflict arises when EU R&D programmes in effect privilege a few large firms, when they are mainly determined by experts detached from, and caring for, large firms, or when they require too much administrative work for participation.

An additional possible grey area between the two policies at stake concerns the intensity of competition prevailing on a market. On the one hand, the industry policy objective of maintaining a minimum technological diversity is likely to generate lower degrees of concentration in the market. This would mean that it comes close to one target of competition policy. On the other hand, the preservation of diversity among national systems of innovation (one way to protect technological variety) might encourage firms to reply to this lack of harmonization by developing as multi-domestic firms. The emergence of multi-domestic firms can lead to a subtle, yet effective, reduction of market competition through the development of coordinated oligopolistic behaviours across borders among the various subsidiaries. In addition, some EU R&D programmes effectively generate the selection and heavy subsidization of a few large firms. This industry strategy not only might distort the market selection process, but also might provoke an increase in market concentration and so ease the appearance of anti-competitive outcomes.

Conclusions

In this section, the coherence among the competition, trade and industry policies in the high-tech sector has been investigated by considering each pair of policies in turn. This exercise revealed the existence of several conflicts and compatibilities. The roots of these frictions often are found in the features of the high-tech sector. These characteristics - mainly, high levels of R&D expenditures, public good features of a crucial intermediary output (knowledge), economies of scale and cumulative learning in innovation and production - are such that the tools used by each policy to attain its own objectives frequently oppose each other.

In the rest of the chapter, we explore that issue in the particular case of the telecommunications services sector.

B. THE TELECOMMUNICATIONS SERVICES SECTOR

Telecommunications services are described in the *Panorama of EU Industry 94*, as 'permit[ting] interactive interconnections between persons, between persons and computers and between machines, through many different media networks such as cable, microwaves and satellite networks. They also permit the diffusion of information from a single point to multiple points such as direct satellite broadcasting for television or data transmission'.

Table 6.1: Telecommunications services in the EU: receipts, surplus, and employment in 1993

Country	1993 receipts (ECU million)	1993 surplus (ECU million)	1993 employment (thousand)
B	3,207.0	270.0	25.6
DK	2,613.0	241.0	17.0
D	35,679.0	-1,738.0	231.0
GR	1,556.0	303.0	26.3
E	.10,193.0	747.0	74.3
F*	25,372.0	899.0	167.8
IRL	1,271.0	118.0	13.0
I	14,872.0	418.0	87.9
L**	164.4	81.3	0.7
NL	5,944.0	n.a.	n.a.
P	1,273.0	61.0	10.0
UK***	20,576.0	2659.0	156.0
EC**	89,626.5	-	898.9
USA**	-	-	575.6
Japan**	-	-	266.1

Source: The 1994 Panorama of the EU Industry.

Notes: * Data linking France Télécom to Cogecom.
** 1991 data.
*** Data concerning British Telecom only; figures for Mercury not available.

The increasing importance of that sector is grasped by means of a few figures reflecting its performances. The revenues of these public telecom operators (TOs) at the EU level amounted to ECU 90 billion in 1991 while their gross investments exceeded ECU 32 billion. The fastest growing subsectors are the mobile communications and the private networks (17 per cent increase between 1988 and 1990).

Another approach to the importance of the telecommunications sector is to assess the extent to which present economic activities depend on the use of information and telematic systems: more than 50 per cent of employment, or six out of ten jobs, are commonly accepted figures.[4] It is expected that the telecommunications sector will be the third largest, after food and drink and chemicals by the year 2000, and that as much as 30 per cent of its revenues would be associated with data and image transmission services.[5] These forecasts have led to the coining of the term 'information society': a society in which information and communication technologies (ITCs) would be an essential support to human activities, could generate as much as 6 per cent of EU GDP by the end of the decade - the annual growth rates of the telecom services and equipment markets being expected to amount to, respectively, 8 per cent and 4 per cent until the year 2000.[6]

The rest of this section is organized as follows: first, key elements characterizing the sector of telecommunications services are described; second, recent technological change and its implications on market configuration are presented; third, the opening up of the market as a consequence of liberalization policy is depicted; fourth, the issue of telecommunications tariffs is examined; finally, information about investments and services quality and diversity is given.

Key Features of the Sector

The sector of telecommunications services is strictly regulated at each national level. An important result of these regulations is that in all but one of the Member States most telecommunications services are exclusively provided by one public telecom operator (TO) forced to comply with a set of obligations (such as provision of universal service, along with financial contributions to certain public R&D expenditures and to the national budget). Another outcome of these regulations has been the development of a European telecommunications services market which is fragmented along national boundaries.

International telecommunications services are organized by means of a very stable regulatory mechanism which stipulates how revenues are shared among international carriers. This mechanism was devised by the International Telecommunications Union (based in Geneva).

Modifications are brought to it when perceived as desirable by the ITU members and are adopted by its members during one of the world

---

4 See European Parliament (1993), p. 3, and Sun and Pelkmans (1994), p. 6.

5 See European Parliament (1993), p. 3, 4.

6 See Sections 3.6 and 5.A of the White Paper 'Growth, Competition, and Employment', CEC (1994a).

telecommunications conferences organized by the ITU. The revenues of each international carrier depend on the size of the international traffic it carries and on the tariffs set by the various carriers. Trade surplus or deficit in telecommunications services are largely determined by the differences existing among these diverse tariffs.[7]

Table 6.2: Telecommunications services: distribution of main lines

Country	Lines per 100 hab. 1980	Lines per 100 hab. 1991	Country	Lines per 100 hab. 1980	Lines per 100 hab. 1991
B	24	41	DK	42	58
D*	26	49	GR	23	39
E	18	31	F	25	49
IRL	13	27	I	21	38
L	35	48	NL	33	47
P	10	21	UK	29	46
USA	-	51.5	Japan	-	45.2

Sources: European Commission, SEC(92) 1050 final, p. 32.
The 1994 Panorama of the EU Industry, p. 25-16.
Note: * figures referring to former West Germany.

The primary responsibilities of the TOs are the provision of the infrastructure and terminals necessary for telecommunications services as well as their maintenance. The infrastructure consists of the transmission networks (copper cables, optic fibres, satellites, etc.) and of the switching units (public or private, analogous or digital). The primary telecommunications service and terminal remains the telephone: 80 to 90 per cent of the public TOs' revenues is derived from basic telephony.[8] However, the variety and the sophistication of telecommunications services and terminals have been increasing over the last 15 years due to a sequence of technological innovations: fax, videotex, audiotex, mobile phone, radiopaging, visioconference, etc.

The vocal telephony service is run by a monopolist - namely the public TO - in all Member States except in the UK. There, a private TO, Mercury Communication, has been authorized to operate next to the public TO, British Telecom, since 1984. The average level of penetration of basic telephones in the EU (42.2 lines per 100 habitants) is close to that

---

7 The EU usually faces a surplus with its main partner, the USA, because the international communication tariffs of its Member States are high.

8 The telex service developed as an important complement to telephone services after the Second World War but its use is steadily decreasing as new services provide similar possibilities with higher speed and quality. Consequently little more will be said about it.

observed in Japan (45.2) and not too far from that of the USA (52.2). This EU level of penetration resulted from a 5 per cent average growth rate of extension and penetration of the EU network over the period 1982-92 (in terms of main junction lines per subscriber). Two groups of users are usually distinguished: the residential customers and the business customers. The latter are more important than the former in terms of requirements and consumption: about 45 per cent of the basic telephony revenues come from business consumers although they own only 26 per cent of the total number of phone lines.

Recent Technological Change and Implications for Market Configuration

The market configuration has been substantially modified by a series of technological findings that occurred in the telecommunications technologies as well as in fields previously not related to it, such as computer and optic fibre technologies. The main developments are in transmission and switching techniques (from analogous mode to digital mode), in transmission support (fibre optics and satellite), and in advanced softwares and terminals.

The digitalization of information signifies that the information is transformed into bits (series of impulsion of the type 0 or 1). This implies that effective handling of the information is eased as well as made uniform across types of information (voice, data or image). In turn, it simplifies the switching operation (reducing the costs of its monitoring and maintenance) and allows for new sorts of transmission supports to be used in networks.

One of these new supports is the optic fibre, made of glass and capable of conveying light. The technology of fibre optics evolved independently of the telecommunications technology. Its industrial applications were mainly developed by the glass industry (especially by Corning, an American firm) as one additional and promising application for glass. Due to digitalization, optic fibres can be used for transmitting information under the form of light impulsions. The major advantages of this type of transmission are its speed (about one million times faster than with traditional copper cable), its reliability and its low costs.[9]

Developments in satellite technology lead to the manufacturing of more powerful antennae and more durable satellites, the exploitation of new frequency bands (10/20 GHz and 20/30 GHz; plus the experimentation of the 40/50 GHz band), and the reduction in earth station size due to the reduction in antenna size.[10] The benefits from these innovations will mostly be observable in the point-multipoint telecommunications applications because the point-point applications that the satellite networks used to handle are being more and more served by optic cable networks.[11]

The contributions of microelectronics and computer technology relate to the elaboration and design of advanced software and terminals. This software is needed to manage the digital commutation units, to monitor the private as well as public communication networks, and to elaborate new services.

The electronic information services are part of these new services; they are also called advanced services or value-added services.[12] These services are mostly demanded and used by business customers, especially by those (such as lawyers, accountants, tax advisors, bank and insurance employees, etc.) whose profession requires frequent access to external information sources. The type of services demanded by the business community are financial, business, scientific and technological information; those demanded by residential customers are entertainment services and information services (news, sports, financial).

---

9 An example of the impact of the higher efficiency of this new support is the re-allocation of the transatlantic telecommunications traffic after the installation of an optic cable network across the Atlantic Ocean: away from the satellite network (which had previously expanded in response to the low quality of the transatlantic analogous cable network) towards the optic fibre network. See the 1990 Green Paper on a Common Approach in the Field of the Satellite Communication in the European Community.

10 The diameter of new antennas varies now between 0.5m to 2.5m instead of about 30m as previously. See the 1990 Green Paper on a Common Approach in the Field of the Satellite Communication in the European Community.

11 Satellites will remain important in handling point-point radio mobile communications in remote areas where terrestrial infrastructure is lacking. See the *Financial Times* Survey, 'Telecommunications in Business', 15 June 1994, p. VI and the *Financial Times* Survey, 'International Telecommunication', 17 October 1994, p. X.

12 VANS is the corresponding acronym; it stands for value-added network services.

Table 6.3: Electronic information services in the EU

	1991	growth (%) 90/91
Employment	28,805.0	8.5
Turnover (ECU million)	3,283.0	12.2
Geographic distribution of online revenues in %:		
- National consumption	34.7	39.4
- Intra-EC trade	36.0	35.3
- Total EC domestic	70.7	37.3
- Exports	29.3	18.2
Turnover by subject content, in %:		
- Finance	63.9	3.7
- Business	27.4	24.5
- Science, technology, medicine	3.2	94.0
- Government	3.3	143.0
- Other	2.2	295.7
Turnover by services, in %:		
- Online information services	90.9	14.3
- Offline information services	9.1	4.9

Source: The 1994 Panorama of the EU Industry.

To have access to the desired information, business customers mainly use online ASCII databases and CD-Roms whereas the residential customers use cheap and user-friendly technologies such as audiotex and videotex.[13] The use of telecopy (also called facsimile or fax) and CD-Roms is well spread across both consumer groups.[14] The present dominance of the facsimile as a text-based messaging technology is justified by the huge amount - 46 billions - of pages sent and received by fax in 1993.[15] Another service developing fast among business and government administration users is Electronic Data Interchange (EDI) and electronic mail. These last two value-added services allow their users to improve business efficiency by substituting electronic forms for their paper-based counterparts.[16]

13 The audiotex service is accessible by means of a dial tone multi-frequency telephone and provides information services by means of recorded messages as well as other applications of general interest. The videotext service requires the availability of a terminal and of a regular telephone and provides various services; possibilities include information services, tourism and shows, reservation services, entertainment services, up to home-banking and home-shopping services. It is mainly available in France (80 per cent of the existing videotex infrastructure in the EU) where it is called Minitel.

14 An interesting review of the evolution of the market for electronic information services was made part of the IMPACT Program. See COM(93), 156 final.

15 See the *Financial Times* Survey, 'Telecommunications in Business', 15 June 1994, p. VII.

16 For more information, see the *Financial Times* Survey, 'Telecommunications in Business', 15 June 1994, p. VII.

Table 6.4: Information services market by delivery of support in the EU

Million ECU	1990	1995	Average % growth/yr 1990/95
ASCII Terminal	1,580	3,100	14
Videotex	300	600	15
Audiotex	220	580	21
CD-Rom	20	220	6
Total	2,120	4,500	16

Source: The 1994 Panorama of the EU Industry.

Mobile telecommunications have increased a lot over the last ten years; it is the fastest growing segment of telecommunications services market.[17] This increase was first due to the introduction of public cellular radiotelephony and later continued because of technological innovations (digitalization of mobile radiotelephony) which generated costs reductions and quality improvements.

The three most common mobile services are: private mobile radio, radiopaging, and analogous cellular radiotelephony. Digital cellular radiotelephony in Europe is based on the same pan-European norm GSM (Global System for Mobile Communications).[18] The coherence that this norm generates at the European level for digital cellular telephony (as opposed to the lack of a clear standard in the USA) proves to be a key factor in exporting the GSM to Eastern Europe, to the Middle East and the Asia/Pacific region (including, China, Hong-Kong, Singapore and Taiwan).[19] However, the low number of commercial agreements among digital cellular network operators still limits the possibility of roaming (i.e., the possibility of using the network of other digital cellular operators in the same country and/or in other countries).[20] New and/or more efficient digital mobile services are being developed; efforts sponsored by the European Telecommunications Standards Institute are made to design

[17] Mobile radio telecommunications have existed in Europe since the 1940s, but they have rapidly expanded since the mid-1980s. The number of users of the three most common services have increased by more than 20 per cent in 1991, with a 40 per cent increase for analogous cellular radiotelephony. This last service represents more than 90 per cent of the whole EU mobile radio market. See the Green Paper on mobile telecommunications, COM (94) 145 final. At the world level, cellular phone subscribers increased to 32 million between 1986 and 1993 with an annual growth rate of 45 to 59 per cent. See also the *Financial Times* Survey, 'Telecommunications in Business', 15 June 1994, p. III.

[18] The GSM standard was elaborated through cooperative R&D efforts sponsored by the EU. The number of its subscribers is still smaller than that of analogous cellular radiotelephony which benefits from an important installed basis.

[19] See the *Financial Times* Survey, 'Mobile Telecommunications', 17 September 1994, p. III.

[20] See the 1994 Green Paper on Mobile Telecommunications, p. 128 and the *Financial Times* Survey, Mobile Telecommunications, 17 September 1994, p. VIII.

pan-European standards for them so as to maximize interoperability and interconnections.

Table 6.5: EU analogous and digital cellular radiotelephony

Country	Anal. Norm	Anal. Suscribers (thousand)	Av. growth rate -yr	Digital Subscribers (thousand)	GSM Introduction Date
B	NMT450	66	14%	-	-
DK	NMT450 NMT900	47 185	-6% 23%	TO:6 DMT:15	03-92 07-92
D	C-Netz	807	9%	D1:190 D2:260	07-92 07-92
E	NMT450 TACS900	59 180	-11% 82%	-	-
F: FT SFR	RC2000 NMT450	331 125	1% 23%	FT:15 SFR:7	07-92 07-92
IRL	TACS900	50	25%	-	-
I	RMTS TACS900	35 950	-33% 39%	1	10-92
L	NMT450	0.9	0%	3.4	07-93
NL	NMT450 NMT900	27 170	4% 33%	-	-
P	C-Netz	30	30%	-	-
UK:BT M	TACS900 TACS900	711 895	23% 19%	1	12-91

Source: 1994 Green Paper on Mobile Telecommunications, p. 82

The main technological consequence of these innovations is that each type of transmitted information (voice, data or image) no longer requires the use of a specific network (respectively, telephone, telex or packet switching). In other words, a same network (often referred to as ISDN, Integrated Service Digital Network, or its future version, broadband ISDN) allows for the integrated distribution of all three information types. The potentials of such an ISDN network are described by experts as revolutionary.[21] The multiple applications and services made possible by this network are expected to influence various aspects of life: work thanks to teleworking; education thanks to distance learning; research thanks to networks among universities and research centres; road circulation thanks to traffic management systems; air transportation thanks to air traffic control; health thanks to healthcare networks; public procurement thanks to electronic tendering.[22] Most of these services (for example, long-distance learning, long-distance medical diagnosis) are already

---

[21] See, for example, the 1994 White Paper on Growth, Competitiveness and Employment, section 3.6, and the 1994 Bangemann Report.

[22] See the Bangemann Report (1994).

operational on a small scale, providing evidence of their possibilities and economic feasibility.[23] The issue is thus no more whether or not such services will emerge, but when and how they will spread as well as their impact on society.

Another crucial effect of these innovations is observed on the structure of the supplier side of the market. Firms mastering neighbouring technologies with growing importance for telecommunications as well as firms developing new telecommunications techniques try to enter the telecommunications service sector. They exert pressure on EU and national authorities to obtain a progressive liberalization s developing new telecommunications techniques try to enter the telecommunications service sector. They exert pressure on EU and national authorities to obtain a progressive liberalization of the new services markets. This last effect supplements the call for deregulation coming from the USA and the UK.[24] However strong these calls and pressures, the degree of effective liberalization in the EU Member States is low on average, slowly increasing under the pressure of the EU legislation and under that of business customers.[25]

The Liberalization Process

The liberalization of the telecoms equipment market demanded by the 1988 EU Directive (88/301/EEC) was completed with a delay of three years due to a slow implementation in four countries (Belgium, Denmark, Germany and Ireland). Indications of an increase in competition following this directive are seen in price reductions and in an

---

23 See the *Financial Times* Survey, 'Telecommunications in Business', 15 June 1994, p. XII.

24 In the USA the commercial monopoly, AT&T, was dismantled in 1984 and since then the provision of long-distance calls and value-added services is open and competitive. (For a quick recall and assessment of the effects of the AT&T deregulation on its telecommunications services activities and on its telecommunications equipments productions, see the Communication of the Commission of 25th June 1992 concerning the European Telecommunications Equipments Industry: Situation, Stakes, and Propositions of Actions.) In the UK, a private TO Mercury received, in 1984, a licence to operate in parallel with British Telecom in all telecoms services. It is interesting to notice the difference in regulatory measures surrounding these two liberalizations in long-distance call activities. In the UK customers are automatically connected with British Telecom unless they ask otherwise. In the USA customers must choose their long-distance carriers on their own. This is said to explain why British Telecom still keeps 90 per cent of that market while AT&T market share is now 65 per cent due to fierce competition from MCI, Sprint, and other long-distance carriers. See the *Financial Times* Survey, 'International Communications', 17 October 1994, p.VI.

25 See next section for a description of the major modifications of the EU telecoms policies and legislations.

augmentation of product diversity affecting, for example, mobile telephone handsets as well as switching units.[26]

The extent of the liberalization of all non-voice services (i.e., VANS) market to be achieved by 1990 according to the EU Directive (90/388/EEC) is still limited. New entrants complain about the lack of available leased lines as well as about the prices charged by public TOs to let them have access to these lines.[27]

In some countries, the movement towards liberalization initiated by the EU legislation has expanded to other telecom services that can still be legally provided on the basis of exclusive rights. This is especially visible in the area of mobile telephony. Several countries have allowed - or plan to allow - a duopoly for digital cellular telephony by selling a second licence to a private firm which would provide the service in competition with the public TO (which has the first licence). Where mobile phone operators compete, prices decrease and the different equipment-tariff packages offered to consumers reflect strategies used by the operators to differentiate one from another.[28] The situation in the UK, where four mobile telephony operators compete, illustrates this well. In 1993, competition led the price of one minute of daytime call in the London region to fall from 33p to 20p and then to 16p. It also pushed some operators to offer free local calls on specific times and days, or as part of the monthly subscription rate.[29]

---

26 See, for example, the *Financial Time* Survey, 'Telecommunications in Business', 15 June 1994, p. III. According to the head of Siemens' public communication networks group, prices for transmission and switching equipment have fallen, in real terms, by about 7 per cent during the last three years. See the *Financial Times* Survey, 'International Telecommunications', 17 October 1994, p. IV.

27 See the 1992 Review of the Telecommunications Sector by the European Commission, p. 21-2. Sun and Pelkmans (1994) provide the following evidence: 'The cost of a 200 km leased line between the UK and France is more than eight times more expensive than a leased line of the same distance within the UK only (*Financial Times*, 24 February 1994)'; 'European wide-area connections or WANs (especially leased lines) can account for as much as 80 per cent of the total cost of setting up a network to link remote sites. This compares to about 35 per cent in the US (*Communications Week International*, 7 February 1994)'; 'At present, more than 80 per cent of the EU's high-speed leased lines are located in the UK .... For the rest of the Union to catch up with the UK, an "infrastructure gap" equivalent to 130,000 circuits will have to be filled. This represents a five-fold increase on present levels. (Ungerer, H., 1993, 'Reconciling Telecommunications Liberalization and Trans-European Networks', Keynote Address, CEPS Focus on European Telecommunications and Competitiveness, 9 November)'.

28 See the comparisons of GSM digital cellular tariffs among AELE countries on p.V of the *Financial Times* Survey, 'Telecommunications in Business', 15 June 1994.

29 See the *Financial Time* Survey, 'Telecommunications in Business', 15 June 1994, p. III.

Another aspect of the supply-side structure change is the setting up of joint ventures and consortia among major TOs of different countries.[30] These TOs justify such collaborative strategies as are necessary to reach the critical size and the sufficient geographical spread needed to benefit from liberalization and essential in order not to lose in the globalization process expected to occur in the telecom services. However, authorities in charge of competition fear that these alliances give too much market power to their members and hinder future competition in the market. In the last two years three global alliances proposing ambitious projects emerged. First, an alliance, called Concert, between British Telecom (UK) and MCI (second largest long-distance operator in the USA). Its objective is to develop one-stop voice and data services for multinationals. It has been approved by the US Department of Justice as well as by its UK equivalent. Second, an alliance, called Atlas, among Deutsche Telekom, France Telecom and Sprint (third largest long-distance operator in the USA). Its objective is an efficient handling of telecommunications services for multinationals. It has not yet been approved by either the American or the EU antitrust authorities. Third, an alliance, called Worldsource/Unisource, among the public TOs of Sweden, Switzerland, the Netherlands and Spain, and AT&T. It is aimed at merging their international telecoms network in order to supply one-stop international telecom services. In addition there are several consortia of less importance, such as the alliance among Air Touch (USA), British Telecom (UK), and two Spanish banks (Airtel-ASR) for exploiting the second GSM licence in Spain, or the alliance between British Telecom (UK) and Ving (D) to build a network to offer data services to large corporate clients.

Besides mergers and alliances, the conduct of a telecommunications services supplier includes tariffs setting, investments in infrastructure, investments in research, delivery of telecom services and the obligation to fulfil certain regulatory requirements (such as supply of universal service at affordable rates and minimal financial contribution to the government budget).

Issues of Pricing

The tariffs proposed to users by any European TO are regulated by government and national authorities. The tariff of a service is usually

---

30 See the *Financial Times* Survey, 'International Telecommunications', 17 October 1994, p. XI.

composed of three elements: a connection charge (i.e., a fee for installing the connection between the user and the network), a subscription charge to be paid per period (every month or every two months) for keeping the right to use the connection and for having the services available, and a charge per call which differs according to the duration of the call, the time of the call (day or night, working days, weekends or holidays, etc.) and the location of the person who is called (within the local area, within the country, or abroad). For international calls, the tariffs and procedures according to which the revenues are shared among TOs are derived from rules and recommendations issued by an international organization, the International Telecommunications Union (ITU), and from bilateral agreements between firms or network owners. The core of the international charge is a sharing tax which serves as a basis for the revenues of the TOs. This tax is shared among the TOs of the countries through which the call transits (i.e., the countries of origin, of destination and of transit, if any).

The principal characteristics of the EU tariffs structure for basic telephony are:[31]

- The prices of local and national calls are low (i.e., below cost) and those of international calls are high (i.e., well above cost).[32] The revenues from these high prices are partly used to subsidize the local and national call activity. The use of cross-subsidies has traditionally been justified as a means of increasing the number of subscribers to a given network so as to comply with the 'universal service' requirement and to exploit positive network externalities. That prices are not oriented to the costs is made possible by the monopoly structure for basic telephony.
- A strong frontier effect exists for intra-EU calls. This effect shows in various ways. First, a 3-minute international call can be as much as 2.5 to 3 times more expensive than a national call of comparable distance in peak time periods (and up to 5 or 6 times in off-peak periods). Second, the price of a call often varies a lot

---

[31] In order to understand the pricing behaviour of the public TOs, it would be ideal to obtain information on their cost structures. Unfortunately this type of information is considered to be confidential and is not accessible.

[32] Historically international calls were more expensive to supply and so required to be charged a high rate. The introduction of new technologies in the 1960s and 1970s reduced the production costs of these calls. However, the prices of these calls were maintained at their initial levels and the additional revenues from not adjusting the price to the costs were invested elsewhere in the network.

according to the country from which it originates; in particular, the price of a call in one direction can differ from that in the opposite direction by a factor of up to 2.

- Divergence of practices among EU countries: some charge the same rate for all calls made to any country within the EU (i.e., independently of the distance, but still depending on the time of the call) whereas others do not.
- Few discounts (i.e., small percentage of reduction as well as low number of hours during which some reduction applies) are offered in night-time and weekend tariffs for intra-EU telephony compared to national telephony.

The increase in competition in the long-distance call activities in the USA and the UK has led to a series of price-cutting moves that have benefited the customers of these countries.[33] This has also had an impact on the prices offered by European public TOs. Indeed as they did not revise international tariffs downwards while the costs were decreasing, new technological devices emerged to by-pass the TO monopoly charges.[34] And large business customers - using international calls intensively and bringing the most revenues to these TOs - started to use these devices and/or switch to the extent possible to rival TOs proposing lower prices. Consequently part of the traffic flows now reflects which TOs offer the most favourable rates although these flows are not justified on the basis of actual costs. Another outcome of these traffic diversions (which do not contravene any competition rule) is the loss of revenues for high tariff TOs.[35]

The numerous inefficient or perverse effects of the distorted tariff structure for telephony generated in 1988 a consensus among EU and national authorities in charge of telecommunications: to progressively orient the tariff structure towards costs. This led to efforts towards re-balancing charges across services according to their costs. Between 1980 and 1991, the tariffs decreased by about 2 per cent in real terms, probably

---

33 See the *Financial Times* Survey, 'Telecommunications in Business', 15 June 1994, p. II

34 New technologies make possible traffic diversions. First, some TOs extend their network (mainly via satellite links) and so are able to offer international call services with a minimum transit on other TOs' networks. They benefit from their investment by charging less than would otherwise be charged because their lower prices attract intensive phone users. Second, equipment providing an automatic 'call-me-back' feature is developed. This device leads to an automatic re-dial of any incoming call that originates from a country in which telephone charges are higher than those prevailing in the incoming country.

35 See the 1992 Review of the Telecommunications Sector by the European Commission, p. 21.

reflecting a similar reduction of costs: connection charges, subscription charges, and prices of long-distance calls decreased while the prices of local calls increased. The modification in prices varied according to the countries and the type of network at stake.[36] Additional improvements included the progressive generalization of pricing calls according to duration and the introduction of flexibility in the definition of local areas. The latter is aimed at reducing anomalies in tariff structure that may occur with calls among neighbours located in different calling areas. The first reduction in international taxes took place in 1992, others followed, and further ones are to be expected.[37] Some of these future reductions will affect the price of transatlantic calls because of the important increase in transmission capacity resulting from the installation of optic cables across the Atlantic Ocean. However, besides all these changes, the intra-EU frontier effect remains quite strong and scope for further intra-EU tariff reductions exists.[38]

The issue of pricing is especially delicate for new telecom services in the EU. First, to find the adequate price level for these services matters: they should not be too low so as to allow the reimbursement of substantial initial investments and they should not be too high so as to attract rapidly a large customer base.[39] Second, a conflict of interest emerges between the incumbent TOs and the entrants' suppliers. One reason explaining this conflict is that most new services require access to the existing infrastructure owned almost exclusively by public TOs. The other reason is that these new services generate a move away from old services exclusively provided by the public TOs. The EU TOs have thus little incentive to provide entrants with fair and quick access to the infrastructure because they do not want to lose revenues from the old

---

[36] Reductions are usually larger on the digital network than in the electro-mechanic one.

[37] Indeed, according to some observers the level of present sharing taxes does not reflect real costs and derives from cartel behaviour on the part of major public and private TOs. The percentage of tax - 65 per cent to 85 per cent on a per unit price of expensive intra-EU calls in 1991 - does not invalidate this fact. See European Commission, SEC(92) 1050 final p. 16.

[38] This is illustrated by the statistics found in the 1992 Review by the European Commission (p. 19): between 1984 and 1992 US interstate telephone tariffs fell on average by 9.7 per cent per year in real terms, while between 1980 and 1990 intra-EU tariffs fell on average by 3.5 per cent per year in real terms.

[39] In mobile telephony, prices have on average decreased (60 per cent of GSM operators reduced their price between June 1993 and June 1994) but in some places they have increased. See the *Financial Times* Survey, 'Telecommunications in Business', 15 June 1994, p. V.

services and because they also provide these new services.[40] Third, the issue of universal service has to be clearly addressed. Today the public TOs are obliged to provide this service, which is known to be unprofitable in several segments of the market. If new operators are allowed to compete with the incumbent public TOs for profitable advanced and value-added services, they will reduce the revenue basis of the TOs. In order to prevent any competition distortion and maintain the quality of the universal service, new operators, too, should in some ways share part of this service burden. No precise agreement has been reached yet about how to regulate such an obligation.[41] The combination of the three factors just mentioned has had an important repercussion on the pace of introduction of new services - too slow - in the EU as well as on their prices - too high. It is observed that in the UK where effective liberalization is at an advanced stage, the introduction of new services has been fast and that competition has led to price reductions.[42]

Substantial investments in infrastructure have been observed in all EU countries. They have mainly been carried by the public TOs. Part of these investments is used to improve the network: modernization of switching centres so as to generalize direct international calling and thus make it cheaper on the one hand, and upgrading of existing transmission equipment so as to reduce transmission costs and to make the price of a call less dependent on distance on the other hand. The rest is aimed at expanding the network in areas which are not yet well served (low density population areas and areas difficult to reach) as well as installing the new

---

[40] Evidence has been found that public TOs often hinder the opening up of the market and distort competition in various ways. The case of cross-subsidies by the Deutsche Telekom illustrates this well: transfer of DM 1.9 billion from protected services to competitively supplied services. According to the EU Competition Commissioner, firms which have evidence concerning the abuse of dominant position by their TOs refuse to lodge formal complaints for fear of reprisals. See the *Financial Times* Survey, 'Telecommunications in Business', 15 June 1994, p. IV.

[41] See Sun and Pelkmans (1994). Notice that the experience of liberalized telecom markets, such as in Sweden or the UK, suggests that the cost of universal services is not as high as public TOs would like politicians and regulators to believe. In these liberalized markets the provision of universal services has not worsened with the increase of competition in long-distance telecommunications and firms active in these services have not shown signs of lower profitability. These facts would mean that public TOs need the maintenance of their monopoly status for other reasons than universal services, such as to fulfil their financial contribution requirement, to hide an employment policy or inefficient management. See the *Financial Times* Survey, 'Telecommunications in Business', 15 June 1994, p. IV; the *Financial Times* Survey, 'International Telecommunications', 17 October 1994, p. II, IV, XII.

[42] See the *Financial Times* Survey, 'International Telecommunications', 17 October 1994, p. VI.

special lines and switching units required to provide advanced services. Two categories of such lines are distinguished: those for the Integrated Services Digital Network (speed of voice telephone call is 64 kilobytes per second and high-speed transmission reaches 2 megabytes per second) and those of the broadband network (transmission speed allowing for high through-put such as video messages: 140 megabytes per second). Bits of an ISDN network are built slowly especially in large urban areas in which there is sufficient demand for the services carried by the ISDN. Elements of a broadband network are developed as part of experiments.[43]

Although the EU policy provides a useful framework and support for introducing new technology-based networks, the '1992 Review of the Situation in the Telecommunications Services Sector' of the European Commission indicates that the development of these networks is insufficient and suboptimal. First, the number of lines supplied for new services provision is low and its growth rate is weak. This leads to lengthy waiting lists (up to several years) for installing these lines and for connecting them to the basic infrastructure in many places. Second, a major issue of intra-EU interoperability and interconnection among the various existing bits of ISDN arises because all Member States do not choose the same standard. These two factors result in an unequal offering of new services across the EU. The EU framework has been used to prevent further lack of intra-EU interoperability in other advanced applications. Success is achieved in mobile telephony where a pan-European standard, GSM, has been adopted; further similar efforts are made to reach a consensus concerning broadband transmission standards.

Investments, and Services Quality and Diversity

Public TOs invest mainly in two areas: infrastructure and R&D. Total gross investments by EU public TOs have increased over the last decade.

---

[43] The cost of the required investments in networks for the 1994-95 period is ECU 20 billion for installing the broadband network and ECU 15 billion for upgrading the ISDN network. See the table: 'Trans-European Telecommunications Networks: Propositions' in Section 3.6. of the 1994 White Paper on Growth, Competitiveness, and Employment.

Table 6.6: Telecommunications Services: Gross Investments (million ECU)

Country	1980	1991	Country	1980	1991
B	426.3	668.7	DK	250.4	355.7
D	3,956.9	11,870.2	GR	177.8	440.9
E	1,175.4	4,846.9	F	4,028.5	4,959.7
IRL	190.6	222.1	I	2,052.4	6,499.9
L	17.9	51.6	NL	510.8	1,312.0
P	106.5	426.6	UK	2,030.5	3,659.1

Source: The 1994 Panorama of the EU Industry. p.25-14.

This increase is especially visible in Portugal, Spain, Greece and Germany (after reunification) and reflects the need for these countries to expand and/or upgrade their network. The main reason for the increase in investments is the digitalization of telecommunications and its implications. First, it required substantial investments in the research and development of the digitalization techniques. Then it induced large investments in upgrading the infrastructure accordingly: construction of digital switching units and installation of optic fibre networks.

Investments in telecommunications R&D by public TOs vary across the EU. In some countries, such as France, the TO is the largest contributor to private R&D in the telecommunications sector whereas in others, such as Germany, the equipment manufacturers are the largest investors. On average, the public TOs contribute between 20 and 25 per cent to R&D expenditures in the telecommunications sector (a low percentage of which is used to finance external R&D). However, close examination of the national R&D systems reveals that in all countries there exists a close cooperation between public TOs and manufacturers.[44]

The provision of telecommunications services can be described by means of its quality and diversity. Studies on the European telecom sector highlight how the TOs' price-setting policy and their infrastructure and R&D investment strategies have led to a lower quality and a reduced diversity of their services compared to what is available in the USA.[45] The lower quality is mainly reflected through a longer waiting period before connection (whether for basic telephony or new services), a smaller number of public phone boots, lower density of the network in terms of traditional and new transmission lines, and higher frequency of

---

[44] For more detail, see Grupp and Schnöring (1992).

[45] The UK in which liberalization started in 1984 with the authorization for a private carrier to supply telecommunications services, is considered as the EU state offering the best price-quality-diversity combination. See the *Financial Times* Survey, 'Telecommunications in Business', 15 June 1994, pp. IV and X.

interferences or interruptions. The reduced diversity results from a slower pace of adoption of new services. This is mainly caused by the regulatory context giving exclusive rights to one TO and so protecting it from strong competitive pressures towards infrastructure modernization and product innovation. In particular, the tariff structure that has arisen in that context is identified as the source of a vicious circle: high prices discourage demand; this in turn provides low incentives to invest in infrastructure and new services and requires the maintenance of high prices in order to recover costs.

The quality and the diversity of telecom services in the EU has improved - especially as regards basic telephony - since the 1987 Telecommunications Green Paper and the expression of a European will to make telecommunications a priority. As has been shown in preceding paragraphs, the result of several policy measures adopted by the EU and the Member States is an increase of competition in the terminal equipment and value-added service markets after their liberalization. In these markets, competition and marketing innovations by incumbent and new participants have led to cost reductions which in turn benefited customers through lower prices (especially those of customer premises, equipment and mobile telephony). However, as various reports indicate, many more efforts have to be made in order to reach a satisfactory situation in terms of pricing, supply of, and access to, high-speed lines and diversity and volume of new advanced services.[46]

This brief survey of the telecommunications services sector first reveals that a stream of technological innovations have been taking place in this sector, substantially modifying its role in the economy. It also points out the difficulties generated by existing national regulations and public TOs' behaviour of adjusting to, and efficiently exploiting, this technological dynamic. In response to the technological change and the growing awareness of the role of telecommunications services in economic growth and competitiveness, the EU authorities acted towards creating an environment which would allow the EU to benefit from this evolution. In the next section, the EU policies concerning the telecommunications services sector are described.

---

[46] See, for example, the 1992 Review of the Telecommunications Services Sector by the European Commission and the 1994 Bangemann Report.

C. THE DEVELOPMENT OF THE EU POLICIES IN THE TELECOMMUNICATIONS SERVICES SECTOR: TRADE, INDUSTRY AND COMPETITION POLICIES

European policy in the sector of the telecommunications services was almost non-existent until the 1980s. Indeed, until then this sector was excluded from the scope of the common market policy and remained the exclusive domain of the Member States and the relevant national authorities. This was reflected in the fragmented state of the EU telecommunications services market.

Concerns grew about the ability of such a segmented market to adjust to, and efficiently exploit, the burst of major innovations in switching, transmission and equipment technologies in the 1970s. Indeed the costs of developing and implementing these technologies are so substantial that no Member State national market is large enough for its public TO to be able to recoup these costs. In addition the efficiency of some new services is likely to be impaired if they happen to be developed separately along different standards, making intra-EU interoperability and interconnection difficult, costly and leading to long delays.

It is in response to these concerns that the Commission began to have an active policy concerning telecommunications in the middle of the 1980s. In the rest of this section, the sequence of policies adopted by the EU authorities is set out. First, the policies of the period from 1984 to 1987 are presented as those of the first phase. Then the measures decided as a result of the adoption of the 1987 Green Paper on Telecommunications are summarized as those of the second phase. This is supplemented by the examination of the pre-competitive R&D policy measures taken since 1987.

The First Phase

In 1984 a first phase started, during which preparatory works and preliminary initiatives took place.

The programme that was at the basis of the first phase comprised five lines of action. One line of action was aimed at the initial coordination of future development of networks. It included efforts towards developing the ISDN, stimulating the ongoing transformation of the existing phone network into a fully digital network, setting the premises for introducing broadband communication and developing digital mobile communication and a pan-European mobile communication network. A second line of action concerned the setting up of European-wide open standards for terminal equipment as a way to progress towards a Community-wide terminal equipment market. A third point of that first phase was the promotion of collaborative pre-competitive and pre-normative R&D and the definition of an important programme for cooperative R&D in the field of telecommunications (RACE). A fourth set of actions dealt with the introduction of advanced services and improved networks in less favoured peripheral regions. The consensus that telecommunications may serve as a tool to ease the economic and social development of these regions constituted the starting point of the STAR programme. The last aspect of that phase consisted of efforts towards reaching a common EU position in international discussions with the objective of defending the EU interests in telecommunications.

This first phase thus shows a series of preliminary steps mainly geared towards harnessing new technologies by means of industrial policy measures. The construction of a unique market for telecom services, however, was not the explicit target of these various initial measures. The actions taken during the first phase and the results of the various studies they commended created a general consensus about the importance of telecommunications for EU economic growth and prosperity. This in turn led to the second phase which began in 1987.

The Second Phase

The target of that second phase was a reform of the sector and the elaboration of a global concept for its development so as to establish a properly functioning internal market which could sustain the efficient and timely development of new services and networks.

The first step of that second phase was the enlargement of the EU telecommunications policy with the adoption by the Council of the Green Paper on Telecommunications in 1988. This adoption implied the expansion of the policy in two ways: first, regulatory conditions were included, and second, competition was to be progressively introduced in the sector. A second consequence of this adoption was the full integration of the EU telecommunications policy into the 1992 programme for internal market completion.

Six objectives for the achievement of a Community-wide open telecommunications market were identified in this Green Paper and subsequently implemented via the adoption of a series of directives shaping the regulatory environment in the field of telecommunications.[47] The measures taken in these decisions reflects an approach combining liberalization and harmonization.

The first objective was the liberalization of the supply and provision of terminal and network equipment. The main directives achieving this objective are the Commission Directive of 16 May 1988 on competition in the markets in telecommunications terminal equipment (88/301/EEC, OJ L 131/73, 27.05.88), the Council Directive of 29 April 1991 on the approximation of the laws of the Member States concerning telecommunications terminal equipment, including the mutual recognition of their conformity (91/263/EEC, OJ L 128/1,23.05.91), and the Council Resolution on the development of the common market for satellite communications services and equipment (92/C8/01, OJ C 8/1, 14.01.92).

The second objective was the liberalization of services, with the temporary exception of public voice telephony (including fax) and the operation of the basic network. This objective was achieved mostly via the Commission Directive of 28 June 1990 on competition in the market for telecommunications services (90/388/EEC, OJ L 192/10, 24.7.90).[48]

The third objective was the separation of the regulatory and operational functions in order to create efficient market structures.

The fourth objective was to ensure open access conditions to networks and interworking and interconnection (Open Network Provision). This objective was enabled essentially by the Council Directive of 28 June 1990 on the establishment of the internal market for telecommunications services through the implementation of open network provision (90/387/EEC, OJ L 192/1, 24.7.90), the Council Directive of 5 June 1992 on the application of open network provision for leased lines (OJ L 165, 19.06.92). These two directives define the principles according to which services providers and users can have access to telecommunications networks and public services. Their objective is to guarantee an access that is harmonized, objective, transparent and non-discriminatory across the EU and among call-users and services providers.

The fifth objective was the stimulation of European standardization. The Commission supported three lines of actions: i) promotion and determination of standards that are believed to be 'pro-competitive'; ii)

---

47 Many directives, decisions, regulations, recommendations and resolutions related to telecommunications have been adopted since 1984. Only some of the major directives will be mentioned in the text.

48 Telex, mobile telephony, radiopaging and satellite services were excluded from the scope of this directive and thus were not liberalized. Intelligent fax, videotex and data networks were liberalized in early 1993.

encouragement of the use of European standards in public procurement; iii) prevention of adoption of standards by Member States which the Commission believes will inhibit the flow of trade.[49] The creation of the European Telecommunication Standards Institute (ETSI) was the major action in this field. This Institute was founded in 1988 as a place favouring interactions for the elaboration of technical specifications. It is in permanent contact with other European and international organizations in charge of norms and standards in the field of telecommunications, such as CEN/CENELEC or CCITT.[50]

The sixth and last objective was the full application of competition rules to the sector. The Council Directive of 17 September 1990 on procurement procedures of entities operating the water, energy, transport and telecommunications sectors (90/531/EEC, OJ L 297/1, 29.10.90) is one of the decisions that take care of this issue. The Guidelines on the application of EEC competition rules in the telecommunications sector (91/c233/02, OJ C 233/2, 06.09.91) published by the Commission provided its viewpoint concerning the global approach to this issue of how to apply EEC competition rules to this sector.

The implementation of these various directives is supervised by the Commission. With regard to competition in the telecommunications services sector, a summary of the evolution of the relevant EU legislation is provided on a yearly basis in the annual competition reports. In these reports the degree of implementation of these liberalization and harmonization directives is also described.[51] Actions taken against Member States that are not complying with the implementation deadlines

---

49 See Besen (1990).

50 A major achievement of the cooperative standardization efforts is the design of a pan-European norm for digital cellular telephony, GSM. The GSM norm is the main standard for digital cellular telephony in the EU and is developing with success in the rest of the world. See *supra*.

51 See, for example, the 19th Report on Competition Policy (point 226), the 20th Report on Competition Policy (points 54-60, and 355), the 21st Report on Competition Policy (points 20-25, 8-82, 323-324, appendix II) and the 22nd Report on Competition Policy (points 30-37, and 511).

are mentioned. Later the date of compliance to the directives is signalled.[52]

The EU authorities' concern to increase competition in the telecommunications services sector also shows in their attentive handling of mergers and joint ventures among telecom firms. Joint ventures aimed at developing a pan-European digital cellular mobile telephony system, such as the consortium ECR 900 among AEG Aktiengesellschaft (from Germany), Alcatel NV (of Franco-Dutch origin), and OY Nokia (from Finland) were given negative attestation on the basis of Article 85, para. 3. Another example of granting exemption on the basis of Article 85, para. 3 occurred in the field of radiopaging.[53] Ambitious alliances among major TOs (such as between British Telecom and MCI, or among Deutsche Telekom, France Telecom and Spring) are under investigation.

Simultaneously, decisions were taken and efforts were made to continue and expand the set of actions started as part of the third and fourth lines of actions of the first phase: the promotion of collaborative pre-competitive and pre-normative R&D and the definition of an important programme for cooperative R&D in the field of telecommunications (RACE) and the introduction of advanced services and improved networks in less favoured peripheral regions.

The Continuity of the Pre-Competitive R&D Policy

The major Community R&D programme in the telecommunications sector, RACE, is a ten-year programme adopted by the Council on 14 December 1987, the goal of which is the global development of integrated broadband communication.[54] The strength of the project would lie in getting all the parties concerned about the evolution of telecommunications

---

52 For example, regarding the implementation of the directive liberalizing the terminal equipment market, the 19th Report identified Belgium, Denmark, Germany and Ireland as countries that still imposed restrictions on the supply of the first telephone set. The 20th report indicated that Denmark, Germany and Ireland lifted these restrictions and that infraction procedures were still in force against Belgium and Spain. The 21st Report mentions that these two countries have abandoned their exclusive rights to supply the first telephone set. See the 19th Report on Competition Policy (point 226), the 20th Report on Competition Policy (point 355), and the 21st Report on Competition Policy (point 323).

53 See the case of the joint venture between Irish Telecom and Motorola targeting the creation, promotion and exploitation of a radiopaging system for Ireland. See the 20th Report on Competition Policy (points 59 and 60).

54 See the Council Decision of 14 December 1987 on a Community programme in the field of telecommunications technologies, research and development (R&D) in advanced communications technologies in Europe (RACE programme) (88/28/EEC, OJ L 16/35, 21.01.88).

services (public TOs, equipment manufacturers, suppliers of new services, etc.) to cooperate extensively.

The first five-year phase (1988-92) was part of the second R&DT Framework Programme and its budget amounted to 405 Million ECU. The objective of this first phase was to promote the competitiveness of the telecommunications equipment and services industry so that consumers could benefit, without any delay and at low cost, from all telecom services necessary to sustain economic growth, employment and competitiveness.

During the 1988-92 years, the focus of the RACE project was twofold. On the one hand, cooperative efforts were made to speed up the harmonization of the European infrastructure and to elaborate common functional specifications for the integrated broadband (high-capacity) communication networks and technologies carrying voice, data and image signals. One satisfactory outcome was the transmission of several hundred specification projects to various European and international normalization authorities. On the other hand, collaborative R&D work was done to implement the asynchronous transfer mode (ATM) for high-speed switching in digital communications, to improve techniques to manage networks, and to develop technologies and norms for HDTV and digital video. In addition, collaborations between RACE and other pan-European R&D programmes such as Eureka or COST took place so as to optimize R&D in the field of telecommunications.

Additional R&D cooperative programmes studying the use of advanced telecommunications services in other sectors started at the same time: AIM in the field of medicine, DELTA in the field of education, DRIVE in the field of transport. Also, specific R&D programmes were launched then for electronic data interchange, for developing information services (IMPACT programme), for assisting EU less-favoured regions in telecommunications development (STAR programme, followed by Programme Télématique).[55] Steps were made towards a common approach to the introduction of High Definition Television (HDTV); this

[55] The STAR programme benefited from a Community aid of nearly 770 million ECU for the period 1987-91. This programme heavily promoted investments in infrastructure (80 per cent of the budget was allocated to it) and stimulated the access to advanced telecommunications services by firms of the less favoured regions (using the remaining 20 per cent of its budget). The Programme Télématique with a budget of 200 million ECU for 1991-93 continued the actions started under STAR aimed at introducing advanced telecommunications systems into firms.

pan-European collaboration stopped later because the technique chosen for this cooperation turned out to be suboptimal.[56]

The results of RACE's first phase were assessed as positive and the lines of action for the second phase (1993-97) were adopted in June 1991 so as to ensure continuity.[57] While the first phase was more oriented towards evaluating the various options for integrated broadband communications (IBCs), the second phase is geared towards preparing the effective introduction of IBCs and further developing applications, services and techniques for network operation and management. The Community cooperative R&D activities in the field of telecommunications services (mainly RACE and Programme Télématique) were integrated into a global effort towards trans-European telecommunications networks by means of the adoption of the third Framework Programme.[58]

Towards a Third Phase

As required by the 1990 Directives concerning competition in telecoms services and ONP framework (90/387/EEC, and 90/388/EEC) the results of the EU telecoms policy as well as the situation in the field of telecommunications were assessed in 1992.[59] It was agreed that the report summarizing these evaluations would become the basis for a major round of consultations among the various parties involved in the telecommunications services sector. The issue of the debate was the type of policy to be adopted for the future, given the growing importance of telecommunications: either to stop the liberalization process, or to implement an extensive regulation for tariffs and investments, or to fully liberalize all vocal telephony communications, or to partially liberalize them.

---

56 The EU cooperative efforts focused on an analogous mode of transmission. Their outcomes would most likely have been dominated by the results of other works based on a digital mode of transmission (and taking place in the USA). The major European firms that were involved in the analogous approach to HDTV have also been, and still are, participating in the R&D aimed at a digital HDTV.

57 See the Final Report Concerning Phase 1 (1988-1992) of the Ten-year Programme RACE, COM(93) 118 final, Brussels, 30.03.93.

58 See the Council Decision of 7 June 1991 adopting a specific research and technological development programme in the field of communication technologies (1990-94) (91/352/EEC, OJ L 192/8, 16.07.91). See the Council Decision of 7 June 1991 adopting a specific research and technological development programme in the field of telematic systems in areas of general interest (1990-94) (91/352/EEC, OJ L 192/8, 16.07.91).

59 See Commission of the European Communities, '1992 Review of the Situation in the Telecommunications Services Sector', SEC(92) 1048 final, Brussels, 21.10.92.

The round of consultations took place in late 1992 and early 1993.[60] This first led to a nuanced assessment of the situation in the telecommunications services sector. It was concluded that the special and exclusive rights held by TOs in each Member State (except the UK) caused EU telecom services to be underdeveloped.[61] Then participants unanimously voted in favour of a total liberalization of public vocal telephony. Finally a list of recommendations for the future development of the telecommunications services sector was issued, including a request for a precise calendar of the evolution of the regulation (with well-defined steps).

In response to the consultations, the Commission established a two-phase calendar in April 1993, which was adopted by the Council in July 1993. The first phase (1993-95) would aim at reinforcing the implementation of existing legislation and at preparing future pieces of regulation. The main objectives of future legislations are the complete liberalization of public vocal telephony by 1 January 1998 (with some derogations for Spain, Portugal, Greece and Ireland up to 2003, and for Luxemburg up to 2000) and necessary amendments to the EU regulatory framework for telecoms (especially concerning tariff structures, network interconnections and access conditions, and universal services). The second phase (1996-98) would target the implementation of these new regulations.

Since the beginning of the first phase, reports on the concept, and the supply, of universal service in the telecommunications sector, a Green Paper on mobile communications and the first part of a Green Paper on the liberalization of telecommunications infrastructures and cable TV networks have been published.[62] (Legislation on the basis of these documents is expected in 1995).

The Council Resolution adopted at the end of 1993 reflected the position of the EU authorities as regards the universal service and the various problems to be tackled in order to prepare for its liberalization. In that resolution, universal service is defined as a minimum service of specified quality available to all users at an affordable price. The reduction of the divergence between tariffs and costs is viewed as necessary for two reasons. First, to alleviate the bottlenecks created by the non-cost orientation of the tariffs, and second, to reduce distortions to effective

---

60 See the Commission's communication to the Council and the Parliament about these consultations, COM(93) 159 final, Brussels, 28.04.1993.

61 The identified bottlenecks are a lack of advanced services, the low availability of high-capacity leased lines, high cross-border tariffs, and insufficient cost-orientation of the tariffs.

62 See respectively COM(93) 543 final, Brussels, 15.11.93, COM(94) 145 final, Brussels, 27.04.1994, and COM (94) 440 final, Brussels, 25.10.1994.

competition between incumbent TOs and new entrants.[63] The delicate issue of financing local and subscriber charges if cross-subsidies between international and local calls are to be substantially reduced will need to be carefully investigated.[64] The solution to this problem should satisfy two criteria. First, low-income households and rural areas should not be excessively affected by this tariff rebalancing. Second, inefficient new service suppliers not burdened by the universal services obligations should have no incentive to enter. To devise such a solution will require the evaluation of the costs of meeting these obligations. This task is likely to be difficult because these universal services obligations differ among Member States in terms of definition and implementation.

The Green Paper on mobile communication first provides a thorough assessment of the mobile communication situation in the EU as well as abroad from a technical and a regulatory point of view. Successful achievements, such as the creation of the efficient GSM digital norm, are pointed out and are contrasted with existing problems, such as the limited possibility of roaming, the lack of interoperability, or the difference in licence procurement procedures. Then it defines the fundamental principles and lines of actions for the future EU strategy and regulatory framework in mobile communications.

The Green Paper on telecommunications infrastructures consists of two parts. The first part focused on assessing the situation, on identifying the policy principles to be followed and on establishing a plan of action (with a specific calendar). Present regulations concerning the use of existing infrastructures - those of public TOs and those of alternative carriers, such as railways, cable TV - are shown to create many constraints and so prevent an efficient and extensive use of existing infrastructure. An intervention aimed at lifting these constraints is presented as necessary to allow liberalization measures to be implemented in due course. In particular it is recommended that cable TV and railways operators could use their infrastructure to provide VANS and cross-border corporate voice communications within closed user groups (CUGs, which typically

---

63 One example of such a competition distortion is the incumbent TO's use of its revenues earned in monopoly markets to subsidize its operations in competitive market segments. A case of such internal cross-subsidies by Deutsche Telekom was investigated by the Federal Cartel Administration in Germany. It turned out that Deutsche Telekom channelled about DM 1.9 billion from its monopoly business to its data service division which is subject to market competition. See the *Financial Times* Survey, 'Telecommunications in Business', 15 June 1994, p. IV.

64 The magnitude of these cross-subsidies is estimated at about ECU 16 billion per year. See Sun and Pelkmans, 1994.

include a firm's headquarters and its subsidiaries and/or its suppliers).[65] The adoption of such a recommendation would create a regulatory-backed incentive to invest in new or upgraded infrastructure and so would help to increase the number of high-speed digital leased lines across the EU. The augmentation and improvement of infrastructure is viewed as desirable to allow the development of value-added services and to prepare for full liberalization of vocal telephony. The second part - to come - should prepare for the debate concerning the issue of infrastructure regulations, after which public vocal telephony will be completely liberalized in 1998.

In addition, during the same period, the White Paper on 'Growth, Competitiveness, Employment - The Challenges and Ways Forward into the 21st Century' acknowledged the importance of the development of an information society and of trans-European networks.[66] Information and communication technologies are identified as its foundations, having the potential to promote a steady and sustainable growth, increase competitiveness, open new job opportunities and improve the quality of life.[67]

Reflection on this issue was continued by a group of experts led by Commissioner Bangemann; its outcome was the submission of the report 'Europe and the Global Information Society: Recommendations to the European Council' to the European Council in June 1994. This report supplements the White Paper analysis and provides concrete recommendations for action. In particular, the need to accelerate the liberalization process and the achievement and preservation of universal service is emphasized. Also the roles of the public authorities and of the private sector are defined. The former should set new rules for safeguarding competition in the telecommunications sector and should control their implementation. The latter should develop the information infrastructure and finance it. In addition, arguments are put forward to encourage such substantial and quick investments: multiplicity of their impacts in various aspects of society (ten applications are described) and necessity of not falling behind the USA and/or Japan in the race towards a successful information society.

---

65 This broadening of infrastructure would not be extended to the entire voice market until 1998.

66 See Chapter 3 and Chapter 5 Section A in the White Paper on 'Growth, Competitiveness, Employment - The challenges and ways forward into the 21st century', Brussels, 1994.

67 See C.1.1. and C.1.2. *supra*. See also the 1994 White Paper on Growth, Competitiveness, and Employment and the 1994 Bangemann Report.

Beginnings in Telecom Services Trade Policy

European trade policy in the telecommunications services sector could not really start before 1988 since the telecoms policy assignment was purely national until then. However, expectations of a trade policy role for the EU in the close future concerning telecommunications services were already justified in 1986 when the Uruguay Round was inaugurated in Punta del Este. Indeed, the themes of services (including telecommunications services) and intellectual property rights were on its agenda for the first time.[68]

Trade in telecommunications services, like trade in other services, differs from trade in goods. Indeed, services can be exported in the traditional sense of the term only marginally; most of the time they require the presence of their supplier on the territory where they will be sold. Consequently usual trade barriers for goods (such as tariffs, quantity restraints, etc.) are often not relevant. Instead, barriers to trade in services result frequently from administrative restrictions or organizational dispositions, such as abusive norms, licence procedures, cartels, access restrictions to the distribution systems, etc. These types of restriction are more difficult to detect and control than the quantitative or tariffs restriction type seen in goods trade. Therefore the measures to be taken towards liberalizing the trade in services are likely to be more difficult to design and implement than reductions in tariffs.

In December 1993, the European Commission signed the Final Act of the Uruguay Round. The latter incorporates the General Agreement on Trade in Services (GATS), the equivalent of GATT for all services of all sectors (except those supplied as part of the exercise of government

68 The Final Act of the Uruguay Round of Multilateral Trade Negotiations contains important developments in these two areas: an Agreement on Trade-Related Aspects of Intellectual Property Rights (TRIPs) was reached and a Decision on Negotiations on Basic Telecommunications was adopted. See GATT (1994) and Hoekman (1993).

power).[69] Among other things, this signature represents a measure of trade policy for telecoms because the telecommunications services are covered by the GATS.[70]

The EU trade position implied by the GATT Final Act signature reflects its desire for a progressive liberalization of the trade in telecoms. However, the timetable which progress towards free trade will take place in the telecommunications services is unknown.[71] In addition, negotiations will start on a bilateral basis with the hope that they will prepare the ground for multilateral negotiations.

The Commission is already involved in negotiations on basic telecom services in the context of GATS and is actively participating in discussions addressing related issues such as intellectual property rights protection and mutual recognition agreements.[72]

This review of the main policy measures taken by the EU in the telecommunications services sector seems to highlight two facts: the first one concerns the evolution of EU telecoms policy since its beginning, the second one relates to the comparison between the political decisions and their implementation.

The sequence of policy measures taken by the EU as regards telecom services reveals a shift in its focus. During the early years (1984-88), industrial policy dominated the sector and its measures were mainly directed towards technology achievements. The emphasis was on collaborative pre-competitive R&D in the techniques viewed essential for future development and on the elaboration of pan-European standards and technical specifications to ensure interoperability and interconnections. Since 1988, competition policy has been given priority and its measures

---

69 From GATT, GATS borrows the various requirements and disciplinary rules (Art. II to Art. XV), such as most-favoured nation clause, transparency requirement, specific commitments *vis-à-vis* developing countries, etc. Two important modalities according to which GATT Members should comply with their specific commitments are expressed in Art. XVI and Art. XVII: the former concerns market access and the latter refers to non-discriminatory treatment of non-nationals. Art. XIX sets the progressiveness of the services trade liberalization. See Houard (1994), pp. 97-101.

70 The cable distribution and the diffusion of radiophonic and televisual programmes are exempted from the application of GATS measures. This conflicts with the definition of GATS's scope ('all services of all sectors except those connected to the exercise of governmental power'). It is too early to say how this conflict will be solved. See Houard (1994), p. 101.

71 The schedule of the series of successive negotiations aimed at designing the measures that will lead to a progressive increase of liberalization is not determined. Only a deadline exists: at most five years after the entry into force of the World Trade Organization Agreement. See Houard (1994), pp. 97 and 100.

72 For additional details, see European Commission, COM (94) 347 final.

have aimed at developing a properly functioning internal market for telecom services. The two lines of action adopted to achieve this goal have been liberalization and harmonization.

The comparison between the policy decisions and their implementation shows some discrepancy. On the one hand there exists a global consensus among all interested parties that in order to benefit fully from the fast technological evolution telecommunications services should be quickly liberalized and that adequate regulations should be adopted. On the other hand effective implementation of the EU directives dealing with the liberalization and harmonization of telecommunications services are continuoually observed to be slow.

In the next section, the relationships among the trade, industry and competition policies are examined in terms of coherence and conflicts.

D. ANALYSIS OF THE COHERENCE AND CONFLICTS AMONG THESE POLICIES

The interactions among trade, competition and industry policies in the telecommunications sector are observed from the viewpoints of both goals and instruments. The analysis of the policies' coherence and divergence is made along the following outline. First, a key aspect of the existing coherence among the three policies is expressed: competition in the telecom services market is identified as crucial. Second, the relationship between competition policy and industrial policy is examined, highlighting the role of standardization. Third, the interactions between competition and trade policies are analysed, revealing much coherence in terms of objectives and pointing out potential conflicts. Finally, the role of standards as a potential tool to improve the coherence among the three policies is explained.

The Competition Priority

The study of the European policy measures affecting the telecommunication services sector clearly indicates that competition as a goal has become the priority of the European authorities. The 1987 Green Paper on Telecommunications, the 1992 Review of the Situation in the Telecommunications Services Sector, and the 1994 Bangemann Report all identify an increase in competition in the supply of telecommunications services as desirable. Such a competition increase is viewed as an essential means to optimally adjust to the rapid technological evolution and to guarantee firms the access to efficient communication services and equipment so as not to lose on the communication-related productivity ground and be ready for the information society challenge.

Market competition as a goal is stimulated and increased by two types of competition policy instruments: liberalization measures and harmonization measures. The former set of measures is aimed at progressively dismantling the exclusive rights regulations existing in most Member States. Such regulations led to the emergence of one national public TO in each country and this monopolistic structure has been more and more perceived as suboptimal. The objective of the liberalization is the opening up of the sector to new operators and service suppliers. The goal of the second set of measures is twofold: first, the creation of interoperability and interconnections among old networks, among new networks and among new and old networks, and second, the harmonization of regulations (such as procedures to obtain network or services licences, etc.). The purpose of these measures is to stimulate and make possible the completion of an efficient internal telecom market and an effective increase in competition. Indeed Community-wide services could not be guaranteed solely by the enforcement of competition rules and the freedom to provide services because of the existence of twelve technically diverging national networks. This explains the need to supplement liberalization measures with harmonization measures to ensure interoperability.

The competition priority and the target of full liberalization in telecoms is unanimously agreed by all parties having interests in telecoms.[73] This general consensus is also reflected in the White Paper 'Growth, Competitiveness, and Employment' and in the Bangemann Report. Thus there seems to be no conflict on that point; there is even an agreement on the need to accelerate the liberalization.

However, a lack of coherence appears between the expression of that will to liberalize the sector and the rate at which steps towards liberalization are actually implemented. Indeed, the debate started about 10 years ago and today several key achievements - already pointed out as important in the 1987 Green Paper on the Development of the Common Market for Telecommunications Services and Equipments - have not yet been fully realized. Evidences of slow, or even absence of, implementation abound: for example, mailing by the Commission of formal warning letters to several Member States for failing to implement

---

[73] See the report on the general consultations organized by the European Commission, COM(93) 159 final, Brussels, 28.04.93.

the competition in the Telecommunication Terminal Equipment Market Directive and the ONP Leased Line Directives; slow compliance to these warning letters; separation between regulatory and operational functions improperly implemented; weak reduction of the tariff border effect; new suppliers being denied the right to provide new formally liberalized services; and so on. This suggests the existence of a strong political resistance in the Member States to implement the various liberalization and harmonization directives.

This slow implementation appears to be caused mainly by structural factors: some related to the supply-side of the market and others connected to political principles followed in assigning tasks and functions between the EU and the Member States. On the supply-side of the telecoms services market, management and organizational features developed during the monopoly period (such as cross-subsidization, etc.) and the obligation to fulfil requirements that are not directly related to telecoms (such as financial contribution to the national budget, employment policy, etc.) are factors which have made, and make, the necessary modifications towards liberalization hard to enforce.

In terms of political distribution of competences, the principle of subsidiarity seems to have played a role in the discrepancy between the directives and their implementation.[74] The investigation of this fact is the object of a recent CEPS Working Document by J.-M. Sun and J. Pelkmans.[75] According to these authors, the presence of significant cross-border externalities has weakened the possibility that subsidiarity leads to a rapid and efficient directives implementation. Three important cross-border externalities are described as characterizing the telecommunications services sector. First, each additional subscriber to the network increases the value of the network for the existing users. Second, the functioning of one country's telecom network influences the operations of other countries' networks as these networks are interconnected for the provision of international services. Third, the tariff-setting procedure for international services (as organized through the

---

[74] Subsidiarity is defined by Sun and Pelkmans as 'an assignment principle which, given a set of policy objectives, is used to determine the optimal level of government at which various public economic functions should be undertaken.' According to these authors, subsidiarity 'assigns policy-making and implementation powers to local government, except when this would likely be ineffective, inefficient, inimical to others, or demonstrably unnecessary'. See Sun and Pelkmans (1994), p. 2.

[75] This paragraph summarizes the main ideas of Sun and Pelkmans' contribution and refers the interested reader to the initial document: Sun, J.-M. and J. Pelkmans, 'Why Liberalization Needs Centralization: Subsidiarity and EU Telecoms', CEPS Working Document No. 88, July 1994.

ITU) creates a significant externality for the users reflected in the tariff frontier effect (cross-border tariffs being more expensive than similar calls within national borders). The charge that users calling abroad must pay includes a rate fixed by the foreign country where the call ends, and users have no control on this foreign tax. The existence of these cross-border externalities suggests that the collection of twelve schemes of implementation, each optimal at its own local level (i.e., within the Member State) will not correspond to the optimal implementation at the European level. The first reason is that local actions are not able to internalize these cross-border externalities. The second reason is that a voluntary and credible policy coordination among Member States which could overcome this fragmentation is unlikely to emerge given the complexity of the coordination problem and given the beggar-thy-neighbour behaviour that these externalities permit.[76]

A similar problem of timing arises concerning the harmonization of the sector. In that matter too, the speed of achievement does not correspond with the theoretical consensus: the former is slow while the latter is supportive of an accelerated harmonization. The reasons for this discrepancy are partly to be found in the numerous divergences existing among the installed networks as well as in the diversity of standards and regulatory procedures among the Member States. These factors make the necessary changes towards harmonization costly in two ways: the design and construction of interoperability and interconnection interfaces, and the search for a compromise about which standards and regulatory procedures to follow. The bearing of telecommunication standards upon economic competition is not only complex but also ambivalent. Both pro- and anti-competitive effects - sometimes concurrently and in a common market - can be generated by a given standardization activity.[77]

The difference between the dates of policy decisions (i.e., vote of directives) and the dates of their effective implementation at the Member States level is likely to have undesirable consequences on the level of competition in the telecom services sector. Indeed the slow pace of

---

[76] The authors propose a similar, but more detailed and nuanced, discussion to argue that the presence of these cross-border externalities constitute a strong rationale for actions at the EU level. They also show that the need for a centralized action is reinforced by the impossibility of a voluntary and credible coordination among Member States. In addition they illustrate how the present telecoms situation reflects the various implementation problems that subsidiarity can not easily overcome in the telecom services sector. Finally they reach the conclusion that European telecoms should be assigned to the EU level of government if the sector is to be successfully liberalized. See Sun and Pelkmans (1994).

[77] For a statement about pro- and anti-competitive effects of interface standardization, see David (1992a).

effective liberalization gives time to incumbent public TOs to strategically use the present revenues from exclusively provided telecom services in ways apt to distort competition. One such strategic behaviour able to impede competition is the use of the incumbent's present revenues from non-liberalized services to subsidize its operation in the competitive segment of the telecoms market.[78] Evidence of such behaviour was found in Germany by the Federal Cartel Administration: Deutsche Telekom had subsidized its data services division (under competition) by up to DM 1.9 billion using its monopoly revenues.[79] Another strategic use of these revenues from protected services is to invest in new services and infrastructures. The explicit justification is the need to modernize the networks and improve services availability. But a complementary and implicit reason is the desire to build barriers to entry against expected new entrants, before the public vocal service liberalization is fully completed. These investments should give an important first mover advantage to the incumbents and help them to maintain their dominant position for a while after the liberalization deadline.[80] It is to be noted that this type of strategic behaviour adds to a substantial, already existing barrier to entry to public vocal telephony: the well-established base of incumbent TOs for protected services and networks.

Another feature of the telecoms policy implementation is its localization and that of future investments. In that aspect, too, some incoherence has been observed between the EU political will to promote and support the development of less favoured regions by means of telecommunications and the implementation of the telecoms directives at the Member State level. Of particular interest is the localization of the investment in new ISDN and broadband networks. On the one hand these high-capacity networks are presented as a key element to help less favoured regions to develop and overcome the gap created by the distance between the countries' major activity centres. On the other hand investments in ISDN and broadband networks are made in major urban areas. Consequently these areas attract new activities even more than before because the existence of

---

[78] For new entrants, to sue incumbent TOs for unfair practices such as cross-subsidies between protected and competitive services operations is a costly and slow process because of legal requirements and procedures (often impeded by the lack of clarity in TOs' accountancy and the lack of dedication of the regulatory body when it remains too close to the TO).

[79] See the *Financial Times* Survey, 'Telecommunications in Business', 15 June 1994, p. IV.

[80] See the *Financial Times* Survey, 'Telecommunications in Business', 15 June 1994, p. IV and Mobile Telecommunications', 17 September 1994, p. VIII. See also Sun and Pelkmans (1994).

sophisticated telecom services and infrastructures is viewed as important and matters in the decision to locate new business.

The Necessity of Standards: Industrial Policy 'Behind the Scene'

Given the initial regulatory situation and the technical evolution in the sector, competition policy has been identified as the most adequate policy to fulfil the objectives chosen by the European authorities for the telecommunications services. Consequently industrial policy in the telecom sector has been subjected to a secondary role: its measures should never impede the pursuit of greater competition. This is reflected, for example, in the restriction of cooperative R&D agreements to pre-competitive stages whenever possible. The scope of industrial policy has been the promotion of cooperative R&D in telecommunication technologies and its related applications and the elaboration of pan-European norms.[81] The emphasis has been on standardization as a means of contributing to the harmonization efforts required by the competition policy.

The selection of a standard is a delicate task. When there is a large amount of uncertainty about the technical and economic merits of many variants, a first phase should typically involve experimentation.[82] After this period of experimentation one, or perhaps a small number of variants emerge as 'standard practice' or 'dominant design'. After this first phase the selection then can be passive, i.e. through the competitive market mechanism. Or it can be active, such as when a dominant economic or political actor decides that a particular variant should become the standard. Reality shows that the selection of the best design among the few remaining ones is frequently fortuitous (rather than the product of a systematic exploration of the merits of all possible variants): either the result of historical circumstances or the outcome of the strategic capabilities of certain agents.

When the development of a standard conforms to such a pattern, problems of selection and of timing are rather difficult. Industrial policy

---

81 See, for example, RACE and Programme Télématique for cooperative R&D, and GSM and aborted HDTV for standards.

82 The first phase, also called the extensive learning or 'learning from diversity' phase, involves experimentation with a variety of standard options. The objective is to gain a broad knowledge about as many potential avenues of development as possible, and then on this basis, make a sensible choice regarding which avenues are likely to be effective and are worth keeping for further investigation. Through the (negative) results of the experimentation this phase leads to the elimination of certain avenues of development.

then should aim at building organizational systems involving a coordinated set of decentralized experimental projects, mechanisms and procedures for exchanging and distributing information produced in the course of these projects, and a centralized procedure of assessment to decide the standard to be selected and the timing to switch to the standardization phase. However such an organizational design is rather difficult to establish.[83]

The European experience of norms selection for telecoms is based on setting up such an organizational system. Its outcome confirms the above description. On the one hand the success of GSM pleads in favour of a centralized procedure. On the other hand the failure of HDTV suggests the greater efficiency of the market.[84] This refers to the issue of which policy, interventionist (i.e. industrial) or free market (i.e. competition), should prevail in the establishment of standards. In the case of the telecommunications services, the EU authorities seemed to have given priority to competition when a centralized standard turned out to be suboptimal compared with what the market developed and when the latter did not threaten pan-European interoperability.

Interactions Among Trade and Competition Policies

The question of conflict or coherence between trade policy and competition policy concerning the telecommunications services sector should be quick to settle. The reason is that the EU trade policy concerning these services is so recent that little material needs to be examined. In principle, coherence seems to prevail up to now among the measures adopted by these two policies. Both policies follow a liberalization approach as shows in the GATS and various EU directives. On the one hand EU competition policy steps towards liberalization offer opportunities for new telecom services suppliers to enter the market as well as for TOs operating in one Member State to enter other Member States' telecoms market. On the other hand EU trade policy moves towards liberalization seek to expand the scope of the telecoms market opening up to other non-EU trade partners on a reciprocal basis. That is,

---

83 One of the main problems to overcome is the incentive for agents to free-ride on participating in experimental projects (knowing that the final information will be widely shared in any case).

84 The HDTV case reveals the possibility that the central authority picks an inferior technology: the European cooperative efforts worked on an analogous mode standard whereas private initiatives in the USA started - somewhat later - on digital mode standards. The European authorities abandoned their project when its inefficiency became obvious.

non-EU TOs can enter the EU telecom services market only if EU TOs can equivalently enter the telecom services markets of these non-EU TOs.

However, the outcome of this double commitment to liberalization in terms of increase in effective competition is uncertain for two reasons. First, negotiations to implement the GATS in the telecommunications services sector are to take place initially on a bilateral basis, and such an approach is likely to generate a mosaic of bilateral agreements reflecting the power of their parties more than an attempt to ease and optimize world trade in telecom services. In addition, differences in national systems for intellectual property rights protection might seriously interfere with reaching satisfactory conclusions during the bilateral (and later multilateral) agreements concerning telecom services requested by the GATS.

Second, the expectations of a globalization of the telecom services market and trade have led to a splurge of international strategic alliances among major public TOs within the EU and between the EU and the USA. The main justification generally given by the members of these alliances is the need to combine assets (especially, networks) and skills in order to be able to provide on a world scale the quality and diversity of services required to face the global competition to come. Although there is definite scope for efficient synergies and task re-allocations, the concentration of market power induced by these strategic alliances constitutes a severe threat to future competition. Indeed, the successful conclusion (including legal approval from relevant antitrust authorities) of these mega-alliance agreements before the sector complete liberalization may put the emergence of a competitive EU telecoms market at risk by destroying all incentives for potential newcomers to enter this market. If this occurs, the supply side of the EU market is likely to be effectively reduced to a few alliances; this would generate an adequate context for collusive behaviour at the EU level.

American and European antitrust authorities are busy with assessing the desirability of each one of these alliances. Their task is extremely difficult. On the one hand, the sector of telecommunications services receives a continuous flow of substantial technological innovations (many of them are not yet commercialized and new ones keep coming). This flow of innovations alters the structure of the supply at the same time as these strategic alliances influence the stream of inventions. The combined impact of this two-way interaction on potential competition is almost impossible to forecast. Therefore, to assess in advance the pro- and anti-competitive effects of these alliances is complex. On the other hand, pressures may arise from the government and/or industry lobbies to allow some alliances even though they are evaluated as anti-competitive from a domestic point of view. To justify their demand these authorities and pressure groups are likely to refer to the need to give the national industry a means of entering foreign markets perceived as closed and to participate in global competition. In the absence of a world antitrust authority, the risk of an escalade of strategic alliances exists. That is, governments authorize alliances - although assessed as apt to distort competition - as a response to similar authorizations in rival trade blocs (with the first country to move being motivated by the desire to extract foreign surplus). Such a scenario would parallel the well-known results of the strategic trade literature:[85] active strategic industrial policy by all countries can lead to suboptimal equilibrium when there exists no institution forcing countries not to adopt actions that are individually appealing but collectively inefficient.

Another aspect of the interactions among competition and trade policies concerns the relationship between harmonization and trade liberalization, the other pillar of competition policy. According to David (1992a), to achieve harmonization within free-trade areas like the EU is likely to be a long and exhausting process. The reasons are the complexity of telecommunications standards and their potential interactions with national economic interests. Indeed, standards that encourage the growth of international trade in telecommunications equipment and services are likely to create immediate winners and losers. In addition, because few countries have progressed very far in their efforts to privatize telecommunications, harmonization may generate direct conflicts of interests between policy-makers in charge of negotiating harmonization agreements and policy-makers responsible for state telecommunications enterprises. These facts suggest that a probable outcome of such harmonization agreements is the erection in effect of non-tariff barriers. They also hint at the deep difficulties to be expected in coming years during the implementation process of the harmonization agreements in the telecom services sector.

Standards as a Potential Tool to Increase Coherence Among these Policies

Given the respective definitions of the three types of policies (competition policy referring to the EU as a single market, trade policy revealing the

---

85 See Dixit (1987).

EU as an agent in the world competition, and high-tech sector industrial policy considering the EU as a system of innovations) standards seem to be able to play a critical role in ensuring a greater coherence among these policies with regard to the telecommunications services sector. First, competition policy needs standardization to achieve harmonization in the telecommunications services sector. Second, trade policy needs standardization as a focusing device allowing national technical resources and organizational capacities of the telecommunications services sector to be efficiently integrated in the world competition. Third, industrial policy needs standardization to generate positive network economies through an increase in interoperability and compatibility among the various telecommunications networks and equipment.

Standardization, however, is only potentially a tool for ensuring coherence because of the possibility of some policy bias in the procedures of standardization. For instance, the HDTV is an example of trade policy bias in the standardization procedure whereas numerous cases of standards introduced too early (and consequently ending prematurely the experimentation phase) are examples of a competition policy bias.

Nonetheless the establishment of decentralized procedures and of mechanisms of coordination for the elaboration of anticipatory standards still appears as one of the most efficient ways to improve the coherence of the three policies in the telecommunications services sector.

CONCLUSIONS

The investigation of the telecommunications services sector, as one of the high-tech sectors, allows the identification of typical problems that EU policy-makers have to handle when a sector evolves rapidly from a technological point of view and when the objective is to create an efficient internal market. First, R&D activities have to be efficiently organized when it comes to the development of systems and networks. Indeed, the proper functioning of these techniques at a pan-European level requires interoperability and interconnection (which have to be taken into account as early as at the R&D level). In the same way the selection of norms which are connected to this R&D policy matters, but there is no recipe for a guaranteed successful outcome. Second, the technology dynamics exerts a strong pressure on the regulatory environment. The coordination of the regulatory decisions resulting from this pressure is necessary in order to avoid the erection of non-tariff barriers. Third, the globalization of trade demands a careful evaluation of how to face increased competition from abroad. In a sector where networks matter, private responses to the globalization challenge include the creation of strategic alliances. The emergence of such global alliances is a difficult question to be dealt with by antitrust authorities because the impact of these alliances on potential competition is hard to predict given the various forces altering the structure of the market.

In the particular case of the telecommunications services sector, EU policy-makers have reached a consensus about the objective which should be given priority: competition. However, closer examination indicates that this consensus has not been enough to achieve the desired liberalization and harmonization. First of all, lags between the directives and their implementation are often important. Causes are found among structural factors. Second, the need to maintain a reasonable degree of effective competition at the EU level seems to conflict with some of the strategies adopted by EU firms to remain competitive in the world market. The way antitrust authorities are going to solve this dilemma is not known yet; it is likely that their decision will have an important impact on how the sector is going to evolve. Third, standardization seems to have a role to play in improving the coherence among the trade, industry and competition policies in the telecommunications services sector; however, its implementation is difficult.

REFERENCES

Bangemann, M. et al. (1994), 'Europe and the Global Information Society: Recommendations to the European Council', June, reprint in *Cordis focus*, Supplement 2, 15 July 1994.

Besen, S. (1990, 'The European Telecommunications Standards Institute', *Telecommunications Policy*, December, pp. 521-30.

Cawson, A., K. Morgan, D. Webber, P. Holmes, and A. Stevens, (1990), *Hostile Brothers: Competition and Closure in the European Electronics Industry*, Oxford: Clarendon Press.

Cawson, A., G. Shepherd, and D. Webber (1990), 'Governments, Markets, and Regulation in the West European Consumer Electronics Industry', in L. Hancher and M. Moran (eds), *Capitalism, Culture and Economic Regulation*, Oxford: Clarendon Press.

Commission of the European Communities (1990a), *Les programmes communautaires de recherche*, 2nd edition, Bonn: Economica Verlag, May.

Commission of the European Communities (1990b), 'Livre vert sur une approche commune dans le domaine des communications par satellites dans la Communauté européenne: Vers des systèmes et des services à l'échelle de l'Europe', Communication by the Commission, COM(90), 490 final, Brussels, 25 June.

Commission of the European Communities (1992a), 'Tarifs des télécommunications dans la Communauté: Vers l'orientation des tarifs sur les coûts et l'ajustement des structures de prix', Communication by the Commission, SEC(92) 1050 final, Brussels, 25.06.92.

Commission of the European Communities (1992b), 'L'industrie européenne des équipements de télécommunications: situation, enjeux, propositions d'action', Communication by the Commission, Brussels, 25 June.

Commission of the European Communities (1992c), '1992 Review of the Situation in the Telecommunications Services Sector', Communication by the Commission, SEC(92) 1048 final, Brussels, 21 October.

Commission of the European Communities (1993a), 'Programme de R&D sur les technologies de pointe dans le domaine des télécommunications en Europe (RACE): Rapport final concernant la Phase 1 (1988-1992) du programme décenal RACE', COM(93), 118 final, Brussels, 30 March.

Commission of the European Communities (1993b), 'Programme IMPACT: Les événements et les développements les plus importants qui ont eu lieu sur le marché des services d'information électroniques 1991', Report by the Commission to the Council, to the European Parliament and to the Economic and Social Committee, COM(93) 156 final, Brussels, 19 April.

Commission of the European Communities (1993c), 'Communication au Conseil et au Parlement Européen sur la consultation sur l'examen de la situation dans le secteur des services de télécommunications', COM(93), 159 final, Brussels, 28 April.

Commission of the European Communities (1993d), 'Développement d'un service universel dans un environnement concurrentiel, Proposition de Résolution du Conseil sur des principes en matière de service universel dans le secteur des télécommunications', Communication by the Commission to the Council, to the European Parliament and to the Economic and Social Committee, COM(93), 543 final, Brussels, 15 November.

Commission of the European Communities (1994a), *Croissance, compétitivité, emploi: les défis et les pistes pour entrer dans le XXIe siècle: livre blanc*, Luxemburg.

Commission of the European Communities (1994b), *Panorama of the EU Industry 94*, Luxemburg.

Commission of the European Communities (1994c), 'Vers un environnement de communications personnelles: Livre vert sur une approche commune dans le domaine des communications mobiles et personnelles au sein de l'Union Européenne', Communication of the Commission, COM(94), 145 final, Brussels, 27 April.

Commission of the European Communities (1994d), 'Europe's Ways to the Information Society. An Action Plan', Communication from the Commission to the Council and the European Parliament, and to the Economic and Social Committee and the Committee of Regions, COM(94), 347 final, Brussels, 19 July.

Commission of the European Communities (1994e), 'Livre vert sur la libéralisation des infrastructures de télécommunications et des réseaux de télévision par cable (1e partie: Principe et calendrier)', Communication of the Commission, COM(94), 440 final, Brussels, 25 October.

Dasgupta, P. and P.A. David (1992), *The new economics of science*, CEPR Discussion Paper no. 320, Stanford University.

David, P.A. (1991), *Reputation and agency in the historical emergence of the institutions of "open science"*, CEPR Discussion Paper, no. 261, Stanford University.

David, P.A. (1992a), *The Economics of Compatibility Standards and Competition - A Report to the German Monopolies Commission*, Cologne, January.

David, P.A. (1992b), *Knowledge, property and the system dynamics of technological change*, World Bank Annual Conference on Development Economics, Washington DC.

David, P.A. and D. Foray (1994), *Accessing and expanding the science and technology knowledge-base: a framework for interpreting available quantitative measures*, OECD-DSTI-CSPT.

David, P.A., and D. Foray (1995), *Institutions, Incentives and the Nature of Externalities in the Process of Knowledge Generation*, Conference in honour of G.B. Richardson, Oxford University, St. John's College, January.

David, P.A., D. Mowery and E. Steinmueller, 'Analysing the economic pay off from basic research', *Economics of innovation and new technology*.

David, P.A. and G. Wright (1991), *Resource abundance and American economic leadership*, CEPR Discussion Paper, no. 267, Stanford University.

Dixit, A. (1987), 'Strategic Aspects of Trade Policy', in T.F. Bewley (ed.), *Advances in Economic Theory: Fifth World Congress*, Cambridge: Cambridge University Press.

European Parliament (1993), 'Emerging Technologies - Information Networks and the European Union -', Directorate General for Research Working Papers, Economic Series W-11, Luxemburg.

Eymann, A., and L. Schuknecht (1993), 'Antidumping Enforcement in the European Community', in J. Finger (ed), *Antidumping: How It Works and Who Gets Hurt*, Ann Arbour: The University of Michigan Press, pp. 221-39.

Financial Times Survey (1994a), 'Telecommunications in Business', 15 June.

Financial Times Survey (1994b), 'Computer Networking', 28 June.

Financial Times Survey (1994c), 'Mobile Telecommunications', 17 September.

Financial Times Survey (1994d) 'New Broadcast and Communication Media', 4 October.

Financial Times Survey (1994e), 'International Telecommunications', 17 October.

GATT (1993a), *Trade Policy Review: European Communities 1993*, vol. 1, Geneva: General Agreement on Tariffs and Trade.

GATT (1993b), *Trade Policy Review: European Communities 1993*, vol. 2, Geneva: General Agreement on Tariffs and Trade.

GATT (1994), *The Results of the Uruguay Round of Multilateral Trade Negotiations*, Geneva, June.

Grupp, H., and T. Schnöring (1992), 'Research and Development in Telecommunications', in *Telecommunications Policy*, January/February.

Harel, T., and L. Soete (1993), *Industrial and Competition Policy in the EC*, report prepared for the United Nations Industrial Development Organization, Merit: Maastricht, February.

Hoekman, B. (1993), 'New issues in the Uruguay Round and Beyond', *The Economic Journal*, 103, pp. 1528-39.

Houard, J. (1994), 'Le GATT et l'Uruguay Round', *Tendances Economiques*, no.6, May.

IDATE (1994), *Réseaux*, no. 8, Special 200, November, pp. 20-21.

Jaffe, Henderson and Trajtenberg (1993), 'Geographic localization of knowledge spillovers', *Quarterly Journal of Economics*.

Machlup, F. (1984), *The economics of information and human capital*, Princeton University Press.

Murphy, A. (1990), *The European Community and the International Trading System*, vol. 2, CEPS Paper no.48, Brussels: Centre for European Policy Studies.

Nicolaides, P. (1993), *The Trade Policy of the European Community: Legal Basis, Instruments, Commercial Relations*, Maastricht: European Institute of Public Administration.

OECD (1993a), *Assessing the Effects of the Uruguay Round*, Paris: OECD.

OECD (1993b), Trade and technology: issue paper', DSTI/STP.

Ordover, J., and W. Baumol, 'Antitrust Policy and High-Technology Industries', *Oxford Review of Economic Policy*, vol. 4, no.4, pp. 13-34.

Pelkmans, J. (1994), 'The Significance of EC-1992', *The Annals of the American Academy of Political and Social Sciences*, no. 531, January, pp. 94-111.

Romer, P. (1993), 'Implementing a national technology strategy with self-organizing industry investment boards', Brooking Papers.

Sapir, A., P. Buigues, and A. Jacquemin (1993), 'European Competition Policy in Manufacturing and Services: a Two-Speed Approach?', *Oxford Review of Economic Policy*, vol. 9, no. 2, pp.113-32.

Soete, L., 'National Support Policies for Strategic Industries: The International Implications', Merit Working Paper no.91-006.

Soete, L., and A. Arundel, *An Integrated Approach to European Innovation and Technology Diffusion Policy: a Maastricht Memorandum*, Luxemburg.

Stiglitz, J. (1991), 'Social absorption capability and innovation, CEPR Discussion Paper, no. 292, Stanford University.

Sun, J.-M., and J. Pelkmans (1994), 'Why Liberalisation Needs Centralisation? Subsidiarity and EU Telecoms', CEPS Working Document no. 88, July.

Weder and Grubel, 'The new growth theory and Coesan economics: institutions to capture externalities', *Weltwirtschaftliches Archiv*.

Discussion

David Deacon

INTRODUCTION

The authors have presented a useful historical summary and factual overview of Community policy in the field of telecommunications and the interaction between trade, competition and industry policies. At the risk of oversimplifying they state that originally industry policy dominated with R&D programmes and harmonization. Competition policy now seems to predominate with the current liberalization programme but trade policy will play a bigger role in future in the framework of GATS and globalizing markets.

I will comment on this chapter from my point of view as a competition practitioner - trying to applying the Community competition rules in a reasonable manner to a sector that is in the throes of rapid and far-reaching technological and regulatory upheavals inside the Community and where globalization and internationally dimensioned strategic alliances are of growing importance.[1] As the chapter shows, the analysis of the sector is complex and the interaction of the three Community policies in question - industry, trade and competition - have to be taken into account in order for any individual policy to be applied coherently, thereby avoiding possible contradictions. The recent G7 conference underlines the importance of the sector and the coming together of the three policy areas.

By final word of introduction I must admit that I am optimistic about the coherent application of the three Community policies. I see them as necessary complements. Much has been written on the conflict of industry and competition policies. However, the Treaty is quite clear. In Article 3(g) it states that in order to achieve the basic goals of the

[1] The author's duties inside the Commission involve coordination of individual cases of the rules of competition to all sectors. As such he has no specific knowledge of the telecommunications sector. The author is therefore grateful for the comments of Miguel Pena of the telecommunications unit in DG IV. All errors and omissions are the author's.

Community there shall be 'a system ensuring that competition in the internal markets' is not distorted.

Furthermore, Article 130 states that industry policy shall be applied 'in accordance with a system of open and competitive markets'.

The Commission put the flesh on these legal structures in two important documents - the White Chapter on Growth, Competitiveness and Employment[2] and its Communication on Industry Policy.[3] Both these documents see the maintenance of effective competition through vigorous competition policy as an essential element to wider Community competitiveness. This theme is also found in Commissioner Van Miert's declaration to Parliament[4] and in a recent Competition Reports.[5] The Bangemann Report underlines the specific role of competition for telecoms. In fact the industry policy programmes for telecommunications described by the authors are not only not contradictory to competition policy, but are in fact prerequisites for competition. Take, for example, the programmes to define open standards and interoperability, without which the Union would remain 12, now 15, different but separate telecommunication networks.[6]

As regards competition and trade policies, again I see them as complementary. Trade policies have a twofold effect. First, they aim to open up the Community and third markets by reducing tariff and other barriers - they therefore widen competition. Second, they protect Community industry from destructive or unfair competition, which can normally only occur because of a failure of competition policy in a third country. On the one hand countervailing duties are imposed on imports that have received what would be illegal subsidies in the Union and are recognized as such under the GATT. On the other hand anti-dumping duties protect EU industry from practices that would normally be made impossible by the application of competition rules from companies operating in a market economy.[7] Thus the 'protectionist' side of trade policy is mainly to compensate EU firms from companies in third

---

2 Bulletin of the EC Supplement 6/93.

3 'An industrial competitiveness policy for the European Union'. Bulletin of the European Union Supplement 3/94 - COM(94) 3/9 final.

4 Hearing of European Parliament, 16 January 1995.

5 XXIII Report on Competition Policy 1993 European Commission pt 17-26 and 150-161.

6 This is not to deny that all standardization is procompetitive - some can be detrimental and have a foreclosure effect. This debate is beyond the scope of my remarks.

7 In fact inside the Community internal market there is no anti-dumping, only competition policy. Similarly there are no countervailing duties against subsidies, only a Community state aids policy.

countries not subject to effective competition rules. In the long run it therefore promotes competition.

LIBERALISATION: A NECESSARY BUT NOT SUFFICIENT CONDITION FOR COMPETITION

In telecommunications, it is clear that liberalization (i.e. the abolition of exclusive rights which give rise to legal monopolies) must be applied before any competition can take place. An ambitious programme going up to 1998 with the liberalization of voice telephony is described in the chapter.[8] However, the introduction of real competition implies much more than a mere programme of the translation into national law of Community directives abolishing legal monopolies in the different Member States. To arrive at a situation where the benefits of competition can be really felt, takes both time and the vigorous enforcement of the rules of competition. Without this latter we risk the incumbent monopolist using both his market power and control over conditions of access to his network to prevent the emergence of potential competitors. Where previously the monopoly telephone operator could hide behind a legal monopoly, after liberalization he could abuse his dominant position to prevent entry. Competition in this sector is all the more difficult to get started up because, unlike most industries, new entrants depend on the incumbent's network to which the price of access is absolutely vital. Unfortunately the chapter does not go into this aspect, where the experience of Mercury in the UK shows how difficult it is to get competition beyond the legal possibility to become fully effective. Neither does the chapter explore methods employed in third countries - such as the more radical solution employed in the USA by the splitting up of AT & T into regional Baby Bells.

In fact many issues need to be resolved to make competition effective beyond the classic application of the rules of competition. For example:

- whether in addition to competition rules there needs to be an EU telecoms regulator to determine the price of network access or whether the same result can be achieved via the coordination of existing regulators. In fact the complementarity of regulation and competition could be usefully explored in the chapter.

---

8 The liberalization of voice telephony is of absolutely crucial importance to the sector and should not be underestimated.

- decisions have to be made on contributions for the funding of the universal service obligation, which is rapidly becoming an effective way for incumbents to defend their entrenched position. However, certain commentators now imply that the financial burden of this universal service obligation is not as heavy as has been implied[9] and could be used by incumbents to block entry.
- a decision needs to be made in the EU on the liberalization of the infrastructure along with that of their associated liberalized services. Competing infrastructures are the best way to facilitate entry and bring about the industry policy advantages of extra investment and capacity forecast in the Bangemann Report.[10] In fact US experience in 'long' lines would suggest that parallel networks are the best way to create both really effective competition and new value-added services.
- major political decisions need to be made because competition requires tariff rebalancing, i.e. tariffs should reflect costs, which is not the case at the moment. This is politically sensitive as in most Member States business is *de facto* subsidizing private households.

In fact the issue of the introduction of effective competition as opposed to its mere legal possibility, on which the chapter focuses, is directly linked to industry and trade policy. Without effective competitive pressure on the monopolist we are unlikely to see the reduction in prices or the extra capacity generated for new innovative value-added services that industry needs. Furthermore, unless entry becomes a *de facto* as well as *de jure* possibility, third countries will continue to perceive our markets as foreclosed and be understandably reluctant to open up their markets to EU companies. In fact this consideration appears to have been a factor in the USA in favour of permitting the cooperation between BT and MCI because the UK market was regarded as an open one.[11]

NEED FOR MARKET ANALYSIS TO ASSESS ALLIANCES

The chapter discusses the growing importance of strategic alliances and other forms of cooperation in this sector, where companies are positioning

---

9 See, for example, John Kay of London School of Economics, *Daily Telegraph* 16 February 1995, 13 February 1995, p. 7 (European edition).

10 These issues are treated in the two Green Papers on infrastructure (COM 94/440 and COM 94/682) which also treat financing of the universal service and interconnection problems. These Green Papers are based on publicly available studies.

11 See also *Financial Times*, Monday 27 February 1995, p. 16 (European edition) where the USA proposes to open its telecom market but only to investors from already liberalized countries. Al Gore at G7 conference.

themselves for global markets. In fact there are some extremely important cases either recently decided - BT and MCI - or currently under consideration - Atlas, a cooperation between French and German Telecom and Sprint. The chapter states 'Therefore to assess *in advance* [emphasis added] the pro- and anti-competitive effects of these alliances is extremely complex', and that 'the concentration of market power induced by these strategic alliances constitutes a severe threat to future competition'. Finally the chapter adds that the arguments will be advanced by the parties and some governments that alliances having anti-competitive effects may be defended as necessary to enter new markets or to compete on a global scale. According to the chapter there appears to be a conflict between competition and industry policy in the global market context. Unfortunately the chapter does not develop any analytical framework which will allow the Commission, or any other antitrust enforcement agency, to make an assessment of these alliances *before* they are consummated or to avoid possible contradictions between trade, competition and industry policies. Because of their structural nature the Commission is obliged to work on the basis of *forecast* economies/synergies and *forecast* effects on the market. Although mistakes can be made, especially on such dynamic markets, the Commission has to assess their impact on the relevant market and balance the gains and losses.

This can be done, as the BT-MCI decision of the Commission shows.[12] It is an example of how the Commission brought potential conflicts into a coherent policy. In fact it is likely that the Commission will not react favourably to alliances where domestic markets are closed, as this may serve only to aggravate the difficulty of eventually introducing competition.[13] Because Commission decisions are subject to judicial review by the Court of First Instance and subsequently the Court of Justice, it is unlikely to be able to approve agreements that seriously prejudice effective competition inside the Community. Furthermore the creation of a European champion at the price of eliminating effective competition on the EU market goes against the spirit of the new EU industry policy. Rather, effective competition is seen as a way to train Community firms to fight on wider markets.[14] Where, however, the

---

12 OJ L 233 of 27.08.1994.

13 See, for example, declaration of Mr Van Miert to G7 on Information Society. *Financial Times*, 28 February 1995, p. 16 (European edition).

14 See also Michael Porter, *Competitive advantage of nations*, New York: Free Press, 1990.

market is truly global all EU firm can be allowed to cooperate because competition within the Community is not prejudiced.[15]

There are also two other factors to be taken into account when discussing alliances. First, alliances may be the only way for EU service providers to break out of their role as essentially domestic monopoly service providers and enter the new fast-moving globalizing services market. Second, we are starting to see alliances between on the one hand non-telecoms companies who have or can easily build physical networks (railway, electricity, energy companies) but have no experience of telecom services and on the other hand telecom service providers who have the know-how to exploit these new alternative infrastructures. Such alliances can be procompetitive and show the complementarity rather than conflict of industry, trade and competition policies.

POTS BECOME PANS - A LOOK TO THE NOT TOO DISTANT FUTURE

Similar forward-looking analysis is required by the Commission when it has to examine the emerging but increasingly important interface between telecommunications, media and computing. If the forecases are to be believed, the form of delivery, type and quantity of media in the homes will be revolutionized and domestic telecommunications will change from the current POTS (plain old telecommunications services) to PANS (pretty amazing new services). Whether ownership of the wires or cables that deliver these services will become relatively less important compared to the services offered, remains to be seen, i.e. will telecom wires be like motorways, where any traffic that pays the toll can pass. This convergence of sectors is already confronting Community competition policy with its sensitive interaction with industry policy and particularly for media with trade policy. In fact the Commission's second negative merger decision concerned Deutsch Telecom and the two leading German pay TV/media companies (Bertelsmann and Kirch) which would have foreclosed the market.[16] It concerned directly industry policy because of

---

[15] See Philips/Thomson/Sagem (Press Release IP/93/32 of Commission and XXIII Competition Report point 215) where all Community firms having interests in Liquid Crystal Displays were allowed to put together their efforts because of the intense competition not only on world markets but also on Community markets from several powerful Japanese producers.

[16] Case IV M 469 MSG 9.11.94 published O.J. L 364, 31.12.1994. Interestingly enough the only other negative merger decision to date has also been in high technology - construction of aircraft. IV M 053 DE HAVILLAND/Aerospatiale-Alenia of 2 October 1991; published L 334, 5.12.91 p. 42.

the link to digital HDTV.[17] Some discussion of these aspects would have rendered the chapter more useful for practitioners who have to analyse such cases, as would the Community policy towards telecoms in the PECOS (former East European state economy countries), with its links to trade policy.

CONCLUSIONS

The chapter is a useful summary of the state of play in telecommunications and the interaction between competition, trade and industry policy. There are some omissions, notably no mention is made of the Commission Communication on Telecommunications Equipment[18] which highlighted the close industry, competition and trade policy links between telecommunications equipment and services. This is a particularly important high-technology industry where the Community has several world class players - Alcatel, Siemens, Nokia, Ericsson - and where the Community is faced with restructuring - see Siemens/Italtel, Teletrra and GEC/Plessey/Siemens. In these cases structural links between national champion telecom equipment producers and monopoly service providers have to be examined, in the context of liberalizing but still essentially monopoly service markets and the opening up of public procurement for telecom equipment.[19]

In fact many of the problems identified in the chapter are already or have already been involved in cases and policies before the Commission. The chapter's usefulness would have been enhanced if it had ventured to look forward and made policy suggestions via a more quantitative and analytical, rather than descriptive, framework. Many apparent contradictions between trade, competition and industry policy in fact disappear or become clear when the real market situation is analysed in the individual case. Finally, liberalization should not be equated with competition; it is in fact only the first of many steps.

---

17 The issue of cable TV and its infrastructure is a crucial issue for the future of telecoms. Penetration of the domestic market in Europe by cable TV, although not as advanced as in the USA, is growing rapidly. An alternative infrastructure network is thus in the making.

18 SEC (92) 1049 Brussels 15 July 1992, 'The European Telecommunications Equipment Industry', Communication from the Commission.

19 In fact the chapter appears to confuse the opening up of public procurement for telecom equipment (switching gear, etc.) with the abolition of exclusive rights of telephone service operators for terminal equipment (handsets etc.). Furthermore, if effective competition is introduced for services, there will be less need for public procurement rules as all service providers will be obliged by pressure of competition to buy the most cost-effective equipment rather than simply rely on a national champion equipment producer.

7. Pharmaceuticals

Gernot Klepper

1. CHARACTERISTICS OF THE MARKETS AND PUBLIC POLICY

1.1. Market Characteristics: The Pharmaceutical Industry

The world market for pharmaceuticals is approximately evenly divided between Europe, North America and the rest of the world. The most important producers of pharmaceuticals are also located in the United States, Japan and the European Union. In 1991, the United States did produce pharmaceuticals with a value at factory prices of approximately 39 billion ECU, compared to Japan with 34 billion ECU (BPI, 1993). The largest producer is the EU with more than 62 billion ECU. The most important producers within the EU are France, Germany, Italy and the UK (see Figure 7.1).

Figure 7.1: Turnover of the pharmaceutical industry in the EC (million ECU, 1990)

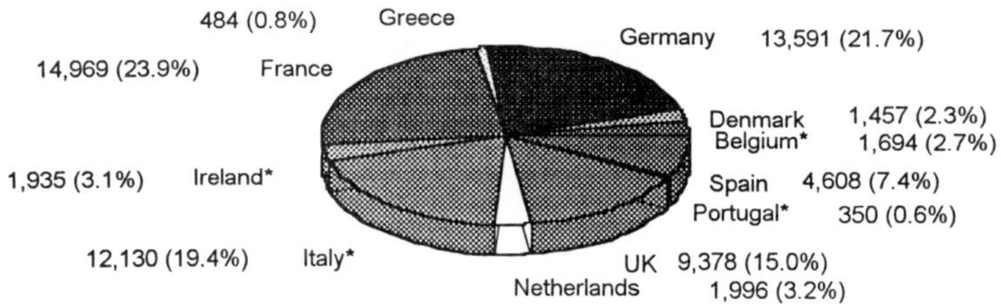

Note : * values for 1989.
Source : EUROSTAT, 1993.

The size distribution of companies shows a particular pattern which is similar throughout the industrialized countries. There is a relatively small number of global firms which dominate pharmaceutical markets and then there is a large number of small firms producing mostly for local or national markets. The roughly 100 global firms originate mostly from the United States, Germany, Switzerland and the UK. They perform most of the R&D of the world's pharmaceutical industry and dominate the market for prescription drugs. For example, the top 100 pharmaceutical firms covered 80 per cent of the pharmaceutical market in Germany in 1991 (BPI, 1993). In the smaller companies very little R&D is undertaken, which to a large degree is dictated by the technology of pharmaceutical R&D and production.[1] The world's pharmaceutical industry therefore shows a two-tier structure in which the global firms are responsible for the R&D and consequently dominate the market for patent-protected prescription drugs whereas the smaller firms serve local needs or they compete with generics against the new products.

Trade in pharmaceuticals

Markets for pharmaceuticals are truly global in nature. This becomes evident if one looks at trade figures. Table 7.1 summarizes the exports and imports of the major Member States of the EU. The EU overall has a large trade surplus in pharmaceuticals compared to the manufacturing industry overall, as do the large producers such as France, Germany and the UK. The pharmaceutical markets are characterized by a large number of submarkets for different therapeutic groups of medicines which are rather unrelated as far as the determinants of demand are concerned. This explains the large degree of intra-industry trade. The second characteristic is the dominance of global companies in the industry. If only for these reasons, it is not surprising that there is intensive trade in pharmaceutical products.

---

1 See section 1.2 for a discussion of this issue.

Table 7.1 Trade in Pharmaceuticals in the EC (1991, US$ m.)

Country	Exports	Imports
Benelux	3,557	3,308
Denmark	1,287	557
France	3,956	3,085
Germany	6,575	4,227
Italy	1,629	3,030
UK	4,516	2,422
Rest EU	2,061	2,426
Total EU	23,581	19,055

Source: OECD, *Trade by Commodities*, 1993; SITC 54.

The export shares of the different member countries of the EU vary strongly. Small countries like Denmark or Belgium export a very large proportion of their output, whereas larger countries with larger domestic markets naturally exhibit lower export shares. Germany, for example, had an export share of 39.3 per cent in 1992 (BPI, 1993). With the exception of the Mediterranean countries, including Italy, the members of the EU have a trade surplus in pharmaceuticals. European exports also seem to be highly concentrated on particular products. The EIU study (EIU, 1991) reports that the top ten drugs exported from the EC in 1989 amounted to US$7,773m. which is almost one-third of all European exports. This also indicates that trade is often dominated by the global companies and even within companies by a few or even one of their best-selling drugs.

The competitiveness of the pharmaceutical industries is illustrated by the Revealed Comparative Advantage (RCA).[2] Figure 7.2 shows the RCAs for the major countries of the EU and of the other two large producers, the United States and Japan. The comparative advantage *vis-à-vis* other industries of the EU as a whole is rather small. However, there are a few countries which stand out. Denmark and the UK show a large RCA - comparable to that of the United States. Italy has a large negative RCA indicating its below average competitiveness, but its RCA is still not as low as that of Japan.

2 The RCA is computed as $RCA_{ij} = \ln(X_{ij}/M_{ij}) - \ln(\Sigma_j X_{ij}/\Sigma_j M_{ij})$ with i=country and j=product groups of manufacturing.

Figure 7.2: Revealed Comparative Advantage (RCA) for pharmaceuticals (selected countries, 1991)

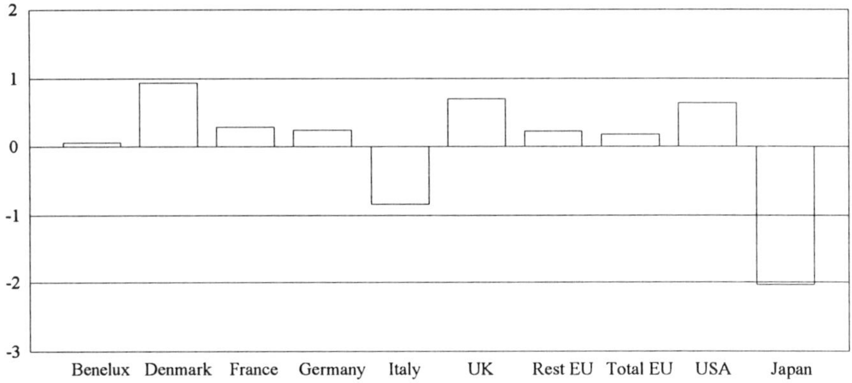

Source: OECD, *Trade by Commodities*, own calculations.

The geographical distribution of exports and imports of pharmaceuticals is relatively evenly divided between the EU and the rest of the world. Figure 7.3 shows that roughly one-half of all EU exports are intra-community exports and the other half (53 per cent) leaves the EU. This trade pattern is very similar for the United States (57 per cent exports to non-EU countries). Exports of Germany and Denmark are more oriented towards non-EU countries with above 60 per cent just like Japan. These numbers indicate that there seem to be no trade barriers which would effectively discriminate against non-EU suppliers like the United States or Japan. At the same time, the similarity in trade patterns of EU member countries on the one hand and the USA as well as Japan on the other hand also seem to indicate that the internal market is no more integrated than the world market in general. The pattern of imports is similar to the export pattern in such a way that the variation within the EU member countries is no different from that of the United States or Japan.

Figure 7.3: Trade patterns for pharmaceutical products (export and import shares to non-EU countries, 1991)

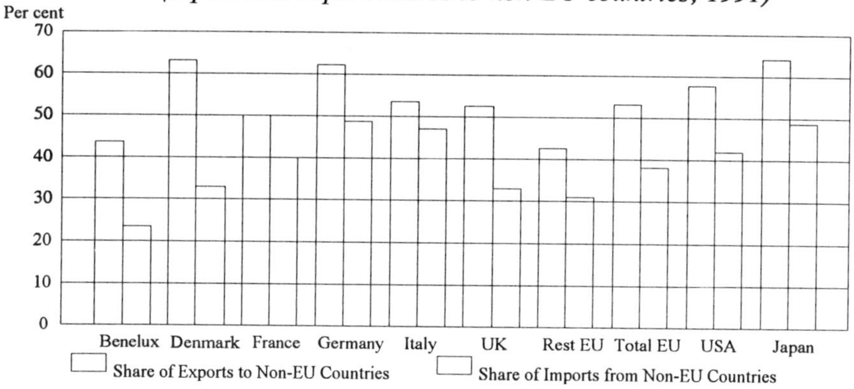

Source: OECD, *Trade by Commodities*, own calculations.

Figure 7.4 shows the importance of pharmaceutical exports relative to total manufacturing exports. Two point one per cent of the EU Member Countries manufacturing exports are pharmaceuticals, which is higher than the OECD average of 1.87 per cent. The export ratios vary considerably among the EU countries, with Denmark showing the highest percentage of almost 6 per cent. Only Italy is below the OECD average, with 1.1 per cent. A look at intra-EU export shares, i.e. intra-EU pharmaceutical exports divided by intra-EU manufacturing exports, reveals that - with the exception of Denmark - all countries have higher export shares for pharmaceuticals in intra-trade than for total manufacturing exports. This could indicate that European pharmaceutical markets are more integrated than the markets for other manufacturing products. However, given the intensive regulation in pharmaceutical markets (see section 2.1), integration is an unlikely explanation. It rather seems to indicate that the large product differentiation which is typical for the pharmaceutical industry has led to this comparatively high level of internal trade, not the least because high-income countries show a more diversified consumption pattern than lower-income countries.

Figure 7.4: Pharmaceutical exports relative to manufacturing exports for total exports and intra-Community exports

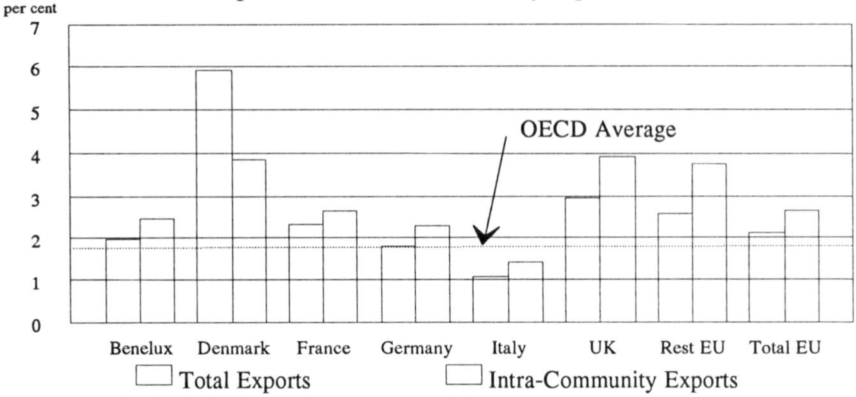

Source: OECD, *Trade by Commodities*, own calculations.

Parallel trade

There is one particular form of intra-community trade which deserves special attention, the so-called parallel imports and the reimports. They are much discussed because of the different perceptions about their role in pharmaceutical markets. The producers of pharmaceuticals claim that parallel imports and reimports exploit those price differences between countries which are induced by national price controls, tax differences, as well as exchange rate fluctuations and thus 'export' these price controls in uncontrolled markets. They see this as a threat to their profitability (Burstall, 1985). The European Court, however, has ruled in several cases that parallel imports and reimports are legal activities even if the price differences are not the result of corporate actions but of government regulations.

There exist different forms of parallel trade. Pharmaceutical companies producing a drug in a particular country will export this drug to foreign wholesalers at a specific ex-factory price which may be different from the price they charge to domestic wholesalers. This price difference could, for example, be induced by price controls in the domestic market. This price difference will be exploited by wholesalers who buy from local wholesalers in the producing country just those products with large price differences and export them 'parallel' to the 'official' exports which come directly from the pharmaceutical company and which are sold abroad at a price different from the domestic one.

Reimports are imports of drugs which are manufactured in a high price country, e.g. Germany. The German producer exports these drugs at lower prices - because of profit-maximizing price discrimination or because of price controls - to another country. The reimporter then buys these drugs from foreign wholesalers and reimports them back into Germany where they are sold at a lower price than the official supplies of the manufacturer.

No official statistics exist for the amount and flow of parallel imports and reimports in the EU but a study commissioned by the European Commission has estimated their extent. Table 7.2 shows the estimated sales of such imports in the countries with relatively high prices. The combined imports of pharmaceuticals of the four countries listed in Table 7.2 amount to between 370 and 436 million ECU in 1990. The share of these imports in the national markets varies strongly. The European average of 2 per cent is determined by a large market share in the UK with 8 per cent and probably the Netherlands with between 5 and 10 per cent. The German market - although it did have among the highest prices at that time - has a very small market share of about one per cent, which is likely to be attributable to the especially tight regulatory framework for product authorization, trademark rules, and the rules for drug prescription and retail sales.[3]

Table 7.2: Estimated sales of parallel imported pharmaceuticals and their market shares in the EC, 1990

Country	ECU	Share of Prescription Medicines in %
Denmark*	n.a.	n.a.
Germany	85-100	1
Netherlands	50-100	5-10
United Kingdom	235	8
European Community	370-436	2

Note: * First sales occurred at the end of 1990. Source: EC (1992).
Source: EC (1992a).

Compared to the total imports of pharmaceuticals in these countries parallel imports and reimports contribute little to overall trade. They probably vary around 5 per cent. If one looks at intra-EC trade - which would represent the relevant comparison - the numbers tell a different story. For example, the share of parallel imports and reimports on the

3 See section 2.1 below for further details.

total intra-EC imports of the UK is quite substantial with about 15 per cent. In the Netherlands they amount to around 8 percent and in Germany to below 5 per cent. At least in the UK and the Netherlands - and probably also in Denmark by now - such import shares may already exert enough pressure on prices at the margin in order to partially level off price differences. The change in price differences, however, not only depends on the arbitrage through parallel trade and reimports but also on price regulations.[4]

1.2. Production Processes

Pharmaceutical companies are engaged in a risky environment. The profitability of a company depends on its ability to successfully develop a new chemical entity with superior therapeutic characteristics and to market this drug in a profitable way. The success of both of these activities can hardly be predicted with accuracy. The R&D process itself is exposed to considerable uncertainties. Thousands of chemicals will be investigated before an entity is found which promises to become a powerful medicine. Only then will further R&D in pre-clinical and clinical testing be invested. The probability of finding a new chemical entity with a given effort has recently improved with the advances in gene-technology and the new knowledge in immunology. Also the likelihood for a new chemical entity to pass pre-clinical and clinical tests has risen somewhat above the previous 30 per cent for the United States.

At the same time, investment requirements necessary to develop a new product have increased dramatically. The total R&D costs of introducing a new chemical entity comprise the out-of-pocket costs as well as the opportunity costs of time until the product can be sold and the investment earns returns. For R&D performed in the early 1980s in the United States, the direct R&D costs were estimated to be $114m. and the costs of capitalizing these outlays amounted to $117m., totalling R&D investments measured in 1987 dollars of $231m. for every new product.[5] This is a remarkable increase against just $6m. (at 1990 prices) during the 1960s.[6]

Once the new chemical entity has been developed there are two distinct production processes. First, the active ingredients are produced as bulk ware and then they need to be converted into dosage form. These two processes need not be carried out at the same place, or even be close to

4 See section 3.1. for a discussion of the determinants of price differences.
5 Grabowski and Vernon (1992).
6 See Grabowski/Vernon (1992).

the R&D centres in which the ingredients have been developed. The production of active ingredients usually involves some economies of scale, whereas the conversion into the dosage form can be localized to a large degree because only a few economies of scale are involved in this activity.

The technological characteristics of the different production steps have important implications for the location of production facilities. The R&D centres are predominantly located in traditional centres of pharmaceutical research - i.e. Germany, Switzerland and the USA - although the UK has been paid particular attention, especially by non-EC companies. In the UK, the national regulations for drug reimbursements have favoured R&D undertaken inside the country. In addition, the lack of a language barrier and low wages for researchers may also have contributed to the attractiveness of the UK as a location for R&D, especially for American companies.

The technology of producing the active ingredients is largely independent of the particular endowment of a country with specialized factors such as research skills or technological know-how, such that other factors such as wage costs and tax or export promotion policies may influence the decision by global firms to locate this production step in a particular country. The same is true for the conversion of the active ingredient into dosage form which can, but need not, take place near the market. This ease of locational choice for these two production steps is important in the internal market which represents a particularly unrestricted environment for such foot-loose activities. It also tends to invite discriminatory practices of regulating agencies which could use their influence to combine their regulatory duties and objectives with industrial policy aspects.

If one were to translate these features into a stylized picture of the production process of research-oriented pharmaceutical companies, the following might be an appropriate description. A firm is faced with very high start-up costs of R&D, which are sunk. Given the considerable uncertainty about the probability of success of this activity, several R&D projects need to be undertaken at the same time in order to maintain the financial viability of the company. A largely fixed cost share is also spent on the sales force. The production variable, namely marginal costs, is then most probably constant. Although the pharmaceutical industry does not report cost figures within this framework, Table 7.3 indicates the cost structure of German and foreign firms in Germany as they are reported by the German association of the pharmaceutical industry. These sunk costs are only part of the fixed costs since for those chemical entities which have been turned successfully into a pharmaceutical product, production facilities for bulk production as well as for the conversion into dosage form need to be established.

Table 7.3: Composition of costs for pharmaceutical companies operating in Germany (1990, in per cent)

Type of cost	German Firms	Foreign Firms
R&D	19.4	9.9
Licences	1.7	2.2
Production	39.0	47.8
Scientific Information and Advertising	15.1	21.7
Distribution	9.2	8.1
Administration	8.4	6.9
Internal Interest	1.8	1.0
Other	5.4	2.4
Total	100.0	100.0

Source: BPI (1993).

Since foreign firms often do not undertake the R&D in Germany their cost share of R&D is significantly lower. For German firms R&D amounts to almost 20 per cent. This share is about 22 per cent in firms with a total turnover of more than DM 150m. per year, i.e. the truly innovative companies. The smaller companies have R&D cost shares between 4 and 8 per cent depending on their size (BPI, 1993). If one adds the other fixed costs such as those for scientific information and advertising or the administration costs to those of R&D, then well over 50 per cent of total costs can not be varied.

Since the riskiness of R&D requires a company to simultaneously undertake several research projects with direct costs well beyond $100m. (see above) it is clear that only very large corporations can in the long run survive such a competitive environment with the existing technology. As long as there is no fundamental change in the technology of developing and producing pharmaceuticals, the two-tier system of a few large global companies and a larger number of non-research firms will prevail. These non-research firms will either produce drugs under licence for a local market which the licence holder does not want to serve or they produce out-of-patent drugs which do not require any large research facilities. Since the bulk production as well as conversion into dosage forms involve little economies of scale these firms could be rather mobile and entry and exit from the industry is relatively easy.

The only limiting factor for the smaller companies may be the sales force. The marketing of pharmaceuticals usually requires complete coverage of the relevant decision-makers on the demand side, i.e., the physicians who prescribe the drugs, and direct access to them. The sales force necessary to meet this requirement may be rather large depending on the size of the market. Hence, the product range of the company also needs to be beyond a certain threshold level. Often corporate restructuring efforts are concerned with getting this market coverage which only firms with local experience will have.[7]

1.3. Market Structure

Pharmaceutical markets are special not only on the supply side, which has already been indicated by the specific production technology, but also on the demand side. The demand for pharmaceuticals is - except for the non-prescription drugs which are determined by the consumer himself - determined by a complex net of intermediaries before they are consumed by the patient. First of all, a physician needs to prescribe the drug indicated by his diagnosis of a particular illness. This decision will, however, not only be influenced by the - subjective or objective - therapeutic value of the drug but often also by the financing agency such as national health insurance systems or national health services. Positive or negative lists for drugs reimbursed, drug budgets allocated to physicians or price-sharing rules for patents, introduce price considerations into the decision. The extent to which prices enter the physician's prescribing behaviour varies with the institutional framework in the different member countries. The price elasticities of demand for pharmaceuticals will consequently vary among countries, yet they are generally considered to be much lower than price elasticities for 'normal' commodities.

The supply side is determined by the two-tier structure of producers and their technological characteristics which have been described above. For the research-oriented companies the long-term survival of the company can only be assured if it can produce important innovative drugs at regular intervals. Given the probabilities of success on the R&D side as well as on the marketing side, which can hardly be influenced, the R&D centres need to develop more innovations to compensate for the possible commercial failure of a particular drug. A study of American innovations shows that only the top two deciles of new drugs introduced are actually

---

7 For a discussion of different strategies in the pharmaceutical industry see EIU (1991).

profitable on the market; the others are essentially subsidized by the successful innovations (Grabowski and Vernon 1992). It would be impossible, however, to cut down on the rate of innovation because the R&D process can not predict which of the new chemical entities will turn out to be a commercial success. The stochastic nature of this process is illuminated first of all by the frequent changes in the ranking of the largest pharmaceutical producers by turnover. A successful new product can push a company way up and it could fall after the patent for such a product runs out.[8] The world's top-ranking global firms therefore constantly change positions but rarely does a new one enter or an established producer disappear.

The second phenomenon is the emergence of global firms with turnovers of well beyond two billion dollar, and - given their R&D shares of at least 10 per cent - R&D expenditures of more than $200m. per year. In addition, many of these companies are subsidiaries of even larger chemical firms which gives them an additional financial cushion to insure them against periods of little or commercially unsuccessful innovations. It is estimated that not more than 50 of these global companies will survive in the long run given the size of the market and the R&D investment necessary to secure a continuous flow of profitable products.

Defining the competitiveness of pharmaceutical markets is difficult in view of this situation. Compared to other industries, there exists in the world market a relatively large number of companies competing against each other with new products. Since there do not exist serious trade barriers in the important markets of Europe, North America and Japan, there is no reason to suspect that competition does not work. The two-tier structure of the industry also creates price competition by the smaller firms in the market through generics and other local pharmaceuticals.

On the other hand, the markets for the different products of the large pharmaceutical firms falling in several therapeutic groups are to a large degree separated. Therefore, the economies of scope on the supply side are not matched by differentiated product demands with high cross-price elasticities. On the contrary, the cross-price elasticities among drugs belonging to different therapeutic groups are zero. Consequently, the large number of products supplied by a single company are all supplied in separate markets - which are commonly subsumed under the heading 'pharmaceutical market' but are from an economic point of view not related at all. The competition in these submarkets - especially those for

---

8 A famous example is Glaxo's Zantac which became the world's best-selling drug with almost $2.4 billion turnover in 1989.

ethical drugs - is quite limited, with only a small number of suppliers and often a virtual monopoly of one supplier. The contradiction is therefore that there is a large number of suppliers for pharmaceuticals overall, but there are only very few suppliers in an isolated submarket.

Table 7.4: Market share of top brand and top five brands in various therapeutic submarkets, 1982 in per cent*

Submarket	France	Germany	UK
Cardiovascular			
Myocardial Agents	25/60	20/67	35/80
Peripheral Vasodilators	15/43	15/45	- /-
Beta-Blockers	17/40	15/50	22/85
Hypotensives	33/60	25/60	- /-
Anti-Ulcer Treatment	80/-	68/-	70/-
Psycholeptics			
Tranquillisers	26/70	26/68	26/80
Hypnotics	21/70	- /-	24/86
Analgesics	33/75	10/36	14/36
Systemic Antirheumatics	20/60	20/50	18/65
Systemic Antibiotics	25/35	7/23	26/46
Anti-Asthmatics	- /-	21/41	35/77
Diuretics	32/79	33/70	25/69

Note: * The first number refers to the top brand, the second to the top five brands.
Source: Burstall (1985).

Burstall (1985) has assembled an interesting set of data from unpublished information about this concentration of products in the different therapeutic groups for the early 1980s. Table 7.4 shows the share of the top-selling and the five top-selling products in 12 therapeutic groups in France, Germany and the UK. They already show a high concentration in several submarkets although the therapeutic groups of Table 7.4 still cover several distinct therapies for which the products mentioned here may not even compete against each other. So these numbers probably still underestimate the market power of a company in a specific therapeutic group.

To conclude, the market structure of pharmaceutical markets can hardly be characterized by one of the standard market forms. The demand side is largely determined by the complex regulation of the whole health system which divides demand decisions among different agents, physicians, health managers and patients and thus limits the price sensitivity of demand. On the supply side an ambivalent picture emerges since the global companies often have a virtual monopoly in relevant submarkets resulting in profitable sales of this particular product. On the other hand, the nature of pharmaceutical research forces them to pursue a large number of research projects of which only very few end up with a new pharmaceutical and of those even fewer will turn out to be commercially successful. Hence the profits in the successful product need also to subsidize other commercially less successful innovations as well as the unsuccessful research.

1.4. Geographical Features

A comparison of extra-EU trade of EU member countries with those of other countries can indicate whether the European market is any different from other markets in the rest of the world. Figure 7.3 has shown the percentage of exports and imports of pharmaceuticals with non-EU origin, relative to total exports/imports. In addition to the members of the EU, the same information is computed for the United States and Japan. It is evident that the variation of the share of extra-EU exports or imports across the member countries is no different from the exports or import shares of the Unites States or Japan to non-EU countries. This also indicates that the access of pharmaceutical firms to markets of Member States is about as good as that of the United States and Japan, or in other words, these data indicate that no apparent discrimination of foreign non-EU suppliers exists.

Figure 7.5: Share of the national market by Swiss and US firms (1984)

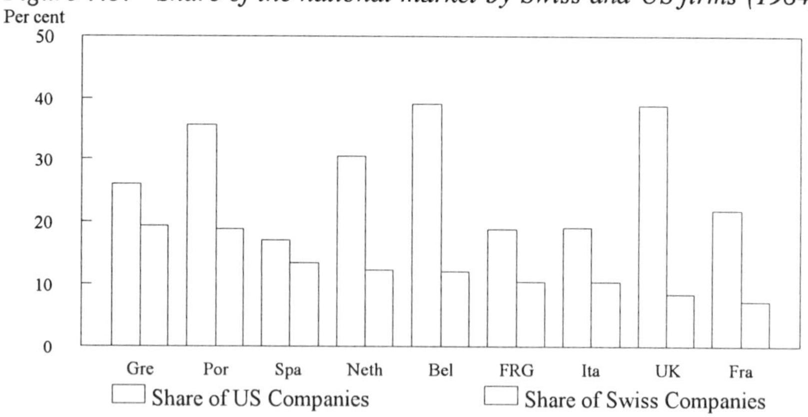

Source: Own calculations from data by Siberston (1990).

A similar picture of little discrimination emerges if one looks at the share of Swiss - or American - owned firms in the different markets of the

EU. In Figure 7.5 not only imports but also domestic production of foreign subsidiaries is measured in terms of market shares. American companies generally have a larger variation across the Member States than the Swiss firms. In particular, Belgium, Portugal and the UK are preferred markets for US firms, probably for different reasons in each case. Apart from a few special cases such as Ireland as a tax haven for bulk production and the UK for her highly qualified, low wage, and English-speaking research community, the markets of member countries do not seem to indicate any remarkable anomalies.

2. POLICY INTERVENTION IN THE PHARMACEUTICAL SECTOR

2.1. Existing Regulations

Not only pharmaceutical markets but also the whole pharmaceutical sector are subject to intense regulation extending through the whole product life. It starts with the laws governing the patenting of new chemical entities, then goes on to the marketing approval of new drugs. The marketing itself is subject to national regulations governing wholesale channels and wholesalers' margins. At the retail level, pharmacies are regulated in many different ways in the Member States. Finally, the sales force of the pharmaceutical producers is also restricted by rules of conduct at the European and at national levels.

Once a product can be sold in this system, it may be subject to price controls. It is also possible that, instead of controlling the product price, profits or costs of producing the product will be controlled by a regulatory body. Finally, when the drug reaches the final consumer, the patient's or the prescribing physician's decision may be controlled and influenced by the specific reimbursement rules which apply to the drug in question. Although no one country engages in all of these possible regulations, all countries apply at least some regulations.

The most prominent examples of this whole system of regulations are summarized in Table 7.5. The separation into the three areas of health, industrial, and commercial and competition policy is somewhat arbitrary since most policies possess aspects and side effects which cut across these boundaries. For example, drug authorization procedures might as well be included under health policies since they are imposed in order to protect the safety and efficacy of drugs. But at the same time the way in which this authorization is handled will have industrial policy aspects as well and, incidentally, the European efforts to harmonize drug approval are caused almost exclusively by industrial policy concerns and not by health concerns. This ambiguity of policy arenas also creates in some cases a duplication of national and supra national regulations.

Table 7.5: Policy interventions in the pharmaceutical sector

Health Policies	Industrial Policies	Commercial and Competition Policies
Cost Controls	Drug Authorization	Market Access
Price Controls	Patent Laws	Transparency
Profit Controls	Tax Concessions	International Harmonization
Positive/Negative Lists		
Reimbursement Rules		
Prescription Rules		
Aut-Simile-Clauses		

The interventions in the product life of a pharmaceutical are imposed by different regulatory agencies. Some of them are on a purely national level, some are exclusively given to supra national bodies like the EU. In many cases, however, there is no clear-cut assignment of regulatory responsibilities to a national or European agency. This is not only true across different regulations, e.g. patent laws and reimbursement, but is also the case within a regulation such as marketing approval for which national as well as multistate or centralized procedures are available. Therefore, the pharmaceutical sector in the EU is neither harmonized nor particularly decentralized such that it is impossible to speak of a hierarchy from local to national and to intra-community regulations. This mix of responsibilities between national and community-wide regulations also influences significantly the functioning of pharmaceutical markets, especially as far as the creation of a true internal market is concerned.[9]

National and local regulations

One of the important national concerns is the rising costs of health services, in particular of pharmaceuticals. Many different national regulatory systems have been invented to keep the rising drug prices under control. On the supply side, these interventions range from straight price controls to profit controls and to more indirect measures such as voluntary price restraints, as in Germany during the last few years.

---

9 See section 3.1 for a normative analysis of this regulatory system.

Measures which try to influence the demand side consist of a limit on the total expenditure for pharmaceuticals of a national health insurance system. Indirect pressure is also exerted through positive lists in which an insurer reimburses only those pharmaceuticals which are in the list, hence those drugs which in the eyes of the insurer are overpriced would be eliminated. Similarly, a negative list excludes the listed items from the reimbursement scheme of an insurer. More persuasive instruments are 'transparency lists' in which all drugs are catalogued in therapeutic groups in order to inform the prescribing physician about the most inexpensive treatment and thus improve competition among suppliers. In some countries, pharmacies are not required to choose the cheapest product among identical active ingredients (aut-simile-clause); in others this is mandatory. Through such measures, out-of-patent drugs especially would come under more competitive pressure from generics. Also, reimports and parallel imports would exert pressure to equalize prices across national markets if the aut-simile-clause extended to such products.

The other major area of national regulation is the approval of pharmaceuticals for sale within national borders. Safety, efficacy and quality of a pharmaceutical are to be controlled by the authorizing agencies. Additional regulations often concern specific requirements for patent information and packaging design. An important factor for product and price competition are the trademark rules. There is - especially in Germany which has trademark rules favourable for the industry - an intensive debate on the logic of trademarks in the pharmaceutical sector. The WHO proposes to name pharmaceuticals after the active ingredients which they contain. The German pharmaceutic industry's association, on the other hand, criticizes this approach as an 'expropriation' (BPI, 1993) of property rights on product designs. This regulation has important implications for the competition between generics and out-of-patent products, but also between parallel imports (reimports) and 'official' company sales because a trademark allows a company to differentiate products with identical ingredients, and often identical dosage and form, simply by name or packaging design.

Cost-control regulations as well as authorization procedures can have more than the direct intended effect of keeping down prices and securing a safe, efficient and high quality supply of pharmaceuticals. These regulations can be used in such a way as to discriminate between domestic and foreign producers or between domestically produced and imported pharmaceuticals. There exists little hard evidence for a planned and systematic use of such discriminatory practices but it is often alleged that some countries engage in such activities. A report by the Bundesverband der Arzneimittel-Importeure - the German Parallel Importers Association - has found that out of 20 newly introduced drugs, 14 had a brand name in Germany which did not correspond to any other name in the rest of the EU.[10]

One example of an indirect discriminatory incentive has been the profit control in the UK and the price determination and product authorization in France which has been reported by Burstall (1985) in the 1980s. Companies producing inside France are reported to have a better chance of getting a quick authorization and more favourable prices than foreign producers. This has been supported by a surprising statistic. If one takes the ratio of local production by foreign-owned companies to imports, the following picture emerges. Most European countries had a low ratio in 1980, e.g. the Netherlands 0.1, Germany 1.3, the UK 2.4, and Belgium 0.25. There are, however, two outstanding countries: France with a ratio of 15.7 and Portugal with 19.0; in addition, Italy has a ratio of 6.0.[11] Hence, for some reason the markets in France, Portugal and Italy are not served through imports but through local production of foreign subsidiaries. It is difficult to find explanations other than the existence of discriminatory practices of the authorities in these countries.

In the UK the permitted rate of return on sales to the National Health Service for many years was based on the contribution which cost factors such as investment, value added, research, and exports made to the UK economy (Earl-Slater, 1993). This, of course, favoured locally produced pharmaceuticals. Whether these practices are still in place is unknown. Also, it is not clear to what extent they have indeed helped the domestic industry since the UK has developed one of the most competitive pharmaceutical industries in the EU whereas France - which has also favoured local production through authorization and pricing procedures - has not been nearly as successful.

The particular success of the Irish pharmaceutical industry is due to their targeted industrial policy which grants concessions on income and profit taxes for export earnings. Consequently, Ireland has become one of the major exporters relative to the size of the country, the companies being mainly local subsidiaries of foreign firms (Burstall, 1985). It is also alleged that this industrial policy has led to some degree of distorted transfer pricing in order to get even larger tax breaks (EIU, 1991).

---

[10] See EC (1992a).

[11] From a study by the OECD, quoted from Rigoni et al. (1985).

Community regulations

The historically developed regulations of national pharmaceutical markets and industries have resulted in an extremely diversified set of rules which in many respects have become an obstacle for the creation of the internal market in the EU. The fragmentation of markets made entry for foreign firms costly and offered established firms the opportunity to segment European markets, which has become evident from the large price differences (EC, 1991). The EC therefore has tried to find a balance between - on the one hand - the sovereign concerns of member countries in controlling their health systems and - on the other hand - the harmonization necessary to create an internal market for pharmaceuticals.

The main areas of intervention are therefore:

- the control of discriminatory practices of regulatory agencies,
- a harmonization of rules for market access,
- competition and trade-related rules, and
- the patent laws.

The EU has not harmonized the working of the health systems of the member countries. However, in order to eliminate as far as possible the use of cost and price controls as instruments of industrial or trade policy the so-called 'Transparency Directive' (89/105/EC) has been implemented. It requires national agencies to make transparent the rules as well as the decisions with respect to the reimbursement and pricing of pharmaceuticals. It sets a time limit of 90 days within which marketing licences with price regulation are to be granted. A list of those pharmaceuticals which are under administered prices needs to be published at least once a year. The macroeconomic reasons for introducing price stops on all pharmaceuticals or on specific therapeutic groups need to be substantiated on a yearly basis. Member States which exercise profit controls need also to inform the Commission about the profit margins, the rules for computing them, and so on. Finally, each Member State must present a list of those pharmaceuticals which can be reimbursed through the national health system and make transparent which products are excluded from the reimbursement.

One of the central issues in creating an internal market and in promoting the free movement of goods is the harmonization of products. Market access for pharmaceutical products, which has in the past been regulated by independent national laws, has now partly moved towards a centralized system. To this end, the Commission has introduced a number of directives. In 1993 the Council issued a regulation and three directives concerning the marketing approval of pharmaceuticals.[12] These decisions offer pharmaceutical companies the option of using a centralized authorization procedure which grants a Community-wide approval for a particular drug.[13] In the alternative decentralized procedure the approval is granted by a national authority whose decision should be mutually recognized by all Member States. In cases of disagreement, a binding European arbitration is envisaged. This harmonization of market access regulations has an important impact upon the segmentation of national markets by making products with different national registrations not only physically homogenous but also legally, thus influencing the degree in which these products are tradable between states.

Increasing development and authorization times for new pharmaceuticals have resulted in continuously falling times in which the patent can be effectively used. The effective patent lives of products have been reduced to 7 to 8 years world-wide. The EC has reacted to the policies extending effective patent lives in the United States and Japan by issuing an additional patent protection certificate which prolongs the effective patent life of a pharmaceutical to up to 15 years. The 'Supplementary Protection Certificates' (SPC's)[14] expand the original patent by a maximum of 5 years. An SPC is granted by each national patent authority upon a formal request by the manufacturer and is granted for those drugs which have a proven development time of more than 5 years.

2.2. Community Experience in Applying the Policies

The regulations concerning the pharmaceutical industry and pharmaceutical markets have been introduced by the European Community only recently and in many cases are still in the process of being implemented in national law within the Member States such that it is still too early to assess their impact. Additional difficulties arise from the fact that the industry's activities are not well documented as far as official publications are concerned. Most of the information of older studies is also based on company data which are not publicly accessible. This section on Community experience will therefore contain little hard

---

[12] Regulation No. 2309/93, Directives 93/39/EC; 93/40/EC; and 93/41/EC.

[13] This process is mandatory for biotechnology products.

[14] Regulation No. 1786/92.

evidence on the experience with the new regulations but somewhat speculative predictions about their impact.

Competition policy

The EU has not followed an active competition policy in the pharmaceutical sector. The production technology and R&D specific risks require firm sizes which can survive only in a global market. Therefore only a small number of global firms compete in the market for innovative products but their competition is not hampered by national trade or entry barriers so that this competition is indeed global in nature. If some competition is distorted through measures of national agencies protecting domestic companies through discriminatory pricing or marketing approval, the Transparency Directive has at least made it more difficult to continue such practices.

The protection and promotion of small firms is a different matter, the reason being the dichotomizing two-tier structure of the industry. The global firms innovate and supply globally sold products; the smaller non-R&D firms supply local, regional or national markets with specialized products or products for which they have not done the R&D themselves. Whether these firms can survive in an increasingly globalized market and under now increased patent protection of new pharmaceuticals depends on a number of factors. One important component is the speed at which new products are brought into the market. This is so because such products will be supplied by the global innovative firms. Hence more new products will also strengthen their market power and reduce the competitiveness of local and generic products, and - vice versa - slower product innovation will protect the price-competitive older pharmaceuticals which are supplied by the local companies or medium-sized producers of generics.

The projected rate of innovation in the pharmaceutical industry has been falling world-wide, probably due to the increasing cost of R&D as well as the tightened standards for marketing authorization. On the other hand, gene technology is expected to become the source of a new generation of powerful pharmaceuticals, thus potentially increasing the rate of innovation in the industry. It is impossible to predict which effect will dominate within the pharmaceutical R&D, but whichever way innovation goes it will determine the competitive position of the innovative companies *vis-à-vis* the smaller non-research firms and it will determine the price levels which depend on the degree of price competition through out-of-patent drugs compared to the quality competition of the global companies.

Another factor determining the competitiveness of the smaller firms *vis-à-vis* their global competitors is the transparency of the market and the price sensitivity of demand. The attempts of the EU to harmonize packaging sizes and the content of patent information will enable even smaller firms to take advantage of the larger internal market. Also the proposed freedom for wholesalers to cross national boundaries in their activities may also lead to a wider diffusion of local products and to more competition. These effects are still speculative since these harmonizations are not yet all implemented and it will take quite some time until the first statistics will reveal results.

Finally, the costs, speed and administrative barriers for getting marketing authorization for generic products is an important factor in determining the ability of the non-innovative companies to compete with the patented products. The EC-Directive 87/21/EC greatly simplifies market authorization for products which have already been authorized for other producers - usually the previous patent holder - by not requiring the whole clinical and pre-clinical test evidence to be presented for a second time. Thus it is possible for generics producers to secure a quick supply of out-of-patent drugs at competitive prices.

Reimporters and arbitrage opportunities may also be looked at as a competition problem in that free entry into the distribution channels, i.e. the pharmacies, may be restricted through marketing regulations as in Germany or through supply restrictions of the producers through the wholesalers from which the reimporters usually buy. If the barriers to arbitrage come from regulations such as trademark rules or non-existent aut-simile-clauses international price competition is not increased through the policies of the EU. The harmonized registration procedure, on the other hand, would ease arbitrage opportunities because it effectively creates identical products independently from the country in which they are introduced. Since national registration is still available for companies as long as no bio-technology products are involved, they might still choose separate registration in each country in order to preserve the opportunity to price discriminate between national markets. This problem could become non-existent if indeed a harmonized internal market were created in pharmaceuticals.

In summary, the EU's regulations of pharmaceutical markets have increased the competitiveness by lowering the authorization costs and by speeding up the authorization process for the producers of generics. More international price competition will be introduced through the European-wide registration procedure. Whether the Supplementary Protection Certificate will increase competition remains an open question.

Industrial policy

Patent laws belong to the crucial institutional framework in which the pharmaceutical industry works. The development of new drugs is costly and risky such that sufficient R&D investment will only be raised and eventually earned if the new products are protected from competition for a sufficiently long time. Figure 7.6 shows that the innovative performance of the European pharmaceutical industry has been falling since the late 1970s, when measured in terms of new chemical entities . This has taken place mostly at the expense of the Japanese industry. The incentives for investigating in R&D for new products depends on the benefits and costs which a company experiences through such activities. Since R&D expenditures are to a large extent technology driven, the market power of the new product in its market segment is of particular importance. The innovative value of new pharmaceuticals consists of the product and not the production process, such that it is often quite easy to copy these drugs. Consequently, patent protection is of particular importance for the extent and success of innovative pharmaceutical companies.

Figure 7.6: New chemical entities 1961-1990 (Share of World-wide Introductions in %)

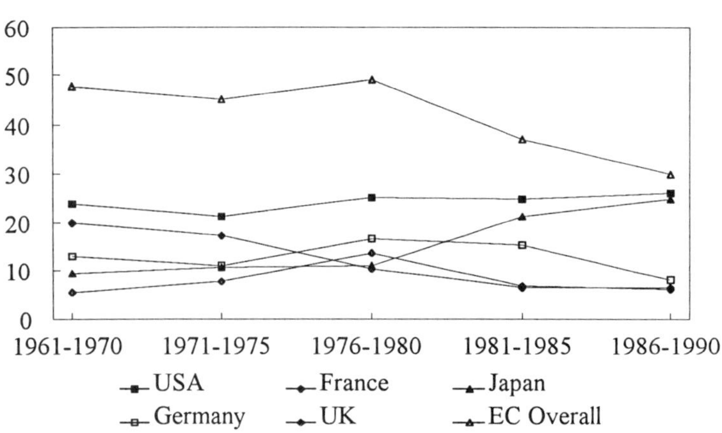

Source: BPI (1993).

New chemical entities which are patented in the EU generally have a patent life of 20 years,[15] compared to 17 years in the United States. The formal patent life is misleading for pharmaceuticals, however, since the effective patent life - measured from the time of the marketing of the product - is significantly lower. In Germany, the effective patent life is claimed to be around 7.7 years out of the 20 years (BPI, 1993). In the UK, the Association of the British Pharmaceutical Industry even claims that the 'true effective patent life was only five years'.[16] The parallel decline in effective patent lives in the United States was alleviated by a number of measures there, such that patents can effectively be used for about 9 years (EIU, 1991).

Additional effective patent protection in the EU will come from the improved certification systems which will cut the time it takes the authorization agencies to approve a new drug. These measures shorten development times and will thus extend the time in which the drug can be marketed under the protection of the patent.[17] The savings in opportunity costs of approval times are substantial. Grabowski and Vernon (1992) have estimated that a reduction in approval times of one year per new chemical entity in the United States will save $19m. which is roughly 8 per cent of their estimated total R&D costs.

The newly introduced SPC will increase the effective patent life to a maximum of 15 years such that the incentives for doing R&D will increase and the competitive position of European companies *vis-à-vis* their mainly American, Japanese and Swiss competitors is restored. Thus the patent extension is part of an industrial policy for the big research-oriented firms. The smaller non-R&D companies, however, will necessarily get access to the out-of-patent products at a later time, thus reducing the market potential for generic products. The SPC is therefore a mixed blessing for the industry as a whole.

The new certification procedures - harmonized European registration for high-technology products and mutual acceptance of national registration if a company so wishes - also have positive effects for the industry in terms of easier, less costly and speedier access to national markets than the previous national registration systems which often had different procedures and documentation requirements. This will undoubtedly be considered a successful industrial policy.

---

15 Ireland has only 16 years of patent protection.

16 Quoted from EIU (1991).

17 See the next section.

However, there is also the other effect of harmonized certification: it creates through arbitrage an internal market for pharmaceuticals and a tendency for equal prices throughout the EU. This runs at least partly against the interests of the global companies, which prefer segmented markets over unsegmented markets as long as the profits from market segmentation exceed the costs which are imposed by the segmented markets such as multi-registration of products. This market segmentation yields higher profits and is under many circumstances preferable to uniform markets, in particular if some of the low-priced markets might not be served because of insufficient demand. It also has distributional consequences since the low-demand markets - e.g. because of low-income levels - would be served by low prices in a segmented market framework whereas the prices would be higher for those low-income consumers in a unified market.

The new certification procedures are not obligatory - except for the high-technology products - such that a company can still choose a particular marketing and pricing strategy through the choice of the certification. A company could obtain authorization through the EC or through mutual recognition and thus serve the whole European market with an identical product. It could also get this product certified separately in each state, possibly under different names, and could thus maintain segmented markets. As long as this freedom of choice remains, the harmonized certification will not be able to complete the unification of pharmaceutical markets in the EC.

Commercial policy

The area of commercial policy is particularly difficult to assess since an explicit policy of this kind does not actually exist. The EU does not protect European companies against foreign competition. Formal trade barriers do not exist. Only some possible but difficult to prove discrimination by national regulatory agencies is reported which may even be legitimized to some extent by rules of the EU. Article 30 of the treaties prohibiting discriminatory trade barriers within the internal market is qualified by Article 36 which allows national regulations violating Article 30 - among other reasons - if they are introduced in order to protect the public health of the citizens of a Member State.

Despite the non existence of formal trade barriers, markets for pharmaceuticals are still segmented to a large degree. Price differences are still significantly larger than for other industrial products. Empirical estimates are extremely difficult because the industry's output consists of a huge number of different products which on the demand side is accompanied by different consumption patterns. It is therefore very difficult to define identical consumption baskets with a significant market share which can adequately represent price levels in the member countries of the EU.[18] Table 7.6 summarizes some current price comparisons which should be treated with the necessary caution.[19]

*Table 7.6: Retail prices for pharmaceuticals in the EC**

Country	1989[a]	1991[b]	1993[b]
Portugal	61	n.a.	67
France	68	n.a.	53
Spain	69	n.a.	94
Greece	71	n.a.	85
Italy	78	n.a.	96
Belgium	85	n.a.	116
Luxembourg	95	n.a.	97
United Kingdom	110	125	123
Ireland	118	130	133
Netherlands	131	134	148
Denmark	141	143	133
Germany	146	111	105

Notes: * EC average equals 100.
[a] EIU (1991) quoted from *Consumer Choice.*
[b] BPI, current issues.

The development of price differences in the Member States has been mixed. Some, but not all, low-price countries have prices moving towards the community average. In the high-price countries, only Denmark and Germany have falling prices between 1989 and 1993 whereas prices in Ireland, the Netherlands and the UK have actually increased. The overall development, however, tends towards less price dispersion if one takes the coefficient of variation of prices. It has been falling from 0.298 in 1989 to 0.258 in 1993.

---

[18] There has been intensive discussion about the appropriateness of empirical price comparisons in the 1970s when the public has become aware of the large price discrimination by pharmaceutical firms paired with the introduction of tight price controls especially in southern Europe. See WIdO (1984) or Glismann and Seusing (1975) and the response by the German pharmaceutical industry which has commissioned a rival study, PROGNOS AG (1984).

[19] Especially as they have been published by interested parties in the pharmaceutical markets.

The causal relationship between the change in prices in the different Member States and the change in regulations is impossible to determine. Too many changes have taken place at the same time; pressure on prices through national insurance agencies, more price-sensitive demand by physicians, increased arbitrage, more transparency in price controls and many more factors may have contributed to this fall in price differences. The variations in the different countries also indicate that the peculiar mix of policies in each Member State may have determined the varying development of prices.

It should also be mentioned that even an averaging out of price differences in the EU does not mean that the average prices have been falling. In fact, in Germany prices have been increasing slightly below the inflation rate but not fast enough to indicate that the strong fall of the German price in the European average from 146 in 1989 to 105 in 1993 could have been accompanied by falling European prices. It is more likely that the European average has increased and tended towards the high-price countries. This is the more likely if one considers that price controls in more open markets will need to decrease such that the net effect of all regulations is an increase in average prices.

3. NORMATIVE APPROACH

The net of regulations within the pharmaceutical sector, both concerning the supply of drugs as well as their demand, belongs to the most intensive one of all industries in the EU. This situation does not differ much from that in all other industrialized countries. All national governments need to find a compromise among the different public and private interests in the pharmaceutical sector. These interests consist among others in:

- securing a safe supply of pharmaceuticals;
- containing the costs of the national health system;
- strengthening the innovative capacity of the pharmaceutical industry;
- maintaining or improving the competitiveness of the pharmaceutical industry.

Many of these objectives conflict with each other, thus making regulation a politically controversial activity as shown by the conflicts surrounding the reform of national health systems in many countries.

The challenge for regulating the pharmaceutical sector within the European Union becomes even more demanding as the national regulations need to be matched by European regulations. The responsibility of the European Community to create the single market within this tight national regulatory framework is particularly difficult if most of the national regulations can not be harmonized despite the fact that they may effectively limit the free movement of goods. For this reason, the measures taken by the Community often only indirectly address the problem in hand. The following normative analysis will therefore first present a stylized picture of the issues which relate to the completion of a single market in pharmaceuticals. It will then analyse the likely effects of the interplay of the different policy initiatives. This analysis will necessarily be confined to a qualitative assessment since most initiatives of the Community have been implemented just recently so that empirically verifiable effects can not yet be expected. Finally, some tentative conclusions will be drawn.

3.1. Completing the Single Market

The pharmaceutical markets in Europe have been given particular attention because they are characterized by the largest price differences - compared to other products - among Member States. These price differences were interpreted as a sign for an insufficient integration of pharmaceutical markets. Since no formal trade barriers exist for pharmaceuticals in the EU, the lack of integration - or in other words, the apparent market segmentation - must stem from other regulations which prevent the free movement of goods or which might restrict competition. Others have also argued that the price controls in many member countries have artificially created these price differences (BPI, 1993).

In fact, the apparent lack of price equalization for pharmaceuticals needs to be attributed to a specific mix of different national and European regulations in the Member States and not to one single impediment to the free movement of goods within the Community. This mix consists of the national regulatory systems of drug marketing - beginning with the approval of drugs, to the trademark regulations, the organization of the marketing channels, and ending with the prescription practices of physicians - and the regulations directed towards controlling the expenditure of national and other health systems for drugs - in many countries through price controls. Incidentally, neither of these regulations have been completely harmonized by the recent directives of the Commission of the EU. Instead, the Transparency Directive tries to eliminate discriminatory price controls - but not price controls in general -

through requiring regulatory agencies to make public the criteria on which they base their decisions. Similarly, the different initiatives for an easier and more harmonised drug approval go only part of the way towards a single market for pharmaceuticals, because they still leave open the option of national drug authorizations and thus of market segmentation through product differentiation along rational boundaries.

The question then is, how do these different regulations interact with each other and what allocative result do they produce? In terms of EU policies it is of interest whether the regulations in the different policy arenas will supplement each other or whether they conflict in terms of their goals. In the case of pharmaceuticals, a strict distinction between competition, industrial and commercial policy is of little help for a normative analysis, since the regulations can not always be attributed to a specific policy arena. Therefore, three issues will be raised here. First, will the mix of European regulations achieve a true internal market in which all pharmaceuticals can move freely? Or, in other words, which are the essential regulations for achieving this objective? Related to this, one can ask what the likely welfare impacts of such an internal market would be. The second question is concerned with the interaction of the internal market programme and specific objectives of industrial policy and competition policy. These may well represent conflicting interests in terms of profitability, welfare and distributional issues. Finally one could then ask: could a different set of European policies have achieved the objective of creating an internal market for pharmaceuticals together with a healthy and predictable environment for pharmaceutical companies?

Figure 7.7: Price discrimination, arbitrage and price controls

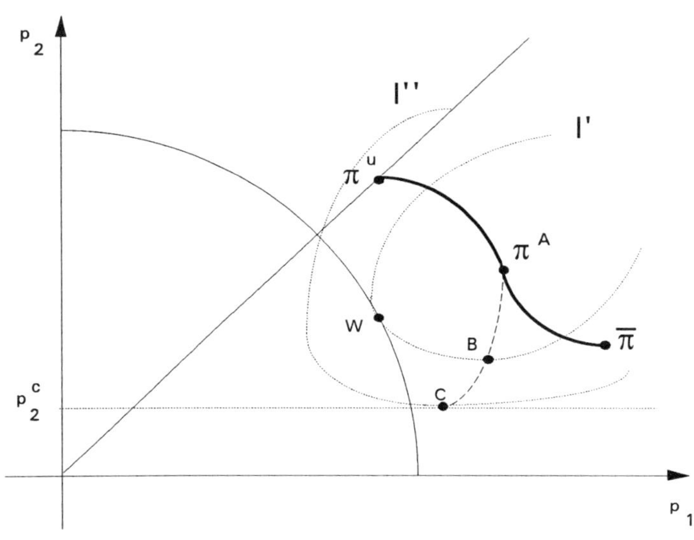

The interplay of national and European authorization procedures with the regulations for the free movement of goods, and national price regulations can be shown in the following simple model of price determination in an oligopolistic market.[20]

Suppose there are two countries, 1 and 2, in which oligopolistic firms compete by setting prices for their products, p_1 and p_2. These markets differ by having different demand curves with different demand elasticities, e.g. because of different income levels or different drug reimbursement rules. If the two markets are completely segmented, i.e. there is no opportunity to exploit the price difference through arbitrage, and if there are no price controls in either of the two markets, then the prices can be chosen freely by firms so as to maximize company profits. The discriminating prices in this case would be given by the point $\bar{\pi}$, i.e. country 1 is the high-price country with a low demand elasticity compared to country 2 in Figure 7.7.

On the other extreme, a regulatory framework in which there is a completely free movement of goods, i.e. arbitrage is costless, uniform prices will prevail in both countries and the prices chosen by the firms will be given by the point π^u. Ideally, the internal market would be represented by a situation in which point π^u is reached. Again, this requires that there are no national price controls. Prices in country 1 would be lower and those in country 2 would be higher than under a regime of completely segmented markets.

If in a situation of costless arbitrage and without trade barriers price controls are introduced by one country - e.g. country 2 - prices would fall in both countries because arbitrage will ensure that the new prices would be on the 45°-line below π^u. Hence, price controls by national governments could still be maintained but would lower the profit margins of the companies.

Of course, these two extreme cases do not correspond to the actual situation within the EU. Arbitrage opportunities are not completely free but are costly. For products which are authorized through the centralized procedure, arbitrage costs are relatively small if local marketing restrictions of reimported products are not in place. Nationally registered products may have higher arbitrage costs because they need to become registered in the country which they enter as reimports or parallel imports. Often they need to become repackaged for adding appropriate patient information etc. Hence, depending on the type of product, the

---

[20] The following analysis is based on Klepper (1992) where the formal model and the proofs are also presented.

regulatory framework, and the registration procedure which it has undergone, different prices in the two markets will be chosen by the firms. The profit-maximizing price combinations under different arbitrage costs are illustrated by the line $\pi^u\pi^A\bar{\pi}$ in Figure 7.7. The point π^A corresponds to one possible configuration of national and European market regulations. Any policy initiative towards, for example, a more harmonized registration of drugs will lower arbitrage costs and therefore will move prices along this line towards π^u. Under normal conditions for demand, this move will be accompanied by falling prices in the 'high-price country' and by rising prices in the 'low-price country'. It is therefore clear that even without price controls some degree of price dispersion will prevail between countries as long as arbitrage is hampered by administrative barriers.

If, in addition to the institutional framework governing the authorization and the marketing of pharmaceuticals, a country uses price controls to keep the costs of the health system under control, the optimal price combination will be governed by the administered price in the controlling country. In Figure 7.7, the price p_2 is fixed by the government at p_2^c such that the optimal response by firms is to set the price in country 1 in such a way as to come to point C. In C the highest isoprofit line I' is reached given the price restriction in country 2.

A relaxation of price controls in country 2, i.e. rising prices p_2, will be accompanied by price changes in country 1 as well. For increasing but still government-controlled prices the optimal price combinations will move along the line $CB\pi^A$ to π^A where price controls would be completely removed.[21] The optimal price policy in country 1 of the companies can not be predicted in general. In the illustration in Figure 7.7 both prices rise with the reduction in price controls. However, it also possible that p_1 falls as a reaction to a higher p_2 because the change in prices in country 1 depends essentially on the shape of the cost curve of arbitrage.

Reimports and parallel imports are currently managed in such a way that reimporters need to buy their supplies from wholesalers almost secretly, against the interests of the pharmaceutical producers. Consequently, an expansion in sales by arbitrageurs will become increasingly difficult since their demand will become easier to detect by the producers who often, as

21 Point B does not even represent a second-best allocation from a global welfare perspective. If company profits of I' were to be achieved, the optimal price control would be in point W where the welfare indifference curve is tangent to the isoprofit line. See Klepper (1992) for details.

a consequence, cut off such supplies. This situation would translate into a convex cost function for arbitrage and this convexity in turn would result in a positively sloped path $CB\pi^A$ in Figure 7.7. Hence, a relaxation of price controls in country 2 would be accompanied by rising prices in country 1 as well. The reason, of course is, that the pressure on prices in country 1 through arbitrage has been lowered such that the producers can more easily exploit the inelastic demand in country 1.

Figure 7.8: The effect of persistent price controls on profits

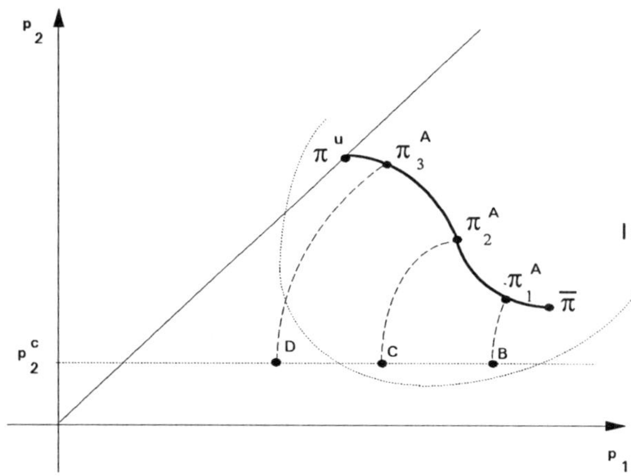

The European initiatives to implement through the multi-state authorization and the European registration of drugs more homogeneous products which can move more cheaply between member countries corresponds to a lowering of arbitrage costs and therefore towards more uniform prices. Price controls by national governments, however, may still be in place despite these changes in the registration procedures. The prices in the member countries will therefore not move along the line $\pi^u\pi^A\bar{\pi}$ in Figure 7.7 but will stay in the price-controlled country at their administratively set level.

Figure 7.8 illustrates this case. An increasing harmonization of products through the regulation of authorization procedures would, in the presence of price controls in country 2 at p_2^c, be accompanied by price changes represented by a move from B over C to D, i.e. the prices in country 1 would fall and those in country 2 would not change such that the price difference between countries would fall as well. If the price controls were not in place the prices in the two countries would move from π_1^A over π_2^A

to π_3^A, i.e. prices in country 1 would fall as before but those in country 2 would rise not through the lowering of price controls but through the completion of the internal market alone. This would increase the incentives of country 2 to maintain her price controls in order to protect herself from the loss in consumer surplus from a more integrated market.

As long as country 2 maintains its price controls the move from B towards D (Figure 7.8) is accompanied by falling profits of the producers of pharmaceuticals. Eventually the profits may fall to zero or become negative if the price-controlled market were still to be served. In Figure 7.8 this would happen if the harmonization of products were so much advanced that - without price controls - prices corresponding to π_3^A would be chosen. However, with price controls at p_2^c, point D should be chosen yielding losses for the firms as it is indicated by the isoprofit line I=0. Therefore such markets may not be served at all by the producers and as a result the harmonization of authorization could make it impossible to maintain price controls at the previous level.

3.2. Conflicts Between the Internal Market Program and Industrial Policy

The previous analysis has already highlighted the fact that a completion of the internal market for pharmaceuticals together with the continuation of price controls in some Member States seems to be incompatible in the long-run with other objectives, such as those of supporting an innovative pharmaceutical industry and maintaining its international competitiveness. Several factors of the initiatives towards an internal market thus interact with the competitiveness of the industry and the industrial policy measures of the EC. The attempts towards creating an internal market through a reform of the authorization procedures in order to allow the free movement of products between Member States directly and indirectly influence the profitability of the industry and - through profits - its potential to regain its competitiveness in innovative products. Through this channel the internal market programme also influences industrial policy objectives.

The central policy in moving towards an internal market consists of the - still partial - harmonization of product authorization. In the previous section the impact of this policy on arbitrage, price differences, and on the possibility to maintain national price controls, has been discussed. Whereas a harmonized drug authorization will lower the cost and time for getting the approval of new products, it became clear that this will also reduce the cost of arbitrage, thus exerting increased pressure on price differences between national pharmaceutical markets. This pressure alone would lower the profitability of product sales in the Community since less of the consumer surplus can be extracted by the firms through price discrimination.

In addition, the national price controls will distort the profitability even more if they are maintained and the markets become more integrated at the same time. Then there is not only an equalization of prices but also a downward pressure within the European market towards the price in the controlled markets. Of course, it is hoped that the harmonization of pharmaceutical markets will indirectly increase the political pressure on national governments to reduce such price controls and move towards uniform and free prices. This parallel evolution of more market integration and less price intervention will have mixed effects in terms of profitability, because lifting price controls raises profits and more arbitrage lowers profits. In the end it is not at all clear how these different effects will balance out in determining the profitability of the pharmaceutical industry.

The issue of price controls is connected with distributional and political economy considerations which make it difficult to find matching interests in industrial policy objectives and the internal market. The high fixed costs of the pharmaceutical industry through large R&D investments and other indivisible costs make it easy to control prices in a submarket by forcing a firm towards marginal cost pricing, as long as the fixed costs can be recouped in other uncontrolled markets. The issue of price controls then boils down to a distributional question of who pays for the R&D. Incidentally, most of the European R&D relative to the production is performed in the high-price countries as Table 7.7 indicates.[22]

[22] These numbers should also be taken with the necessary caution. As an example, the German Pharmaceutical Industry Association reports R&D expenditures relative to turnover of 15.4 per cent (BPI, 1993) which is far greater than the numbers from the European Federation of Pharmaceutical Producers from which the numbers in Table 7.7 are derived.

Table 7.7: R&D investments in the Member States of the EU

	R&D (mio ECU)	R&D (in % of Production)
Belgium	206	11.2
Denmark	173	15.9
France	1,578	11.8
Germany	1,471	9.8
Greece	-	-
Ireland	-	-
Italy	1,008	9.1
Netherlands	221	14.1
Portugal	-	-
Spain	191	3.4
United Kingdom	1,786	16.6
Total EC	6,584	10.6

Source: EC (1993).

It therefore seems politically sensible for countries with little or no industrial R&D to try to force the financing of the R&D expenditures upon the consumers in those countries in which the global firms are located.

The attempts of the EU to create an internal market in pharmaceuticals are faced with diverging interests from two groups of countries. Those countries without an R&D-intensive industry will prefer to push consumer interests by trying to obtain imported drugs or locally produced drugs - but developed in a foreign country - at the lowest possible price. Thus, they have little reason to push for more integration and harmonization of pharmaceutical markets. For these countries, health policy also becomes an area of indirect commercial or trade policy.

The countries hosting R&D-intensive companies, on the other hand, are unlikely to support further harmonization as long as persistent price controls will lead to strong profit reductions as soon as the opportunities for market segmentation are reduced and arbitrage becomes easier. They will therefore still offer a national registration of drugs in order to give firms the opportunity to secure at least the profitability of their home markets. Their industrial policy objectives can not be served by the existing regulations since they do not effectively remove the above-mentioned price controls. National registration of drugs becomes an industrial policy for securing the competitiveness of the national industry. This, however, is achieved at the cost of the domestic consumers of pharmaceuticals.

The initiatives of the EU interfere very little with those national health regulations which are concerned with reimbursement and pricing of pharmaceuticals. This fact, however, will in the short run impose substantial costs upon the industry if at the same time the unification of markets through a harmonization of products is to be pushed further, e.g. through a mandatory European drug authorization. Then arbitrage will force prices towards the low levels in the most regulated markets thus threatening the competitiveness of the industry. The internal market programme would, by creating more openness, run into conflict with its industrial policy interests of recreating the environment for a financially viable industry which can compete in innovative products with non-European firms. Even if the pressure on prices through a reduction in the price differences will eventually make national price controls impossible to implement, the intermediate costs of more uniform prices paired with price controls may have its social costs. From an industrial policy perspective it would be desirable that the harmonization of products throughout the Community should be accompanied by stronger attempts to reduce national price controls.

Another indirect aspect of the move towards a harmonized authorization for a unified market is related to competition and industrial policy objectives. It has just been shown that the impact of the internal market programme on the profitability of the industry will be ambiguous thus also having an ambiguous effect on the incentives for performing and financing R&D. In addition to this effect on the global innovative firms, the easier authorization of generic products will also increase price competition from the non-patented products by giving the generics producers timely and less costly access to the market. This increases competition between the large and the smaller companies in the internal market but it also potentially reduces the expected profitability of R&D by reducing effective patent lives. The increase in effective patent lives through the SPC will, however, compensate for this reduction.

The relationship between the industrial policy objective of maintaining the innovative capacity of the global firms and the opportunity to introduce more price competition into the different submarkets by giving the non-R&D firms faster access to new products remains delicate. In pharmaceutical markets with relative inelastic demand elasticities because of the complex system of demand determination, price competition becomes a powerful control for monopolistic pricing. At the same time, the innovation rents are negatively related to the degree of price competition, such that a balance needs to be found between the length of effective patent lives and the extent of price competition by the smaller firms. Economic analysis has little to offer as to which rate of innovation would result in a welfare-maximizing balance between the innovation rents and price competition. In this sense, industrial policies and competition policies are necessarily in a conflict which can not be resolved even through a coherent design of policies.

REFERENCES

Boroch, Wilfried and Dieter Cassel (1993), 'Integration regulierter Märkte; Das Beispiel eines einheitlichen EG-Arzneimittelmarktes', in Helmut Gröner and Alfred Schüller (eds.), *Die europäische Integration als ordnungspolitische Aufgabe*, Gustav Fischer Verlag, Stuttgart, 359-78.

BPI, *Pharma-Daten,* Bundesverband der Pharmazeutischen Industrie, Frankfurt, current issues.

BPI (1993), *Pharma Jahresbericht 1992/93,* Bundesverband der Pharmazeutischen Industrie, Frankfurt.

Burstall, M.L. (1985), *The Community's Pharmaceutical Industry,* Commission of the European Communities, Office for Official Publications, Luxemburg.

Earl-Slater, Alan (1993), 'Pharmaceuticals', in Peter Johnson (ed.), *European Industries - Structure, Conduct and Performance,* Edward Elgar, Aldershot, 75-100.

EC (1991), 'The Economics of 1992', *European Economy*, No. 35.

EC (1992a), *Impediments to Parallel Trade in Pharmaceuticals within the European Community*, EEC Reference IV/90/06/01, Luxemburg.

EC (1992b), *Die Regelung der Arzneimittel in der Europäischen Gemeinschaft*, Band 1, Luxemburg.

Economist Intelligence Unit (EIU) (1991), *Europe's Pharmaceutical Industry - Tackling the Single Market*, Special Report No. 2085, London.

EU (1994), *Mitteilung der Kommission an den Rat und das Europäische Parlament über die Leitlinien einer Industriepolitikfür den Arzneimittelsektor in der Europäischen Gemeinschaft,* Com(93) 718, Brussels.

EUROSTAT, *Struktur und Tätigkeit der Industrie*, Theme Energy and Industry, Series C, current issues.

Glismann, Hans H. and Ekkehart Seusing (1975), 'Probleme internationaler Preisvergleiche - Pharmazeutische Produkte', *Die Weltwirtschaft*, No. 2, 176-90.
Grabowski, Henry G. and John M. Vernon (1992), 'The Costs and Returns to Pharmaceutical Research and Development', *Rivista internazionale di Scienze sociali*, No. 3, 347-58.
Klepper, Gernot (1992), 'Pharmaceuticals: Who's Afraid of '1992'?', in L. Alan Winters (ed.), *Trade Flows and Trade Policy After '1992''*, Cambridge University Press, Cambridge, 150-69.
PROGNOS AG (1976), *Internationale Markt- und Preisvergleiche im Pharmabereich*, Basel.
PROGNOS AG (1984), *Einzelstaatliche Preisregulierungen und die Folgen für den EG-Pharmamarkt*, Basel.
Rigoni, Raymond, et al. (1985), 'Pharmaceutical Multinationals - Polemics, Perceptions and Paradoxes', *IRM Multinational Reports*, January-March 1985, John Wiley & Sons, Chichester.
WIdO (Wissenschaftliches Institut der Ortskrankenkassen) (1984), *Der europäische Arzneimittelmarkt*, WIdO-Schriften, Vol. 6, Bonn.

Discussion

Elisabeth Waelbroeck-Rocha

The chapter by Dr Klepper on the coherence of EC competition, trade and industrial policies in the pharmaceutical sector rightly stresses the very complex structure of this market. On the supply side, the market is characterized by a dichotomous, two-tier structure, with a few large firms responsible for most of the R&D and for innovation, operating alongside a large number of small and medium-sized firms mainly producing off-patent drugs, often for local markets. On the demand side, there are different types of economic agents having different preferences and choice criteria, these agents being the patients, the physicians themselves and the health insurers.

Both on the demand and on the supply side, the market is dominated by a complex web of regulations related to national reimbursement rules, pricing, trademark rules, market access conditions and patenting procedures, all of these reflecting different responses to concerns over health and safety.

As is also well illustrated in the chapter by Dr Klepper, the market for pharmaceuticals is constantly changing, as drugs come off-patent after a few years. When this happens, the products come under intense pressure from generics. Typically, when a high-selling drug comes off-patent, its sales value can be halved within a very short time span.

Finally, the industry is characterized by high development costs, and continuous innovation is key to success. This implies that, more than in most other sectors, there is a need to maintain high profits to finance R&D.

Starting from this, there is a presumption underlying Dr Klepper's analysis which is that the present high degree of fragmentation of the EU market not only allows the national regulatory authorities to discriminate between domestic and foreign producers, or between domestically produced and imported pharmaceuticals, but also makes it possible for the firms themselves to discriminate through prices to maintain high profits.

The implication is that, in reducing market segmentation, the achievement of a single European market for pharmaceuticals combined with an active competition policy might have negative effects on profits, hence on R&D and innovation, and on the sector's relative competitiveness in world markets. Based on the financial results of the world's top 25 pharmaceutical companies, one can, however, challenge both the assumption that market segmentation enables EU firms to generate abnormal profits and the fact that there is a direct link between profits and R&D. In Europe, for every year from 1991 to 1993, R&D as a share of turnover of the top firms in the sector has been higher than that of the top US firms, despite the fact that the average operating profit of the larger US firms as a share of turnover was greater than that of EU firms. In 1992, for example, the average return on sales of the top European pharmaceutical producers was 14 per cent, which compares with a figure of 15.9 per cent for the top US firms, and 5.6 per cent for the only Japanese company in the top 25 world ranking. At 11.8 per cent, however, the R&D/turnover ratio of the EU firms was well above that of the US firms, which was 10.5 per cent in the same year. The greater market segmentation in Europe compared to the USA thus does not translate into comparatively higher profits by EU companies, although this did not prevent the latter from investing more as a share of turnover than their US competitors. The (positive) correlation between R&D and profits is thus not as direct or absolute as is often believed.

Turning to the analysis of the coherence of economic policies in the pharmaceutical sector, this can be done along four different dimensions: (1) Are the policies internally consistent? (2) Are they mutually consistent? (3) Do they meet their objective? (4) Are they consistent over time?

In his chapter, Dr Klepper focuses mainly on the coherence of EU policies along the first three of these dimensions. The chapter reviews the set of regulations in place at EU level, and discusses whether these are internally consistent (i.e. whether policy measures contradict, neutralize or reinforce each other), whether they are mutually consistent (in particular whether trade policies are consistent with industrial policies), and whether they fit the overall goals of an appropriate health policy, the latter being defined as a policy which:

- secures a safe supply of pharmaceuticals;
- contains the costs of national health systems;

- strengthens the innovative capacity of the European pharmaceutical industry;
- maintains or improves the competitiveness of Europe's pharmaceutical industry.

The main conclusions that are reached by Dr Klepper are that:

- given the structure of the market, there is no reason to suspect that competition does not work, even though there can be very few competitors in some market segments; indeed, the two-tier structure of the industry creates price competition by the smaller firms through generics and other substitute products;
- competition policy has an influence on the rate of innovation, hence on the competitiveness of the industry; in particular, the rules for market authorization influence the level of R&D by the sector;
- by lowering the authorization costs and by speeding up the authorization process for generics producers, EU regulations of pharmaceutical markets have increased the sector's competitiveness;
- the EC's competition and industrial policies are, however, not fully consistent: the SPC Directive conflicts or at least has opposite effects to those of the Marketing Approval Directive, in that by extending the period of patent protection the former extends the period under which innovative drugs are protected from competition, whereas the aim of the second (the Marketing Authorization Directive) is to speed up access to the market to other producers - in particular generics producers - to increase market competition;
- more importantly, the completion of the internal market for pharmaceuticals together with the continuation of price controls in some Member States is, in the long run, incompatible with objectives such as the support of an innovative pharmaceutical industry and the maintenance of its international competitiveness.

There are, however, a number of issues related to the coherence of trade, competition and industrial policies in the pharmaceutical sector which are not dealt with in the above chapter. For instance, it makes little reference to the Intellectual Property rules, nor to the discussions surrounding their inclusion in GATT. More importantly, neither in this nor in other chapters has there been much reference to the effects of economic policies on company strategies; in other words on the 'spill-over' effects of policy measures on industry structure and on the competitive environment.

Pharmaceutical companies, like all companies, are not passive economic agents. Looking at the consistency of industrial, competition and trade policies over time involves looking at the companies' response to the regulatory changes and understanding how these will affect the structure of the industry and the competitive environment.

Within Europe, the pharmaceutical companies' present strategies reflect the fact that:

- it is the self-medication market which is the fastest-growing pharmaceutical segment;
- there is a trade-off between present and future government spending on health which the pharmaceutical producers ought to capitalize upon (this is linked to the benefits of health prevention measures and the costs of non-compliance to medical treatments);
- not only do the rates of growth of these two market segments differ, but the distribution and marketing channels are also completely different in the non-prescription and in the prescription pharmaceuticals markets respectively.

As a result, companies are adopting very different strategies on the ethical product's market segment than on the self-medication market segment.

On the ethical products market, there is a clear shift in focus as companies increasingly avoid 'me-too' drugs in order to specialize on niche segments in which they believe they enjoy a comparative advantage. The companies can thus benefit from a quasi-monopoly situation in their niche segment during the period of patent protection, sometimes even after as many companies are now producing their own generics. The shift in focus of ethical drugs producers is often accompanied by a separation of the 'research' and 'development' functions, with companies engaging in the 'development' phase only when they believe that there is a sufficiently large market for the products and that there is a high probability of the drug being reimbursed. When these two conditions are fulfilled, indeed, they can enjoy a rapid rate of return on their investment.

In parallel to this increased specialization trend amongst the top companies, which tends to reduce the number of players in given market segments, a number of ethical drugs producers are actually reducing their emphasis on the ethical drugs market in order to concentrate on the more profitable and fast-growing self-medication market. This is further reducing the number of key players in the ethical drugs markets.

In the OTC (over-the-counter) segment of the market, in contrast, the types of strategies that pharmaceutical producers are pursuing should a priori lead to increased competition. Nevertheless, because there is pressure on prices and profits from national governments seeking to limit the rise in health-care costs and because there is increased competition as more and more producers are seeking to enter this market, some of the larger OTC producers are responding by trying to expand their control of down-stream activities, for instance distributors and health management organizations (HMOs). The trend is particularly visible in the USA, where a number of pharmaceutical companies have recently acquired HMOs. This trend may progressively spread to Europe, starting in the countries where the distribution of pharmaceutical products is less regulated (as in the UK, for example). The number of trans-European alliances or mergers amongst drug distributors has itself increased significantly in the past years, such that alliances at EU level account for 55 per cent of the market in France, 50 per cent in the UK and 45 per cent in Germany. In some cases, there was a direct involvement of the pharmaceutical producers themselves. The risks are high that a continuation of this trend would squeeze pharmaceutical producers from the market, in particular the more local firms and the producers of generics which have no 'ethical drugs' branch. This has obvious implications for the future conduct of EU competition policy.

The above discussion of the coherence between policies over time leads to the conclusions that the present regulatory stance results in company behaviours which are a potential threat to the competitive environment. This emphasizes the importance of looking not only at the internal and mutual consistency of policies, but also at their consistency over time, by taking into account the companies' reactions to given policy mixes and anticipating the implications that these will have on future industry structure.

Index